AF789464

Borderlines in Private Law

Borderlines in Private Law

Edited by

WILLIAM DAY
JULIUS GROWER

OXFORD
UNIVERSITY PRESS

OXFORD
UNIVERSITY PRESS

Great Clarendon Street, Oxford, OX2 6DP,
United Kingdom

Oxford University Press is a department of the University of Oxford.
It furthers the University's objective of excellence in research, scholarship,
and education by publishing worldwide. Oxford is a registered trade mark of
Oxford University Press in the UK and in certain other countries

© the several contributors 2024

The moral rights of the authors have been asserted

All rights reserved. No part of this publication may be reproduced, stored in a retrieval system, or transmitted, in any form or by any means, without the prior permission in writing of Oxford University Press, or as expressly permitted by law, by licence or under terms agreed with the appropriate reprographics rights organization. Enquiries concerning reproduction outside the scope of the above should be sent to the Rights Department, Oxford University Press, at the address above

You must not circulate this work in any other form
and you must impose this same condition on any acquirer

Public sector information reproduced under Open Government Licence v3.0
(http://www.nationalarchives.gov.uk/doc/open-government-licence/open-government-licence.htm)

Published in the United States of America by Oxford University Press
198 Madison Avenue, New York, NY 10016, United States of America

British Library Cataloguing in Publication Data
Data available

Library of Congress Control Number: 2024936385

ISBN 9780198888710

DOI: 10.1093/9780191995200.001.0001

Printed and bound by
CPI Group (UK) Ltd, Croydon, CR0 4YY

MIX
Paper | Supporting responsible forestry
FSC® C013604

The manufacturer's authorised representative in the EU for product safety is Oxford University Press España S.A. of El Parque Empresarial San Fernando de Henares, Avenida de Castilla, 2 – 28830 Madrid (www.oup.es/en or product.safety@oup.com). OUP España S.A. also acts as importer into Spain of products made by the manufacturer.

Dedicated to the memory of Alexis Grower, a proud lawyer.

Preface

This book's origins lie in the debates which its editors shared while teaching seminars on the Advanced Private Law paper on the 2021–22 Cambridge LLM. The most difficult and recurring aspects of those debates frequently related to areas on borderlines between different constituencies of private law (such as questions of concurrent liability in either contract and tort or contract and unjust enrichment) or where those constituencies responded to similar issues in different ways (most pronounced, perhaps, in the idea that 'we do this at law, but that in equity'). We considered that it was worth asking whether these difficulties arose at least in part *because* they were on borderlines of private law (perceived or actual) and that there would be a benefit in examining a range of borderlines in private law so as to identify, explore, and offer different perspectives on how to resolve or manage such doctrinal tensions. And so this project began.

A secondary aim of this book was to respond to a current controversy in private law about whether, in legal academia, grand theories are being pursued at the expense of 'practical' or 'reflexive' scholarship which engages with the actual reasoning in cases and assists practitioners and judges in developing and applying the common law.[1] Many private law academics would probably see themselves as pursuing some form of 'interpretative theory', aiming to enhance the understanding of doctrinal law by identifying those features which are more or less important and so giving it an 'intelligible order'.[2] However, that is a broad church. There is clearly a spectrum ranging from more black-letter scholarship which makes sense of evolving case law by reference to broader principles and policy considerations to more theoretical approaches that are much less grounded in or concerned with the detail of doctrinal rules, whilst at the same time still offering an interpretation of contract law, tort law, and so on.

To provide a structure for this book, we picked five common organising subjects of private law (contract, tort, unjust enrichment, property, and equity) and invited contributions along the borderlines between each of them. As noted in a number of chapters in this book, this is undoubtedly a schema of which Peter Birks would have strongly disapproved, having famously argued that private law should instead be mapped by reference to causative events, namely consent, wrongs, unjust enrichment, and other.[3] Yet private law can be mapped in more than one way and,

[1] Andrew Burrows, 'Judges and Academics, and the Endless Road to Unattainable Perfection' (The Lionel Cohen Lecture, 25 October 2021); Jane Stapleton, *Three Essays on Tort* (OUP 2021).

[2] Stephen Smith, *Contract Theory* (OUP 2004) 5.

[3] Peter Birks, *Unjust Enrichment* (2nd edn, OUP 2005) 21–28.

given our desire to produce a publication that may also be useful to those in the business of the application of the law (solicitors, barristers, and judges), we considered that it would be much better to structure the borderlines around topics which would be recognisable and applicable in the *practice* of law and the determination of real-world private law disputes.

The chapters of this book underline the breadth of approaches within interpretative theory, ranging from doctrinal-focused analyses (see the contributions by Janet O'Sullivan, Graham Virgo, William Day, and, from a comparative angle, Helen Scott) to more philosophical arguments (see the contributions by Rory Gregson, Nicholas McBride, Alexander Waghorn, and Sarah Worthington) and to those somewhere in between (see the contributions of Ben McFarlane and Julius Grower). Given our desire that this project encourage dialogue between academics and the judiciary, we are delighted also to have a number of chapters from senior judges which respond to and consider the arguments made in the academic contributions. These are from Lady Carr (on the borderlines around tort law), Mrs Justice Cockerill (the borderlines around contract law), Mr Justice Foxton (the borderlines around the law of unjust enrichment), Mr Justice Fancourt (the borderlines around property law), and Mr Justice Marcus Smith (the borderlines around equity).

First drafts of our academic chapters were discussed at a conference held at Downing College, Cambridge on a sunny 3 April 2023.[4] There was an enjoyable and lively debate between the academics, and between the academics and the judges, with the judges then drafting their contributions after the conference with the benefit of those interactions. The formal part of the day ended with presentations from Lord Sales and Robert Stevens reflecting more broadly on the operation of borderlines in private law, and which are also published in this collection as the first and last chapters.

We are both very grateful to everyone who has participated in this project, and also to OUP for supporting it through to publication. We must also acknowledge, appreciatively, the financial support from both the Yorke Fund in Cambridge and the Faculty of Law at the University of Oxford for the conference at Downing.

William Day (Downing College, Cambridge)
Julius Grower (St Hugh's College, Oxford)
December 2023

[4] Appropriately enough, given the subject matter of the conference, we were in that part of Downing College known as West Lodge, formerly the home of FW Maitland as the chair of the Downing Professor of the Laws of England.

Contents

Table of Cases

UNITED KINGDOM

OTHER JURISDICTIONS

Australia

Canada

South Africa

New Zealand

Table of Legislation

EUROPEAN UNION

Contributors

Academic Contributors

William Day is Fellow of Downing College, Cambridge and Barrister at 3 Verulam Buildings, London.

Rory Gregson is Fellow and Tutor in Law of Merton College, Oxford and Associate Professor of Law at the University of Oxford.

Julius AW Grower is Ann Smart Fellow and Tutor in Law of St Hugh's College, Oxford and Associate Professor of Law at the University of Oxford.

Nicholas J McBride is Fellow of Pembroke College, Cambridge.

Ben McFarlane is Fellow of St John's College, Oxford and Professor of English Law at the University of Oxford.

Janet O'Sullivan is Vice Master and Fellow of Selwyn College, Cambridge and Professor of Private Law at the University of Cambridge.

Helen Scott is Fellow of Downing College, Cambridge and Regius Professor of Civil Law at the University of Cambridge.

Robert Stevens is Fellow of Lady Margaret Hall, Oxford and Herbert Smith Freehills Professor of English Private Law at the University of Oxford.

Graham Virgo is Master of Downing College, Cambridge and Professor of English Private Law at the University of Cambridge.

Alexander Waghorn is Assistant Professor of Law at the London School of Economics.

Sarah Worthington is Professor of Law at the London School of Economics and Downing Professor Emeritus of the Laws of England at the University of Cambridge.

Judicial Contributors

Lady Carr is Lady Chief Justice of England and Wales.

Mrs Justice Cockerill is a High Court Judge assigned to the Commercial Court in the King's Bench Division.

Mr Justice Fancourt is a High Court Judge assigned to the Chancery Division.

Mr Justice Foxton is a High Court Judge and Judge in Charge of the Commercial Court in the King's Bench Division.

Lord Sales is a Justice of the Supreme Court of the United Kingdom.

Mr Justice Marcus Smith is a High Court Judge assigned to the Chancery Division and President of the United Kingdom Competition Appeal Tribunal.

1
Borderlines in Private Law: An Introduction

Lord Sales

It was a pleasure to attend the conference which generated this edited collection. I learned a lot from the papers circulated and the conference presentations. As appears from a number of the chapters in this book, the notion of borderlines is intimately connected with the idea of taxonomy in law. Both are aspects of the very basic impulse to treat legal doctrine as a topic of study and debate. From the perspective of a judge (I mean any judge, but perhaps this is particularly true for an appellate judge in an apex court) doctrine and taxonomy matter, so understanding the borders of concepts and principles and how they interact with each other really matters as well. It should also be emphasised that the formulation of doctrine is hard. One has to take account of many different perspectives, both practical and conceptual, to formulate a good, or even passable, legal rule or standard. Accordingly, I find the carefully reflective debates in these chapters thought-provoking and inspiring. Also, it has to be said, rather overwhelming, in terms of reminding me how little I know and how much remains for me to learn and think about.

Why does taxonomy matter in law? In my view it is for three basic reasons, each of which bears on me as a judge. First, it is an axiom of justice that like cases should be treated alike. But to resolve disputes in accordance with a law that gives effect to principles of justice we need detailed and specific criteria to identify what cases are to count as being alike.

Secondly, lawyers need to be trained. A legal culture has to be created with its own distinct modes of thought which provide the basis for certainty and predictability in the application of legal rules. Legal culture is the foundation for the sense given by a legal system, as Karl Llewellyn and many others have emphasised.[1]

[1] On the importance of legal culture for the regular application of legal rules, particularly in common law and equivalent environments, see, eg, Patrick Atiyah and Robert Summers, *Form and Substance in Anglo-American Law: A Comparative Study of Legal Reasoning, Legal Theory and Legal Institutions* (OUP 1987) 355; Max Weber, *Economy and Society*, vol 2 (University of California Press 1979) 759, 794; Roger Cotterrell, *Law's Community: Legal Theory in Sociological Perspective* (OUP 1995) 170. In William Scheuerman, *Frankfurt School Perspectives on Globalization, Democracy and the Law* (Routledge 2008) 43, it is argued that in international arbitration, where the flexible standards of the *lex mercatoria* may be applied, a certain amount of regularity and predictability is achieved as a result of 'the relative homogeneity of legal decision-makers and the fact that arbitrators and international business share relatively similar social interests and ideological views'.

Lord Sales, *Borderlines in Private Law: An Introduction* In: *Borderlines in Private Law*. Edited by: William Day and Julius Grower, Oxford University Press. © Lord Sales 2024. DOI: 10.1093/9780191995200.003.0001

Llewellyn explains how the lawyers are adepts in exercising a craft and how law embraces 'the skill and the traditions of the crafts of law, the ways of seeing, thinking, feeling, doing, and duty in and into which the craftsmen—the body of craftsmen—have been reared'.[2] The law controls what a judge does 'in good part by moulding in advance his sense of "what is sense"'.[3] It is through taxonomy that lawyers are trained to think as lawyers. Law involves the application of a technically trained sense of right.[4] I do not wish to exempt judges from being trained and taught to think through taxonomy. Emphatically not. I am acutely aware of the time factor in being a judge. You have to get through the business before the court in a reasonable time. A judgment is not a research paper. You are educated by the arguments you hear. You need to rely on a basic orientation given by a taxonomy which is commonly understood by you and counsel presenting arguments in the case—and then, when the argument is finished, you have to write.[5]

Thirdly, and related to the second point, as a judge (particularly an appellate judge) you are very conscious that when writing a judgment you are yourself potentially reproducing or modifying the taxonomy which the legal system will use. You need to have a good understanding of the law's taxonomy in order to do that consciously and with a proper appreciation of the effects you may be producing. Law is complex. You see only a part of the forest in one case, and it is easy to make a misstep. So taxonomy is important when considering the guidance function of a judge, particularly at the level of an apex court providing strategic guidance for the legal system as a whole. We need to be able to fit our rulings into the existing framework in a coherent way, or to be able to give good reasons when we choose to modify it. Otherwise, we will produce unintended disruption and uncertainty. But we also want the guidance we give to be followed, and that is best achieved when the taxonomy we seek to apply or reformulate makes sense to other lawyers, as well as being capable of being made acceptable to the general public.

In the light of these points, I offer four short reflections on themes which strike me as emerging from the chapter. First, to speak of borders in private law is to invite deeper reflection on what a border might look like and what functions it serves. Broadly speaking, it is helpful to think of a typology involving three kinds of border:

(1) A hard border in a strong conceptual sense. I take Ben McFarlane's chapter on the relationship between law and equity as an illustration of this.[6] On

[2] Karl Llewellyn, *The Common Law Tradition: Deciding Appeals* (Quid Pro 1960) 185.
[3] ibid 202.
[4] The phrase is taken from Carleton Kemp Allen, *Law in the Making* (OUP 1927) 193.
[5] For discussion of how legal rules orientate the ways in which a judge may approach a case and obviate the need for them to invent solutions from scratch or to revert to underlying principles or reasons for adopting a rule in the first place, see, eg, Cass Sunstein, *Legal Reasoning and Political Conflict* (OUP 1996) and Frederick Schauer, *The Force of Law* (Harvard University Press 2015).
[6] See ch 12.

his account, common law property rights and equitable rights are not in direct competition in a way which would require one to establish a border between them to govern when one or the other takes precedence. Rather, the point to be made about the relationship between these two areas of legal doctrine is that one needs to understand the conceptual world in which the two fit together and complement each other, and how indeed the common law provides the necessary conceptual framework within which the equitable rules have scope to apply. It is only on the basis of the common law's own framework of rights and obligations that it is possible to understand the equitable rules. Aspects of this sort of relationship between areas of legal doctrine are also touched on in William Day's chapter on unjust enrichment and contract,[7] especially where he discusses cases where the intention of the parties is irrelevant. As he points out, where there has been payment of a debt by legal compulsion or by a surety, that is the foundation for a claim against the primary obligee. The two sets of rules (governing when a debt is discharged and when a claim arises to recoup the payment) do not conflict with each other; the latter depends upon the due operation of the former.

(2) A hard border, but in a softer conceptual sense, where there is a potential conflict between legal regimes, methodologies, and solutions and one or other regime, methodology, or solution has to be chosen. Here, one comes up against the justified pre-eminence of contract as a legal category. If the parties have chosen the rights they wish to have under the regime which gives them that choice, it potentially means the law should apply a hard border to give effect to that choice and give priority to the contractual regime. One encounters this in the regions where contract law and the law of unjust enrichment appear potentially to overlap.[8] Similar choices may fall to be made in regions where contract law and tort law potentially overlap, if the force of the contract is taken to be so great as to displace the application of tort law.[9] There are aspects of this theme in, to mention just two, William Day's chapter[10] and Janet O'Sullivan's chapter.[11]

(3) Situations where the border is porous and soft and legal categories overlap, so that two may be capable of applying alongside each other. This is the sort of area where concurrent duties in tort and contract apply,[12] or where equity produces a shadow law of contract as described by Julius Grower in his

[7] See ch 9.

[8] *Pan Ocean Shipping Co Ltd v Creditcorp Ltd (The Trident Beauty)* [1994] 1 WLR 161 (HL); *Barton v Morris* [2023] UKSC 3, [2023] AC 684; *HEB Enterprises Ltd v Richards* [2023] UKPC 7.

[9] *Tai Hing Cotton Mill Ltd v Liu Chong Bank Ltd* [1986] AC 80 (PC).

[10] See ch 9.

[11] See ch 3.

[12] *Henderson v Merrett Syndicates Ltd* [1995] 2 AC 145 (HL); *Manchester Building Society v Grant Thornton UK LLP* [2021] UKSC 20, [2022] AC 783.

chapter.[13] These are problematic zones precisely because there is no hard border. So they force us to question more closely what the exact parameters of the categories are and how they should be allowed to operate alongside each other in a coherent manner. These border areas pose interesting but difficult questions for the formulation of doctrine, and for an appellate court they are fraught with danger when trying to give guidance.

Secondly, it really matters why we ask the categorisation question. Usually this relates to the practical consequences. We need a form of categorisation which unites rights and remedies in a coherent regime, serving the same objectives. But, in addition, statutes may be laid as templates on top of the common law so as to introduce their own very important practical consequences. For example, statute may impose limitation periods in relation to underlying common law or may require compliance with formalities for the formation of contracts or the transfer of property rights. Statute can thus have important consequences, which are superimposed by the legislature rather than arising as organic creations of the common law, and the existence of these regimes puts external pressure on the common law categories where they have to be slotted into a statutory pigeonhole.

In this regard, difficulties have arisen in working out how a developing common law category like unjust enrichment should be accommodated within limitation statutes which do not refer to it.[14] Similarly, limitation statutes refer to the categories of contract and tort, which do not necessarily accommodate the intermediate concept of assumption of responsibility very well.[15] Such statutes pose questions of categorisation for their own purposes. This can work in strange ways, potentially taking one back to older forms of categorisation in the common law. An example of this is the examination of whether contributory negligence as a defence applied in contract as well as tort.[16] The statutory question asked under the Law Reform (Contributory Negligence) Act 1945 required the courts to go back to earlier case law and schemes of categorisation in order to determine in what circumstances a defence of contributory negligence had been available, leading to the conclusion that it had been available (and so was now available) in cases where there were concurrent duties of care in both contract and tort. In the early nineteenth century, the categories of tort and contract were not so fixed and impermeable as they are now.

[13] See ch 4.

[14] *Test Claimants in the Franked Investment Income Group v HMRC* [2020] UKSC 47, [2022] AC 1.

[15] See the discussion of the form of liability in *Hedley Byrne & Co Ltd v Heller & Partners Ltd* [1964] AC 465 (HL) as based on old conceptions of assumpsit duties, in Paul Mitchell, '*Hedley Byrne & Co Ltd v Heller & Partners Ltd* (1963)' in Charles Mitchell and Paul Mitchell (eds), *Landmark Cases in the Law of Tort* (Hart 2010); see also Lord Sales, 'Pure Economic Loss in the Law of Tort: The History and Theory of Assumption of Responsibility' (Annual Tort Law Research Group Lecture, Ontario, 26 September 2022).

[16] *Wilson v Merry & Cunningham* (1868) LR 1 HL Sc 326 (HL); *Forsikringsaktieselskapet Vesta v Butcher* [1989] AC 852 (HL).

In the context of the application of the 1945 Act, previous classification systems had to be retrieved and understood in order to show that the contract/tort divide is *not* critical for the purposes of that statute.

Thirdly, a significant factor is how the common law has developed new categories and, still more fundamentally, new ways of conceiving of its own explanatory framework. It can be argued that with current debates about the borders of contract, tort, and unjust enrichment we are still coming to terms (as it seems, amazingly) with the move from a taxonomy based on the forms of action to a taxonomy based on substantive legal concepts and substantive justifications for legal results. A recent decision concerning the operation of the Limitation Act 1980 in relation to the law of nuisance and pollution from an oil spillage illustrates this: *Jalla v Shell International Trading and Shipping Co.*[17] It continues to matter that nuisance is an action on the case, according to the old forms of action, so that damage is the gist of the cause of action. This is an embedded feature of the tort, drawn from the ancient scheme of classification of forms of action, which underlay the analysis for limitation purposes. The old forms of action in assumpsit indicate that there are species of binding undertaking which go wider than contractual promises, as discussed by Nicholas McBride.[18] Similarly, assumption of responsibility reasoning, rooted in this form of action, provides the background for questioning aspects of the modern law of tort, as Janet O'Sullivan does in her chapter:[19] in cases of liability for defective buildings, it seems odd that the builder is not subject to an assumpsit duty of care (even though he has most obviously assumed responsibility for the construction), but a building inspector is. How do these two rules fit together?

With the change in the basis of taxonomy from grouping categories around the forms of action to grouping them around substantive rights and obligations, one is dealing with a profound paradigm shift of the kind described by Thomas Kuhn in relation to science.[20] The common law is an amalgam of, on the one hand, materials located in, and the product of, specific periods and, on the other, modern ways of conceiving how the materials should fit together and be explained. These perspectives are in tension. An account of borderlines in the common law has to have a historical dimension as well as a theoretical dimension. The common law never starts from scratch, from a tabula rasa. Borders in legal taxonomy have to take account of legal theory as it has emerged and is expounded currently, but they also have to fit with existing materials (understood in light of their historical specificity) in order to make the best overall interpretive sense of these two dimensions of the common law.

17 [2023] UKSC 16, [2023] 2 WLR 1085.
18 See ch 6. And see, eg, *Lejonvarn v Burgess* [2017] EWCA Civ 254, [2017] BLR 277.
19 See ch 3.
20 Thomas Kuhn, *The Structure of Scientific Revolutions* (University of Chicago Press 1962).

Fourthly, there are potential dangers in adopting an overly strict approach to legal taxonomy. Partly by reason of its historical development, partly by reason of the sheer width of interests and values which it recognises and seeks to accommodate, the common law categories are somewhat baggy and capacious. They are not always defined with precision, and a significant part of the common law's practical capacity to do justice and adapt to changing social conditions might be lost if they were. There may sometimes be value in having a rather loose taxonomy, as a heuristic for organising ideas or providing the starting point for thinking about potential issues which might arise, as distinct from providing a strict definition of a unitary cause of action. The saga of the development of the law of unjust enrichment exemplifies this. The elements of enrichment, at the expense of the claimant, which is unjust, and the absence of any relevant defence, may not define a cause of action.[21] However, in a difficult and unfamiliar area, judges may be assisted by having a loose framework of things to think about, even if having thought about them they find that they do not ultimately provide the answer to the problem at hand.

Judges and lawyers need assistance to orientate themselves on the legal map, and it is not necessarily helpful to send them back into a wilderness of single instances such as the law of restitution seemed to be before Robert Goff and Gareth Jones began their project of trying to identify a coherent set of underlying substantive principles.[22] It is not satisfactory to conceive of the common law just as a collection of historically located decisions. The parallel search for explanatory principle is vitally important. Principle provides structure, coherence, and determinate guidance to assist in deciding new cases. Judges need help to orientate themselves in what may be unfamiliar territory. Although the elements identified in unjust enrichment claims may not define a cause of action, they may assist with the effort of orientation and in identifying important issues which require consideration, so that they are not inadvertently left out of account. It is not obvious that, conceived in this loose taxonomical way, it would be helpful to abandon this sort of categorisation.

[21] See ch 7.

[22] Robert Goff and Gareth Jones, *The Law of Restitution* (Sweet & Maxwell 1966).

2

Contract's Borderlines

Mrs Justice Cockerill

At the conference that preceded this book, the segment which I introduced can be seen as operating as a loop: contract/tort, tort/equity, and back to contract via equity/contract. This arrangement lends a specious appearance of harmony. On the other hand, the chapters in this book concerned with contract's borderlines to which I have been asked to write a response are very different in nature and indeed texture.

Janet O'Sullivan, operating on the contract/tort borderline produced one of the chapters which, as I joked, was right at the top of the judicial list of 'articles likely to make my life easier'.[1] The joke was perhaps a little unfair on others because the borderline she examined is one which genuinely does manifest in practical terms with considerable frequency; whether in the limitation context on which she focused her fire, or in the world of jurisdiction and choice of law. Adopting her geographical analogy, the contract/tort borderline is perhaps the Alsace–Lorraine of legal borderlines.

Janet's chapter applies a rigorous analysis to the difficulty which has emerged via the decision in *Henderson v Merrett Syndicates Ltd*,[2] where the House of Lords found a way to decide that Lloyd's Names, beggared by the losses suffered from a 'concatenation of catastrophes',[3] should (via an intriguing take on *Hedley Byrne & Co Ltd v Heller & Partners Ltd*)[4] be able to claim financial loss caused by negligent performance of services. That borderline, and that specific issue on it, is one which is particularly resonant for me: my first major case in practice was *Deeny v Gooda Walker*,[5] and I recall that the concerns which are thrown into relief in Janet's analysis did not go unexpressed at the time.

Our analysis, as representatives of the agents in the firing line, perhaps lacked the purity of her approach. It also lacked *Robinson v PE Jones (Contractors) Ltd*,[6] which, by its conclusion that there is no concurrent duty in the context of a

[1] See ch 3.
[2] [1995] 2 AC 145 (HL).
[3] *Deeny v Gooda Walker* [1996] LRLR 183 (QB) 193 (Phillips J), adopted in *Arbuthnott v Feltrim Underwriting Agencies Ltd* [1995] CLC 437 (QB) and *Brown v KMR Services Ltd* [1995] CLC 1418 (CA). Actually, my phrase at the time, and I still proudly claim authorship of it.
[4] [1964] AC 465 (HL).
[5] See n 3.
[6] [2011] EWCA Civ 9, [2012] QB 44.

Mrs Justice Cockerill, *Contract's Borderlines* In: *Borderlines in Private Law.* Edited by: William Day and Julius Grower, Oxford University Press. © Mrs Justice Cockerill 2024. DOI: 10.1093/9780191995200.003.0002

negligent building contractor, offers an excellent resonator for testing the soundness of the *Henderson* approach. Janet's analysis is compelling, as is her view that the disjunction in the results is hard to defend and that the *Hedley Byrne* analysis in *Henderson* has not aged well. Where I might part company with her is the suggestion that an answer lies via the Law Commission's now almost forgotten 2001 proposals for reform of the law of limitation.[7] The vibrancy of the debate which remains on those is illustrated by the reasons for abandonment: they were felt by many interest groups to involve unworkable costs.[8] And at the risk of sounding Cassandra-like, the opportunities afforded by hearing expert evidence explaining other jurisdictions' attempts to harmonise their limitation regimes tends to suggest that in this specific context of this borderline we will ever be, as Janet says, 'crying for the moon'.[9]

A theme within the discussions at the conference more generally was the extent to which we debate within the existing taxonomy or spread our wings and look for a new one. This was very apparent in Nicholas McBride's chapter,[10] over which the shadow of Peter Birks loomed large. Nicholas posited equity as the world of primary obligations and tort as that of secondary obligations; and at the same time (perhaps counterintuitively) equity as bestowing rights against right-holders while tort gives rights in respect of people and their natural capacities. Adopting this approach, he suggested the possibility that we may adopt a new taxonomy in future, leaving the labels of tort and equity behind, like shed snakeskins which are no longer needed. A similar approach was almost equally apparent in William Day's contract/unjust enrichment chapter,[11] which seeks to persuade us to focus far more closely on the reasons why a transfer of value may be normatively defective, which may lead to a different interaction with the law of contract as between different types of restitutionary claim, rather than utilising the intention-based analysis which is central to the current approach.

However, as Lord Sales noted in discussion at the conference, the approach which leaves traditional categorisations behind seems in danger of ignoring the practical utility of law in a world where many day-to-day users of it are not professionals in or even enthusiasts for it. It also neglects the economic effect which the uncertainty inherent in a change of taxonomy would inevitably bring. Again and again we hear from the largely international users of the Commercial Court that one of the main things which brings them to this jurisdiction is the certainty and predictability of the law.[12] The Commercial Court was created against a backdrop

[7] Law Commission, *Limitation of Actions* (Law Com No 270, 2001).
[8] HC Deb 19 November 2009, vol 501, col 12WS.
[9] See, eg, *Lombard North Central plc v Airbus Helicopters SAS* [2021] EWHC 2025 (Comm).
[10] See ch 6.
[11] See ch 9.
[12] Over 50 per cent of cases in the Commercial Court have no domestic parties; 75 per cent have at least one international party. A similar state of affairs pertains across much of the Business and Property Courts.

where insufficient predictability of outcomes was stultifying business.[13] Research for the Ministry of Justice in 2015 highlighted the quality and certainty of English Law in the top five reasons for choosing to litigate in this jurisdiction.[14] That plays out in economic consequences highlighted by the recent Oxera Report for Legal UK on the value of English law to this country, which pointed out that indirectly 'the law adds economic value by increasing predictability of outcomes and hence growth in the volume of transactions in an economy' and that 'value generated for the UK is maximised when internationally mobile transactions are governed by English law, and when UK legal services are used (whether the contract specifies the jurisdiction of the courts of England and Wales, or a UK-seated arbitration)'.[15] Taxonomy matters in practical and economic terms.

But, of course, taxonomy is imperfect. Julius Grower's chapter highlights the way in which contract and proprietary estoppel, which should be conceptually distinct, have crept close to the point where proprietary estoppel can be said to be operating in some respects at least as a 'shadow law of contract'.[16] He notes that in the context of gratuitous promises proprietary estoppel appears now to have 'the ability to enforce de facto undertakings which for one reason or another contract is reluctant to' and suggests that equity has here crept beyond its proper role of supplementing or mitigating the common law of contract, pushing towards a 'civil war' of inconsistency.

It may be this tendency on the part of equity to tread on the toes of contractual principles which has in part given birth to that heterodox estoppel (there are of course much less courteous descriptions):[17] contractual estoppel. It is perhaps ironic that the concept of estoppel, which the modern lawyer instinctively associates with equity, should have become the voice of that most traditional of contractual doctrines, freedom of contract. It is no secret that I have expressed some concerns about contractual estoppel as a doctrine, in particular the way in which it has emerged with little supporting analysis to orient the decision-maker.[18] But reflecting on the question of contractual borderlines with equity, in particular via Julius Grower's chapter and Lord Sales' 2019 lecture on the interface between contract and equity,[19] combined with the passionate pro-contractual estoppel advocacy of Alexander Trukhtanov,[20] gives pause for thought.

[13] For a full account, see <www.commercialcourt.london/origins2> accessed 10 October 2023.

[14] Eva Lein and others, 'Factors Influencing International Litigants' Decisions to Bring Commercial Claims to the London Based Courts' (Ministry of Justice Analytical Series 2015).

[15] Oxera for LegalUK, 'Economic Value of English Law' (2021).

[16] See ch 4.

[17] See, eg, Gerard McMeel, *The Construction of Contracts* (2nd edn, OUP 2011) 26.76 ('illegitimate species of estoppel') and Gerard McMeel, 'Documentary Fundamentalism in the Senior Courts: The Myth of Contractual Estoppel' [2011] LMCLQ 185, 206–07 ('a myth which must be exploded').

[18] Sara Cockerill, 'Contractual Estoppel: the Case for Coherent Principles' [2022] JBL 189.

[19] Lord Sales, 'The Interface between Contract and Equity' (Lehane Memorial Lecture 2019).

[20] Alexander Trukhtanov, *Contractual Estoppel* (2nd edn, Hart 2022).

As Lord Burrows has noted,[21] contractual estoppel is a part of the law of contract and not a creation of equity. It is, at its simplest, as stated by Aikens LJ in *Springwell Navigation v JP Morgan Chase*: 'If A and B enter into a contract then, unless there is some principle of law or statute to the contrary, they are entitled to agree what they like.'[22] What the doctrine appears to be doing, via a mechanism which we instinctively (but wrongly) associate with equity,[23] is reasserting traditional contractual norms.

One interesting question to which little attention has been given is why such a doctrine is needed given the wealth of authority on contractual construction and the well-established nature of contractual norms. The answer is not entirely clear. Most obviously it emerged in answer to circumstances where the intervention of equity has distanced results from literal contractual interpretations. The paradigm here is *Lowe v Lombank*,[24] where an elderly widow accepted a salesman's assurance that a (dangerously defective) car was practically perfect in every way, and signed an acknowledgement that she had inspected the car and confirmed it was in good working order. The perceived unconscionability of an orthodox result drove the outcome. The best efforts of subsequent legal minds have failed to produce a convincing explanation for the result by reference to orthodox contractual principles,[25] but it spawned a series of cases[26] where estoppel by representation principles were used in the commercial sphere to short-circuit non-reliance clauses. Trukhtanov thus hailed the advent of contractual estoppel as 'the long overdue correction of just such an aberration which lingered after consumer protection policy distorted general contract law in *Lowe v Lombank*.'[27]

Another reason for the rise of contractual estoppel appears to be one founded in litigation dynamics: it offers an efficient route through what has now become the regular deployment of (equitable) estoppel by convention arguments as a backstop to issues of contractual construction. That itself is a facet of litigation which has been created by the combination of nuanced or purposive approaches to contractual construction and the routine survival (courtesy of modern technology) of extensive pre-contractual negotiations which can offer ballast for such arguments.

[21] Andrew Burrows, *A Restatement of the English Law of Contract* (2nd edn, OUP 2020) 78.

[22] [2010] EWCA Civ 1221, [2010] 2 CLC 705 [143]. Derided as 't-shirt philosophy' in Gerard McMeel, 'The Impact of Exemption Clauses and Disclaimers: Construction, Contractual Estoppel and Public Policy' in Andrew Dyson, James Goudkamp, and Frederick Wilmot-Smith (eds), *Defences in Contract* (Hart 2017) 258.

[23] Trukhtanov (n 20) 7.16 notes that 'late 19th century estoppels have been developed exclusively in equity. This has engendered an inclination to apply equitable standards to anything that claims to be an estoppel.' See, eg, the Supreme Court in *Tinkler v Revenue and Customs* [2021] UKSC 39, [2022] AC 886 [28] (Lord Burrows) coming close to eliding estoppel with unconscionability.

[24] [1960] 1 WLR 197 (CA).

[25] With a wide variety of possibilities being offered and no two judges agreeing on the correct analysis.

[26] See, eg, *EA Grimstead & Son Ltd v McGarrigan* [1998–99] Info TLR 384 (CA); *Watford Electronics Ltd and Sanderson CFL Ltd* [2001] EWCA Civ 317, [2001] 1 All ER (Comm) 696.

[27] Trukhtanov (n 20) 1.33.

It is also a facet of modern litigation which, because of the need to deal with what is often an evidential morass, has often complicated and increased the length and cost of determining issues of contractual construction. The fact that the doctrine of contractual estoppel has been used over such a spread of factual areas illustrates the extent to which a tool in favour of orthodox analysis and capable of offering a route to summary judgment is felt to be needed.[28] It is certainly right that the contractual estoppel sceptics can be seen as speaking from a perspective which is so influenced by concerns for the day-to-day contract user (such as individuals like Mrs Lowe and SMEs) that it might not be unfair to call it protectionism, though to call it, as Trukhtanov does, 'unadulterated protectionism masquerading as legal discourse' is harsh.[29] In essence, therefore, the position we have reached on contractual estoppel may be seen as the law of contract fighting back in another area in which equity has been overstepping its proper bounds.

But the tension which feeds such overstepping also feeds into a theme which seemed to me to emerge from these chapters: the extent to which taxonomy develops on its historical base and how, as it develops, certain approaches become a poor fit and then require adjustment. Contractual estoppel has been felt to be both a significant change and a controversy precisely because there is now so marked a sensitivity in relation to consumer protection and avoiding the hard-edged result in cases where contractual negotiation is either not a reality or not evenly balanced. Freedom of contract works harshly, consumer protection legislation fails to keep up (or revised limitation legislation fails to be enacted), and so mitigations via tort or equity step in. But problems occur when they move beyond mitigation into substance. The structure becomes like the Crooked House pub of recent notoriety: braced and reinforced and shored up into a semblance of itself, but some way from the original conception.

In a similar way, going back to the particular contract/tort borderline discussed by Janet, one sees the echoes of the arguments derived from forms of action, such as assumpsit. One also sees the way that the division between construction and other professional services has emerged, in part because of the very significant crisis (with thousands of human faces) caused by the Lloyd's spiral issues of the 1990s and in part because of a residual historical sense of the 'bread and butter' or 'blue collar' nature of the construction industry. But, as O'Farrell J has rightly noted in *Sheffield Teaching Hospital Foundation Trust v Hadfield Healthcare Partnerships Ltd*,[30] the increase in complexity and specialisms both generally in the modern world and specifically in such areas erodes the factual distinctions upon which both the taxonomy and the specific distinction are based.

[28] See, eg, *Fine Care Homes v National Westminster Bank plc* [2020] EWHC 3233 (Ch); *Aquila WSA Aviation Opportunities II Ltd v Onur Air Tasimacilik AS* [2018] EWHC 519 (Comm); *BSkyB Ltd v HP Enterprise Services UK Ltd* [2010] EWHC 86 (TCC), 129 Con LR 147.

[29] Trukhtanov (n 20) 1.33.

[30] [2023] EWHC 644 (TCC), 207 Con LR 95 [78].

A similar but contrasting problem of concepts struggling with the developments of the modern world presents itself in the context of fiduciary relationships. A number of the chapters highlight the extent to which, when confronted with a contract/tort or contract/equity borderline, judges instinctively reach for the concept of fiduciary relationships to justify an exceptional approach or a tweak to orthodoxy. Janet O'Sullivan reminds us how the reasoning of *Hedley Byrne* has its roots in a concept of the fiduciary relationship, and how this was explicitly alluded to and apparently seen as some form of reassurance by Lord Browne-Wilkinson in *Henderson*.

There are a number of problems with this approach, not the least of which is our lack of full understanding of the fiduciary relationship. Nicholas McBride's chapter notes Evan Fox-Decent's thinking, warning against an apparent tendency towards making the fiduciary ideal 'an interpretive ecumenical theory of everything',[31] which becomes as meaningless as assumption of responsibility. The answer is plainly not one of simple elision. Many will be familiar with Birks' view, which saw the concept as springing from the medieval custodial grant of land. More recently however, Joshua Getzler has traced how medieval (one might almost say chivalrous) concepts of loyalty did not take a straight line into the law on fiduciary duties;[32] rather, a more amorphous set of relationships sometimes labelled as fiduciary (at common law as well as in equity)[33] was narrowed down and became fused in the nineteenth century with a moralising regulatory approach.

But that approach was based on a world which was different and a world view which we increasingly question. It also depends upon the acceptability of a clear line being drawn where certain persons and professions are held to particularly high standards, with stringent equitable remedies including, for example, a wide-ranging obligation to account linked neither to causation of the gain by the fiduciary position nor to the possibility of the principal being able to make the same gains. The acceptability of that clear line and the seriousness of the consequences appear likely to have been dependent in part upon the nature of the different world: the smaller number of professions and smaller range of obligations in the nineteenth century. And, certainly, when one looks at the factual background of the nineteenth-century cases in which the boundaries and consequences of fiduciary duty are spelled out, the fact patterns are stark: the defrauded widow relying wholly on apparently reputable professionals looms large. In that context the policy reasons which underpin the breadth of the obligation to account *do* make

[31] Evan Fox-Decent, 'New Frontiers in Public Fiduciary Law' in Evan Criddle, Paul Miller, and Robert Sitkoff (eds), *Oxford Handbook of Fiduciary Law* (OUP 2019).

[32] Joshua Getzler, 'Fiduciary Principles in English Common Law' in Criddle, Miller, and Sitkoff (eds), *Oxford Handbook of Fiduciary Law* (n 31).

[33] A point also made by Nicholas McBride, by reference to Paul Finn, 'Public Trusts, Public Fiduciaries' (2010) 38 FL Rev 335.

sense. Modern commentators continue to overwhelmingly support that policy justification.[34]

However, there is room for doubt. Life is now not so binary. As David Richards LJ noted in *Wood v Commercial First Business Ltd*,[35] in the modern world '"Fiduciary duty" is a protean term, capable of covering a wide range of different rights and obligations'. The *Oxford Handbook of Fiduciary Law* illustrates this, with chapters on fiduciary principles in agency, trust, corporate unincorporated entities, charities and non-profits, banking, investment advice, pensions, employment, bankruptcy and insolvency, family, legal representation, public offices, and international law.[36]

Consequently, in the modern world there can be a disjunction between the legal incidence of fiduciary status (and its serious repercussions) derived from nineteenth-century norms and what might reasonably be expected by a contemporary actor. It may not be surprising if in some contexts where fiduciary duties do in law occur, those involved may be unaware of this, seeing themselves subjectively as constrained only by the contractual ties which are more obvious to them. Take, for example, a case where for financial reasons a number of sophisticated international individuals form a small company for the purpose of doing business with other international individuals, each individual being a director. Do they subjectively expect that their obligations extend beyond contract to fiduciary obligations? It is quite possible that they do not. And yet that is the result.[37]

An element of judicial discomfort with this state of affairs occasionally becomes visible. Two well-known cases are *Regal (Hastings) Ltd v Gulliver*[38] and *Boardman v Phipps*.[39] More recently, in *Murad v Al-Saraj*,[40] three individuals were buying a hotel as a joint venture. One of them lied about the fact that he was making his contribution by way of a commission he was being paid for arranging the deal. Two members of the Court of Appeal expressed considerable discomfort with the operation of the secret profits rule,[41] with Arden LJ floating the possibility of a relaxation of the rule against secret profits and with Clarke LJ, drawing on the approach of the High Court of Australia in *Warman International Limited v Dwyer*,[42] advocating the opening of the door to a defaulting fiduciary being able to show that

[34] See Matthew Conaglen, 'The Nature and Function of Fiduciary Loyalty' (2005) 121 LQR 452; Matthew Conaglen, 'Strict Fiduciary Loyalty and Accounts of Profits' (2006) 65 CLJ 278; Irit Samet, 'Guarding the Fiduciary's Conscience: a Justification of a Stringent Profit-Stripping Rule' (2008) 28 OJLS 763; Mitchell McInnes, 'Account of Profits for Breach of Fiduciary Duty' (2006) 122 LQR 11; Lusina Ho, 'Deemed Performance in Account of Profits' in Peter Devonshire and Rohan Havelock (eds), *The Impact of Equity and Restitution in Commerce* (Hart 2019) 183.

[35] [2021] EWCA Civ 471, [2022] Ch 123 [36].

[36] Criddle, Miller, and Sitkoff (eds), *Oxford Handbook of Fiduciary Law* (n 31).

[37] See, eg, *Recovery Partners v Rukhadze* [2018] EWHC 2918 (Comm), [2022] EWHC 690 (Comm), [2023] EWCA Civ 305.

[38] [1967] 2 AC 134 (HL).

[39] [1967] 2 AC 46 (HL).

[40] [2005] EWCA Civ 959.

[41] ibid Arden LJ at [82] and Clarke LJ at [158].

[42] (1994) 182 CLR 544 (HCA).

another approach would better meet the justice of the case. That door has been left ajar more recently in *Recovery Partners v Rukhadze*,[43] but it awaits the arrival of a suitable case in the Supreme Court.[44]

At present the rules which we observe as regards the obligations of fiduciaries arise from an approach which says (with Lord Sales) that 'equity imposes fiduciary obligations for reasons which are normatively independent of contract'.[45] But the result creates tension in some places by subsuming into the moralistic starting point of equity responsibilities that are certainly more obviously and arguably better seen as common law contractual obligations. What this perhaps illustrates is that while familiar divisions and concepts have huge importance there can be a limit to the utility and safety of traditional taxonomies. While we keep largely to the labels and concepts hallowed by long use, we need to be careful about a reflexive use of them and we may need to spend more time with the alternative taxonomies as a means of analysis in the hard cases on the borderlines.

43 [2023] EWCA Civ 305.
44 ibid [111] (Popplewell LJ).
45 Lord Sales (n 19) 15.

3
Contract | Tort

Janet O'Sullivan

I. Introduction

Geographical borderlines are not the product of coherent theory or principle. Frequently a national border is contested, whereby the same piece of land is claimed by two states;[1] elsewhere national borders defy logic, as where a straight line suddenly kinks,[2] or an area outside physical borders is nonetheless included in a state's territory.[3] Oddities of this kind can only be explained by understanding history and context. The same applies to borderlines between legal concepts, none more so than the question of whether a claimant can sue their contractual counterparty in tort for breach of a contractual obligation of reasonable care. Where claims for personal injury and property damage are concerned, concurrent tort liability is uncontroversial: a private doctor can be sued in the tort of negligence just as much as a National Health Service doctor.[4] But in claims for pure economic loss, concurrent liability in tort is available for some negligent breaches of contract but not others. This chapter will explore this contested, unprincipled borderline.

Just as with our geographical anomalies, this doctrinal issue can only be understood from a historical perspective, but also in its practical context. That context is worth explaining at the outset, before embarking on a discussion of the authorities. It is that, in practice, a plea of concurrent tort liability is almost entirely driven by the different *limitation* rules for actions for breach of contract and for the tort of negligence, whereby time starts to run for breach of a contractual obligation to take reasonable care at the date of breach, but not until the date of damage for the equivalent tortious obligation. Since, in a pure economic loss claim, breach and damage are frequently separated by a long time period, it is common to find a claimant out of time for their contract action but not for a tort claim. The perverse effect of the different limitation start dates is exacerbated by the fact that the latent

[1] eg, the dispute between the United Kingdom and Mauritius over the Chagos Islands, the subject of the International Court of Justice's 2019 opinion entitled 'Legal Consequences of the Separation of the Chagos Archipelago from Mauritius in 1965'.

[2] eg, the north-western boundary of South Africa with Namibia and Botswana.

[3] Extremely common when overseas territories are concerned, but sometimes just an oddity, such as the part of the United States of America known as Point Roberts, a pene-exclave of Washington surrounded on all sides by Canadian territory.

[4] See generally Jonathan Morgan, 'Equality at the Contract-Tort Boundary: Levelling Up or Levelling Down' (2022) 38 PN 135.

Janet O'Sullivan, *Contract* | *Tort* In: *Borderlines in Private Law.* Edited by: William Day and Julius Grower, Oxford University Press. © Janet O'Sullivan 2024. DOI: 10.1093/9780191995200.003.0003

damage provisions in section 14A of the Limitation Act 1980, under which the time of the accrual of the cause of action may be postponed until after the claimant has the relevant knowledge, apply only to tortious and not to contractual negligence. This is why claimants have sought to invoke the tort of negligence to sue their contractual counterparty, and is why they met with support from the House of Lords in *Henderson v Merrett Syndicates Ltd*,[5] when previously English law took the view that contract formed an exclusive code.[6] Lord Goff in *Henderson* conceded that the more principled approach would be for incidental rules such as the limitation regimes to be reformed into a more logical shape, but that this was 'perhaps crying for the moon', concluding that 'with the law in its present form, practical considerations of this kind cannot sensibly be ignored'.[7] Alas, lawyers have had to persist with crying for the moon in the three decades since *Henderson*, because the Law Commission's 2001 report, *Limitation of Actions*,[8] which proposed reforms to rationalise the inconsistencies between claims for tortious and contractual negligence, was never implemented.

II. Two Concurrent Liability Claims—A Stark Contrast

In *Henderson*, the House of Lords held, on a preliminary issue, that Lloyds investors ('Names') could bring proceedings in the tort of negligence against their managing agents, in connection with the agents' negligent management of the syndicates, which caused significant financial loss to the Names. These claimants, who had concurrent (but time-barred) claims for breach of contract, were known as the 'Direct Names'. As will be seen, Lord Goff achieved this result by expanding the conventional understanding of the scope of *Hedley Byrne & Co Ltd v Heller & Partners Ltd*,[9] from solely covering negligent misstatement to potentially catching negligent performance of services. He likewise reasoned that *Hedley Byrne*'s 'assumption of responsibility in circumstances akin to contract' rationale applied *a fortiori* to defendants undertaking responsibility in an 'actual contract' with the

[5] [1995] 2 AC 145 (HL). Lord Goff said, at 185:

> If concurrent liability in tort is not recognised, a claimant may find his claim barred at a time when he is unaware of its existence. This must moreover be a real possibility in the case of claims against professional men, such as solicitors or architects, since the consequences of their negligence may well not come to light until long after the lapse of six years from the date when the relevant breach of contract occurred.

[6] In *Tai Hing Cotton Mill Ltd v Liu Chong Bank Ltd* [1986] AC 80 (PC) 107, Lord Scarman famously remarked: 'Their Lordships do not believe that there is anything to the advantage of the law's development in searching for a liability in tort where the parties are in a contractual relationship.' However, it should be noted that this was in the context of a plea to recognise a tortious duty of care that was more extensive than the obligations contained in the parties' (banking) contract.

[7] *Henderson* (n 5) 186.

[8] Law Commission, *Limitation of Actions* (Law Com No 270, 2001).

[9] [1964] AC 465 (HL).

claimant, otherwise the law would countenance 'the startling possibility that a client who has had the benefit of gratuitous advice from his solicitor may in this respect be better off than a client who has paid a fee'.[10] The one restriction was that concurrent tortious liability is 'subject only to ascertaining whether the tortious duty is so inconsistent with the applicable contract that, in accordance with ordinary principle, the parties must be taken to have agreed that the tortious remedy is to be limited or excluded'.[11]

In contrast, in *Robinson v PE Jones (Contractors) Ltd*,[12] the claimant contracted with the defendant building contractors to purchase a house, still under construction at the time of the contract, in Prestbury, near Macclesfield. Twelve years after the house was built, defective flues[13] were discovered, that had to be rebuilt at considerable expense to the claimant.[14] A claim for breach of contract was time-barred, so the claimant sued the defendant in tort for this pure economic loss. The ratio of the case was that the contract contained an exclusion clause that was inconsistent with any possible liability in tort, which the trial judge held was reasonable under the Unfair Contract Terms Act 1977. The trial judge therefore struck the claim out, and the Court of Appeal dismissed the appeal.

For our purposes, what is significant is Jackson LJ's discussion of the underlying question, whether a builder who negligently breaches a contract and causes financial loss to their contracting counterparty can in principle be concurrently liable in tort, thereby giving the claimant a route to redress that is not time-barred. Jackson LJ distinguished *Henderson v Merrett* as covering different ground:

> It is perhaps understandable that professional persons are taken to assume responsibility for economic loss to their clients. Typically, they give advice, prepare reports, draw up accounts, produce plans and so forth. They expect their clients and possibly others to act in reliance upon their work product, often with financial or economic consequences.
>
> When one moves beyond the realm of professional retainers, it by no means follows that every contracting party assumes responsibilities (in the *Hedley Byrne* sense) to the other parties co-extensive with the contractual obligations. Such an analysis would be nonsensical. Contractual and tortious duties have different origins and different functions. Contractual obligations spring from the consent of the parties and the common law principle that contracts should be enforced. Tortious duties are imposed by law, as a matter of policy, in specific situations.

10 *Henderson* (n 5) 185.
11 ibid 194.
12 [2011] EWCA Civ 9, [2012] QB 44.
13 The flues had not been constructed in accordance with good practice, or in accordance with the building regulations in force at the time of construction.
14 His claim was for £35,000.

> Sometimes a particular set of facts may give rise to identical contractual and tortious duties, but self-evidently that is not always the case.[15]

Jackson LJ countenanced the possibility (as dictated by precedent) that a building contractor might 'assume responsibility' so as to attract *Hedley Byrne/Henderson v Merrett* concurrent liability, but asserted that:

> In the present case I see nothing to suggest that the defendant 'assumed responsibility' to the claimant in the *Hedley Byrne* sense. The parties entered into a normal contract whereby the defendant would complete the construction of a house for the claimant to an agreed specification and the claimant would pay the purchase price. The defendant's warranties of quality were set out and the claimant's remedies in the event of breach of warranty were also set out. The parties were not in a professional relationship whereby, for example, the claimant was paying the defendant to give advice or to prepare reports or plans upon which the claimant would act.[16]

Can we account for this different treatment? Here we need to first turn to the underlying purely tortious rules, normally hostile to liability for pure economic loss. *Robinson* sits in the line of cases applying that general rule, namely those involving latent defects in real property, where the English courts have categorically ruled out negligence liability for pure economic loss,[17] that is the cost of repairing the defect or the diminution in value of the property.[18] This prohibition applies whether the tort claim is against the defaulting builder[19] or others involved in the construction process such as local authority surveyors exercising statutory powers under building regulations.[20]

In contrast, there is one enclave[21] where negligence liability in tort for pure economic loss is exceptionally permitted, namely the line of cases derived from *Hedley Byrne & Co Ltd v Heller & Partners Ltd*.[22] Originally, this was rationalised

[15] *Robinson* (n 12) [75]–[76].
[16] ibid [83].
[17] As opposed to personal injury or damage to other property, which is straightforwardly recoverable.
[18] In *Robinson* (n 12), Stanley Burton LJ said, at [92]: 'In my judgment, it must now be regarded as settled law that the builder/vendor of a building does not by reason of his contract to construct or to complete the building assume any liability in the tort of negligence in relation to defects in the building giving rise to purely economic loss.'
[19] *D&F Estates Ltd v Church Commissioners for England* [1989] AC 177 (HL).
[20] *Murphy v Brentwood DC* [1991] 1 AC 398 (HL).
[21] Jane Stapleton, *Three Essays on Tort* (OUP 2021) 53, is critical of this enclave, asking 'why tort law gives certain non-vulnerable commercial claimants this economic free ride, while in physical manufacture cases they are left to their own [devices]?'.
[22] *Hedley Byrne* (n 9).

as a particular exception involving negligent *misstatement* falling short of deceit;[23] discussion therefore centred around the reasons why words, rather than deeds, gave rise to difficulty in applying ordinary negligence principles. Lords Reid and Hodson in particular articulated the problem in this way. It was in this context that an exception was, in theory,[24] recognised, which concerned professional persons making statements in circumstances 'akin to contract'[25] when they had undertaken responsibility for them and realised the other party would be relying on them. So Lord Morris explained that 'if someone possessed of a special skill undertakes, quite irrespective of contract, to apply that skill for the assistance of another person who relies upon such skill, a duty of care will arise. The fact that the service is to be given by means of or by the instrumentality of words can make no difference.' This reasoning reflected Denning LJ's dissent in *Candler v Crane, Christmas & Co*,[26] which was rehabilitated and adopted by the House of Lords.

Robinson and *Henderson* represent the intersection of these two, conflicting, lines of authority. We now have a very peculiar situation, as reflected in Jackson LJ's *dictum* that a builder under a 'normal' building contract (or contract to sell a house still under construction) owes no concurrent tortious duty to their contractual counterparty but might do so if 'the claimant was paying the defendant to give advice or to prepare reports or plans upon which the claimant would act'.

This *dictum* undoubtedly represents the law; it has been applied in numerous subsequent cases[27] and is adopted uncritically in the leading practitioner's text on building contracts.[28] But it demonstrates the irrational landscape in this area. Consider a domestic building containing a latent defect, causing pure economic

[23] In other words, the boundary of *Derry v Peek* (1889) 14 App Cas 337 (HL).

[24] As is well known, the discussion of general principle in *Hedley Byrne* was *obiter*. The actual result was that the defendant bank disclaimed responsibility for the credit reference it gave, and both Lord Morris and Lord Devlin suggested that, even if there had been no disclaimer, there might not have been a duty of care on the facts.

[25] The House of Lords were untroubled by the fact that the credit reference was not given by the bank in exchange for any consideration. This may reflect judicial scepticism about the requirement of consideration, but it is more likely a recognition that the giving of a credit reference is not the banking equivalent of a gift. As Lord Devlin put it, at 529:

> It may often be material to consider whether the adviser is acting purely out of good nature or whether he is getting his reward in some indirect form. The service that a bank performs in giving a reference is not done simply out of a desire to assist commerce. It would discourage the customers of the bank if their deals fell through because the bank had refused to testify to their credit when it was good.

[26] [1951] 2 KB 164 (CA).

[27] See, eg, *Broster v Galliard Docklands Ltd* [2011] EWCH 1722 (TCC) and *Thomas v Taylor Wimpey Development* [2019] EWHC 1134 (TCC).

[28] Vivian Ramsey and Stephen Furst (eds), *Keating on Construction Contracts* (11th edn, Sweet & Maxwell 2023) 7-06ff.

loss when discovered by a subsequent owner. English law imposes no tortious negligence liability on the primary wrongdoer, the negligent builder, who created the defect, nor on the local authority surveyor who negligently failed to spot the defect at the time of construction; moreover there is highly unlikely to be contractual liability on the vendor (other than in the very unlikely event of an express warranty). However, a surveyor or valuer who negligently fails to spot the defect at the time of the owner's purchase *does* incur negligence liability under *Hedley Byrne* to the subsequent owner, potentially even where the valuation was commissioned by the mortgagee and the report contained a disclaimer of liability to anyone else.[29] The allocation of risk reflected in this pattern seems the wrong way round and is difficult to defend.

Why do we speak of intersection, given that *Robinson* did not involve negligent misstatement? The reason is that the law was extended in *Henderson*, expanding *Hedley Byrne* from its original enclave of 'negligent misstatements'[30] to cover 'negligent performance of services'.[31] This expansion is itself controversial and has been subjected to cogent criticism. For example, Andrew Burrows points out that 'once one moves from statements to the performance of beneficial services, a complaint of negligently caused pure economic loss naturally embraces a complaint of failure to benefit'.[32] This in turn means that there is nothing *independent* about the tort cause of action, to justify concurrent liability: 'Any idea that the law of tort simply imposes an obligation to use reasonable care where the defendant is performing services, analogously to its imposition of liability for statements, fails to provide any convincing justification for why the defendant is held liable not merely for harmful interference but also for a failure to benefit the plaintiff'.[33] Simon Whittaker is similarly critical, regarding the decision on the facts as justifiable, but decrying the breadth of Lord Goff's explanation of the principle, apt to catch failure to perform and, more seriously, to support a duty of care where the contract was silent on the matter.[34]

[29] *Smith* [1990] 1 AC 831 (HL).

[30] Stapleton (n 21) 52 describes *Henderson* as an investment decision case, but one that does not involve reliance by the claimant on the defendant's advice, and rather where it is 'the defendant himself, who decides to commit the claimant's funds to a transaction that is less lucrative than one in which the funds would have been invested if the defendant had not relied on his own impugned investment judgement'.

[31] Judgment in *Henderson* was given on 25 July 1994. *White v Jones* [1995] 2 AC 207 (HL), which was also not a case of negligent misstatement, followed on 16 February 1995.

[32] Andrew Burrows 'Solving the Problem of Concurrent Liability' (1995) 48 CLP 103, 119.

[33] ibid 121.

[34] Simon Whittaker, 'The Application of the "Broad Principle of *Hedley Byrne*" as between Parties to a Contract' (1997) 17 LS 160, 187:

> It is submitted that where liability under *Hedley Byrne* is put in terms of a negligent misstatement given by a person who can foresee that it will be relied on rather than in the broader terms of an 'assumption of responsibility' in the sense of an agreement to perform a service for the other party, then there is nothing inconsistent in finding a duty of care under *Hedley Byrne*

III. Default Rules and Exceptions—A Logical Fallacy

We will return to whether Lord Goff's 'assumption of responsibility' reasoning can justify the inconsistent default position in *Robinson*'s 'normal' building contract case. For now, it is worth pausing to note a logical fallacy in the approach adopted in *Robinson*, which is central to the argument in this chapter.

The House of Lords in *Hedley Byrne* carved out the circumstances where a duty of care might, exceptionally, apply for pure economic loss, in response to the way the case was argued: the boundaries of the tort of deceit and the problem of *words* operating differently from *deeds*. An exception for statements made (in circumstances 'akin to contract') by a professional or another party in a special relationship with the claimant, relied on by the latter, is a coherent, exceptional category of liability in that context. But though the reasoning makes sense in its context, it has spawned a logical fallacy. Where economic harm is inflicted by negligent deeds not words, the default rule is *not* 'no liability unless there's deceit'; it is (for example) 'no liability for negligent construction of a defective building'. The *Hedley Byrne* exception relates to a different default rule. It is therefore illogical to assert that the only circumstances in which a builder can be liable for negligently building a defective house will be if the facts can be strained into an analogy with a professional writing a valuation report or giving investment advice.

This is not a basis on which to criticise the reasoning in *Robinson*: the Court of Appeal was bound by the case law ruling out negligence liability for builders causing pure economic loss, so the only possible exception was one within the *Hedley Byrne* enclave. But as an academic exercise, it is valuable to explore whether this really is the only common law exception available, or whether the law *should* consider afresh the question of whether a builder can exceptionally be (concurrently) liable in tort for breach of the implied term of reasonable care owed to their contracting counterparty.

The analysis will proceed as follows. First, it will ask whether the arguments offered in *Henderson* apply equally or justify ruling out concurrent liability for *Robinson*'s 'normal' building contracts. Secondly, it will explore whether, in the *Robinson* fact pattern, the concept of 'assumption of responsibility' provides any meaningful assistance. Thirdly, it will consider the proper context for discussion of *Robinson* (the 'no liability' default rule for defective construction work causing pure financial loss) and ask whether any exceptions to that 'no liability' default rule should be recognised, in concurrent contractual and purely tortious cases.

but no express or implied duty of care in contract. By contrast, however, to the extent to which a defendant's having 'assumed responsibility' for doing something is to mean that he 'agreed to do it', then it is submitted that it is much more difficult to hold that a party 'agreed to do it' for the purposes of the tort but did not 'agree to do it' for the purposes of the contract.

IV. Analysis of the Inconsistent Fact Patterns

A. Do the Arguments Offered in *Henderson* Justify Ruling Out Concurrent Liability for *Robinson*'s 'Normal Building' Contracts?

Most obviously, *Robinson* involved precisely the same limitation problem as *Henderson*: the claimant could not have discovered the existence of the defendant's breach before the contractual limitation period expired. As has been seen, this was the explicit motivation for the House of Lords' decision in *Henderson*. More generally, cases of defective building work involve the same high risk of latent defects, and long periods between breach and damage, as negligent professional advice cases such as *Henderson*. Andrew Burrows exposes the reasoning in *Henderson* to cogent criticism, but ultimately supports it as a sensible way round the limitation problem: 'The pragmatic solution is to allow plaintiffs to evade those unwarranted disadvantages by framing what is in essence a contractual claim as a claim in tort.'[35] It is hard to see why the same pragmatic justification should not apply in a 'normal' building contract case.

As a matter of authority, Lord Goff in *Henderson* did not discuss the question of concurrent liability for negligent breach of a building contract. This was not in issue and would have been a surprising inclusion, given the relatively recent affirmation of the general prohibition on purely tortious liability in this context in *D&F Estates*.[36] His acceptance of concurrent liability in a *Hedley Byrne* fact pattern was, however, expressly based on the seminal first instance decision of Oliver J in *Midland Bank Trust Co Ltd v Hett, Stubbs & Kemp (A Firm)*,[37] a professional negligence action brought concurrently in tort (for limitation reasons) against solicitors, but where the reasoning approving concurrent liability was not confined to the professional negligence context.[38] Of course *Midland Bank* also predated the prohibition on negligence liability for defective building work in *D&F Estates*, where *Dutton* was expressly overruled. The point is simply that the boundary of the *Hedley Byrne* exception that was applied in *Henderson* is not, as a matter of authority, absolutely set against extension to building contracts.

This is confirmed when we see that the extended *Hedley Byrne* principle has been applied since *Henderson* (and thus of course post *D&F Estates*) in areas extending beyond negligent misstatement and the performance of professional advisory services, into those much closer to *Robinson*'s normal building contracts.

35 Burrows (n 32) 122.

36 *D&F Estates* (n 19).

37 [1979] Ch 384 (Ch).

38 eg, Oliver J cited with approval the judgment of Lord Denning MR in *Dutton v Bognor Regis UDC* [1972] 1 QB 373 (CA) 394 which 'in the clearest terms' said that 'the fact that the defendant [building contractor] is the vendor, so that the relationship between him and the purchaser is a contractual one, clearly does not . . . exclude a parallel liability in tort'.

For example, in *Barclays Bank plc v Fairclough Building Ltd (No 2)*,[39] a specialist cleaning company was subcontracted to carry out industrial cleaning of asbestos roofing on warehouses, but did so negligently, causing asbestos slurry to run onto the buildings and surrounding area. Their contracting counterparty claimed a contribution to the cost of the remedial work, and this claim succeeded. Citing *Henderson*, Beldam LJ held: 'A skilled contractor undertaking maintenance work to a building assumed a responsibility which invites reliance no less than the financial or other professional adviser does in undertaking his work. The nature of the responsibility is the same though it will differ in extent.'[40]

Perhaps a more convincing ground of distinction lies in the *fiduciary* roots of the *Hedley Byrne* principle, beginning with the House of Lords in *Nocton v Lord Ashburton*,[41] distinguishing the requirement of deceit in *Derry v Peek*,[42] where the parties were in a fiduciary relationship. Lord Browne-Wilkinson in *Henderson* emphasised the fiduciary context of the decision as a justification for extending *Hedley Byrne* to concurrent cases, stating:

> The extent and nature of the fiduciary duties owed in any particular case fall to be determined by reference to any underlying contractual relationship between the parties . . . The existence of an underlying contract (e.g. as between solicitor and client) does not automatically exclude the general duty of care which the law imposes on those who voluntarily assume to act for others.[43]

Although historically important, fiduciary status is not a precondition for liability under *Hedley Byrne* today.[44] But it does explain why professional negligence came to be regarded as the paradigm example of its application—the liability of solicitors, valuers, accountants, and other professional advisers. It is, however, worth noting that, in the twenty-first century, there is no longer a clear divide between 'white collar' professionals with quill pens and 'blue collar' builders with grubby overalls. In the recent case of *Sheffield Teaching Hospital Foundation Trust v Hadfield Healthcare Partnerships Ltd*,[45] O'Farrell J declined to strike out a third party claim against a construction company in respect of a concurrent duty of care in tort, noting that it is:

> [R]ight to question, as a matter of law, whether there is any basis on which building contractors should be distinguished from other professionals when

39 [1995] PIQR P152 (CA).
40 ibid 167.
41 [1914] AC 932 (HL).
42 *Derry* (n 23).
43 *Henderson* (n 5) 206.
44 For an extreme example, see *Chaudhry v Prabhakar* [1989] 1 WLR 29 (CA). Note, though, that the defendant conceded the existence of a duty of care, a concession (rightly) criticised by May LJ.
45 [2023] EWHC 644 (TCC).

> ascertaining whether there has been any *Hedley Byrne* assumption of responsibility. The range of recognisable professions generally has expanded since *Hedley Byrne* and *Henderson*, with the introduction of new technologies and industries, greater research and understanding, and improvements in the training and standards of specialist areas of work. In particular, within the construction industry today there are many disciplines of special skill and expertise which could be described as professional.[46]

B. Do We Gain Any Assistance from the Concept of 'Assumption of Responsibility'?

O'Farrell J refers to the core question, namely the meaning of 'assumption of responsibility' in this context, since under the law as it stands after *Henderson* this represents the only exception where pure economic loss is recoverable. As we have seen, Jackson LJ in *Robinson* concluded that the facts revealed 'nothing to suggest that the defendant "assumed responsibility" to the claimant in the *Hedley Byrne* sense. The parties . . . were not in a professional relationship whereby, for example, the claimant was paying the defendant to give advice or to prepare reports or plans upon which the claimant would act.'[47]

To the layman, it would be surprising—startling even—to be told that, when they make a building contract with a builder, paying the builder to build a house for them or to sell them a house under construction, the law does not regard that builder as 'assuming responsibility' to them. When asked to explain why not, very few lawyers would attempt a convincing explanation. It should be conceded that most lawyers would also intuit that not every negligent breach of contract attracts concurrent liability in tort, so there must be a test to discriminate between them. The big question is: is 'assumption of responsibility' the appropriate test?

Lord Goff in *Henderson* said that, 'especially in a context concerned with a liability which may arise under a contract or in a situation "equivalent to contract", it must be expected that an objective test will be applied when asking the question whether, in a particular case, responsibility should *be held to have been assumed* by the defendant to the plaintiff'.[48]

The concept is undoubtedly objective, in the sense that it does not turn on the defendant's subjective attitude to whether or not they are undertaking responsibility. But beyond that, no guidance is offered on how the reasonable observer would make this objective judgement. In fact, Lord Goff's phrase 'held to have

46 ibid [78].
47 *Robinson* (n 12) [83].
48 *Henderson* (n 5) 181 (emphasis added).

been assumed' lets the cat out of the bag—this is a judgement for the court, the criteria for which are opaque in the extreme.

It is therefore not surprising that the concept of 'assumption of responsibility' is much derided, as a meaningful test for liability in this context. Writing before *Henderson*, Barker encapsulates the problem perfectly:

> The language of 'voluntary assumption' is particularly slippery in this respect and judicial interpretations of what it is for a defendant to 'voluntarily assume' a responsibility vary in strength. Sometimes, they mean that the defendant has impliedly promised the plaintiff that he will take care in his conduct; at others, that the defendant has exercised a degree of 'choice' of some kind. More recently, judges have interpreted the phrase to mean no more than that the defendant has voluntarily 'acted'.[49]

Since *Henderson*, many commentators have noted that Barker's criticism is even more compelling. Jonathan Morgan rightly points out that it is 'most unfortunate that inconsistent and insufficiently rigorous invocation of assumption of responsibility by the courts leaves its true nature in doubt. Current practice is open to the charge of fictitious, disingenuous "deemed assumption" (itself, of course, a contradiction in terms).'[50] Jane Stapleton is likewise damning:

> What is the coherent normative justification for a tort entitlement in these cases[?] . . . Much appellate mention is made in this regard of the notion of the 'assumption of responsibility' by the defendant. Yet how this phenomenon is to be identified in the facts, short of an explicit statement of acceptance of legal responsibility for the economic risk, has not been made clear by the courts. This leaves the suspicion that the notion is no more than an opaque conclusionary label.[51]

For these commentators (and the present author), trying to decide whether a builder 'assumes responsibility' in the sense required for the tort of negligence is a pointless exercise, obscuring the real concerns that drive the perverse borderline we currently see. But others do attempt to defend the concept as a meaningful one—could their analysis provide a defensible answer to the question of whether a builder assumes responsibility, in the technical sense, to their contracting counterparty?

First, we should note Paul Mitchell's brilliant explanation that liability under *Hedley Byrne* can be understood as a direct descendant of the ancient assumpsit action, representing the 'middle ground' between contract and tort, though of

[49] Kit Barker, 'Unreliable Assumptions in the Modern Law of Negligence' (1993) 109 LQR 461, 462.
[50] Morgan (n 4) 152.
[51] Stapleton (n 21) 61.

course from many centuries before lawyers would have thought in those substantive terms.[52] David Ibbetson has explained to me that the question of whether an action in assumpsit was available against a builder who built a defective house is as difficult a question of legal history as our contemporary conundrum! In short, the answer shifted depending on the century; Ibbetson suggested the answer was probably 'yes' before the sixteenth century, but more problematic thereafter.[53] Mitchell certainly cites case law that extends into our territory, in particular the case of *Elsee v Gatward*,[54] where the Court of King's Bench held that a carpenter was liable in assumpsit for mis-performance, namely causing pure economic loss by using the wrong materials. Overall, there is no clear prohibition on liability for builders in the historical development from the assumpsit action.

Among contemporary analysts, Nolan offers the most vociferous support for the concept of assumption of responsibility as a meaningful legal test, whilst conceding that the concept has not been used consistently by the courts:[55]

> The end result is that when a negligence lawyer talks about an 'assumption of responsibility', she could mean any of three different things: (1) the taking on of a task, including by beginning performance of it ('role' responsibility, and the second sense of 'undertaking'); (2) the acceptance of a legal duty (which is to say, an acceptance of responsibility in the 'legal responsibility' sense); or (3) the giving of a promise or assurance (the first sense of 'undertaking'). Furthermore, it seems to me from reading the cases that judges have ascribed all three of these possible meanings to the phrase, and indeed sometimes have ascribed more than one of these meanings to it in the same judgment.[56]

Reviewing the cases, Nolan concludes in favour of the first of these possibilities: 'it seems clear that by far the most plausible way of characterising the conduct that, at least prima facie, triggers that conclusion is that A has *taken on a task or job* for B',[57] and later '[w]hat matters is that A has taken on the task, not how A has done so'.[58] For Nolan, this formulation explains the element of 'privity' inherent in the

[52] Paul Mitchell, '*Hedley Byrne & Co v Heller & Partners Ltd*' in Charles Mitchell and Paul Mitchell (eds), *Landmark Cases in the Law of Tort* (Hart 2010)

[53] See the discussion of the emergent action of assumpsit in the context of what would be regarded today as contractual and/or tortious disputes in David Ibbetson *A Historical Introduction to the Law of Obligations* (OUP 1999) 130–51.

[54] (1793) 5 TR 143.

[55] Donal Nolan, 'Assumption of Responsibility: Four Questions' (2019) 72 CLP 123. At times, Nolan goes beyond the usual approach to considering alternative points of view, eg, at 158, by expressing a 'degree of frustration with much of the recent scholarship on this question, which to my mind takes a somewhat narrow and blinkered view of the law'.

[56] ibid 129.

[57] ibid 129 (emphasis added).

[58] ibid 133.

concept,[59] but it is immediately apparent that 'assuming responsibility for a task' encompasses virtually every contractual promise of work, including the construction of a building, a matter which Nolan does not discuss.

Kit Barker (writing before *Henderson* was decided),[60] identified the same model of assumption of responsibility in the case law[61] and described it as the weakest model, meaning nothing more than that the defendant was acting voluntarily, a requirement already essential for negligence liability. As a test for when liability should be imposed, he concluded, it is a fiction: 'We are left none the wiser about the considerations which are pertinent to duty in cases of economic loss, misstatement, or omission. In order to say something which is true, the courts have reduced the strength of what they say beyond the point at which it is in the slightest bit useful.'[62]

Nothing in *Henderson* or in the case law following it provides any satisfactory response to this conclusion. Instead of persisting with the fruitless exercise of trying to work out whether the legal test for assumption of responsibility catches a builder making and performing a building contract, it is better to abandon this exercise and confront the correct default rule, when considering the *Robinson* fact pattern.

C. Exceptions in the Appropriate Context: The 'no Liability' Default Rule for Defective Construction Work Causing Pure Economic Loss

Rather than seeking to force the fact pattern of *Robinson* into an exception designed in the context of liability for negligent misstatement, using the inapt tool of assumption of responsibility, we should consider the question in its proper context. *Should* the law recognise any exceptions to the prohibition on negligence liability for defective construction work causing pure economic loss and, if so, in what circumstances? At first glance, where negligent deeds rather than negligent words are concerned, the case for liability seems stronger, as Tony Weir averted to in his seminal contemporary critique of *Hedley Byrne*: words are the 'weakest form of act'.[63]

As an academic exercise, it is important to consider the policy implications[64] of 'creating' new exceptions to a general default rule of no liability. It is not entirely

[59] The defendant must have assumed responsibility *to the claimant*, cf *Banca Nazionale del Lavoro SPA v Playboy Club London Ltd* [2018] UKSC 43, [2018] 1 WLR 4041.

[60] Barker (n 49).

[61] Citing, eg, *Reid v Rush & Tompkins Group plc* [1990] 1 WLR 212 (CA) 229: 'The concept of voluntary assumption of responsibility as used in the Hedley Byrne case seems to me to refer to an act by a defendant whereby he voluntarily does something, which affects the plaintiff, and it is such an act that a reasonable man would recognise that in the circumstances he is required to perform it with due care' (Ralph Gibson LJ).

[62] Barker (n 49) 474.

[63] Tony Weir, 'Liability for Syntax' (1963) 21 CLJ 216.

[64] In the sense of considerations of both interpersonal justice and community welfare, as illuminated in Andrew Robertson, 'Policy-Based Reasoning in Duty of Care Cases' (2013) 33 LS 119.

clear whether the current Supreme Court would agree,[65] but it seems appropriate to do so where (notionally) the court is being invited to revisit an existing default rule. As Lord Reed said in *Robinson v Chief Constable of West Yorkshire Police*:

> Where the existence or non-existence of a duty of care has been established, a consideration of justice and reasonableness forms part of the basis on which the law has arrived at the relevant principles. It is therefore unnecessary and inappropriate to reconsider whether the existence of the duty is fair, just and reasonable (*subject to the possibility that this court may be invited to depart from an established line of authority*).[66]

This in turn raises something controversial, namely Lord Goff's *dictum* in *Henderson* that 'once the case is identified as falling within the *Hedley Byrne* principle, there should be no need to embark upon any further enquiry whether it is "fair, just and reasonable" to impose liability for economic loss'.[67] This is problematic when it is sought to extend *Hedley Byrne* liability to a novel factual situation, and indeed is routinely ignored.[68] In any event, we are exploring the negligent construction of defective property default rule in its own terms, not attempting to squeeze it into a *Hedley Byrne* claim.

On this assumption, can we identify features of a building contract case such as *Robinson* that might, exceptionally, justify an exception to the default rule of no liability for pure economic loss derived from *D&F Estates*? Can we justify another 'pragmatic solution'[69] where the claimant and defendant were contracting counterparties, but the claimant's contractual action is out of time? Although in a sense this is an illogical structure, since what is being considered is *tort* liability, we will concentrate first on the question of concurrent tort liability in the *Robinson* fact pattern, then cross-check with purely tortious fact patterns, such as where the claimant is not the first purchaser from the negligent defendant.[70]

The most obvious feature of *Robinson* is that the claimant was a *consumer*, having contracted with the defendant building company to purchase a house which

[65] See Janet O'Sullivan 'Negligence, Policy and "Novel Exceptions"' in Jodi Gardner and others (eds), *Politics, Policy and Private Law*, vol I (Hart 2023).

[66] [2018] AC 736 [26] (emphasis added).

[67] *Henderson* (n 5) 181.

[68] The 'fair, just and reasonable' enquiry was central to the reasoning of, eg, the Court of Appeal in *Patchett v Swimming Pool & Allied Trades Association Ltd* [2009] EWCA Civ 717, [2010] 2 All ER (Comm) 138. The court concluded that a *Hedley Byrne* duty of care was not owed by a trade association regarding statements on its website.

[69] Recall Andrew Burrows' ultimate acceptance of *Henderson* as a 'pragmatic solution' to the limitation problem.

[70] Or where the work is performed gratuitously, though this is not likely to be a common problem (cf credit references), although note *Lejonvarn v Burgess* [2020] EWCA Civ 114, [2020] 4 WLR 43. In that case the Court of Appeal held that an architect giving gratuitous advice had no contractual liability to the claimant but owed a duty of care in tort under *Hedley Byrne*.

was then under construction. Writing extra-judicially after *Robinson*, Jackson LJ averted to the statutory regime for contracts for services, in an attempt to explain the different treatment of builders and professional advisers:

> Whilst there are always problems in drawing the line, there is a discernible distinction between those who design buildings and those who construct buildings. The former provide a service and are subject to the implied term [of reasonable care and skill] contained in s. 13 of the Supply of Goods and Services Act 1982. I doubt that the latter are providing a service within the meaning of s. 13.

It is unclear whether the same conclusion would apply today where, as in *Robinson*, the claimant making the contract is a *consumer*, given the subsequent enactment of the Consumer Rights Act 2015 ('CRA'), but it seems inherently unlikely that it would be so excluded, given that the regime is designed to maximise protection for consumers. Although the CRA reproduces the concept of a 'contract for services',[71] it does so in the context of a core definition of 'consumer contract' as one made between a trader[72] and a consumer.[73] Since a building contract with a consumer will now count as a contract for the supply of a service, this means that an implied contractual obligation of reasonable care and skill cannot be excluded.[74]

All this is perhaps only tangentially relevant to the question of whether a court should recognise an exception to *D&F Estates*, but it does set the question in its contemporary context of particular vigilance to protect consumers. Parliament has acknowledged the particular vulnerability of a consumer dealing with a trader. We should explore whether this theme should be reflected in the recognition of a duty of care in tort owed by a builder to a consumer in respect of domestic building work, concurrent with their contractual obligation of reasonable care. What are the features of the consumer/building contractor relationship calling for such exceptional treatment?

The first feature to consider is the consumer purchaser's reliance on the builder and the reasonableness of that reliance. Away from the concurrent liability pattern and in a purely tortious context, the courts have held that a valuer instructed by the mortgagee cannot disclaim liability to a consumer purchaser 'at the lower end of the housing market' who relies on the mortgage valuation, but can do so to 'purchasers of an expensive property whether residential or commercial'.[75] The

[71] The regime is contained in ss 48–57, which reproduce the basic implied terms that were previously in the Supply of Goods and Services Act 1982, and include additional, new protections for consumers.

[72] S 2(1): 'A person acting for purposes relating to that person's trade, business, craft or profession, whether acting personally or through another person acting in the trader's name or on the trader's behalf.'

[73] S 2(2): 'An individual acting for purposes that are wholly or mainly outside that individual's trade, business, craft or profession.'

[74] S 57, as opposed to being subject to a test of reasonableness under the Unfair Contract Terms Act 1977 as in *Robinson* itself.

[75] *Smith* (n 29) 872; contrast *Scullion Bank of Scotland plc (t/a Colleys)* [2011] 1 WLR 3212 (CA).

expressed reason[76] for the generosity in the former case is that the defendant will know that a 'potential mortgagor seeking to enter the lower end of the housing market'[77] would be unlikely to be able to afford a separate survey report. If it is reasonable to assume that a domestic purchaser at the lower end of the housing market will not be able to afford their own survey, this must surely imply an equivalent understanding that such a purchaser, where contracting directly with the builder, will be reasonably relying on the builder.[78] Ironically, it transpires that the property in *Robinson* was a large, expensive detached home,[79] meaning that analogising from the reasoning in *Smith v Eric S. Bush*, protecting the 'lower end of the housing market' does not help to justify concurrent liability in tort on *Robinson*'s particular facts. But there are other features of the consumer/building contractor relationship that apply more generally to all consumer purchasers.

In particular, consumers' lack of any meaningful opportunity to negotiate or influence the terms on which they deal with the building contractor is significant. In *Involnert Management Inc v Aprilgrange Ltd*,[80] Leggatt J averted to an analogous feature of the claimants' position in *Henderson* (his concern was primarily with the 'Indirect Names', namely those not in a direct contractual relationship with the defendants, but the point is of general relevance):

> It is fair to say that Lord Goff did not spell out expressly the features which distinguished the contractual arrangements for underwriting at Lloyd's from cases such as his example of an ordinary building contract where the existence of a comparable contractual chain is inconsistent with an assumption of responsibility. It is noteworthy, however, that in *Henderson v Merrett* the relevant contractual structure was fixed by law . . . a name was required to contract with a members' agent by entering into a prescribed form of agency agreement, and the members' agent was in turn required to enter into a prescribed form of sub-agency agreement with a managing agent. The names therefore had no choice about the extent of the contractual rights conferred on them and no opportunity to bargain for any contractual rights directly against the managing agents.[81]

[76] It should also be noted that, although technically not in a contractual relationship with the defendant valuer, Mrs Smith indirectly paid his fee, having reimbursed her mortgagee.

[77] *Smith* (n 29) 872. For the same reason, the valuer's disclaimer was held to be unreasonable under the Unfair Contract Terms Act 1977.

[78] It is recommended that a purchaser of a new-build home commissions a 'snagging survey' before committing to buy, but many will not do so.

[79] In an early draft of this chapter, I glibly described the house bought by Mr and Mrs Robinson as 'modest', implying that it would meet the description of the 'lower end of the housing market'. I am grateful to my colleague Nicholas McBride, who commentated on my paper at the conference, for putting me right. He discovered that the property in question is now valued at about £900,000, having last been sold in September 2021 for £750,000.

[80] [2015] EWHC 2225 (Comm), [2016] 1 All ER (Comm) 913.

[81] ibid [287].

It might be argued that this justification—the claimant's lack of choice over the terms—applies *a fortiori* in a case involving a domestic building contract or purchase off-plan from a builder, as in *Robinson*. Stapleton disputes Leggatt J's justification for liability in *Henderson*, arguing that although it is true that the Indirect Names would not have been able to get direct contractual protection from the defendants, that did not make them vulnerable, 'because they could have walked away from the commercial arrangement on offer . . . These were non-vulnerable investors who chose to enter a risky commercial arrangement.'[82] In contrast, consumer purchasers (like the Robinsons) are buying a home, not investing for profit. It is implausible to expect them to bargain with a builder or developer over the terms of the transaction—in that sense at least they are 'vulnerable' and deserve the protection of the tort of negligence.

A final exceptional feature to note is that, unlike many instances of pure economic loss caused by defective building work, the facts of *Robinson* involved a potentially *dangerous* defect. The problem with the flues came to light because a British Gas service engineer conducted a test to check that the gas fire was effectively drawing combustion products from the room in which it was located. As Jackson LJ explained, '[t]he family room gas fire failed that test. The service engineer recorded this and he also recorded that the gas fire had a "poor flue run". Both gas fires were disconnected for safety reasons.'[83] This is significant because it emphasises the constraint on the part of the claimant to carry out the remedial work. But it is also significant when we consider the historical development of tort liability for defective building work in the era of *Anns v Merton LBC*,[84] and the subsequent reversal of that development by the House of Lords in *D&F Estates*,[85] then *Murphy v Brentwood DC*. The House of Lords' reasoning in the *Anns* era did not emphasise the purely economic nature of the claimant's loss, but rather the dangerous nature of the defect (inadequate foundations), justifying the award of damages as, in effect, preventative or anticipatory damages to avoid 'personal injury that hasn't happened yet'.[86] This particular treatment of dangerous defects was heavily criticised in *D&F Estates* and was not preserved when *Anns* was overruled

[82] Stapleton (n 21) 56.
[83] *Robinson* (n 12) [15].
[84] [1978] AC 728 (HL).
[85] *D&F Estates* (n 19).
[86] In *Anns* (n 84) 759–60, Lord Wilberforce said:

> If classification is required, the relevant damage is in my opinion material, physical damage, and what is recoverable is the amount of expenditure necessary to restore the dwelling to a condition in which it is no longer a danger to the health or safety of persons occupying and possibly (depending on the circumstances) expenses arising from necessary displacement. On the question of damages generally I have derived much assistance from the judgment (dissenting on this point, but of strong persuasive force) of Laskin J in the Canadian Supreme Court case of *Rivtow Marine Ltd v Washington Iron Works* [1973] 6 WWR 692, 715.

This cannot explain the aberrant decision in *Junior Books Ltd v Veitchi Co Ltd* [1983] 1 AC 520 (HL).

in *Murphy*. The criticism noted its novelty, and its potential to undermine conventional negligence principles, as Lord Oliver explained in *D&F Estates*:

> It has to be accepted either that the damage giving rise to the cause of action is pure economic loss not consequential upon injury to person or property—a concept not so far accepted into English law outside the *Hedley Byrne* type of liability ... or that there is a new species of the tort of negligence in which the occurrence of actual damage is no longer the gist of the action but is replaced by the perception of the risk of damage.[87]

This allegation of novelty was a principal strand of the reasoning that lay at the heart of the rejection of *Anns*, and thus of *Dutton*. It is essentially a re-categorisation argument, that the Lords in *Anns* did not appreciate how much of a drastic extension in the law they were making, that they had aligned the facts (in an impermissible way) with future personal injury, failing to appreciate that those facts were properly to be categorised as pure economic loss. Three decades later, it might be thought that recognising a limited exception, allowing for (concurrent) liability in tort for negligent breach of a consumer building contract leading to a *dangerous* defect, would not radically destabilise the law of negligence.

It is very important to acknowledge the other principal strand in the reasoning in *D&F Estates*, and later *Murphy*, namely the interrelation between negligence liability and the statutory regime in the Defective Premises Act 1972 ('DPA'). This is essentially a deference argument: that Parliament in the DPA set the boundaries and limitations of tort liability for defective building work, and the common law should not subvert that, which the House believed it had done in the regime under *Anns*. As Lord Bridge put it in *D&F Estates*,

> The statutory duty imposed by the Act of 1972 was confined to dwelling-houses and limited to defects appearing within six years. The common law duty, if it existed, could not be so confined or so limited. I cannot help feeling that consumer protection is an area of law where legislation is much better left to the legislators.[88]

The statutory duty owed by any 'person taking on work for or in connection with the provision of a dwelling' is a strict one, to 'see to it that the work which he takes on is done in a workmanlike or, as the case may be, professional manner, with proper materials and so that as regards that work the dwelling will be fit for habitation when completed'.[89] This chapter cannot begin to do justice to the theoretical debate about the deference argument: whether the common law should regard the

[87] *D&F Estates* (n 19) 213.
[88] ibid 208.
[89] Defective Premises Act 1972, s 1(1).

boundary of a statutory regime as precluding development outside it, or whether that is an important gap-filling function of the common law.[90] For these purposes, it is worth pointing out those gaps—that the statutory duty only applies to 'dwellings' and only to defects that render a dwelling 'unfit for human habitation'. The courts have been relatively generous about the meaning of this latter phrase,[91] so it is possible that it would be broad enough catch the dangerous flue in *Robinson*, although only the gas fire in one room (the family room) failed the appropriate fume test.

There is a final, and very pertinent, twist to this discussion of whether an exceptional concurrent duty of care in negligence should be recognised, on the fact pattern of *Robinson*. Until recently, the statutory duty under the DPA added nothing to the analysis, because it suffered from the equivalent limitation difficulty to a claim for breach of contract: six years from the date the dwelling was completed, with no secondary limitation period once latent defects became discoverable. In a nice irony, given our 'crying for the moon' context,[92] this limitation period has recently been significantly extended, as part of the legislative response to the Grenfell Tower disaster. Under the Building Safety Act 2022 ('BSA'), the limitation period for claims under the DPA has been extended to thirty years retrospectively for claims accruing before 28 June 2022 and to fifteen years for claims accruing after 28 June 2022. This means that the question of whether or not a particular claim falls within the DPA now becomes of crucial significance.[93] This may, in time, resolve the need for a common law exception to *D&F Estates*, in the *Robinson* fact pattern of consumer building cases involving dangerous defects.[94] The fact that Parliament has (exceptionally) intervened does demonstrate the unfairness of the result in a case like *Robinson*, an unfairness that has little to do with the boundaries of *Hedley Byrne* liability.

The preceding discussion, of a potential exception to the default prohibition on negligence claims for pure economic loss in the context of defective building work, of course applies equally to pure tort claims, namely where there is no concurrent

[90] Lord Goff's approach to limitation in *Henderson* (n 5).

[91] eg, in *Rendlesham Estates plc v Barr Ltd* [2014] EWHC 3968 (TCC), [2015] 1 WLR 3663 (which concerned mould and damp in a residential block of flats), Edwards-Stuart J said, at [68]:

> In my judgment, for a dwelling to be fit for habitation within the meaning of the Act, it must, on completion (without any remedial works being carried out): (a) be capable of occupation for a reasonable time without risk to the health or safety of the occupants: where a dwelling is or is part of a newly constructed building, what is a reasonable time will be a question of fact (it may or may not be as long as the design life of the building); and (b) be capable of occupation for a reasonable time without undue inconvenience or discomfort to the occupants.

[92] *Henderson* (n 5) 186.

[93] Not just the meaning of 'unfit for human habitation' but also of 'dwelling'—would it catch student accommodation, for example?

[94] Similarly, the Building Safety Act 2022 contained a requirement for an independent body to deal with consumer complaints regarding newly built homes—the New Homes Ombudsman Service—which will provide some claimants with redress without the need for civil litigation.

contractual claim against the defendant.[95] The most common fact pattern will be where the claimant has acquired an interest in the property from the original owner before the defect has come to light. *Henderson* extended negligence liability to the 'Indirect Names',[96] but thought that this *Hedley Byrne* application would not extend to a case involving a chain of building contracts, such *Simaan General Contracting Co v Pilkington Glass (No 2)*.[97] Here, the head-contractor claimant had deliberately put in place a contractual structure that did not involve a direct contractual link with the defendant and could not look to the law of negligence to 'get round' that contractual structure. *Simaan* seems absolutely correct in its commercial context but, it is suggested, should not rule out negligence liability in the exceptional, domestic, fact pattern we have been discussing, where the claimant had no way of obtaining contractual protection.

V. Conclusion

I find myself in an odd position. If we picture an ideal world where our 'crying to the moon' has been answered, and the limitation rules are rationalised so that there is no advantage in pleading tort in an action for professional negligence, that would leave *Hedley Byrne* to those unusual, non-contractual fact patterns, where liability is actually relatively rare.[98] Here, Tony Weir's contemporaneous criticism of the general principle remains (certainly in commercial cases) as compelling as ever:

> They made bad business deals, having taken only a free opinion before hazarding their wealth in the hope of profit, no part of which, had it eventuated, would they have transferred to the honest person whom they now seek to saddle with their loss. The defectiveness of a system which refuses in such a case to sever the risk of loss from the chance of profit is not obvious.[99]

In contrast, reflecting on the issues in this chapter confirms my view that English law threw the baby out with the bathwater when it ruled out tort liability for the primary wrongdoer in a case of defective domestic building work—namely, the builder.[100] In other words, a coherent line could, for many reasons, have been

[95] The Defective Premises Act 1972 duty is owed to 'every person who acquires an interest in the dwelling'.

[96] The subject of fierce criticism by Stapleton (n 21) 56.

[97] [1988] QB 758 (CA).

[98] See Janet O'Sullivan, 'Suing in Tort Where no Contractual Claim Will Lie—a Bird's Eye View' (2007) 23 PN 165.

[99] Weir (n 63) 218.

[100] As put in the opening paragraph of Duncan Wallace, '*Anns* Beyond Repair' (1991) 107 LQR 228:

> There have for many years in the United Kingdom been serious problems of defective work in new buildings. It is often too widespread to be accidental, and cannot be divorced from the fact

drawn between that case and that of the local authority that negligently fails to spot the defect, when exercising its statutory functions under building regulations. Put simply, *Murphy* is much more defensible than *D&F Estates*, and it is a shame that the House of Lords, bent on reversing *Anns*, got its hands on *D&F Estates* first. This issue turns in many ways on the complex regulatory and contractual regimes in the area, objections to 'transmissible warranties', National House Building Council protection and, from now own, the very favourable DPA limitation regime since the BSA. But it is, I think, a worthy issue for an academic discussion as to first principles.

Meanwhile, in the *Hedley Byrne* context at least, as Jackson has said:

> If the Law Commission proposals [with respect to limitation] are adopted, . . . the path will then be clear for the Supreme Court to look again at the issue of concurrent liability. In my view the rights and liabilities of contracting parties should generally be regulated by the contracts which they have made, not by some amorphous and ever expanding law of tort.[101]

Alas we are still 'crying for the moon', and still stuck with an inconsistent borderline while we cry for it.

that such a large proportion of building work is of necessity rapidly covered up, so as to defeat all but the hour-by-hour supervision which only builders themselves can exercise over their employees or sub-contractors.

[101] Sir Rupert Jackson, 'Concurrent Liability: Where Have Things Gone Wrong?' (Technology & Construction Bar Association Lecture, London, 30 October 2014).

4
Contract | Equity

*Julius AW Grower**

I. Introduction

On one view, to suggest that there is a borderline between contract and equity is absurd. After all, in the right circumstances either an injunction or specific performance may be granted as a remedy for breach of contract. Likewise, the possibility of rectification exists to relieve parties from potential hardships entailed by their own erroneous recording of their otherwise legally binding agreements. Each of these interventions is undeniably equitable in nature.

Yet on another view there is a real and meaningful distinction between equity and the law of contract. As Lord Mustill noted in *Re Goldcorp Exchange Ltd*,[1] while the fact that two parties share a contractual relationship 'does not necessarily mean that [one of them] does not also owe fiduciary duties to [the] other [as a consequence of their relative positions]', 'the essence of a fiduciary relationship is that it [involves] obligations of a different character from those deriving from [any] contract [which underpins it]'.[2] Furthermore, and despite several bold attempts to show otherwise,[3] it is clear that (in the extra-judicial words of Lord Sales) 'equity imposes fiduciary obligations for reasons which are normatively independent of contract'.[4] There are thus at least parts of contract and equity which appear to work in a fundamentally dissimilar way to one another. This implies the existence of at least some difference of type or kind, expressible as a borderline or boundary, between them.

How, then, should we make sense of these seemingly contradictory positions? As is often the case with law, the answer lies in the making of a distinction; in this instance between equity's so-called 'concurrent' and 'exclusive' jurisdictions. As Nicholas Tiverios has explained, cases which fall into equity's 'exclusive' jurisdiction are those in which it '[assumes] a particular primary outcome at common law' but '[imposes] a new jural relation on [two] parties' designed to control one

* Thanks are due to Janet O'Sullivan, Eliza Bond, and Martin Dixon. I wish also to acknowledge the general debt of gratitude I owe to my friend and colleague Ben McFarlane, whose work on proprietary estoppel has greatly informed my own understanding of that subject. Any errors are solely my own.

[1] *Re Goldcorp Exchange Ltd* [1995] 1 AC 74 (PC).

[2] ibid 98.

[3] See, eg, James Edelman, 'When Do Fiduciary Duties Arise' (2010) 126 LQR 302.

[4] Lord Sales, 'The Interface between Contract and Equity' (Lehane Memorial Lecture, Sydney, 28 August 2019) 15.

Julius AW Grower, *Contract | Equity* In: *Borderlines in Private Law*. Edited by: William Day and Julius Grower, Oxford University Press. © Julius AW Grower 2024. DOI: 10.1093/9780191995200.003.0004

of those parties' 'insistence on [their] strict legal rights, . . . or powers'.[5] It therefore covers amongst other things the law of fiduciaries and the law of trusts. In contrast, equity's 'concurrent' jurisdiction concerns actions designed to 'aid [in] the enforcement of primary legal rights'.[6] 'In such cases', Tiverios says, 'equitable remedies supplement those at common law, by providing relief in circumstances where common law remedies may be inadequate or non-existent'.[7] This is where rectification, specific performance, and the award of an injunction fit in.

This chapter is about the borderline between equity's 'exclusive' jurisdiction and the law of contract, mostly a set of common law rules and principles. More specifically, it considers the functional closeness of contract and a major part of the modern law of proprietary estoppel.[8] It is therefore both a piece of doctrinal scholarship and a work which raises questions as to the place of equity within our legal system more widely.

Over time, the boundary between equity and contract (such as there genuinely is one) has been somewhat inconsistently managed. Parts of it are guarded jealously and attempts made from either side to alter its position are strongly rebuked.[9] Other portions are more porous, and some go-between has proven possible, not least in the name of adjudicative expediency.[10] Nevertheless, its overall structure has retained some degree of coherence. Indeed, for this reason and to quote one of Lord Sales' extra-judicial reflections once again, 'it is not really possible to understand or state the law [of England] without including Equity as a distinct body of doctrine'.[11] However, in recent years this situation has become appreciably more complex. In at least one significant respect, the distinction between equity's 'exclusive' jurisdiction and the law of contract may now, in substance, be thought to have collapsed. In other words, far from maintaining two more or less separate spheres of influence, there has arisen a region of joint sovereignty between those parts of our legal system.

[5] Nicholas Tiverios, 'Preventing the Infinite Regress: Discretionary, Bars to Relief and the Structure of Equity' (2023) 82 CLJ 350, 352. We might also add immunities to that list. See, eg, *Commonwealth of Australia v Verwayen* (1990) 170 CLR 394 (HCA).

[6] Tiverios (n 5) 352.

[7] ibid 352.

[8] For a full account of its scope, see Ben McFarlane, *The Law of Proprietary Estoppel* (2nd edn, OUP 2020).

[9] See, eg, *Re Wait* [1927] 1 Ch 606 (in which the Court of Appeal held that equitable rights could not arise to undercut the intricate transactional structure established for contracts of sale by the Sale of Goods Act 1897); *Magnus v Queensland National Bank* (1888) 37 Ch D 466 (in which the Court of Appeal denied the relevance of any common-law style causal enquiries when determining the extent of a non-trustee custodian's liability to reconstitute a fund with which they have been charged after its unauthorised disbursement).

[10] See, eg, *Target Holdings Ltd v Redferns* [1996] AC 421 (HL); *AIB Group (UK) plc v Mark Redler & Co Solicitors* [2014] UKSC 58, [2015] AC 1503 (both contract into equity); *White & Carter (Councils) Ltd v McGregor* [1962] AC 413 (HL) (equity into contract).

[11] Sales (n 4) 7.

What matters here is the doctrine of proprietary estoppel and, in particular, what it does in certain (what might be called) 'proto-contractual circumstances': situations involving promises in which, all other things being equal, a promisee would need to procure a promisor's entry into a contract so as to render the promise which has been made to him enforceable per se. This is because through this form of estoppel equity has displayed an ever-increasing desire to give effect to those undertakings itself. Now at one time, the power to do so was thought to be in the sole possession of the law of contract.[12] However, a line of cases starting with *Crabb v Arun DC*[13] and ending (for the time being) with *Guest v Guest*[14] has partially reversed that position. The purpose of this chapter is to assess the extent of that change. What is more, by re-mapping part of the borderline between equity's 'exclusive' jurisdiction and the law of contract, it will argue that, subject to several significant limitations, the former is now running what might be described as a shadow law of contract. It will also sketch out the implications of this development both as a matter of legal principle and policy.

What is to come is divided into three main sections. The first will lay down some basic principles of both the law of contract and the law of proprietary estoppel, then pin down more precisely this chapter's claims about the nature of equity's growing jurisdiction over the enforcement of promises. The second section will demonstrate the now stark functional overlap between those two areas of law as they currently stand. In particular, it will do so through the medium of half a dozen brief examples. The third and final section will raise two concerns about this state of affairs. This is because it is far from clear that as a matter of English law the existence of a shadow law of contract is tolerable.

II. Starting Points

If this chapter's functional comparison between the scope of the law of contract and at least part of the scope of the law of proprietary estoppel is going to succeed, it will need to be clear as to precisely what doctrines it is referring to. Furthermore, in light of the enormous amount of commentary which proprietary estoppel itself has generated, not least since the decision of the Supreme Court in *Guest v Guest*,[15]

[12] See, eg, *Maddison v Alderson* (1883) 8 App Cas 467 (HL); *Foakes v Beer* (1884) 9 App Cas 605 (HL). I leave aside cases in which otherwise gratuitous promises are made formally, under seal, which form a distinct and relatively small category.

[13] *Crabb v Arun DC* [1976] Ch 179 (CA).

[14] *Guest v Guest* [2022] UKSC 27, [2022] 3 WLR 911.

[15] See, eg, Kirsty Potts, 'An Unwelcome Guest? Exploring the Spare Room of Proprietary Estoppel' (2023) 87 Conv 78; Lorren Eldridge, 'Looking a Guest Horse in the Mouth: Proprietary Estoppel in English Law' (2023) 87 Conv 101; Harry Sanderson, 'Proprietary Estoppel in Guest v Guest: Equity at its Most Flexible?' (2023) 139 LQR 187; Brian Sloan, 'Proprietary Estoppel in the Supreme Court: Banquo's Ghost?' (2023) 82 CLJ 13; Alexander Waghorn, 'Promises in Equity and at Law: Proprietary Estoppel after Guest v Guest' (2023) 86 MLR 1504.

there is good reason for it to establish exactly what arguments it is advancing. It is therefore to this that the remainder of this section is devoted.

A. Contract Law 101

The law of contract exists to give effect to certain promises,[16] provided that (1) they are produced by way of an agreement (formed by a corresponding offer and acceptance),[17] (2) both the promisee and the promisor of each promise intend for that promise to be legally binding,[18] (3) the promisee of each promise has provided consideration for that promise,[19] and (4) the promise is certain enough in content.[20] In some cases, in particular those involving promises concerning the sale or other disposition of an interest in land, there may well be an extra requirement that the parties' agreement is sufficiently formalised (usually with the use of writing).[21] Nevertheless, the general rule is that, to be binding, promises which satisfy each of the other aforementioned requirements need not assume any particular form.

Once created, a contract imposes on its parties reciprocal duties to do that which they promised each other they would do.[22] These are sometimes called duties of counter-performance. If one of the parties to a contract fails to perform their duty of counter-performance, they will commit a breach of that contract.[23] When damages would be an inadequate remedy for a breach of contract, the victim of that wrong may seek an (equitable) order for the specific performance of the duty they are owed.[24] In other words, the party who owes the as yet unperformed duty may be ordered (essentially on pain of imprisonment for contempt of court) to do that which is (still) required of them. However, this is an 'exceptional remedy'[25] and will only be awarded in limited circumstances. The default form of relief offered by the law is damages.[26]

[16] Some promises, such as those to commit a crime or those to behave in a sufficiently immoral manner, are excluded from the scope of possible enforcement on the basis of their deleterious content.

[17] *Gibson v Manchester City Council* [1979] 1 WLR 294 (HL).

[18] *Rose & Frank Co v JR Crompton & Bros Ltd* [1925] AC 445 (HL).

[19] *Tweddle v Atkinson* (1861) 1 B & S 393.

[20] *Scammell & Nephew Ltd v Ouston* [1941] AC 251 (HL).

[21] See, eg, s 2(1) of the Law of Property (Miscellaneous Provisions) Act 1989, discussed in *Keay v Morris Homes (West Midlands) Ltd* [2012] EWCA Civ 900, [2012] 1 WLR 2855.

[22] *Photo Production Ltd v Securicor Transport Ltd* [1980] AC 827 (HL) 848 (Lord Diplock).

[23] ibid 849 (Lord Diplock).

[24] *Co-operative Insurance Society Ltd v Argyll Stores (Holdings) Ltd* [1998] AC 1 (HL) 11 (Lord Hoffmann). For a useful account of the different circumstances in which damages have been held to be an inadequate remedy, see Janet O'Sullivan, 'Specific Performance and the Reflective Loss Rule' in Ben McFarlane and Steven Elliott (eds), *Equity Today: 150 Years After the Judicature Reforms* (Hart 2023) 214–17.

[25] *Co-operative Insurance Society Ltd* (n 24) 11 (Lord Hoffmann).

[26] *Photo Production* (n 22) 849 (Lord Diplock).

Admittedly, there is some debate over whether or not breach of contract is actionable per se. Some commentators argue that it is a wrong which does not 'require the proof of consequential loss before substantial damages will be awarded [in response to it]',[27] whereas others take an opposing view. Unfortunately, the subsisting cases are not wholly consistent on this issue. Nevertheless, it seems clear that the usual aim of an unliquidated monetary award in response to a breach of contract is to put the party to whom it is granted, 'so far as money can do [so], in the same situation ... as if the contract [*viz* the so far unfulfilled promise which was made to them] had been performed'.[28]

B. Proprietary Estoppel: The Basics

The doctrine of proprietary estoppel does not enjoy the same degree of conceptual unity possessed by the law of contract, nor anything like it. However, as McFarlane (amongst others) has demonstrated, when trying to navigate the mass of subsisting authorities, a degree of illumination can be achieved by adopting two particular sequential distinctions.[29] The first is between (1) those cases which involve the granting of relief to a claimant on the basis that the defendant acquiesced in a mistaken belief on the claimant's part as to his or her own existing rights,[30] a rule which will operate even in the absence of any promise (or representation) by the defendant as to the nature of those rights,[31] and (2) those cases which necessarily involve the making of either an express or implied promise (or an express or implied representation) by the defendant. The second distinction to be made is from within that second batch of decisions. It is between those cases which turn on a classic estoppel by representation which just so happens to have proprietary effects as between its parties,[32] and those in which some promise (or representation) by one party ultimately leads to the imposition on them of a liability 'which may, but need not, be satisfied by precluding [that party] from asserting a right against [the addressee of their promise or representation]'.[33] Importantly, in this second group of cases, the promisee (or representee) is recognised as having an independent

[27] Robert Stevens, 'Damages and the Right to Performance: A *Golden Victory* or Not?' in Jason Neyers, Richard Bronaugh, and Stephen Pitel (eds), *Exploring Contract Law* (Hart 2009) 176.

[28] *Robinson v Harman* (1848) 1 Ex 850, 855.

[29] See McFarlane (n 8) 1–16.

[30] See, eg, *Willmott v Barber* (1880) 15 Ch D 96 (Ch); *Taylors Fashions Ltd v Liverpool Victoria Friendly Society* [1982] QB 133 (Ch).

[31] McFarlane (n 8) 36–37.

[32] See, eg, *Hopgood v Brown* [1955] 1 WLR 213 (CA). In these cases, the estoppel in issue does not operate as a cause of action but instead works only to prevent one party from denying the truth of a particular state of affairs. For an explanation of how such an estoppel can have proprietary effects, see *Cobbe v Yeoman's Row Management Ltd* [2008] UKHL 55, [2008] 1 WLR 1752 [14] (Lord Scott).

[33] McFarlane (n 8) 6.

cause of action against the promisor (or representor) which might itself result in an order that the promisor (or representor) grant the promisee (or representee) a right in certain property. Indeed, this is why it is with this 'strand' of proprietary estoppel (what Ben McFarlane calls the 'promise-based'[34] strand) that this chapter is concerned.

To obtain relief on the basis of promise-based proprietary estoppel, a claimant must convince a court of four things.[35] The first is that he was made, by the defendant, a promise (or representation) in relation to certain property. The second is that he relied on that communication. The third is that he suffered some detriment as a result of that reliance. The fourth is that it would be unconscionable for the defendant to repudiate their previous undertaking (or representation). Once all this is established, the court will begin to determine what is an appropriate remedy. Traditionally, the guiding principle on this front has been described as the ascertainment and award of 'the minimum equity to do justice [to the claimant]'.[36]

However, as the Supreme Court has recently made clear, that does not mean that equity should either be looking to compensate the claimant for the detriment he has incurred 'as an alternative to fulfilling [his] expectation', or 'choosing in any particular case the cheaper (or more minimalist) alternative, as between [those] two [options]'.[37] Instead, the basic idea is that what must be granted is sufficient to undo 'the unconscionability identified in the promisor's repudiation of his promise [or representation]'.[38] This matters because, as Lord Briggs pointed out in *Guest v Guest*, it is arguable that, all other things being equal, 'the simplest way to prevent the unconscionability inherent in repudiating [a promise (or representation)]' is 'to hold the promisor [(or representor)] to his promise [or representation]'.[39] Indeed, it was for this reason that his Lordship then advanced the following statement of principle:

> The [remedy] stage will normally start with the assumption (not presumption) that the simplest way to remedy the unconscionability constituted by the repudiation is to hold the promisor to the promise. The promisee cannot (and probably would not) complain, for example, that his detrimental reliance had cost him more than the value of the promise, were it to be fully performed.[40]

[34] ibid 7.
[35] See, eg, *Walton v Walton* (CA, unreported, 14 April 1994); *Thorner v Major* [2009] UKHL 18, [2009] 1 WLR 776; *Guest* (n 14).
[36] *Crabb* (n 13) 198 (Scarman LJ).
[37] *Guest* (n 14) [25].
[38] ibid [13].
[39] ibid [61].
[40] ibid [75].

III. The Extent of This Chapter's Claims

As indicated above, it is this chapter's central argument that, subject to several important limits, equity (and, in particular, its 'exclusive' jurisdiction) is now running something of a shadow law of contract. In other words, it is currently providing for the enforcement of certain promises which, all other things being equal, have previously been considered the sole concern of the law of contract. However, it is essential to state that this claim is only one of substance, not of form. When intervening in cases of promise-based proprietary estoppel, the operation of a parallel equitable system of promise enforcement is *not* the judges' self-identified aim. Rather, they say that they are trying to achieve something different. Consider, for example, these words of Lord Briggs in *Guest v Guest*:

> The court's focus on holding the promisor to his promise [is] not aimed at 'protecting' the promisee from [suffering a] detriment, still less compensating for it. It [is] aimed at preventing or remedying the unconscionability of the actual or threatened conduct of the promisor, with the effect, but not the aim, that it [tends] to satisfy the expectations of the promisee.[41]

Instructive, too, are these extra-judicial remarks of Lord Sales:

> It would . . . be a mistake to understand proprietary estoppel as simply a variant of contract law, with detrimental reliance standing in place of consideration as the factor which obligates a person to keep a promise. Instead, the promise-detriment strand of proprietary estoppel constitutes a standalone doctrine targeted at the specific form of unconscionability that arises if a person, A, were wholly free to leave another person, B, to suffer a detriment as a result of B's reasonable reliance on A's promise.[42]

Consequently, to the extent that equity does in fact end up enforcing a defendant's promise, that is (at least from the claimant's point of view) merely an incidental benefit of its intervention in his case. Having said that, and crucially for this chapter's purposes, that does not mean that said enforcement is not in fact taking place. Indeed, it is with the unsettling implications of this reality that the next section will start to grapple.

Two further points of clarification as to the scope of this chapter's claims should also be made. The first concerns what is meant by enforcement. This is because, as a matter of contract law, there are several ways in which a broken promise might

[41] ibid [61].

[42] Lord Sales, 'Proprietary Estoppel: Great Expected and Detrimental Reliance' (Modern Studies in Property Law Conference Keynote Lecture, Oxford, 2022).

be effectuated. An order for specific performance may be available, but, as noted above, that possibility is conditional on damages being an inadequate remedy. Indeed, for that reason, in the majority of cases the victim of a breach of contract must make do with the award of an unliquidated monetary sum. Nevertheless, that amount is still designed to satisfy (in some way) the claimant's underlying interest in their contract's performance. As Lord Reed said in *Morris-Garner v One Step (Support) Ltd*,[43] 'damages for breach of contract are . . . a substitute for performance'.[44] It is only in rare cases, such as those where the claimant cannot prove that they would have been better off as the result of their counterparty's promised conduct, that an alternative measure of relief will be adopted.[45]

In contrast to all this, and in the absence of a statutory power to do so, equity does not usually award unliquidated monetary remedies designed to compensate claimants for their losses.[46] Instead, in keeping with various principles established in the eighteenth and nineteenth centuries, its starting point is normally with gain-focused remedies such as accounts of profit, which are designed to place defendants—not claimants—into the position in which they should have been had they not acted unlawfully.[47] It is true that, over time, a damages-like award of equitable compensation *has* been introduced in some cases, including those involving a breach of fiduciary duty.[48] But there is little suggestion from the authorities that pecuniary awards made after successful proprietary estoppel claims—which may occur when the remedial starting point identified in *Guest v Guest* is departed from—are quantified simply by reference to where the claimant would have been had the defendant made good his promise (or representation). As Lord Briggs noted in that very case, a much more complicated set of considerations is in play:

> The court may have to listen to . . . reasons [advanced by] the promisor . . . why something less than full performance will negate the unconscionability and therefore satisfy the equity. . . . If the promisor asserts and proves . . . that specific enforcement of the full promise, or [its] monetary equivalent, would be out of all proportion to the cost of the detriment to the promisee, then the court may be constrained to limit the extent of the remedy. This does not mean that the court will be seeking precisely to compensate for the detriment as its primary task, but simply to put right a disproportionality which is so large as to stand in the way of a full specific enforcement doing justice between the parties.

[43] *Morris-Garner v One Step (Support) Ltd* [2018] UKSC 20, [2019] AC 649.
[44] ibid [35].
[45] See, eg, *Anglia Television Ltd v Reed* [1972] 1 QB 60 (CA).
[46] See, eg, Peter Millett, 'Proprietary Restitution' in Simone Degeling and James Edelman (eds), *Equity in Commercial Law* (Lawbook Co 2005) 309–10.
[47] See, eg, *O'Sullivan v Management Agency and Music Ltd* [1985] QB 428 (CA) (a case of undue influence).
[48] See, eg, *Mahoney v Purnell* [1996] 3 All ER 61 (QB); *Swindle v Harrison* [1997] PNLR 641 (CA), both applying *Nocton v Lord Ashburton* [1914] AC 932 (HL).

> It will be a very rare case where the detriment is equivalent in value to the expectation, and there is nothing in principle unjust in a full enforcement of the promise being worth more than the cost of the detriment, any more than there is in giving specific performance of a contract for the sale of land merely because it is worth more than the price paid for it. An example of a remedy out of all proportion to the detriment would be the full enforcement of a promise by an elderly lady to leave her carer a particular piece of jewellery if she stayed on at very low wages, which turned out on valuation by her executors to be a Faberge worth millions. Another would be a promise to leave a generous inheritance if the promisee cared for the promisor for the rest of her life, but where she unexpectedly died two months later.[49]

Of course, if remarks like this appeared in a contract law judgment, one might think that they would make the doctrinal private law scholars of this world wince.[50] However, given that the enforcement of the promise in issue in each case of promise-based proprietary estoppel is *not* the aim of any remedial award made in response to its repudiation, but only—from the claimant's perspective—a potentially happy side-effect of it, this should not be particularly surprising. Moreover, the implications of the above for the scope of this chapter's claim about the relationship between contract and equity's 'exclusive' jurisdiction should also be sufficiently clear. It is that there *is* a significant functional overlap between the two areas of law, but only insofar as the law of proprietary estoppel is capable of resulting—advertently or otherwise—in what it now terms the 'specific enforcement'[51] of a defendant's promise. The key comparison is therefore between—on the one hand—those cases where an unperformed promise is contained in a contract which may be the subject of the exceptional remedy of specific performance, and—on the other—those cases in which a promise is detrimentally relied upon in such a way as to make its repudiation unconscionable *and* in which the *Guest v Guest* starting point is not departed from. In the absence of any clear (albeit attenuated) ideal of enforcement behind the award of unliquidated monetary remedies for proprietary estoppel, there is no substantive analogy to be drawn between such relief and damages for breach of contract, at least where such damages are granted

[49] *Guest* (n 14) [75]–[76].

[50] Consider, eg, the result in *Williams Brothers v ET Agius Ltd* [1914] AC 510 (HL) (as regards what Robert Stevens calls 'substitutive damages') and *Supershield Ltd v Siemens Building Technologies FE Ltd* [2010] EWCA Civ 7, [2010] 2 All ER (Comm) 1185 (as regards damages for consequential loss). Having said that, it is clear that skilled judges can (and do) often use the rules on remoteness to protect defendants from at least some types of disproportionate liability *for consequential loss*. See, eg, *Victoria Laundry (Windsor) Ltd v Newman Industries Ltd* [1949] 2 KB 528 (CA). In addition, the position appears to be different when it comes to liquidated damages clauses. See, eg, *Cavendish Square Holding BV v Makdessi* [2015] UKSC 67, [2016] AC 1172.

[51] *Guest* (n 14) [62], [76], and [77] (Lord Briggs).

in order to protect a claimant's 'expectation interest'.[52] Indeed, for this reason no more will be said about either of them here.

The second point of clarification as to the scope of this chapter's claim about the existence of a shadow law of contract can be much more briefly stated. It is that, as things stand, there is *no* overlap between the law of proprietary estoppel and the legal enforcement of promises which *do not* relate to certain property. Thus, while the law of contract can also cover promises for the provision of services and promises to pay over fixed sums, each of which can (in the right circumstances) be the subject of an order for specific performance,[53] there is no authority whatsoever which suggests that the same is true of equity's 'exclusive' jurisdiction. It would therefore be a mistake to argue that there is a *general* substantive overlap between the two areas of law currently under consideration, and this chapter will not do so. Instead, its focus will be limited to what it considers to be the observable duplication of coverage which exists in relation to certain property-focused proto-contractual circumstances. Beyond all this, the limited extent of what is currently equity's shadow law of contract should be kept in mind when it comes to considering the contents of the next section, which begin to evaluate the impact of its existence.

IV. The Borderline (or Lack of it) in Practice

Having talked it up, it is in this section that the existence of the borderline which forms the subject matter of this chapter—or, rather, the fact of its partial erosion—will be substantiated. Indeed, with the use of six brief examples, the full extent of the (admittedly) partial overlap between equity and contract which exists with respect to the enforcement of certain promises will be made clear. The overall point to be made is that, at least in substance, equity is now enforcing some promises which, all other things being equal, would previously have had their legal efficacy determined solely by the law of contract.

As they constitute the paradigm cases of proprietary estoppel, it makes sense to start with promises made in relation to land:

Scenario 1: Intending to create legal relations, A makes B a sufficiently certain oral promise, which is supported by consideration, to transfer B title to certain land. A then refuses to convey his right to B.

[52] Lon Fuller and William Perdue, 'The Reliance Interest in Contract Damages' (1936) 46 Yale Law Journal 52, 54.

[53] See, eg, *Posner v Scott-Lewis* [1987] Ch 25 (Ch) (contract for the provision of services) and *Beswick v Beswick* [1968] AC 58 (HL) (contract for the (regular) payment of a fixed sum to a third party).

Because the subject matter of the parties' agreement is an interest in land, section 2 of the Law of Property (Miscellaneous Provisions) Act 1989 would govern its validity. Section 2(1) provides:

> A contract for the sale or other disposition of an interest in land can only be made in writing and only by incorporating all the terms which the parties have expressly agreed in one document or, where contracts are exchanged, in each.

Here, there has been no writing. This means that A's promise has been insufficiently formalised. At law the upshot of this is crystal clear: as a contract, the agreement between A and B is void.[54] Its terms, and in particular the requirement that A convey his title to B, will be unenforceable by B. This is the settled will of the Crown in Parliament.

Of course, *were* there writing (and therefore a valid contract) the opposite would be true. What is more, as land is unique, damages are almost always said to be an inadequate remedy in cases where one party fails to perform a contractual obligation to convey an interest in such property to another.[55] Thus, subject to the (perhaps unlikely) existence of some other bar to relief,[56] an order for specific performance would almost certainly be available to B.[57] In addition to this, pursuant to the doctrine in *Lysaght v Edwards*,[58] even before A actually conveyed title to the land to B, A would hold his title on some sort of non-express—though notably not wholly unqualified—trust for B.[59]

Importantly, this is very close to the position which could be achieved on the same facts if the unfulfilled promise in issue here were the subject of a successful proprietary estoppel claim, *viz* if B could show that, due to an act of detrimental reliance on his part, it would be unconscionable for A to withdraw from his undertaking.[60] Moreover, in one respect, B's position could in fact be a little stronger than it would be under the law of contract. Assuming that after the parties came to their agreement there had been no change in circumstances sufficiently dramatic to mean that A's repudiation of his promise to B would not in fact be unconscionable

[54] *Firstpost Homes Ltd v Johnson* [1995] 1 WLR 1567 (CA) 1571 (Peter Gibson LJ).

[55] *Mungalsingh v Juman* [2015] UKPC 38 [33] (Lord Neuberger). For an exception to this rule, see the Privy Council's decision in *Loan Investment Corporation of Australasia v Bonner* [1970] NZLR 724.

[56] Such as unclean hands on the part of B (on which see *Quadrant Visual Communications v Hutchison Telephone (UK)* [1993] BCLC 442 (CA)) or the predicted infliction of extreme hardship on A (on which see *Patel v Ali* [1984] Ch 283 (Ch)).

[57] For an example of such an order, see *Palmer v Lark* [1945] Ch 182 (Ch) 185–86 (Vaisey J).

[58] *Lysaght v Edwards* (1876) 2 Ch D 499 (Ch).

[59] See, eg, *Jerome v Kelly (Inspector of Taxes)* [2004] UKHL 25, [2004] 1 WLR 1409 [32] (Lord Walker); *Scott v Southern Pacific Mortgages Ltd* [2014] UKSC 52, [2015] AC 385 [61]–[63] (Lord Collins).

[60] It is no objection to the operation of proprietary estoppel that the parties could, by reducing their agreement to writing, have produced a binding contract but failed to do so. See, eg, *Howe v Gossop* [2021] EWHC 637 (Ch) esp at [48] (Snowden J).

at all,[61] the consideration provided by B in exchange for A's promise[62]—or at least the cost of raising and/or providing it—could constitute such detrimental reliance that an equitable cause of action in respect of that promise's non-performance would be complete.[63] On top of this, as said above, when it comes to determining the appropriate form of relief, the first question as per *Guest v Guest* is whether the 'specific enforcement of the full promise, or [its] monetary equivalent, would be out of all proportion to the cost of the detriment [incurred by B]'.[64] This means that if the consideration provided by B (or at least the overall cost associated with its provision) was substantial enough to prevent a departure from Lord Briggs' starting point, any court in which B brought proceedings would probably accept that 'the simplest way to remedy the unconscionability constituted by [A's] repudiation [of his promise was] to hold [A] to [that] promise'.[65]

Looking at the relevant cases, this seems to mean one of two things. Either the court will make an order that A must convey the title which formed the subject matter of his promise to B,[66] or it will declare that A is holding that title on constructive trust for B.[67] However, in practice, there is little difference between these outcomes. It is trite law that where a court order directs one person to transfer a specific right to another that person holds that right on constructive trust for that other from the moment at which the order is made.[68] Furthermore, in contrast to vendor-purchaser constructive trusts, these trusts do not appear to exist only 'in a qualified sense',[69] nor do they entail 'peculiar duties and liabilities [on the part of their trustees]'.[70] In other words, it seems that the initial interest in the land which B could obtain by bringing proceedings in equity would in fact be slightly stronger than that which he would get if he were simply to sue in contract. In the end, then, it is tolerably clear that, on the right facts, equity's 'exclusive' jurisdiction is capable of achieving what contract is, by statute, forbidden from providing for in the same circumstances: the enforcement, at least in substance, of a particular promise.

Scenario 2: Intending to create legal relations, A makes B a sufficiently certain written promise, which is unsupported by consideration but detrimentally relied upon by B, to transfer B title to certain land. A then refuses to convey his right to B.

[61] On which see *Guest* (n 14) [74]; *Uglow v Uglow* [2004] EWCA Civ 987.

[62] Which *ex hypothesi* was 'sufficient'.

[63] It is also possible that B could have changed his position in good faith by forgoing one or more alternative opportunities to acquire otherwise suitable parcels of land from third parties.

[64] *Guest* (n 14) [76] (Lord Briggs).

[65] ibid [75] (Lord Briggs).

[66] See, eg, *Pascoe v Turner* [1979] 1 WLR 431 (CA); *Walton* (n 35).

[67] See, eg, *Thorner* (n 35).

[68] See, eg, *Maclurcan v Maclurcan* (1897) 77 LT 474 (CA); *Mountney v Treharne* [2002] EWCA Civ 1174.

[69] *Rayner v Preston* (1881) 18 Ch D 1 (CA) 6 (Cotton LJ).

[70] *Earl of Egmont v Smith* (1877) 6 Ch D 469 (Ch) 475 (Jessel MR).

In this case, there is no lack of formality about this arrangement capable of causing section 2(1) of the Law of Property (Miscellaneous Provisions) Act 1989 to block its validity as a contract. However, A's promise would still be unenforceable *as such* because it has not been supported by consideration. As is well known, the provision of consideration by one side in exchange for another's promise is a necessary (but insufficient) ingredient in the creation of a contract.[71] Thus, rather than the fundamental invalidity of A and B's arrangement being a matter of Parliamentary intention, it is in this instance the result of centuries' worth of judicial determinations.

Of course, if there *were* 'sufficient' consideration all would be different. There *would* be a binding contract between the parties and B would almost certainly get an immediate interest in the land under a vendor-purchaser constructive trust. If A failed to convey his title to B as per the terms of their contract, B could seek an order for specific performance and A would be compelled to do just that. Indeed, this would be the case even if the consideration provided to A by B was, to use a term of art, inadequate. This is because the inadequacy of consideration is not in and of itself a reason why a court can refuse to order the specific performance of a contract.[72] B would therefore eventually end up with what was previously A's title.

Once again, though, and significantly, this is essentially the position in which the parties could in fact end up under the law of proprietary estoppel.[73] If the extent of B's detrimental reliance on A's promise was not so grossly disproportionate to the benefit which would be conferred by its 'full enforcement',[74] then, all other things being equal, they might be entitled to just that form of relief. Indeed, if that were so, then, as above, they would in the first instance be awarded (by one of two mechanisms) an interest under a constructive trust of A's title. This, they could easily collapse in their own favour pursuant to the rule in *Saunders v Vautier*.[75]

It is true that how likely it is that B could show that they had sufficiently detrimentally relied upon A's promise is going to be an open question. However, it is worth reflecting on how close the (admittedly distinct) concepts of consideration and detrimental reliance are, or at least can be in the right circumstances. Consider, for example, the nature of contractual consideration itself.[76] On one view it might be thought to have two aspects. The first is a request aspect. The second is a benefit/detriment aspect. Both need to be present for a court to find that a promise is not a bare and therefore unenforceable one.

[71] *Foakes v Beer* (1884) 9 App Cas 605 (HL).

[72] See, eg, *Mountford v Scott* [1975] Ch 258 (CA).

[73] See, eg, *Crabb* (n 13) (in fact a case of an oral promise which was not supported by consideration, but the additional bar to enforceability makes no difference to the point).

[74] *Guest* (n 14) [79] (Lord Briggs).

[75] (1841) 4 Beav 115, 49 ER 282.

[76] An alternative illustration of the distinct nature of consideration and detrimental reliance has already been indicated. While, to create a contract, consideration needs to be sufficient but need not be adequate, and while the inadequacy of consideration is not a bar to the ordering of specific performance, to ensure specific enforcement in cases of proprietary estoppel detrimental reliance must be *both* sufficient *and* sufficiently adequate to avoid a departure from the *Guest v Guest* starting point.

The most famous statement of the law on consideration is perhaps that of Lush J in *Currie v Misa*.[77] In that case, he said that consideration will be provided in exchange for a promise 'either [when there is] some right, interest, profit, or benefit accruing to the [promisor], or some forbearance, detriment, loss, or responsibility, given, suffered, or undertaken by the [promisee]'.[78] Yet this is provably an incomplete account of the rule. Consider, for example, the decision of the Court of Appeal in *Combe v Combe*.[79] In that case, a husband made a promise to his wife during the course of their divorce proceedings that he would pay her an allowance of £100 a year. In reliance on that promise, the wife declined to apply to the courts for an order for maintenance (as she would otherwise have been entitled to). The husband then failed to make any of his promised payments and the wife brought proceedings against him. The judges refused to hold that the husband's initial promise was contractual and so said it was unenforceable by the wife. There was no doubt that the wife had suffered a detriment in reliance on his communication: she had foregone the opportunity to seek legal recourse. But this behaviour had not been requested by the husband. It was therefore incapable of amounting to consideration. Here is part of Denning LJ's judgment:

> Promises of [the] kind [made by the husband] have long been enforced, so long as the act or forbearance [undertaken by the promisee] is done on the faith of the promise and at the request of the promisor, express or implied. The act done is then in itself sufficient consideration for the promise . . .
>
> [But] I cannot find any evidence of any intention by the husband that the wife should forbear from applying to the court for maintenance, or, in other words, any request by the husband, express or implied, that the wife should so forbear. He left her to apply if she wished to do so. She did not do so.[80]

Thus, the scope of Lush J's description of consideration can only be seen as going to its second aspect: the benefit/detriment aspect. It says nothing about the first, the need for a request. Having said that, it is clear from *Currie*, as it is from *Combe*, that the incurrence of a detriment by a promisee in reliance on a promise made by the promisor *is* sufficient to constitute a qualifying burden. This means that in any case like the scenario under consideration, *viz* when there is no lack of formalities, the difference between (1) detrimental reliance which is insufficient to amount to contractual consideration and (2) detrimental reliance which is capable of grounding a claim in proprietary estoppel *and* which is sufficient to secure the

[77] *Currie v Misa* (1874–75) LR 10 Ex 153 (Ex Ch).
[78] ibid 162.
[79] *Combe v Combe* [1951] 2 KB 215 (CA). Consider, alternatively, the implications of the so-called 'request exception' to the rule that past consideration is not good consideration, set out in *Lampleigh v Brathwait* (1615) Hob 105.
[80] *Combe v* (n 79) 221.

de facto enforcement of the promise to which it relates, could be as little as the existence of a request—express or implied—on the part of the promisor.

Scenario 3: With no intention to create legal relations, A makes B a serious and sufficiently certain promise, which is both supported by consideration and detrimentally relied upon, to transfer B title to certain land. A then refuses to convey his right to B.

On these facts, there should be no doubt whatsoever that as a matter of contract law B will have no claim against A. It is trite law that two parties may—perhaps even in writing—work out between themselves the most elaborate set of reciprocal responsibilities, and yet by wishing it to be binding in honour only they can exclude any role for the courts in the enforcement of that agreement.[81] This is because the manifestation of a (mutual) intention to create legal relations is a necessary (but insufficient) element in the formation of a binding contract.[82] The agreement between A and B in this case would therefore be 'unenforceable at law'.[83]

And yet, on the same facts, there is a distinct possibility of at least some contractual-style relief being available in equity. Consider, for example, *Walton v Walton*.[84] There, a mother repeatedly promised her son that if he committed to provide her farm with cheap labour, he would one day inherent that property. Her 'stock phrase', used in response to his occasional requests for improved pay, was: 'You can't have more money and a farm one day'. In time, the pair's relationship deteriorated, and the mother repudiated her undertakings. She also attempted to sell the land in issue to a neighbour. The son brought proceedings seeking to stop that disposition.

At first instance, the judge found against the son. He recognised that the man had been 'hard done by' but held that there 'was nothing unconscionable about his not getting the farm'. Significantly, the judge also found that the words used by the mother when making the promises she did 'were never . . . intended to create a legal obligation [on her part]'. Indeed, as Hoffmann LJ would then observe on appeal, 'in many cases of promises made in a family or social context, there is no intention to create an immediately binding contract'. This is because 'such promises are often subject to unspoken and ill-defined qualifications'. Turning to the facts of *Walton* itself, Hoffmann LJ then stated:

> When [her promise] was first made, [the mother] did not know what the future might hold. Anything might happen which could make it quite inappropriate for the farm to go to [her son]. But a contract, subject to the narrow doctrine

[81] See, eg, *Rose & Frank Co* (n 18).
[82] *Balfour v Balfour* [1919] 2 KB 571 (CA).
[83] *Rose & Frank Co* (n 18) 454.
[84] *Walton* (n 35).

> of frustration, must be performed come what may. This is why [the mother's] promise could not have been intended to become a contract.

However, his Lordship then proceeded to overturn the trial judge's decision and order that title to the farm be transferred to the son. What is more, he did so on the basis of (what he called) 'equitable estoppel'. That set of rules, he stated, 'looks backwards from the moment [at which a] promise falls due to be performed and asks whether, in the circumstances which have actually happened, it would be unconscionable for [that] promise not to be kept'.

In his Lordship's view, what mattered in *Walton* was that, notwithstanding the lack of an intention to create legal relations on the mother's part, she had still made her son an 'unambiguous' promise which was 'intended to be taken seriously'. 'Taken in its context', he added, it was one which she 'might reasonably [have expected] to be relied upon by [her son]'. All other things being equal, Hoffmann LJ said, *that* was sufficient to ground a claim for relief which may include a direction (such as the one that he would actually make) that the promisor's promise '[is] to be kept'.

Of course, one challenge here is that, at least in some circumstances, the distinction between a promise made with an intention to create contractual relations and a promise which is intended to be taken seriously in the relevant sense appears to be vanishingly thin. In cases like *Walton*, where the promise in issue is made with the aim of securing a *quid pro quo* such as the discounted provision of valuable labour from the promisee, it is hard to see how (in addition to detrimentally relying upon that promise) the promisee has not in fact provided consideration for it. His or her rendering of their otherwise marketable time and effort has been *requested* by the promisor. Consequently, if Hoffmann LJ was correct to observe that on such facts it is reasonable for both sides 'to expect that [the promisor's promise] will be kept', it seems that in substance what is being accepted by the promisor at the time of his promising is that, in exchange for some performance on the part of the promisee, he will come under some form of actionable liability to do that which he is undertaking to do. Admittedly, this is not quite the same thing as the manifestation of an intention to come under an immediately binding (and strict) legal duty to the promisee (as would be the case if they shared a contract)[85] but it is also not far off. Regardless of *when* the promisor is subject to some constraint vis-à-vis the promisee in respect of what he pledged to do, in substance that is (or at least may be) the eventual outcome in both cases.

Nevertheless, it must be acknowledged that this point is ultimately incidental to the main issue at hand. The key takeaway is that, howsoever and whensoever it comes into existence, the encumbrance on the part of the promisee imposed by equity in the circumstances under consideration is capable of being given effect to, at

[85] A point noted by Hoffmann LJ in the course of his judgment.

least in substance, in the same way as if he were party to an actual contract. As a result, then, we again have a glimpse of a truth which seems increasingly to be hiding in plain sight. It is that through the law of proprietary estoppel, equity's 'exclusive' jurisdiction is running something of a shadow law of contract. It is giving effect to promises which, all other things being equal, would fall to be enforced (or left unenforced) *as promises* by the common law.

Scenario 4: Intending to create legal relations, A makes B a sufficiently certain promise, which is unsupported by consideration but detrimentally relied upon by B, to transfer B title to certain goods. A then refuses to convey his right to B.

Here there would be no contract between the parties due to the absence of consideration. This means that as a matter of common law nothing would happen as between them. However, the opposite may be true in equity. Assuming that there really was one, in recent years the promise-based strand of the law of proprietary estoppel has decisively transgressed any limit on its scope of application which restricted it to promises made in relation to land.[86] This was acknowledged by Lord Briggs in *Guest v Guest* who stated that 'the aim of [the doctrine] was to prevent the unconscionable repudiation of promises or assurances about property (*usually* land)'.[87] It is also clear from cases like *Thorner* in which, on its true construction, the promisor's promise covered not just his farm, but also his live and dead stock, his agricultural equipment, and his business' cash in the bank. At first instance, John Randall QC[88] (sitting as a Deputy Judge of the High Court) ordered that *all* of that property was held upon bare trust for the claimant.[89] This was overturned by the Court of Appeal,[90] but unanimously affirmed by the House of Lords.[91]

Note that one explanation for at least some of these decisions is that the promise at issue in each of them related to *both* land *and* chattels, such that '[the promisor's] liability to [the promisee was] extended to that other property'.[92] However, this account does not cover all of the authorities.[93] In addition, it is not clear why that extension is justified. Rather, it seems that, when an impugned promise relates to chattels, it is potentially capable of being the subject of a proprietary estoppel claim *in its own*

[86] The two other strands of proprietary estoppel have certainly done so. See, eg, *Fisher v Brooker* [2009] UKHL 41, [2009] 1 WLR 1764 (involving intellectual property rights and the so-called 'acquiescence-based' strand) and *Process Components Ltd v Kason Kek-Gardner Ltd* [2016] EWHC 2198 (Ch) (involving intellectual property rights and the so-called 'representation-based' strand).

[87] *Guest* (n 14) [61] (emphasis added). See, alternatively, [4] or [12].

[88] As he then was.

[89] I am most grateful to John Randall KC for sharing a copy of his unreported order with me. His judgment, without his order, has the neutral citation [2007] EWHC 2422 (Ch).

[90] [2008] EWCA Civ 732.

[91] See, alternatively, *Ottey v Grundy* [2003] EWCA Civ 1176 in which a boat was the subject of a successful proprietary estoppel claim.

[92] McFarlane (n 8) 48, fn 188.

[93] See, eg, *Motivate Publishing FZ LLC v Hello Ltd* [2015] EWHC 1554 (Ch) (a case about intellectual property rights rather than chattels, but for the purposes of disproving the existence of a general rule against claims relating to non-land-adjacent property it still makes the point).

right for exactly the same reason that promises made in relation to land are.[94] It therefore appears that the goods in issue in this scenario *could* be the subject of a free-standing proprietary estoppel claim by B and that, notwithstanding the absence of consideration, a court may end up enforcing A's promise, at least in substance.

Scenario 5: Intending to create legal relations, A makes B a sufficiently certain promise, which is unsupported by consideration but detrimentally relied upon by B, to transfer B a certain shareholding. A then refuses to convey his right to B.

Once again, the absence of consideration means that here there would be no enforceable contract between A and B. Furthermore, in contrast to each of the previous four scenarios, this time A's promise does not even concern property. Unlike the certificates which relate to them,[95] shares themselves are *not* things in respect of which people have rights which are potentially 'exigible against the rest of the world'.[96] Indeed, this is why, without more, it is impossible for one person to sue in conversion a third party whom they believe to have in some way interfered with a shareholding of theirs.[97] Instead, shares are 'a special sub-species of chose in action':[98] they are personal rights (and, in particular, contractual rights) against the company to which they relate.[99] This is why for one party to 'transfer' certain shares (gratuitously or otherwise) to another, the legal procedure which they must go through to effect that change in 'ownership' is a novation involving the relevant company.[100]

Does this legal reality get in the way of B bringing a claim in proprietary estoppel to achieve, or at least try to achieve, the de facto enforcement of A's promise? Possibly yes. After all, in *Thorner v Major*,[101] Lord Walker stated:

> In my opinion it is a necessary element of proprietary estoppel that the assurances given to the claimant (expressly or impliedly . . .) should relate to identified *property* owned . . . by the defendant.[102]

However, on a broader view of the doctrine, there is perhaps a way round this apparently absolutist position. Although it was not a case arising out of any proto-contractual circumstances (but rather one which involved 'a defective voluntary transfer'),[103] in *Curtis v Pulbrook*[104] Briggs J advanced the proposition that, 'in the context of . . .

[94] Indeed, this was a point made by Birss J in *Motivate Publishing*: ibid [61].
[95] Which *can* be the subject of successful conversion claims. See, eg, *MCC Proceeds Inc v Lehman Brothers International (Europe)* [1998] 4 All ER 675 (CA) 686 (Mummery LJ).
[96] Robert Stevens, 'Crypto Is Not Property' (2023) 139 LQR 615, 616.
[97] *MCC Proceeds Inc* (n 95) 699 (Hobhouse LJ).
[98] *Macmillan Inc v Bishopsgate Investment Trust plc* [1995] 1 WLR 978 (Ch) 992 (Millett J).
[99] See Ariana Pretto-Sakmann, *Boundaries of Personal Property* (Hart 2005) 82–83.
[100] See Eva Micheler, 'Legal Title and the Transfer of Shares in a Paperless World—Farewell Quasi-Negotiability' [2002] JBL 358, 360–61 and the cases cited there.
[101] *Thorner* (n 35).
[102] ibid [61] (emphasis added).
[103] *Curtis v Pulbrook* [2011] EWHC 167 (Ch) [43] (Briggs J).
[104] ibid [43].

shares', 'some detrimental reliance by [a] donee upon an apparent although ineffective gift may so bind the conscience of [its] donor [as] to justify the imposition of a constructive trust'.[105] If this is correct, there is no reason to think that it should not also be true in all other possible promise-based proprietary estoppel contexts.

Indeed, it is also worth noting that there *are* decisions which seem to envision the validity of equitable claims in cases in which a promisor has promised a promisee that he would obtain an interest in certain land *indirectly*, that is to say that he would grant the promisee an interest in a company which would acquire title to a particular piece of land. In *Farrar v Miller*,[106] for instance, the Court of Appeal rejected a promisor's attempt to strike out a promisee's claim arising from such facts, and specifically noted that it '[had] not been contended . . . that there can be no proprietary estoppel because any promise made . . . could have related . . . only to the shares in [a] Joint Venture entity'.[107]

Scenario 6: Intending to create legal relations, A makes B a sufficiently certain oral promise, which is unsupported by consideration but detrimentally relied upon by B, to buy B's title to certain land. A then refuses to commit to any written document.

The difference between this scenario and the previous five is that here A is promising to accept a right *from* B, rather than to transfer one *to* B. He has moved from being a seller to a buyer. As in *Scenario 1*, the agreement's lack of formality would be fatal to the existence of any contract. Note, though, that if there *were* a contract, the fact that A's promise was to buy rather than sell land would not necessarily obstruct the making of an order for specific performance.[108]

What, then, of proprietary estoppel? The answer appears to be that no such claim would lie. This is because, even though this chapter has so far spoken simply of promises in relation to property, the cases tend to distinguish sharply between promises to grant another party a right in relation to property and promises to receive a right in relation to the same. Nevertheless, it would be wrong to say that there is no authority at all in support of the proposition that the second sort of promise could be actionable in equity. As McFarlane has noted in detail, in *Salvation Army Trustee Co Ltd v West Yorkshire Metropolitan CC*,[109] that is precisely what happened.[110] Moreover, in *Attorney General of Hong Kong v Humphreys Estate (Queen's Gardens) Ltd*,[111] Lord Templeman described the

[105] ibid [43].
[106] *Farrar v Miller* [2018] EWCA Civ 172.
[107] ibid [52] (Kitchin LJ).
[108] See, eg, *Cogent v Gibson* (1864) 33 Beav 557, 55 ER 485 (specific performance of a contract to buy a certain patent).
[109] *Salvation Army Trustee Co Ltd v West Yorkshire Metropolitan CC* (1980) 41 P & CR 179 (QB).
[110] See McFarlane (n 8) 460–62.
[111] *Attorney General of Hong Kong v Humphreys Estate (Queen's Gardens) Ltd* [1987] AC 114 (PC).

decision in that case as 'clearly right'.[112] Ultimately, the point has not been regularly pushed in court, and that has left some room for debate. However, whichever way the law presently stands, it is useful to be aware of the possibility (or impossibility) of equity's involvement on these proto-contractual facts.

V. Questions and Comments

So, now we know that, in at least certain cases, equity (and in particular the law of proprietary estoppel) is capable of giving effect, at least in substance, to some promises which would ordinarily fall within the purview of the law of contract. More acutely, it has the ability to affect the de facto enforcement of undertakings which for one reason or another contract is reluctant to. This section will set out two concerns about this state of affairs. This is because it is far from clear that as a matter of English law the existence of a shadow law of contract is tolerable.

A. The Relationship of Judge-Made Law and Statute

The most obviously unacceptable consequence of equity's foray into the domain once controlled exclusively by the law of contract is that it has resulted in the existence of an area of judge-made law which is, in substance, directly inconsistent with the terms of a validly enrolled statute.[113] Think back to *Scenario 1*, set out above. In that case, section 2(1) of the Law of Property (Miscellaneous Provisions) Act 1989 would apply with the result that the parties' agreement could not constitute a valid contract (unless and until it was reduced to writing). Until then, it would be void as such an arrangement. A and B would gain no legally enforceable personal rights against one another. More significantly, B would have no entitlement to seek an order for specific performance if A failed (or even threatened to fail)[114] to convey the land to him. He would have no interest under a vendor-purchaser constructive trust either. As the old joke goes, A's promise would not be worth the paper it was written on.

Yet thanks to the operation of the law of proprietary estoppel, there is a real sense in which much of that position (including the most practically significant aspects of it) may still be achieved in equity. After all, although it would not generate a personal right to counter-performance in B's favour, assuming that the extent of B's detrimental reliance was sufficient to mean that the benefit to be conferred on B by the specific enforcement of A's promise would not be disproportionately high, that

112 ibid 127.
113 *Cobbe* (n 32) [29] (Lord Scott).
114 See, eg, *Hasham v Zenab* [1960] AC 316 (PC).

is in the end what would be ordered. A will be instructed to convey title to the land in issue to B, or it will be declared that he holds the same on constructive trust. In other words, in substance if not in form, what will occur is a great deal of what is not meant to happen.

Why is this unacceptable? Well, the 1989 Act was passed in order to further various policy goals (not least the desire to increase certainty in land dealings)[115] and the courts have generally accepted that Parliament considered those goals to be so important that they justify invalidating agreements which, but for the non-incorporation of just one actually agreed-upon term into a particular written document, would amount to a binding contract.[116] It is therefore constitutionally improper for judges to reject those goals and, in substance, disapply the law's contents.[117] Parliament makes the law. The judiciary interprets it. It is true that the process of interpretation can sometimes be robust. But if there is a meaningful distinction between legislation and adjudication, which one might reasonably think there is (and which, more importantly, seems to be something borne out by the cases), then the process of statutory construction must have its limits.[118]

The standard explanation as to why proprietary estoppel claims are not currently ousted by section 2(1) is that the statute applies only to prevent the enforceability of oral promises intended to be binding as part of a contract, not their enforceability for any other reason, including as an incident to the remedying of unconscionability in the relevant sense.[119] Alas, this is not (or at least should not be) seriously sustainable. It is a line of argument which appears to place form over substance. Legislation which sought (1) to suppress *contractual* claims arising in response to promises made about land transfers, but (2) was entirely disinterested in *other* claims which could end up having a number of the same effects, would be irrational. It should not be supposed that Parliament would wish to establish such norms. As Lewison LJ rather delicately put it in *Dudley Muslim Association v Dudley Metropolitan Borough Council*,[120] 'it would be surprising if one could do by

[115] Law Commission, *Transfer of Land: Formalities for Contracts for Sale etc of Land* (Law Com No 164, 1987) esp 5.7.

[116] See, eg, *North Eastern Properties Ltd v Coleman* [2010] EWCA Civ 277, [2010] 3 All ER 528 [42]–[43] (Briggs J).

[117] *Dudley Muslim Association v Dudley MBC* [2015] EWCA Civ 1123 [33] (Lewison LJ).

[118] There *is* s 2(5) of the Law of Property (Miscellaneous Provisions) Act which provides that the rule in s 2(1) does not 'affect[] the creation or operation of resulting, implied or constructive trusts'. Further, Robert Walker LJ's judgment in *Yaxley v Gotts* [2000] Ch 162 (CA) indicates that, as a result, at least insofar as they end in the judicial imposition of a constructive trust, proprietary estoppel claims may disregard the formality requirement in s 2(1). However, the best interpretation of the exception contained in s 2(5) is that it is exists merely to preserve the validity of those trusts, including vendor-purchaser constructive trusts, which arise pursuant to the creation of an appropriately formalised contract for the sale or other disposition of an interest in land, but which are themselves not mentioned in such documents.

[119] See, eg, Lord Neuberger, 'The Stuffing of Minerva's Owl? Taxonomy and Taxidermy in Equity' (2009) 68 CLJ 537, 546; John McGhee (ed), *Snell's Equity* (34th edn, Sweet & Maxwell 2019) 12-046; *Farrar* (n 106).

[120] *Dudley Muslim Association* (n 117).

... estoppel what one could not do by informal contract'.[121] Thus, rather than discriminating between causes of action, the better view is that the 1989 Act is interested in preventing certain outcomes, *viz* the enforceability, at least in substance, of certain oral promises. That being so, there seems to be good sense in Snowden J's view, expressed recently in *Howe v Gossop*,[122] that:

> [While] there is ... doubt [as to whether] Section 2 is intended to affect the operation of proprietary estoppel at all, ... if it did, [it would] only operate as a bar to the grant of equitable relief if and to the extent that such relief had the effect of enforcing, or otherwise giving effect to, the terms of a contract for the sale or other disposition of an interest in land that the statute renders invalid and unenforceable.[123]

B. The Importance of Contractual Imperialism

A second concerning feature of the present law of proprietary estoppel, and in particular its partial overlap with the law of contract, is made plain by *Scenarios 2, 3,* and *4* above. In *Scenarios 2* and *4*, sufficiently formal promises made in relation to land were invalid as contracts because they were not supported by consideration. Indeed, this was so even though the difference between the sort of detrimental reliance sufficient to give rise to an equitable cause of action and contractual consideration itself could, on the right facts, be as little as the existence of an express or implied request on the part of the promisor. In *Scenario 3*, non-enforceability flowed from the lack of an intention to create legal relations on the part of the promisor. This was so although the promisor possessed an intention that their promise be taken seriously, and that, at least in certain cases, the difference between such an intention and (an) *animus contrahendi* is a very narrow one.

To understand why it is troublesome that proprietary estoppel might, at least in substance, be giving effect to certain otherwise unenforceable promises, regard might be had to the mid-nineteenth century demise of the old equitable doctrine of making representations good.[124] By the time of its passing, it was essentially a nascent version of the promise-based strand of proprietary estoppel.[125] Consider, for example, the decision in *Loffus v Maw*.[126] There, an elderly testator had induced his niece to reside with him as his housekeeper on the basis of an oral promise that he would leave her certain real property in his will. Moreover, the old man *did* then

[121] ibid [33].
[122] *Howe* (n 60).
[123] ibid [48].
[124] For one account of its contents, see Paul Finn, 'Equitable Estoppel' in Paul Finn (ed), *Essays in Equity* (Law Book Co Ltd 1985) 62–64.
[125] McFarlane (n 8) 8–9.
[126] *Loffus v Maw* (1862) 3 Giff 592.

produce an appropriate testamentary provision. Unfortunately, he later revoked that document by way of a codicil. After his death, the niece brought an action in the Court of Chancery claiming that, as a result of her efforts in caring for him, '[she was] entitled to have the full benefit' of her agreement with her uncle 'and to have the same duly performed by the persons claiming under his will and codicils'.[127] Sir John Stuart VC agreed. He said:

> It appearing that the [claimant was] induced to render valuable services to the testator on the faith of [his] representation that by doing so she would become entitled to the benefit of [certain property under his] will, the testator had no right to revoke [his will]; and [I] therefore order and decree that [the transfer] in favour of the said [claimant] declared by the [old will] be performed.[128]

Now this chapter is not the place to rehearse the exact course by which the rules applied in *Loffus* were excised from our judge-made law. As others have explained, it took a series of substantial appellate court decisions for that to occur.[129] Nevertheless, it is important to understand *why* that process happened. This is because at least some of the reasons given by the judges in the key cases are just as pertinent to that part of equity's 'exclusive' jurisdiction which currently overlaps with the law of contract.

As Paul Finn has explained, much turned on the fact that judges started to recognise that the law of making representations good 'was pregnant with the potential to enlarge if not outflank the law of contract'.[130] This was a consequence of their view that, 'if equity[,] by enforcing a representation[,] gave it "all the force of a binding contract", this . . . was because the representation was "so made as to constitute the ground of a contract"'.[131] In addition, they also thought that in order to make a promise part of a contract (and therefore enforceable in its own right) it needed to be supported by consideration. Indeed, this point was directly reasserted by both Lord Cranworth LC in *Jorden v Money*[132] and the Earl of Selborne LC in *Maddison v Alderson*.[133] Thus, as McFarlane has explained, the doctrine of making representations good was cast down 'in order to preserve the primacy of the law of contract'—including its rules on consideration—'as a means for the enforcement of agreements'.[134]

[127] ibid 599.

[128] ibid 605.

[129] See, eg, David Jackson, 'Estoppel as a Sword' (1965) 81 LQR 84; Francis Dawson, 'Making Representations Good' (1982) 1 Canta LR 329.

[130] Finn (n 124) 61.

[131] ibid 63–64, quoting *Prole v Soady* (1859) 2 Giff 1 and *Maunsell v Hedges* (1854) 4 HL Cas 1039, respectively.

[132] *Jorden v Money* (1854) 5 HL Cas 185, 214–16.

[133] *Maddison* (n 12) 473.

[134] Ben McFarlane, 'Understanding Equitable Estoppel: From Metaphors to Better Laws' (2013) 66 CLP 267, 292.

But *why* were the judges so committed to the law of contract and, in particular, the need for it to hold some sort of imperium over the enforcement of promises *as promises*? The answer is not directly disclosed in any of the relevant cases. However, with a little reflection it is not too hard to divine. Broadly speaking, both equity's 'concurrent' and 'exclusive' jurisdictions are justified by a quasi-Aristotelian model of the relationship between law and equity. In other words, equitable intervention in either of its two main forms is appropriate when, because of their generality, certain rules of common law would cause some unacceptable type of injustice.[135] Think, for example, of specific performance, which applies when the ordinary rules about how breaches of contract are enforced—which provide for the payment of damages—would not provide the claimant with an adequate remedy. Consequently, when it comes to equity's 'exclusive' jurisdiction, whilst it *is* open to the courts to introduce new jural relations[136] to regulate one party's stickler-ish insistence on their subsisting common law rights, powers, or immunities, it is *not* normally open to its judges to regulate people's legal *privileges* by introducing primary equitable duties which mirror those in existence at law but apply in a wider set of circumstances.[137] To re-work Lord Templeman's famous phrase, that would be equity contradicting, not supplementing, the common law.[138]

A good example of this limitation in action comes from *Great Peace Shipping Ltd v Tsavliris (International) Ltd*.[139] In that case, the Court of Appeal held that there was no separate equitable doctrine of common mistake under which a contract might be rescinded in circumstances where that would be impossible at common law. More specifically, it said that the decision of the Court of Appeal in *Solle v Butcher*[140] was inconsistent with that of the House of Lords in *Bell v Lever Brothers Ltd*.[141] In *Solle*, Denning LJ had claimed that a contract which was unimpeachable at law (on the basis of a common mistake) could still be voidable in equity if its parties 'were under a common misapprehension either as to facts or as to their relative and respective rights, provided that the misapprehension was fundamental and that the party seeking to set [the contract] aside was not himself at fault'.[142] Sadly, as the Court of Appeal in *Great Peace* would explain, the problem here is twofold. Denning LJ did not say what would constitute a fundamental mistake, nor crucially did he explain *why* whatever would count as fundamental in equity was different to (and drawn in wider terms than) that which would count as fundamental

135 See, eg, *Earl of Oxford's Case* (1615) Rep Ch 1, 6–7.

136 Including power-liability relations (as in cases in which a contract has been procured by a non-fraudulent misrepresentation) and disability-immunity relations (as in cases to which the doctrine in *Hughes v Metropolitan Railway Co* (1877) 2 App Cas 439 applies).

137 See also ch 17. (As Tiverios has noted, the doctrine of breach of confidence constitutes an exception to this position. See Tiverios (n 5) 352, fn 12.)

138 *Rhone v Stephens* [1994] 2 AC 310 (HL) 317.

139 *Great Peace Shipping Ltd v Tsavliris Salvage (International) Ltd* [2002] EWCA Civ 1407.

140 *Solle v Butcher* [1950] 1 KB 671 (CA).

141 *Bell v Lever Brothers Ltd* [1932] AC 161 (HL).

142 *Solle* (n 140) 693.

at law. This was an issue because in *Bell* the need for a fundamental mistake was said to be the touchstone for any relief on the basis of a common mistake.

Significantly, the judges in *Great Peace* did not hold that there could never be an equitable jurisdiction to set aside contracts on the basis of a common mistake. Rather, they said, quite correctly, that the jurisdiction which Denning LJ had created was unprincipled in its operation and had to be cast aside. This is because, rather than seeking to temper the hard edges of the common law by going beyond the prima facie application of its rules in some way, it was instead seeking to contradict them.[143] The common law itself has a doctrine of common mistake. Indeed, in a quasi-Aristotelian sense it is equitable in nature.[144] What is more, its judges have made a decision as to what errors are sufficient to entitle mistaken contracting parties to relief. It is therefore not open to equity to second guess that position and in doing so rewrite (to some extent) individuals' primary rights and duties under the law of contract. As Lord Phillips MR said in *Great Peace*:

> The premise of equity's intrusion into the effects of the common law is that the common law rule in question is seen in the particular case to work injustice, and for some reason the common law cannot cure itself. But it is difficult to see how that can apply here. . . . We are *only* concerned with the question [of] whether relief might be given for common mistake in circumstances wider than those stipulated in *Bell v Lever Brothers*. But that, surely, is a question as to where the common law should draw the line; not whether, given the common law rule, it needs to be mitigated by application of some other doctrine. The common law has drawn the line in *Bell v Lever Brothers*.[145]

What is the lesson in all this for proprietary estoppel? The answer is that, at least insofar as it applies in proto-contractual circumstances, it appears not to be supplementing the common law of contract but instead saying that cases like *Maddison v Alderson*[146] and *Balfour v Balfour*[147] were wrongly decided.[148] This is inappropriate because the common law has formed a view on what promises are to be enforceable in their own right, and it is the common law which gets to draw the line. Equity is not acting equitably when it intervenes to say that other promises (for

[143] Indeed, this point was noted by the first instance judge (Toulson J) in *Great Peace*, see *Great Peace Shipping Ltd v Tsavliris Salvage (International) Ltd* (HC, unreported, 9 November 2001) [69].

[144] Though not in the Maitlandian sense that it originates from the jurisdiction administered, before the Judicature Acts, by the Court of Chancery. See Frederic Maitland, *Equity: A Course of Lectures* (Alfred Chaytor and William Whittaker (eds), rev John Brunyate, 2nd edn, CUP 1936) 1.

[145] *Great Peace Shipping* (n 139) [156].

[146] *Maddison* (n 12).

[147] *Balfour* (n 82).

[148] The former is authority for the proposition that, all other things being equal, the provision of consideration by a promisee is essential to render a promise enforceable. The latter demonstrates that, all other things being equal, the existence of a mutual intention to create legal relations is essential to rendering an agreement enforceable.

example, gratuitous promises) should, in substance, be given effect to. Rather, it is pushing large parts of our law of obligations towards an unacceptable level of inconsistency, or what Maitland pessimistically termed 'civil war'.[149] This, in turn, raises good questions as to equity's overall legitimacy, something which all sensible private lawyers should wish to avoid.

VI. Conclusion

Thinking back on the above, much of what has been said should not have come as any real surprise to the reader. The collapse of at least part of the borderline between equity's 'exclusive' jurisdiction and the law of contract caused by the development of the promise-based strand of proprietary estoppel—if not, of course, its current *extent*—has been a feature of English law since that doctrine's creation in the aforementioned case of *Crabb v Arun DC*.[150] There, Lord Denning MR said:

> The basis of... proprietary estoppel... is the interposition of equity. Equity comes in, true to form, to mitigate the rigours of strict law.... What then are the dealings which will preclude [a defendant] from insisting on his strict legal rights? If he makes a binding contract that he will not insist on the strict legal position, a court of equity will hold him to his contract. Short of a binding contract, if he makes a promise that he will not insist upon his strict legal rights—then, even though that promise may be unenforceable in point of law for want of consideration or want of writing—then, if he makes the promise knowing or intending that the other will act upon it, and he does act upon it, then again a court of equity will not allow him to go back on that promise.[151]

The problem here is that his Lordship is aligning equity's response to a situation where two parties share a binding contract with that in which they do not. In other words, he is purporting to treat a party who has a common law liberty to act in a certain way in the same manner as he would a party who is subject to a (preclusive) legal duty in respect of the same conduct. He is thus promulgating something of a shadow law of contract in equity.

Some commentators recognised this fact almost immediately. In what Peter Millett QC[152] called an 'interesting, if intemperate'[153] case note ('When is an Enforceable Agreement Not a Contract? Answer: When it is an Equity') Patrick Atiyah famously argued that the effect of the Court of Appeal's decision in *Crabb*

[149] Maitland (n 144) 17.
[150] *Crabb* (n 13).
[151] ibid 187–88.
[152] As he then was.
[153] Peter Millett, 'Crabb v Arun District Council—A Riposte' (1976) 92 LQR 342, 242.

was to create an equitable route 'to the same result'[154] which, but for various 'outmoded ideas about the . . . nature of the doctrine of consideration',[155] could have been achieved at common law. In particular, he observed that the outcome arrived at via the invocation of estoppel was 'the enforcement of [the] right'[156] which the claimant had been promised by the defendant. And yet the doctrine of promise-based proprietary estoppel marched on and eventually received the imprimatur of the House of Lords in *Thorner v Major*.[157] The scale of the problems caused by its existence, two of which have been identified above, has therefore only increased. Indeed, since the decision of the Supreme Court in *Guest v Guest*,[158] the possibility of restyling this area of law into a smaller, backwards-looking, loss-focused set of rules (aimed primarily at relieving unconscionability by offering equitable compensation to make good the detriment suffered by those who have reasonably relied on non-contractual promises concerning property) has all but passed. This means that as between one part of equity and the law of contract we are now in something of a state of doctrinal deadlock.

It seems inevitable that one day a choice will have to be made. The law as a whole cannot continue to have its cake and eat it when it comes to the enforcement (at least in substance) of certain non-contractual promises. The only question is as to which way it should finally break. As this chapter has explained, there are various reasons to think that the last movement in the judicial drama should be decisively *against* the existence of the promise-based strand of proprietary estoppel (at least as it currently functions). This is not just because it constitutes an example of bad equity (although it certainly *does* do that), but also and perhaps more importantly because it has resulted in bad law.

[154] Patrick Atiyah, 'When is an Enforceable Agreement Not a Contract? Answer: When it is an Equity' (1976) 92 LQR 174, 179.
[155] ibid 174.
[156] ibid 177.
[157] *Thorner* (n 35).
[158] *Guest* (n 14).

5
Tort's Borderlines

Lady Carr[*]

I. Introduction

When we look at the borderlines between the law of tort and other areas of private law, it is easy to see tensions and conflicts. The borderlines are sometimes not neat and tidy; examining them can expose inconsistencies and arbitrary distinctions. One example, illustrated by Janet O'Sullivan in her chapter, is the 'contested, unprincipled' borderline between tort and contract in the context of claims for pure economic loss.[1] In this area, as I will explore, the extent to which the law of tort should be able to play a 'gap-filling' role is a matter of significant controversy and debate. Thought of in this way, it is tempting to see the overlap between different causes of action as a problem that needs to be fixed. If *only* we could resolve the conflict between different areas of private law, the law would work smoothly and consistently. In other words, the borderlines are a 'foe': a problem that needs to be overcome.

However, it is important to remember that there is not always conflict at the borderlines. Sometimes, different areas of private law overlap and interact, *complementing*, rather than *competing against*, each other. A good example of this, as I consider later, is the overlap between the law of tort and property. The 'law of tort' is a broad conceptual category, including causes of action such as negligence, deceit, misrepresentation, defamation, conversion, private nuisance, and occupiers' liability, to name but a few. The principles behind each are influenced by the interests that they protect including, for example, personal injury, economic loss, or property interests. In such cases, the borderlines do not stand as a 'foe', but as a 'friend': they overlap comfortably, adapting the cause of action to suit the facts and circumstances of each case. Alexander Waghorn looks at this in the context of the interaction between property and the law of tort in his chapter, debating the appropriate remedy in a hypothetical case at the tort-property borderline.[2]

* I am grateful to my judicial assistant Thomas Hibbs for his research and assistance in the preparation of this chapter.

[1] See ch 3.

[2] See ch 15.

Lady Carr, *Tort's Borderlines* In: *Borderlines in Private Law.* Edited by: William Day and Julius Grower, Oxford University Press. © Lady Carr 2024. DOI: 10.1093/9780191995200.003.0005

Further, sometimes the borderlines between different areas of private law are too far apart to be meaningful. For example, the law of tort and equity exist in such different spheres that they can be accused of being 'different in the way that Jupiter is different from a post-box: so different that it is stupid to talk about the distinctions between them'.[3] The same accusation could be levied at the interplay between the law of tort and unjust enrichment.[4] Nevertheless, as both Nicholas McBride and Rory Gregson discuss, there is still value in exploring the reasons for such differences.

In this response to the tort chapters presented at the conference at Downing College, I seek to look more closely at the interaction between the law of tort on the one hand and equity, unjust enrichment, contract, and property on the other. I explore contexts where there is tension at the borderlines (where the borderlines are a 'foe'), and other contexts where the overlap is welcome (the borderlines are a 'friend'). To set the scene, I start by asking what it means to label a cause of action as a 'tort': what does this signify, and, therefore, what makes a situation a 'borderline' case? I then turn to each of the four borderlines before offering some concluding thoughts.

II. What is 'The Law of Tort'?

The law of tort is, famously, a disparate area that evades precise definition.[5] Given that tort law protects such a wide range of different interests, and encompasses so many different causes of action, it has been questioned whether labelling a cause of action as a 'tort' has any practical importance.[6] Of course, if we did abandon the category 'tort', there would be no need to talk about borderlines in this piece at all. Nevertheless, it is generally accepted that tort *does* have unifying features, which distinguish it from other areas of private law. These features are threefold: tort law primarily responds to (i) fault-based wrongs; (ii) imposed by law; for which (iii) compensation is the principal remedy. Let us look at each in turn.

First, at its core, tort is concerned with liability for 'civil wrongs'.[7] It is fault-based. By comparison, unjust enrichment does not require negligent wrongdoing at the time that the relevant act is committed.[8] For example, in the seminal case of *Lipkin Gorman (a firm) v Karpnale Ltd*,[9] the court found that the money should be repaid despite the fact that the defendants acted innocently throughout. Similarly, in

[3] See ch 6.
[4] See ch 7.
[5] Gerald Fridman, *Fridman on Torts* (1st edn, Waterlow Publishers 1990) 1.01.
[6] See, eg, Ken Oliphant, 'Against Certainty in Tort Law' in Stephen Pital, Jason Neyers, and Erika Chamberlain (eds), *Tort Law: Challenging Orthodoxy* (Hart 2013).
[7] Andrew Tettenborn (ed), *Clerk & Lindsell on Torts* (24th edn, Sweet & Maxwell 2023) 1-01.
[8] See Peter Birks, *Unjust Enrichment* (2nd edn, OUP 2005) 11-38.
[9] [1991] 2 AC 548 (HL) 559 (Lord Goff).

contract, although parties often do contractually agree to a particular standard of performance (such as reasonable care), liability arises out of breach, regardless of fault. Although there are some strict liability torts, arising in the absence of proven fault (such as the rule in *Rylands v Fletcher*),[10] these are the exception rather than the norm. Many of these cases have been rationalised either under the idea that fault can be assumed, or that it is simply too difficult to prove.[11]

Secondly, tortious obligations are generally imposed by law, rather than by agreement. This is the essence of Professor Winfield's well-known 'will theory': that duties in the law of tort are primarily fixed by the law, whereas in contract they are fixed by the *parties* themselves.[12] Once again, the line is a little blurrier than this. Terms can be implied in contracts by law (for example, the duty of good faith in insurance contracts)[13] and agreements can be struck down for a variety of reasons, such as illegality, mistake, frustration, or restraint of trade. On the other hand, a duty of care in tort can be voluntarily assumed,[14] and, through the doctrine of *volenti non fit injuria*, the risk of harm from tortious conduct can be voluntarily waived.[15]

Thirdly, the primary focus of tort remedies is on *compensation* for loss. As famously declared by Lord Blackburn in *Livingstone v Rawyards*,[16] the purpose of damages in tort law is to 'put the party who has been injured, or who has suffered, in the same position as he would have been in if he had not sustained the wrong'. That is different to the position in other areas of private law. Contract law is focused on achieving the parties' expectations, as made clear in *Hadley v Baxendale*.[17] In the field of equitable wrongs, it is at least arguable that the primary focus is not on loss, but rather on the diversion of an advantage. Take a case of breach of fiduciary duty, such as *Bhullar v Bhullar*,[18] where a director failed to notify his company of an opportunity to acquire additional property. In failing to disclose this information, and instead purchasing the property under the name of his own company, he diverted an advantage to himself. Remedies such as an account of profits and equitable compensation, to academics such as John Gardner, reflect this breach of loyalty.[19]

Having defined what it means to say that a cause of action is brought under the 'law of tort', we can now proceed to look at cases at the borderlines.

[10] (1868) LR 3 HL 330 (HL).
[11] See further John Murphy, 'The Merits of *Rylands v Fletcher*' (2004) 24 OJLS 643.
[12] Sir Percy Winfield, 'The History of Negligence in the Law of Torts' (1926) 42 LQR 184, 197.
[13] *Versloot Dredging BV v HDI Gerling Industrie Versicherung AG* [2016] UKSC 45, [2017] AC 1 [7]–[8] (Lord Sumption).
[14] *Hedley Byrne & Co Ltd v Heller & Partners* [1964] AC 465 (HL).
[15] See, eg, *Morris v Murray* [1991] 2 QB 6 (QB).
[16] *Livingstone v Rawyards Coal Co* (1880) 5 App Cas 25 (HL) 39 (Lord Blackburn).
[17] (1854) 9 Ex 341, 154 ER 145.
[18] [2003] EWCA Civ 424.
[19] John Gardner, *Torts and Other Wrongs* (OUP 2020) ch 1.

III. Borderline Cases

A. Tort and Contract

Of all the borderlines under scrutiny, examination of those lying between the law of tort and contract reveals the clearest, and most common, tension. This is because, if a claimant has no recourse to a claim in contract, their next port of call will usually be the tort of negligence. The classic case is where a party to a contract cannot bring a claim under the agreement because the relevant limitation period has expired.[20] The claimant will then turn to the law of tort, where the limitation periods can operate more generously, as discussed by Janet O'Sullivan in the context of latent defects.[21] An alternative situation is one where a claimant was never a party to the contract, but has nevertheless suffered loss, and is attempting to sue 'through' the contractual chain;[22] again, the claimant will usually turn to the tort of negligence for relief.

Should the claimant who is party to a contract in such situations be able to obtain redress through the alternative route of tort? If a claim could have been brought under a contractual agreement, when is it appropriate to turn to tort? This is an area of obvious difficulty, and different jurisdictions draw the line in different places. German law contains a doctrine of *Vertrag mit Schutzwirkung zugunsten Dritter* (or 'contracts with protective effects to third parties'); French law has a similar concept of *obligations de sécurité* (or 'security obligations': tort-like obligations implied into a contract).[23] The effect of drawing the line in different places, in the words of a leading work in this field, is that 'what is considered a matter of contractual law in one legal system is exclusively governed by tort in another'.[24]

In English law, if a claimant wishes to have recourse under an *existing* contract to which they are not a party, they can do so through the Contracts (Rights of Third Parties) Act 1999.[25] If the claim is brought in negligence, it is now well known that the 'assumption of responsibility' doctrine applies in this situation, which stems back to the revolutionary *Hedley Byrne* decision.[26] The doctrine states that, in the context of negligence claims for pure economic loss, a duty of care will only exist if

[20] As in *Henderson v Merrett Syndicates Ltd* [1995] 2 AC 145 (HL).

[21] The Limitation Act 1980 provides an identical period of six years for claims in both tort and contract (ss 2 and 5). In contract time runs from the date of breach; in tort from the date of damage. However, s 14A of the Limitation Act (as amended) offers a claimant the possibility of bringing a (non-personal injury) claim in tort outside that period. In crude terms, the claimant may be able to avail themselves of a three-year limitation period running from the date of actual or constructive discovery of facts relevant to the cause of action. See further ch 3.

[22] As in *Simaan v Pilkington Glass* [1988] 1 All ER 791 (CA).

[23] See Miquel Martin-Casals (ed), *The Borderlines of Tort Law: Interactions with Contract Law* (Intersentia 2019) 3.

[24] ibid.

[25] See *Linden Gardens Trust Ltd v Lenesta Sludge Disposals Ltd* [1994] 1 AC 85 (HL); *Alfred McAlpine Construction Ltd v Panatown Ltd* [2001] AC 518 (HL).

[26] *Hedley Byrne & Co Ltd v Heller & Partners* (n 14).

A has 'assumed responsibility' to B. There can be obvious unfairness if recovery for pure economic loss is limited to situations where there is a contract. As we see from the speech of Lord Devlin:

> [I]f a doctor negligently advises a patient that he cannot safely pursue his occupation when in fact he can and he loses his livelihood, there is said to be no remedy. Unless, of course, the patient were a private patient and accepted half a Guinea for his trouble: then the patient can recover all. *I am bound to say, my Lords, that I think this is a nonsense.*[27]

Lord Devlin went on to suggest that a duty of care should only be imposed in circumstances 'akin to contract'.[28] Inevitably, this raises the question as to how closely aligned a claim based on 'assumption of responsibility' must be to a *truly* contractual situation. This has been explored in cases such as *Banca Nazionale del Lavoro SPA*.[29] More broadly, it leads to debate about how far the tort of negligence should permeate into quasi-contractual situations, through the concept of assumption of responsibility.

Some lawyers take the view that if the contractual scheme has failed, the law of tort should not readily expand to save the day. Sir Rupert Jackson, for example, has denounced the 'amorphous and ever-expanding law of tort' into situations more appropriately regulated by contract.[30] Janet O'Sullivan's chapter suggests that there would be far less need to turn to 'assumption of responsibility' if the courts aligned the contractual and tortious limitation periods, ending the so-called 'crying for the moon' that was famously discussed by Lord Goff in *Henderson v Merrett Syndicates Ltd*.[31] Others, such as Jane Stapleton, criticise the lack of an 'adequate normative justification' for the assumption of responsibility doctrine, which they suggest signifies 'no more than an opaque conclusionary label'.[32] This idea that no principled interaction between tort and contract can be drawn (and that the assumption of responsibility doctrine is merely a foil for policy arguments) is common in academic circles.

An alternative view is that the 'assumption of responsibility' doctrine *can* be independently justified. Donal Nolan, undertaking a detailed assessment of existing case law, defines it as A 'taking on a task' for B.[33] Interestingly, to support his analysis, he does not view the doctrine merely as a question of how far tort

[27] ibid 517 (emphasis added).

[28] ibid 528–29.

[29] See *Banca Nazionale del Lavoro SPA v Playboy Club London Ltd* [2018] UKSC 43, [2018] 1 WLR 4041.

[30] Sir Rupert Jackson, 'Concurrent Liability: Where Have Things Gone Wrong' (2015) 23 Tort L Rev 3. See also John Fleming, 'Comparative Law of Torts' (1984) 4 OJLS 235, 240–41.

[31] *Henderson v Merrett* (n 20) 186.

[32] Jane Stapleton, *Three Essays on Torts* (OUP 2021) 61.

[33] Donal Nolan, 'Assumption of Responsibility: Four Questions' (2019) 72 CLP 123, 129.

should extend into the contractual sphere. Rather, he criticises as 'reductive' the analysis of the assumption of responsibility as 'contract cases in disguise'; he then emphasises the connection between assumption of responsibility and breach of fiduciary duty.[34] Lord Browne-Wilkinson, in particular, supported such analysis in his decisions: in both *White v Jones* and *Henderson*, he drew a connection between the assumption of responsibility and the 'special relationship' unique to fiduciary duties.[35]

The assumption of responsibility doctrine illustrates clear tension at the tort-contract borderline. There is, however, much more to this debate than a simple conflict between contract and tort, as we see from the academic work. Donal Nolan justifies the doctrine using equity; other work has discussed its historical foundations.[36] Thus, the appropriate scope of the 'assumption of responsibility' is a much more nuanced and multifaceted question and is not *solely* a question of conflict at the tort-contract borderline.

B. Tort and Property

In the previous section, we have seen how the borderlines can create conflict and dissonance, with different areas of private law fighting for conceptual space. But, as stated earlier, not all borderlines work that way. Sometimes the overlap allows different areas of private law to complement, and build upon, one another. The best example of this is the overlap between the law of tort and proprietary interests.

Private nuisance, for example, only becomes a possible claim when an individual has a right to the affected land. [37] In the recent and, some would say, controversial case of *Fearn v Board of Trustees of the Tate Gallery*,[38] it was held that the leaseholders of glass flats could obtain damages in nuisance from the Tate Modern, as the museum had invited visitors to look out on the flats from its viewing platform. The Supreme Court made clear that it was no answer to a claim in nuisance that the museum's land was being used reasonably, or in a way that was beneficial to the public. Tort law, where property is concerned, is about protecting the infringement of rights. As such, the public utility of conflicting uses is irrelevant, going only to the appropriate remedy, including whether or not an injunction should be granted.[39] As the Court said:

[34] ibid 146.

[35] *White v Jones* [1995] 2 AC 207 (HL) 270–72; *Henderson v Merrett* (n 20) 205–06.

[36] See also the historical justification in Lord Sales, 'Pure Economic Loss in the Law of Tort: The History and Theory of Assumption of Responsibility' (Annual Tort Law Research Group Lecture, Ontario, 2022).

[37] *Hunter v Canary Wharf Ltd* [1997] AC 655 (HL) 692 (Lord Goff).

[38] [2023] UKSC 4, [2023] 2 WLR 339.

[39] ibid [121]–[122].

> It is fundamental to the integrity of any system of property rights that . . . the individuals whose rights are infringed or overridden receive compensation for the violation of their rights. In other words, the public interest may sometimes justify awarding damages rather than granting an injunction . . . but it cannot justify denying the victim any remedy at all.[40]

Another example in which the property-tort borderline raises distinct questions is the tort of conversion: a cause of action that can be brought when one person deprives another person of the use and possession of their personal property. It is, to quote Lord Nicholls, 'the principal means whereby English law protects the ownership of goods'.[41] A topical question in the law of conversion is what *type* of property can be converted. A huge amount of private wealth is now held in intangible property, whether that is data held in a hard drive on an electronic device, assets such as Bitcoin and non-fungible tokens (NFTs), emails, and contractual rights.

Answering this question requires us to consider not only the functions of the law of tort, but also the nature and definition of 'property rights'.[42] The current approach, laid out by the Supreme Court in *OBG Ltd v Allan*,[43] is that the tort of conversion only extends to so-called 'documentary intangibles': that is, *physical* assets which represent an *intangible* asset, such as cheques or share certificates. 'Pure intangibles', however, such as Bitcoin or contractual rights, cannot be converted. This has come under a great deal of criticism. In *OBG* itself, Lady Hale and Lord Nicholls criticised the distinction between 'documentary' and 'pure' intangibles as being arbitrary and not aligned with the legal conception of property. In the words of Lady Hale:

> There may be a document evidencing an obligation of a purely personal kind, which ought not to attract a proprietary remedy. On the other hand, there are many debts and some other obligations which can now be readily assigned, attached, form part of an insolvent estate, and enjoy all the other characteristics of property, but which are not represented by a specific document.[44]

The crux of the point is that 'typical' aspects of property, including the ability to exclude others and assign it, are *even more* appropriate to intangible property than they are to some types of tangible property. Further, both intangible rights and chattels are, on this view, equally capable of misappropriation by third parties. As such, conversion should align with and update to modern conceptions of property. Other academics, such as Pey Woan Lee, have made a similar point, namely

[40] ibid [122].
[41] *Kuwait Airways Corporation v Iraqi Airways Co (Nos 4 & 5)* [2002] 2 AC 883 (HL) [77].
[42] See Michael Crawford, 'Contract as Property: Triangles and Tragic Choices' (2023) 82 CLJ 83.
[43] [2007] UKHL 21, [2008] 1 AC 1.
[44] ibid [310].

that conversion is out of step with theoretical ideas of property.[45] The contrary argument, discussed by Simon Douglas[46] and the majority in *OBG*, is that to extend conversion to intangible assets would be a radically wide expansion of the remit of the law of tort for circumstances that are, in essence, situations of pure economic loss; and that intangible assets were not, historically, the focus of conversion.

Thus, whereas we saw division at the contract-tort borderlines, we see development at the property-tort borderline. Property law does not conflict with the law of tort, but rather helps it to develop and fit the facts. More broadly, as modern conceptions of 'property' move forwards, they can be used to develop doctrines in tort law. We see from torts such as nuisance and conversion that, as much as we must discuss and debate the proper scope of tort law, we must also question what it means to be the holder of a 'property' right, as well as what rights and entitlements come with being a property-right holder. So, while one way of looking at the borderlines is as a tension between two areas of private law, sometimes discussing borderlines helps to advance tort into new areas, address new challenges, and protect new interests.

C. Tort and Equity/Unjust Enrichment

Lastly, we can turn to the overlap between the law of tort and equity, and unjust enrichment. I take these two together because the 'borderline' between them is slightly different, and more remote, than the other two. On first glance, it may appear that there is no real 'borderline' between either tort and equity, or tort and unjust enrichment. Tort and equitable wrongs operate in very different spheres, even though certain causes of action (such as misuse of private information and breach of confidence) are analogous.[47] They have different historical roots, different rationales, and give rise to different remedies.[48]

Likewise with unjust enrichment, although this crucially depends on how we define its scope. Historically, the field of 'unjust enrichment' was held to include restitution for wrongs.[49] It was for this reason that it was considered that a claimant

[45] Pey Woan Lee, 'Inducing Breach of Contract, Conversion and Contract as Property' (2009) 29 OJLS 511.

[46] Simon Douglas, 'Converting Contractual Rights' [2008] LMCLQ 129.

[47] See *A v B* [2002] EWCA Civ 337, [2003] QB 195 [4] (Lord Woolf MR); *Campbell v MGN Ltd* [2004] UKHL 22, [2004] 2 AC 457 [14] (Lord Nicholls).

[48] For breach of trust, equitable compensation is available, which is generally seen to be more generous than tort compensation, with no requirement that the loss be foreseeable: *AIB Group (UK) plc v Mark Redler & Co Solicitors* [2014] UKSC 58, [2015] AC 1503. It has, however, been suggested that tort compensation and equitable compensation are converging. Equitable wrongs also open up proprietary remedies through following and tracing.

[49] Charles Mitchell, Paul Mitchell, and Stephen Watterson, *Goff & Jones on Unjust Enrichment* (10th edn, Sweet & Maxwell 2022) 1-03.

had to 'waive' their claim in tort in order to seek a restitutionary remedy.[50] The predominant view now is that unjust enrichment is a distinct category from restitution for wrongs. In the words of *Goff & Jones*, unjust enrichment is a cause of action: the 'event' giving rise to liability. By contrast, restitution for wrongs is the 'remedy'.[51] In this sense, there is very little overlap or tension between tort and unjust enrichment. That is not surprising, because they are functionally distinct. Tort law, as explained above, responds to *wrongs*; whereas unjust enrichment does not require the defendant to be at fault.

Thus, the only sense in which there is a *direct* borderline is in cases where both a claim in the tort of negligence is maintained on the same facts as an equitable wrong or unjust enrichment claim. For example, it has recently become common, in cases where it is held that a bank owed a *Quincecare* duty of care for the execution of payment orders, to claim alternatively that the bank was unjustly enriched.[52] Occasionally, these concurrent claims give rise to disputes, especially where one cause of action is used to circumvent the rules of another. For example, in *Paragon Finance plc v DB Thakerar & Co*,[53] a breach of trust was (strategically) claimed to take advantage of more advantageous limitation rules; the Court of Appeal rejected this attempt.[54]

However, there is a more fundamental and interesting way in which a borderline *does* exist. By looking at common threads of reasoning between tort and equity/unjust enrichment, we can question whether the law of tort should be driven by different rules. This is explored both by Rory Gregson and Nicholas McBride in their chapters of this book. Rory Gregson, for example, explores 'big ideas' in both the law of tort and unjust enrichment, which he uses to question whether each is functioning as it should. He argues that the idea of 'correlativity' (that the claimant's *right* must justify the defendant's *obligation*) is common to both areas. Looking at literature discussing tort law, and finding the principle of 'correlativity' unsatisfactory, he concludes that unjust enrichment was wrong to be influenced by it.[55] In simple terms, we see that criticisms of *reasoning* in tort law are transposed over to influence unjust enrichment.

Nicholas McBride, in an insightful discussion of the relationship between tort and equity, discusses common threads of thinking between tort and equity to suggest that tort should *not* impose liability for public authority omissions. In his words:

[50] Jack Beatson, 'The Nature of Waiver of Tort' in Jack Beatson, *The Use and Abuse of Unjust Enrichment* (OUP 1991).
[51] Mitchell, Mitchell, and Watterson (n 49) 1-02.
[52] See, eg, *Tecnimont Arabia Ltd v National Westminster Bank plc* [2022] EWHC 1172 (Comm).
[53] [1999] 1 All ER 400 (CA).
[54] ibid 414.
[55] See ch 7.

> We have no reason to think that the fiduciary status of public right-holders means that they are subject to an equitable duty of care in exercising their powers. Tort would therefore be going much further than Equity were it to find that public right-holders are subject to a duty of care.[56]

Sometimes, therefore, borderlines do not represent an area of tension or development, as discussed above. Instead, there may be an overlap of common reasoning or judicial thinking, which can influence both doctrines. This more abstract and amorphous borderline is helpful to questioning the scope of the law of tort, as well as some of the principles that underpin it.

IV. Conclusion

In this short response, I have sought to draw together some of the chapters concerning tort's borderlines and to show, overall, how the law of tort interacts with other areas of private law; in essence, to see the different ways in which the 'borderlines' arise. Three points can be made by way of conclusion. First, the most common way in which the 'borderlines' are seen is as areas of tension between tort and another area of private law. For example, the assumption of responsibility demonstrates a key area of tension between tort and contract, asking how far tort should extend when a contract would arguably be required to regulate the situation. Secondly, less commonly, the borderlines emerge as one area complementing and working well with the other, refining the law of tort and allowing unique remedies where, for example, property rights are in play. Thirdly, as we see with the interaction of tort and unjust enrichment and equitable wrongs, it can be hard to see a 'borderline' at all. In such cases, however, much can be gained by exploring common threads of reasoning between very different areas of private law, and questioning whether their underlying principles should be developed.

[56] See ch 6.

6
Tort | Equity

Nicholas J McBride

Lunchtime at All Souls College, Oxford, in the spring of 1997. As I slide into place for lunch opposite Peter Birks, he congratulates me on my appointment to a Fellowship at Pembroke College, Cambridge. 'What will you be teaching?' 'Tort, Contract and Equity'. A slight snort of disdain for the Other Place's peculiarities: 'Hmph. Equity, what's that?' Peter would, of course, have strongly disapproved of this 'Borderlines' project, at least so far as tort and equity are concerned. Insofar as they are different, he would have contended, tort and equity are different in the way that Jupiter is different from a postbox, so different that it is stupid to talk about the distinctions between them. And insofar as they are similar, they are not qualitatively similar in the way that the redness of Mars and the redness of a postbox make them similar. Instead, they are similar in the same way that Mars and Jupiter are similar: part of equity belongs to the same genus as tort, which genus is the law of wrongs. And insofar as tort and equity are similar, talking of borderlines between them undermines what an unrelenting commitment to deciding like cases alike should lead us to do when we come across legal species belonging to the same genus: which is to obliterate any artificial distinctions between them that have the effect of speciating them into different categories.[1]

In this chapter, I will set out two different ways of understanding the divide between tort and equity that escape the force of Peter's challenge to the 'Borderlines' project.[2] Each way of understanding the divide establishes a difference between tort and equity. However, in each case the difference is not such as to make it stupid to talk about it (in the same way that it would be stupid to observe that one difference between Jupiter and a postbox is that Jupiter is a gas giant while a postbox is

[1] See Peter Birks, 'Equity in the Modern Law: An Exercise in Taxonomy' (1996) 26 UWAL Rev 1, 27.

[2] For a third way of understanding the difference between tort and equity, see John Goldberg and Henry Smith, 'Wrongful Fusion' in John Goldberg, Henry Smith, and Peter Turner (eds), *Equity and Law: Fusion and Fission* (CUP 2021) 330, arguing that equity 'operates in a second-order fashion on tort law to limit the ability of actors to take advantage of the rights and powers that first-order tort law confers'. I find this a less interesting theme to pursue for the purposes of this chapter because: (1) it has been dealt with very well by Goldberg and Smith already, and (2) (a Birksian point) I do not think this difference identifies a genuine borderline between tort and equity in that there is no reason why the equitable limits on the operation of tort law could not be generated from within tort law itself, such that it became self-limiting. It is, after all, merely history and not principle that accounts for why tort law does not recognise a 'clean hands' limit on claimants' abilities to bring actions in tort and deals with such issues (if it does at all) under the rubric of 'illegality' instead.

Nicholas J McBride, *Tort | Equity* In: *Borderlines in Private Law*. Edited by: William Day and Julius Grower,
Oxford University Press. © Nicholas J McBride 2024. DOI: 10.1093/9780191995200.003.0006

a metal container). Instead, the difference illuminates something important about the roles that tort and equity each play in the law. But at the same time, understanding the ways in which tort and equity are different allows us to look forward, as Peter undoubtedly did, to a time when our law libraries will no longer be organised around categories such as tort and equity. The Private Law Library of the Future will draw on the 'heap of good learning'[3] represented by tort and equity but will also leave those labels behind. So while Peter may have disapproved of the 'Borderlines' project, I hope he would have been pleased at the conclusion that the project allows me to reach.

But before we plunge into these differences, a boring and cautionary clarification. In talking about the (interesting) differences between tort and equity, I do not seek to give an account of the *whole* of tort or the *whole* of equity. An account of the border between France and Germany does not call for a description of the German towns that lie on the border with Poland, or the Pyrenees that separate France and Spain. Our focus is on the *parts* of equity and tort that abut in an interesting way, and as we will see occasionally overlap.

I. Two Kinds of Obligation

The first difference draws on the distinction between primary and secondary obligations, where a secondary obligation arises out of the breach of a primary obligation.[4] The secondary obligation that classically arises out of the breach of a primary obligation is an obligation to pay the victim of the breach compensation designed to put them, so far as money can do so, in the position they would have been in had the obligation been performed.[5]

The law does respond in other ways to the breach of a primary obligation, but such alternative responses tend to take the form of recognising *liabilities* to pay non-compensatory damages to the victim of a breach of a primary obligation. For example, Stephen A Smith has convincingly argued that there is no such thing as an obligation to pay punitive damages arising out of the breach of a primary obligation; only a liability to do so.[6] His attempt to argue that the same is true of compensation (that there is no obligation to pay it to the victim of a breach, only a liability to be made to pay it)[7] has been more fiercely resisted,[8] and for the purposes of this

[3] A favourite phrase of Peter's, derived from Thomas Wood's *An Institute of the Laws of England* (1720) *i*. See, eg, Peter Birks, 'This Heap of Good Learning: The Jurist in the Common Law Tradition' in Basil Markesinis (ed), *Law Making, Law Finding and Law Shaping: The Diverse Influences* (OUP 1997).

[4] For the origin of this terminology, see Bernard Rudden, 'Correspondence' (1990) 10 OJLS 288.

[5] *Robinson v Harman* (1848) 1 Exch 850, 855 (Parke B) (breach of contractual obligation); *Livingstone v Rawyards Coal Co* (1880) 5 App Cas 25 (HL) 39 (Lord Blackburn) (breach of obligation in tort); *The Albazero* [1977] AC 774 (HL) 841 (Lord Diplock) (breach of either).

[6] Stephen A Smith, *Rights, Wrongs and Injustices: The Structure of Remedial Law* (OUP 2019) 91, 126.

[7] Stephen A Smith, 'Duties, Liabilities, and Damages' (2011–12) 125 Harv LR 1727.

[8] Sandy Steel and Robert Stevens, 'The Secondary Legal Duty to Pay Damages' (2020) 136 LQR 283.

chapter I will assume that the breach of a primary obligation does give rise to an obligation to pay compensation to the victim of the breach.[9]

One way of expressing the difference between tort and equity is to say that equity is concerned with enforcing primary obligations, not secondary obligations; while the reverse is true for tort. Various equitable rules and doctrines demonstrate equity's especial concern with enforcing primary obligations.

First, primary obligations arising in tort and non-monetary contractual obligations are not enforceable at law. If they are enforceable at all, they are enforced in equity, through the award of an injunction or an order for specific performance.

Secondly, while equity only grants an injunction or an order for specific performance to compel performance of a common law obligation when a monetary remedy for breach of that obligation would be inadequate, equity does not adopt the same position in relation to equitable obligations. As Lionel Smith observes, when it comes to equitable obligations, 'equity's traditional aim is to get as close as possible to specific performance, not to award compensatory damages'.[10] As a result, '[i]f the trustee has the trust property, he is not given the option of keeping it and paying compensation. In respect of trust property held by the trustee, a trust is always automatically specifically enforceable.'[11]

Thirdly, such is the general importance attached by equity to the performance of primary equitable obligations, that the courts exercise a general supervisory jurisdiction over the administration of trusts, under which trustees are allowed to ask the courts for directions as to how they should perform their roles as trustees.[12]

Fourthly, it has been repeatedly emphasised in recent years that the process of taking an account, and the remedies flowing therefrom, are designed to uphold the primary obligations of someone charged with managing money for another, and not to give effect to a secondary obligation arising out of breach of those primary obligations.[13] As Lord Millett observed:

> an account is not a remedy for [a] wrong. Trustees . . . are accounting parties, and their beneficiaries . . . do not have to prove that there has been a breach of trust . . . in order to obtain an order for account. Once the trust . . . is established or conceded the beneficiary . . . is entitled to an account as of right. Although like all

[9] I am more sceptical in Nicholas McBride, *The Humanity of Private Law, Part I: Explanation* (Hart 2019) 58–60.

[10] Lionel Smith, 'Equity is Not a Single Thing' in Dennis Klimchuk, Irit Samet, and Henry Smith (eds), *Philosophical Foundations of the Law of Equity* (OUP 2020) 151–52.

[11] ibid 157.

[12] See Richard Nolan, 'Invoking the Administrative Jurisdiction: The Enforcement of Modern Trust Structures' in Paul Davies and James Penner (eds), *Equity, Trusts and Commerce* (Hart 2017); Daniel Clarry, *The Supervisory Jurisdiction Over Trust Administration* (OUP 2018); Susan Kiefel, 'Judicial Advice to Trustees: Its Origins, Purposes and Nature' (2019) 42 MULR 993.

[13] James Edelman and Steven Elliott, 'Money Remedies against Trustees' (2004) 18 TLI 116, 118; Joshua Getzler, 'As If—Accountability and Counterfactual Trust' (2011) 91 BUL Rev 973, 978–79; Charles Mitchell, 'Stewardship of Property and Liability to Account' [2014] Conv 215, 221–24.

equitable remedies an order for an account is discretionary, in making the order the court is not granting a remedy for [a] wrong but enforcing performance of an obligation.[14]

Fifthly, while a fiduciary's obligation to give up a gain they have made to their principal is often said to be triggered by their having committed a breach of fiduciary duty in making that gain, the better view[15] is that the obligation is primary: it does not arise out of a breach of duty, but because fiduciaries are under an obligation not to put themselves in a position where pursuit of their self-interest might lead them to breach a (non-fiduciary) duty that they owe to their principal. Making them give up a gain gives effect to this primary obligation.

Sixthly, where equity does perform a recognisably compensatory function, it does not do so in response to wrongdoing but instead gives effect to what I have called 'compensation without wrongdoing':[16] that is, a primary obligation to compensate the claimant for some loss they have suffered or will suffer if they are not compensated. For example, the constructive trust in *Eves v Eves*[17] arose not because the defendant had done anything wrong by inducing the claimant to rely on his assurance that his house was as much hers as it was his (by doing work on the house), but because he had an obligation to ensure that that work was fairly rewarded. Similarly with the remedies that the defendants (very unusually) could choose between in *Guest v Guest*[18] under the law on proprietary estoppel: whether the defendants gave the claimant a reversionary interest in their farm (subject to the defendants' retaining a life interest) or the monetary equivalent (suitably discounted), the remedy was designed to ensure that the claimant's years of work on the farm were properly rewarded.

By contrast, one of tort's core functions is to give effect to secondary obligations to pay compensation to the victims of torts. So close is the association between tort and compensation that it came to be thought that tort's function was to determine when A would be required to pay compensation to B in a case where A had caused B to suffer loss.[19] This was a mistake which has now been rectified.[20] It is now widely understood that tort determines what primary obligations we owe each other automatically, without anyone having to do anything special for them to arise, and that it gives effect to various secondary obligations and liabilities when

[14] *Libertarian Investments Ltd v Hall* [2013] HKCFA 93 [167].

[15] See Nicholas McBride, *Key Ideas in Trusts Law* (Hart 2023) 85–89.

[16] McBride (n 9) 61–62.

[17] [1975] 1 WLR 1338 (CA).

[18] [2022] UKSC 27, [2022] 3 WLR 911.

[19] For example, my assigned textbook on tort law when I studied the subject in 1989 was Peter Cane (ed), *Atiyah's Accidents, Compensation and the Law* (4th edn, Weidenfeld & Nicholson 1987).

[20] Thanks in particular to Peter Birks, 'The Concept of a Civil Wrong' in David Owen (ed), *Philosophical Foundations of Tort Law* (OUP 1995); Ernest Weinrib, *The Idea of Private Law* (Harvard University Press 1995); various editions of Nicholas McBride and Roderick Bagshaw, *Tort Law* (Pearson Education, beginning in 2001); Robert Stevens, *Torts and Rights* (OUP 2007).

those primary obligations are breached. But while tort determines what primary obligations we owe each other automatically, it does not enforce them: it depends on equity for their enforcement.[21]

Of course, this neat division is somewhat spoiled by equity's getting into the business of enforcing secondary obligations to pay equitable compensation to another in cases where a defendant has breached an equitable duty owed to the claimant.[22] Lord Millett has condemned this development as 'heretical',[23] arguing that equitable compensation is only payable when a primary, specific equitable remedy is not available.[24] Whether heretical or not, this development is certainly novel,[25] and the novelty of this development underscores the point made in this section, that one difference between equity and tort is that equity traditionally concerns itself with enforcing primary obligations while tort focuses on enforcing secondary obligations.

II. Two Kinds of Right

Ben McFarlane and Robert Stevens' work allows us to suggest a second significant difference between equity and tort. Starting with the nature of a trust,[26] and then working outwards to areas such as the law on equitable assignment, McFarlane and Stevens suggest[27] that 'what's special about Equity' is that rights in equity, for the most part, take the form of a 'right against a right'; that is, a right that a right held by someone else be exercised in a particular way.[28]

[21] It might be objected that it is really tort which is enforcing these primary obligations, such that injunctions awardable to prevent someone committing a tort should be regarded as 'part' of tort (and treated as such in the tort law textbooks), and as having flown the nest of equity. If that were so, why is there a 'clean hands' limit on injunctions being awarded against tortfeasors, when tort recognises no such limit on damages being awarded against a tortfeasor?

[22] *Target Holdings Ltd v Redferns* [1996] AC 421 (HL); *Swindle v Harrison* [1997] 4 All ER 705 (CA); *AIB Group (UK) plc v Mark Redler & Co Solicitors* [2014] UKSC 58, [2015] AC 1503.

[23] Lord Millett, 'The Common Lawyer and the Equity Practitioner' in Daniel Clarry (ed), *The UK Supreme Court Yearbook*, vol 6: *2014–2015 Legal Year* (Appellate Press 2015) 183.

[24] ibid 183–84, citing in support *Nocton v Lord Ashburton* [1914] AC 988 (HL) (rescission of a transaction induced by a breach of a fiduciary duty was not available, therefore equitable compensation was awarded instead).

[25] See Lord Browne-Wilkinson's judgment in *Target Holdings* (n 22) 428, observing that the case raised the 'novel point' of whether 'a trustee who commits a breach of trust [is] liable to compensate the beneficiary not only for losses caused by the breach but also for losses which the beneficiary would, in any event, have suffered even if there had been no such breach?'. If it were normal for equity to enforce secondary obligations arising out of breach of an equitable duty, it would be impossible for such a basic question to be regarded as raising a novel point in 1996.

[26] Ben McFarlane and Robert Stevens, 'The Nature of Equitable Property' (2010) 4 J Eq 1; Robert Stevens, *The Laws of Restitution* (OUP 2023) 216–28.

[27] Ben McFarlane and Robert Stevens, 'What's Special about Equity? Rights About Rights' in Klimchuk, Samet, and Smith (eds), *Philosophical Foundations* (n 10).

[28] While the concept of a 'right against a right' is nowadays most associated with Ben McFarlane and Robert Stevens, the palm for first coming up with the idea should go to Lionel Smith, who over twenty-five years ago highlighted the phenomenon of someone having rights 'in' a right held by someone

There are, of course, no such things as 'rights against rights', strictly speaking. Rights are always held against other people. But if we take what McFarlane and Stevens refer to as 'rights against rights' as actually being 'rights against a right-holder', then their thesis about what's special about equity can be accepted: Equity does seem peculiarly concerned with determining when someone (C) will have a right against a right-holder (RH), requiring RH to exercise that right in a particular way. In Hohfeldian terms, C's right will always be a claim-right: a right that RH act in a particular way, corresponding to a duty of RH's to act in that way. The right held by RH, and which is the focus of C's claim-right, may be a claim-right (arising, for example, under the law of contract or the law of tort), but it may also be a legal power (such as a power to transfer title to property to someone else).[29] And, of course, C's claim-right may itself may be the subject of a right held against C as to how that claim-right is exercised. This is the case with a sub-trust, where RH holds assets on trust for C, and C holds her rights under the RH-C trust on trust for someone else.

By contrast, and for the most part, the claim-rights that tort recognises us as having are not rights against right-holders, but rights in respect of people's natural capacities. For example, tort gives me a claim-right against you that you not use your hands to touch me without my consent. It also gives me a claim-right against you that you not use your tongue to tell damaging lies about me to other people to my detriment, or to tell me lies with the object of getting me to act in a particular way with the result that I am so induced to my detriment. When I am in possession of land, tort gives me a claim-right that you not make so much noise that the amenity value of the land is unreasonably reduced. It has been suggested that this particular claim-right will only be held against someone who is in a position to *use land* in such a way as to interfere unreasonably with the amenity value of my land.[30] This is a mistake: the claim-right is held against everyone. If, over an extended period of time, you march a military band playing 'Colonel Bogey' up and down outside my house, then I will be able to use equity to get an injunction against you doing this, and also have tort enforce your secondary obligation to pay me damages equalling a reasonable sum for being made to put up with the noise created by the band.

else: see Lionel Smith, *The Law of Tracing* (OUP 1997) 61–63. See also Lionel Smith, 'Unravelling Proprietary Restitution' (2004) 40 CBLJ 317, 321–22.

[29] Arguing that the right held by RH is often more aptly characterised as a legal power rather than a claim-right, see James Penner, 'The (True) Nature of a Beneficiary's Equitable Proprietary Interest Under a Trust' (2014) 27 CJLJ 473. Ben McFarlane and Robert Stevens accept this modification of their original view in Ben McFarlane and Robert Stevens, 'What's Special about Equity?' (n 27) 194.

[30] This heresy originated in Francis Newark, 'The Boundaries of Nuisance' (1949) 65 LQR 480, 489. It was then picked up by the Court of Appeal in *Hussain v Lancaster City Council* [2000] QB 1 (CA) 15, and now seems to have been endorsed by the Supreme Court in *Fearn v Board of Trustees of the Tate Gallery* [2023] UKSC 4, [2023] 2 WLR 339 [9] (Lord Leggatt) and [158] (Lord Sales).

Had tort chosen to give effect to a rule against people's abusing their rights our second difference between tort and equity would have been obliterated: tort would have recognised as many claim-rights against right-holders as equity does. But in *Bradford v Pickles*[31] and *Allen v Flood*[32] the House of Lords refused to extend tort so as to give claimants claim-rights that defendants not abuse their *private* rights to the claimants' detriment. But it is different with *public* rights. When it comes to public rights, tort like equity *does* recognise the existence of claim-rights against right-holders.

For example, tort recognises that I have a claim-right that a public official not abuse their powers with the intention of harming me, and that I also have a claim-right that a public official not knowingly abuse their powers, knowing that I will suffer harm as a result. Violation of either of those claim-rights will amount to the tort of misfeasance in public office. Similarly, I have a claim-right in tort that the authorities not maliciously prosecute me for a crime with the result that I am unjustly convicted of that crime; the tort being committed by violating that right being malicious prosecution. The extension of the tort of malicious prosecution to cases of maliciously instituting civil proceedings in *Willers v Joyce*[33] might be justified as compatible with the House of Lords' nineteenth-century stance against using tort to give claimants claim-rights that defendants not abuse their private rights to those claimants' detriment. Launching civil proceedings against another is a sufficiently public act—invoking as it does the powers of the courts against that other—that the power to launch such proceedings may be justifiably classified as a public, and not private, power.

So just as our first difference between tort and equity was somewhat spoiled by the courts' starting to give effect to secondary obligations arising out of the breach of a primary equitable obligation, our second difference between tort and equity is slightly undermined by tort's recognising the existence of claim-rights against right-holders where the rights in question are sufficiently public in nature.

III. Linking the Differences

Despite these wrinkles, our two differences between tort and equity are sufficiently marked that the question of whether they are linked is impossible to ignore.

One obvious link between these differences is that because (for the most part) the claim-rights recognised by tort constrain other people's natural capacities, the primary obligations that correspond to those claim-rights can only be enforced by a jurisdiction that acts *in personam*; literally, against the body: forcing someone to

[31] [1895] AC 587 (HL).
[32] [1898] AC 1 (HL).
[33] [2016] UKSC 43, [2018] AC 832.

perform the bodily acts or non-actions that they have a primary obligation to perform in tort.

Under the common law, that *in personam* jurisdiction can be found not in private law (which is confined to enforcing obligations and liabilities to pay money to others), but in the criminal law. Indeed, the core function of criminal law is to compel people to conform to the primary obligations that tort says they owe others. But the criminal law only acts as a general deterrent, punishing people after the event when they are found to have breached a primary obligation under the law of tort with a blameworthy state of mind. Equity is the *in personam* jurisdiction that helps tort out by acting as a specific deterrent: ordering a particular individual to perform their primary obligations under the law of tort under the threat of being sent to prison if they do not.

A deeper link between our two differences between equity and tort can be discerned when we ask: is there something about the nature of claim-rights against a right-holder (equity's speciality) that means the obligations corresponding to those claim-rights need to be routinely enforced in a way that the sort of primary obligations that are the meat and drink of the law of tort never are? I think there is, and the answer to this question lies in the fact that claim-rights against a right-holder usually arise in order to preserve the legitimacy of private law.[34] They exist in order to ensure that rights enjoyed by a right-holder are not used in a way that would bring private law into disrepute. The law therefore has a very strong reason to seek to ensure that claim-rights against a right-holder are observed: a failure to do so automatically endangers the legitimacy of private law.

The same is not true of the primary obligations that arise under the law of tort. A breach of those obligations does not necessarily bring private law into disrepute. What would endanger private law's legitimacy when a primary obligation arising in tort is breached is if private law did not respond *adequately* to that breach, and through the inadequacy of its response showed the breached primary obligation to be 'little more than a sounding brass or a tinkling cymbal'.[35] So in order to preserve the legitimacy of the law, the obligations corresponding to claim-rights against a right-holder need to be specifically enforced, while breach of the obligations that typically arise under the law of tort only needs to be responded to adequately.

Thus the link between our two differences between tort and equity is made out. The claim-rights that equity recognises people as having will be routinely enforced because they are claim-rights against a right-holder and, as such, violation of those rights will always endanger the legitimacy of the law. In contrast, the claim-rights that typically arise under tort (claim-rights in respect of our natural capacities)

[34] See McBride (n 9) ch 6, for an extended discussion of the various private law rules and doctrines which exist to maintain the legitimacy of private law.

[35] *Simpson v Attorney-General (Baigent's Case)* [1994] 3 NZLR 667 (NZHC) 693 (Hardie Boys J, quoting 1 Corinthians 13:1).

will not be specifically enforced unless damages would be an inadequate remedy, because violation of those types of claim-rights will not endanger the legitimacy of the law if the violation can be responded to adequately.

IV. When in Rome

The previous two sections have drawn some clear dividing lines between tort and equity, but at the same time observed how those dividing lines are crossed; first of all, through equity getting into the business of enforcing secondary obligations, and secondly, through tort recognising claim-rights against right-holders where the rights held by those right-holders are public in nature.

However, where equity crosses into territory traditionally governed by tort, it would be foolish of equity not to learn from tort's much longer experience in that area and shape its invading rules and doctrines to mirror those of tort's; and the same is true *mutatis mutandis* where tort crosses into territory traditionally governed by equity. I will spell out the implications of this lesson in relation to: (A) awards of equitable compensation against a trustee who has committed a breach of trust; and (B) the common law liabilities of a public body for failing to exercise its powers to save someone from harm.

A. Equitable Compensation for Breach of Trust

In *AIB Group (UK) plc v Mark Redler*, Lord Reed held that:

> The measure of compensation should . . . normally be assessed at the date of trial, with the benefit of hindsight. The foreseeability of loss is generally irrelevant, but the loss must be caused by the breach of trust, in the sense that it must flow directly from it. Losses resulting from unreasonable behaviour on the part of the claimant will be adjudged to flow from that behaviour, and not from the breach. The requirement that the loss should flow directly from the breach is also the key to determining whether causation has been interrupted by the acts of third parties.[36]

While the amount of compensatory damages payable by a tortfeasor will 'normally be assessed at the date of trial, with the benefit of hindsight'[37] none of Lord Reed's

[36] *AIB Group* (n 22) [135].

[37] *Jobling v Associated Dairies Ltd* [1982] AC 794 (HL). The position in breach of contract cases is more confused, with *Golden Strait Corp v Nippon Yusen Kubishika Kaisha (The Golden Victory)* [2007] UKHL 12, [2007] 2 AC 353 taking a 'date of trial' approach while the need for commercial certainty militates in favour of a 'date of breach' approach.

other rules for assessing the amount of equitable compensation that is payable by a trustee committing a breach of trust apply in the case of someone who has committed a tort.[38]

The foreseeability of loss is plainly relevant, at least where the tort has been committed innocently.[39] The fact that the victim of a tort's unreasonable conduct has contributed to their loss will not prevent the victim arguing that the tort caused that loss.[40] Instead, the damages payable to the victim of the tort will be reduced for contributory negligence—but only where the tort involved the breach of a duty of care owed to the victim.[41] And whether there was a 'break in the chain of causation' between a tort's being committed and the victim of a tort suffering loss depends not on whether there was a 'direct' link between the two, but on whether after the tort was committed a third party or the victim did something to contribute to that loss being suffered and what they did amounted to a deliberate, voluntary, informed, and unreasonable act.[42]

It is difficult to know why Lord Reed would seek to reinvent the wheel when it comes to determining the measure of compensation that is available against a trustee who has committed a breach of trust. It may be that he was uncomfortable with making it so obvious that the courts have embarked on a new method of dealing with errant trustees and preferred a halfway house between tort's approach to determining the scope of a wrongdoer's liability to pay compensatory damages and equity's traditional accounting process for ensuring a trustee lives up to their obligations. However, the better view is represented by Millett LJ in *Bristol & West Building Society v Mothew*, holding that when making a trustee liable to pay equitable compensation for 'breach of the equitable duty of skill and care ... There is no reason in principle why the common law rules on causation, remoteness of damage and measure of damages should not be applied by analogy in such a case.'[43]

B. Public Authority Liability for Omissions at Common Law

While Lord Reed's position in *AIB* represents a model of what should *not* have happened when equity travelled into territory traditionally governed by tort, a much happier picture emerges when we consider what has occurred in cases where tort

[38] For a good review of the current differences in assessing the amount of equitable compensation payable by a trustee in breach of trust and the compensatory damages payable by a tortfeasor, see Paul Davies, 'Compensatory Remedies for Breach of Trust' in Richard Nolan, Kelvin Low, and Tang Hang Wu (eds), *Trusts and Modern Wealth Management* (CUP 2018) 328–38.

[39] Nicholas McBride and Roderick Bagshaw, *Tort Law* (6th edn, Pearson Education 2018) 314–18.

[40] See *Pritchard v Co-operative Group Ltd* [2011] EWCA Civ 329, [2012] QB 320.

[41] McBride and Bagshaw (n 39) 738.

[42] ibid 297–99.

[43] [1998] Ch 1 (CA) 17. See also Steven Elliott, 'Remoteness Criteria in Equity' (2002) 65 MLR 588, 597.

has crossed the equity/tort borderline by determining whether and when people have claim-rights against public right-holders that those right-holders exercise those rights to save them from harm.

As numerous writers led by Paul Finn[44] have observed, where equity recognises people as having claim-rights against public authorities or officials in respect of how they exercise their rights, it does so on the basis that public right-holders hold those rights as *fiduciaries* for others.[45] As such, equity only recognises public right-holders as owing other people or the State obligations of *loyalty* in respect of how they exercise their rights. Such obligations require that public right-holders not exercise their powers for improper purposes or in self-interested ways or stand idly by while those who they are charged to protect suffer harm.[46]

Tort has ended up taking exactly the same position in cases where a public right-holder is sued for failing to save someone from harm. Tort does not recognise any distinctive claim-rights against public right-holders that they exercise those rights to save someone from harm other than a right that the public right-holder not *knowingly* fail to save someone from harm that it was charged with the responsibility of protecting. In such a case, the public right-holder will commit the tort of misfeasance in public office. Outside such a case, the only way tort will recognise that the public right-holder owed someone else a duty to act is if an equivalently situated private person, not equipped with any distinctive rights, would also have been subject to such a duty.[47]

Paul Finn suggests that it is no accident that tort and equity should have ended up taking exactly the same position in respect of what claim-rights can be asserted against a public right-holder *qua* public right-holder. Finn explains that it was originally 'the common law, *not equity*' that was responsible for characterising the relationship between public officials and the public as a 'fiduciary' or 'trust' relationship and for policing that relationship in those terms.[48] It was because of this that the tort (and corresponding crime)[49] of misfeasance in public office was recognised. But then this aspect of the common law was completely forgotten, and

[44] See Paul Finn, 'The Abuse of Public Power in Australia: Making the Governors Our Servants' (1993) 75 Canberra Bulletin of Public Administration 14; Paul Finn, 'The Forgotten Trust: the People and the State' in Malcolm Cope (ed), *Equity: Issues and Trends* (Federation Press 1995); Paul Finn, 'A Sovereign People, a Public Trust' in Paul Finn (ed), *Essays on Law and Government*, vol 1: *Principles and Values* (Law Book Company Ltd 1995); Paul Finn, 'Public Trusts, Public Fiduciaries' (2010) 38 FL Rev 335.

[45] *Bowes v City of Toronto* (1858) 11 Moo PC 463 (discussed in Lionel Smith, 'Loyalty and Politics: From Case Law to Statute Law' (2015) 9 J Eq 130); *Reading v Attorney General* [1951] AC 507 (HL); *Bromley LBC v Greater London Council* [1983] AC 768 (HL) (discussed in Martin Loughlin, *Legality and Locality* (OUP 1996) 231–47; John Barratt, 'Public Trusts' (2006) 69 MLR 514, 533–34).

[46] See Theodore Rave, 'Fiduciary Principles and the State' in Evan Criddle, Paul Miller, and Robert Sitkoff (eds), *The Oxford Handbook of Fiduciary Law* (OUP 2019) 335–37.

[47] *Michael v Chief Constable of South Wales Police* [2015] UKSC 2, [2015] AC 1732.

[48] Finn, 'Public Trusts, Public Fiduciaries' (n 44) 337 (emphasis in original).

[49] For the criminal history, see David Lusty, 'Revival of the Common Law Offence of Misconduct in Public Office' (2014) 38 Crim LJ 337.

it fell to equity to revive, articulate, and give effect to these common law ideas. It was only in the twentieth century that tort recovered from its amnesia; and by rediscovering the long-forgotten tort of misfeasance in public office,[50] it was able to resume enforcing standards of loyalty on public right-holders.

Those who take the view that tort should recognise public right-holders as having a distinctive duty to *take care* to save someone from harm[51] may argue that such a development is actually mandated on the approach advocated for here. This is because, they might argue, fiduciaries are subject to an obligation to take care to exercise their rights for the benefit of those they are charged with protecting. For example, Paul Miller argues that fiduciaries are subject to a 'principle of prudence [that] requires that fiduciaries execute their mandates with due care'.[52] This 'principle of prudence establishes deliberative and attitudinal ideals for decision-making. It also supports a universal duty of care governing the execution of fiduciary mandates.'[53] So if equity recognises that public right-holders *qua* fiduciaries are subject to a duty of care in exercising their rights, so must tort.

However, the better view is (again) set out by Millett LJ in *Bristol & West Building Society v Mothew*, observing that '[b]reach of fiduciary obligation ... connotes disloyalty or infidelity. Mere incompetence is not enough. A servant who loyally does his incompetent best for his master is not unfaithful and is not guilty of a breach of fiduciary duty.'[54] On the tort side of the tort/equity divide, Tony Weir agrees: '[t]he principal thrust of the fiduciary duty is one of loyalty, and while care is always required, loyalty is an issue only when disloyalty is possible, where there is a conflict of interest.'[55] So while it might be the case that fiduciaries characteristically have an obligation to take care in performing their functions, that obligation does not spring from their fiduciary status, but is entirely independent and usually arises out of their 'assuming a responsibility' to their principal to take care. The independence of the obligation to take care is shown by the fact that many people who 'assume a responsibility' to someone else to take care and incur a duty of care to that someone else as a result are *not* fiduciaries, such as building contractors or architects.

Incorporating a 'principle of prudence' *within* the fiduciary ideal and then applying that 'principle of prudence' to the State *qua* fiduciary seems to spring from a discreditable ambition to make the fiduciary ideal an 'interpretive, ecumenical

[50] Originally in Australia, in *Farrington v Thomson* [1959] VR 286 (VSC).

[51] See, eg, Sandy Steel and Stelios Tofaris, 'Negligence Liability for Omissions and the Police' (2016) 75 CLJ 128.

[52] Paul Miller, 'Principles of Public Fiduciary Administration' in Tsvi Kahana and Anat Scolnicov (eds), *Boundaries of State, Boundaries of Rights* (CUP 2016) 266.

[53] ibid 267. See also Rave (n 46) 337–39.

[54] [1998] Ch 1 (CA) 18. See also Paul Finn, 'The Fiduciary Principle' in Paul Finn, *Fiduciary Obligations* (rev edn, Federation Press 2016) 330–31.

[55] Tony Weir, 'The Staggering March of Negligence' in Peter Cane and Jane Stapleton (eds), *The Law of Obligations: Essays in Celebration of John Fleming* (OUP 1998) 129.

theory of everything' that will tell us everything we need to know about how the State should function.[56] Discreditable, because a theory of everything is a theory of nothing: a theory of everything will have to be infinitely manipulable, and therefore unfalsifiable, in order to cover the 'everything' that it seeks to explain.[57]

It follows that we have no reason to think that the fiduciary status of public right-holders means that they are subject to an equitable duty of care in exercising their powers. Tort would therefore be going much further than equity were it to find that public right-holders are subject to a duty of care in exercising their powers. In this area equity is tort's big brother, with the result that, on the approach advocated for here, tort should follow equity rather than seek to lead it.

V. The Private Law Library of the Future

It might be thought that if tort is required to act like equity when it crosses into territory traditionally controlled by equity, and equity is required to act like tort when it crosses into territory traditionally controlled by tort, the distinctions between tort and equity will be set in aspic. However, the opposite is true. We only need to make a firm distinction between tort and equity if tort and equity do the same things, but in different ways—so that 'We do this in tort but that in equity'.[58] If tort and equity start doing the same things and in the same way, it becomes misleading to think about tort and equity as wholly distinct areas of law and necessary to find new words to describe the area of law that is comprised of those parts of tort and equity that do the same things and in the same way.

Current developments allow us to see a new Private Law Library emerging where old titles such as *Clerk and Lindsell on Tort* and *Lewin on Trusts* will be left behind and replaced by—what? A new private law library would have one volume devoted to 'Rights', and within that volume distinguish between rights constraining natural freedoms and rights constraining how people exercise their rights. Another volume on 'Remedies' would distinguish between vindicatory remedies that enable claimants to compel defendants to observe the rights that those claimants have against those defendants, and wrong-based remedies that are available to a claimant where a defendant has violated the claimant's rights. A third section in the 'Remedies' volume would deal with 'free-standing remedies' that are designed neither to uphold someone's rights nor respond to their violation.[59]

[56] Evan Fox-Decent, 'New Frontiers in Public Fiduciary Law' in Criddle, Miller, and Sitkoff (eds), *Handbook of Fiduciary Law* (n 46) 910. See also Evan Fox-Decent, *Sovereignty's Promise: The State as Fiduciary* (OUP 2011).

[57] See McBride (n 9) 28.

[58] A conscious reference to Andrew Burrows, 'We Do This at Common Law but That in Equity' (2002) 22 OJLS 1.

[59] On which, see Nicholas McBride, 'Free-Standing Liabilities' (forthcoming, in a volume edited by Lionel Smith and others honouring the work of Stephen Smith).

Much of the private law we are familiar with could be decanted into just these two volumes. But not all—we would need to emulate Blackstone by supplementing these two volumes with two more, the first on 'Persons' (dealing with the various categories of individual who might be benefited or burdened by private law) and the second on 'Interests' (categorising the different kinds of interests that might give rise to rights against others and how those interests are acquired).

Were we to organise the way private law is understood and taught around the simple categories of 'Persons', 'Interests', 'Rights', and 'Remedies', the language of 'Tort' and 'Equity' would simply drop away, as no longer needed to make sense of, or explain, private law. Moreover, adopting this scheme for thinking about private law would: (1) ensure that the law on what rights we have and what remedies are available to vindicate those rights and to respond to their violation is rationally developed; (2) make for easy comparison between jurisdictions in terms of what those jurisdictions have to say on these issues; and (3) put paid to any talk of there being borderlines between different parts of private law. I think Peter would have approved.

7

Tort | Unjust Enrichment

*Rory Gregson**

I. Introduction

This chapter considers two big ideas which cross the borderline between the law of torts and the law of unjust enrichment. The first big idea is that the law of unjust enrichment is like the law of torts because different unjust enrichment claims, like different torts, are justified by different reasons. This chapter argues that this has an important implication which has not been fully appreciated. Different reasons may justify different rules. Accordingly, classifying a claim as within the law of unjust enrichment says nothing about the rules which should apply to it. Nevertheless, the courts have repeatedly fallen into the trap of assuming that, because a claim is within the law of unjust enrichment, it must be governed by certain rules.

The second big idea is correlativity. This idea states that any duty that D owes to C must be justified by a reason that links the parties, simultaneously justifying both C's right and D's duty. This idea originally emerged in the law of torts, but it recently contributed to radical changes to the law of unjust enrichment in two Supreme Court decisions: *Investment Trust Companies v Revenue & Customs Commissioners* ('*ITC*') and *Prudential Assurance v Revenue & Customs Commissioners*.[1] However, this chapter argues that the idea of correlativity has been pushed too far, and it cannot justify the latter decision.

II. More Like Torts than Contract

In *Barnes v Eastenders Cash & Carry plc*, the UK Supreme Court approved the following passage:

> The reasons why the courts have held a defendant's enrichment to be unjust vary from one set of cases to another, and for this reason the law of unjust enrichment more closely resembles the law of torts (recognising a variety of reasons why a

* I thank Nick McBride and Alexander Waghorn for their written comments on an earlier draft.

[1] *Investment Trust Companies v Revenue and Customs Commissioners* [2017] UKSC 29, [2018] AC 275 ('*ITC*'); *Prudential Assurance Co Ltd v Revenue and Customs Commissioners* [2018] UKSC 39, [2018] 3 WLR 652.

Rory Gregson, *Tort | Unjust Enrichment* In: *Borderlines in Private Law*. Edited by: William Day and Julius Grower, Oxford University Press. © Rory Gregson 2024. DOI: 10.1093/9780191995200.003.0007

defendant must compensate a claimant for harm) than it does the law of contract (embodying a single principle that expectations engendered by binding promises must be fulfilled).[2]

The first half of this chapter argues that the implications of this have not been fully grasped.

A. Different Reasons, Different Rules

The rules governing a legal claim should be shaped by the reasons for that claim.[3] There are at least two good reasons for this. First, as Jeremy Waldron puts it, '[a]pplying a norm to a human individual is not like deciding what to do about a rabid animal or a dilapidated house'.[4] Instead, humans are moral agents. In order to respect their moral agency, the rules that the law imposes on them must be justified by good reasons.[5] Second, if the courts started laying down arbitrary rules, for which there were no good reasons, then this would eventually erode the law's legitimacy, threatening public respect for, and willingness to comply with, the law.[6] Thus, legal rules should not be arbitrary and instead they should be shaped by good reasons.

Different reasons may justify different rules. So if different claims are justified by different reasons, then it may be that they should be governed by different rules. In the law of torts, this is uncontroversial. Different torts are justified by different reasons and so different torts are governed by different rules.[7] To take some uncontroversial examples: different torts demand different levels of fault;[8] some torts

[2] *Barnes v Eastenders Cash & Carry plc* [2014] UKSC 26, [2015] AC 1 [102] (Lord Toulson) quoting Charles Mitchell, Paul Mitchell, and Stephen Watterson, *Goff & Jones: The Law of Unjust Enrichment* (9th edn, Sweet & Maxwell 2016) para 1-08. See also Graham Virgo, *The Principles of the Law of Restitution* (3rd edn, OUP 2015) 60; Andrew Burrows, 'In Defence of Unjust Enrichment' (2019) 78 CLJ 521, 530; Lionel Smith, 'Sources of Private Rights' in Simone Degeling, Michael Crawford, and Nicholas Tiverios (eds), *Justifying Private Rights* (Hart 2020) 145–52; Charles Mitchell, Paul Mitchell, and Stephen Watterson, *Goff & Jones: The Law of Unjust Enrichment* (10th edn, Sweet & Maxwell 2022) paras 1-09–1-13; Robert Stevens, *The Laws of Restitution* (OUP 2023) ch 20.

[3] Stephen Smith, 'Taking Law Seriously' (2000) 50 University of Toronto LJ 241, 249; William Day, 'Restitution for Wrongs: One Step Forwards, Two Steps Back' [2018] RLR 60, 61.

[4] Jeremy Waldron, 'How Law Protects Dignity' (2012) 71 CLJ 200, 210 approved *R (Osborn) v Parole Board* [2013] UKSC 61, [2014] AC 1115 [68] (Lord Reed).

[5] Trevor Allan, 'Procedural Fairness and the Duty of Respect' (1998) 18 OJLS 497, 499–507; Stephen Smith, 'Intermediate and Comprehensive Justifications for Legal Rules' in Degeling, Crawford, and Tiverios (eds), *Justifying Private Rights* (n 2) 75.

[6] Frederick Wilmot-Smith, 'Illegality as a Rationing Rule' in Sarah Green and Alan Bogg (eds), *Illegality After Patel v Mirza* (Hart 2018) 124; Nicholas McBride, *The Humanity of Private Law, Part I: Explanation* (Hart 2019) 199–200.

[7] Lionel Smith, 'Restitution: A New Start?' in Peter Devonshire and Rohan Havelock (eds), *The Impact of Equity and Restitution in Commerce* (Hart 2019) 92–94.

[8] cf *Blyth v Birmingham Waterworks Co* (1856) 11 Ex 781; *Rylands v Fletcher* (1865) 3 Hurl & C 774, 159 ER 737; *Derry v Peek* (1889) 14 App Cas 337 (HL).

require proof of loss[9] whereas others are actionable per se;[10] contributory negligence is a defence to some torts but not others.[11]

In *Barnes v Eastenders*, the Supreme Court said that the law of unjust enrichment 'resembles the law of torts' in that the 'reasons why the courts have held [D]'s enrichment to be unjust vary from one set of cases to another'.[12] Different reasons may justify different rules. So, just like torts, different unjust enrichment claims may be governed by different rules.[13] Thus, Robert Stevens writes that '[w]e cannot reason by analogy from one group of cases to another if the reasons justifying the different claims are not the same'.[14] Or, as Lionel Smith puts it, the law of unjust enrichment contains multiple causes of action, each governed by different rules.[15]

However, courts and commentators often overlook this, and fall into the trap of thinking that a claim must be governed by certain rules because it is a claim in the law of unjust enrichment. To take some examples:

(1) In *ITC*, the Supreme Court held that D's enrichment comes at C's expense if there is a direct transfer of value from C to D.[16] The Court sought to squeeze various unjust enrichment claims into conformity with this test, and so identified various situations which 'the law treats as equivalent to a direct transfer'.[17] These included subrogation cases concerning 'co-ordinated transactions . . . forming a single scheme',[18] and 'situations where the defendant receives property from a third party into which the claimant can trace an interest'.[19] I have argued elsewhere that treating these cases as equivalent to a direct transfer of value is problematic and difficult to square with the result in *ITC*.[20]

(2) In *Menelaou v Bank of Cyprus*, a majority of the Supreme Court said that subrogation does not require C to trace into the discharge of D's debt because 'a claim in unjust enrichment does not need to show a property right'.[21]

[9] *Rothwell v Chemical & Insulating Co Ltd* [2007] UKHL 39, [2008] 1 AC 281 [74] (Lord Scott).

[10] *Entick v Carrington* (1765) 2 Wils KB 275, 291, 95 ER 807, 817 (Lord Camden CJCP).

[11] *Standard Chartered Bank v Pakistan National Shipping Corp (Nos 2 and 4)* [2002] UKHL 43, [2003] 1 AC 959; *Pritchard v Co-Operative Group Ltd* [2011] EWCA Civ 329, [2012] QB 320.

[12] *Barnes* (n 2) [102] (Lord Toulson) quoting Mitchell, Mitchell, and Watterson (9th edn) (n 2) para 1-08.

[13] Andrew Burrows, '"At the Expense of the Claimant": A Fresh Look' [2017] RLR 167; Burrows, 'In Defence of Unjust Enrichment' (n 2) 528.

[14] Stevens, *The Laws of Restitution* (n 2) 416. See also 23, and ch 20 generally.

[15] Smith, 'Restitution' (n 7).

[16] *ITC* (n 1) [43] and [46] (Lord Reed).

[17] ibid [50] (Lord Reed).

[18] ibid [48] (Lord Reed).

[19] ibid [48] (Lord Reed).

[20] Rory Gregson, 'Is Subrogation a Remedy for Unjust Enrichment?' (2020) 136 LQR 481, 494–98.

[21] *Menelaou v Bank of Cyprus UK Ltd* [2015] UKSC 66, [2016] AC 176 [38] (Lord Clarke). See also [50], [53] (Lord Clarke), [92], [96]–[98] (Lord Neuberger), [141] (Lord Kerr and Lord Wilson).

(3) The duty to make restitution of a mistaken payment is strict in the sense that it does not require proof of any fault on the part of D.[22] For this reason, it has been argued that an innocent recipient of misappropriated trust assets should also be under a strict duty to make restitution.[23]
(4) It is sometimes said that 'the defence of change of position is a general defence to all restitution claims (for money or other property) based on unjust enrichment'.[24] It is therefore assumed, without further argument, that it must be possible to raise a change of position defence to a failure of basis claim.[25] However, whether this is correct is controversial.[26]
(5) Conversely, in *Foskett v McKeown*, Lord Millett said that trust beneficiaries' claims to recover the traceable proceeds of misappropriated trust assets are not claims in unjust enrichment. One of his reasons for this was that 'a claim in unjust enrichment is subject to a change of position defence' whereas the beneficiaries' claims are not.[27] Again, this assumes that all unjust enrichment claims are subject to this defence.

These are all illegitimate moves. Unjust enrichments are like torts, in that different unjust enrichment claims are justified by different reasons. Different reasons may justify different rules. As a result, classifying a claim as part of the law of unjust enrichment is not enough to establish that it should be governed by particular rules.[28] Instead, to determine the rules which should apply, courts must look to the reasons for the claim—this particular claim, and not other unjust enrichment claims justified by different reasons.

Despite this, at least two arguments have been offered for why classifying a claim as part of the law of unjust enrichment should still influence the rules which should govern that claim. Each will be considered in turn.

[22] *Kelly v Solari* (1841) 9 M & W 54, 59, 152 ER 24, 26 (Parke B); *Banque Financière de la Cité SA v Parc (Battersea) Ltd* [1999] 1 AC 221 (HL).

[23] *Criterion Properties plc v Stratford UK Properties LLC* [2004] UKHL 28, [2004] 1 WLR 1846 [4] (Lord Nicholls); Lord Nicholls, 'Knowing Receipt: The Need for a New Landmark' in William Cornish and others (eds), *Restitution Past, Present and Future: Essays in Honour of Gareth Jones* (Hart 1998); Peter Birks, 'Receipt' in Peter Birks and Arianna Pretto (eds), *Breach of Trust* (Hart 2002); Andrew Burrows, *The Law of Restitution* (3rd edn, OUP 2011) 424–31; Mitchell, Mitchell, and Watterson (10th edn) (n 2) paras 8-133–8-138. Criticised by William Swadling, 'Ignorance and Unjust Enrichment: The Problem of Title' (2008) 28 OJLS 627.

[24] *Haugesund Kommune v Depfa ACS Bank* [2010] EWCA Civ 579, [2012] QB 549 [122] (Aikens LJ). cf *Test Claimants in the FII Group Litigation v Revenue and Customs Commissioners* [2014] EWHC 4302 (Ch) [315] (Henderson J).

[25] Burrows, *Restitution* (n 23) 544–47 citing *Westdeutsche Landesbank Girozentrale v Islington LBC* [1994] 4 All ER 90 (QB) 946–54 (Hobhouse J).

[26] *Goss v Chilcott* [1996] AC 788 (PC) 799 (Lord Goff); *Depfa* (n 24) [124] (Aikens LJ), [152] (Etherton LJ); *School Facility Management Ltd v Christ the King College* [2020] EWHC 1118 (Comm) [455]–[500] (Foxton J); *Banca Intesa Sanpaolo SPA v Comune Di Venezia* [2022] EWHC 2586 (Comm) [393]–[402] (Foxton J); Stevens, *The Laws of Restitution* (n 2) 359–60.

[27] *Foskett v McKeown* [2001] 1 AC 102 (HL) 129.

[28] Frederick Wilmot-Smith, 'Reasons? For *Restitution*?' (2016) 79 MLR 1116, 1124.

B. High Level Principle

One argument for applying some of the same rules to different unjust enrichment claims is that, at a higher level of abstraction, the claims are united by a single principle. For instance, Lord Burrows has written extra-judicially that:

> At a very high level of generality . . . there is a single normative principle against unjust enrichment . . . The single high level normative principle of unjust enrichment ties together what may be regarded as more specific causes of action which have significantly different normative explanations.[29]

This 'principle of reversing unjust enrichment . . . [enables a] framework of more specific principles and doctrines leading from the root principle to legal decisions'.[30]

Even if this is true, it is not enough to justify applying the same rules to different claims. There is sufficient variation between the principles at the more specific level to justify different rules. For instance, mistake claims and *Woolwich* claims may both be justified—at a high level of generality—by the principle against unjust enrichment. But at a more specific level, they are justified by different principles and so they are governed by different rules. The reason for a mistake claim (the leading theories are C's vitiated intention[31] or the absence of a basis for the enrichment[32]) admits a change of position defence. By contrast, the reason for a *Woolwich* claim (that a public authority should not be able to abuse its power by unlawfully levying tax) would be stultified if a change of position defence allowed a public authority to retain unlawfully levied tax.[33] The specific reasons for the claims vary, so the rules vary. Consequently, if a single principle is to catch all unjust enrichment claims, then it must be stated at such a high level of generality that it is not specific enough to dictate specific rules.

To draw an analogy, Lord Burrows suggests that the law of torts is 'tied together by the single high level normative principle of there being a wrong'.[34] However, he rightly makes no suggestion that this principle is specific enough to justify particular rules applying to particular torts, nor that it justifies applying the same rules to different torts.

[29] Burrows, 'In Defence of Unjust Enrichment' (n 2) 529–30.

[30] Burrows, *Restitution* (n 23) 4–5. See also Virgo (n 2) ch 3; Pablo Letelier, 'Another Civilian View of Unjust Enrichment's Structural Debate' (2020) 79 CLJ 527, 542.

[31] Peter Birks, *An Introduction to the Law of Restitution* (Clarendon Press 1989) 100–01; Burrows, *Restitution* (n 23) 86; Virgo (n 2) 121; Mitchell, Mitchell, and Watterson (10th edn) (n 2) para 1-29.

[32] Peter Birks, *Unjust Enrichment* (OUP 2005) chs 5–6; Stevens, *The Laws of Restitution* (n 2) ch 6.

[33] *FII* (n 24) [309]–[315] (Henderson J).

[34] Burrows, 'In Defence of Unjust Enrichment' (n 2) 529.

C. Default Rules

The current editors of *Goff & Jones* (Charles Mitchell, Paul Mitchell, and Stephen Watterson) offer a second argument for applying some of the same rules to different unjust enrichment claims:

> Differences between the justifications for recovery in different cases make it unsafe to assume that the rules governing each case should always be the same . . . This point should not be overstated, however: many of the rules which collectively form the law of unjust enrichment can appropriately and fairly be applied in a variety of different situations, and the courts should not waste time and effort reinventing them from first principles in every unjust enrichment case, just as they should not reinvent, e.g. the rules governing causation and remoteness in every tort case. There may be good reasons for applying different rules in some tort cases, e.g. because fraudulent and negligent defendants merit different treatment, but it is still an appropriate and effective strategy for the courts to start with one set of rules and then ask when it is appropriate to depart from these. In the same way, the courts should be open to the idea that some unjust enrichment cases may be insufficiently alike to justify carrying rules over from one type of case to another. Nevertheless, this will frequently be a fair and reasonable course for them to take.[35]

This approach is illustrated by the defence of change of position. This is a defence to unjust enrichment claims, except where it would 'stultify', 'subvert', or 'be inconsistent with' the unjust factor.[36] Similarly, *ITC* laid down a rule against incidental benefits: C 'will not normally be [entitled to restitution] where the provision of the benefit was merely an incidental or collateral result of his expenditure'.[37] However, this rule does not apply to all unjust enrichment claims. For instance, cases of 'legal compulsion' or 'secondary liability' are said to be 'justified exceptions' to the rule against incidental benefits.[38]

As such, there is some support for the model of applying default rules to all unjust enrichment claims, and then departing from those defaults where appropriate. However, when the role of default rules is inspected more closely, this model proves to be problematic.

[35] Mitchell, Mitchell, and Watterson (10th edn) (n 2) paras 1-12–1-13.

[36] *FII* (n 24) [315] (Henderson J).

[37] *ITC* (n 1) [52] (Lord Reed).

[38] Burrows, 'At the Expense of the Claimant' (n 13) 177. See also Charles Mitchell, *The Law of Contribution and Reimbursement* (OUP 2003) para 3.31; Burrows, 'In Defence of Unjust Enrichment' (n 2) 542; Stephen Watterson, 'At the Claimant's Expense' in Elise Bant, Kit Barker, and Simone Degeling (eds), *Research Handbook on Unjust Enrichment and Restitution* (Edward Elgar 2020) 285; *Croxen v Gas and Electricity Markets Authority* [2022] EWHC 2826 (Ch) [208]–[209] (Zacaroli J).

Certainly, the editors of *Goff & Jones* are right to say that it would be a 'waste [of] time and effort to reinvent . . . rules from first principles in every . . . case'. Where precedent establishes that a particular rule applies to a particular claim, then a judge is bound by the rules of precedent to apply that rule.[39] In such a case, a default rule has no role to play. Therefore, a default rule is only relevant in a case where a judge is not bound by authority to apply a particular rule. In this kind of case, a default rule seems to operate as a staging post in the judge's analysis: it is a rule which the judge should apply, unless there is some reason to depart from it.

But how does a judge know where to find a default rule? Take Mitchell, Mitchell, and Watterson's example of the rules governing remoteness. In the tort of negligence, only reasonably foreseeable types of loss are recoverable,[40] whereas in the tort of deceit all direct losses can be recovered.[41] Which of these tests, if either, is the default rule for the law of torts? Mitchell, Mitchell, and Watterson suggest that 'fraudulent and negligent defendants merit different treatment', so perhaps the default rule differs according to a tort's fault standard. But this appeals to (unstated) reasons that the law has for responding to fraudulent and negligent conduct. Thus, in deciding where to find a default rule, a judge has to engage with the reason for the claim and identify other claims with similar reasons. Ultimately, the judge must go back to 'first principles'. Far from being a 'waste [of] time and effort', this is a necessary step in the process.

Similarly, how does a judge decide whether to depart from a default rule? Legal rules should not be arbitrary. Instead, they should be conditioned by the reasons for the claim. As such, a judge should look to the reasons for the claim and ask whether these reasons justify a departure from the default rule. Ultimately, the judge must again go back to 'first principles'. This can be illustrated by the change of position defence. It is sometimes assumed that the default rule is that the change of position defence applies to unjust enrichment claims.[42] In *FII*, Henderson J had to decide whether to depart from the default rule and exempt *Woolwich* claims from the defence. In deciding this, he identified the reason for the claim (preventing public authorities abusing their power by unlawfully levying tax) and determined that it would be stultified by the defence.[43] Thus, despite the default rule, the judge still had to identify the reason for the claim and the rules that it demanded.

Consequently, it is not clear that default rules save judges any time or effort. In fact, they seem to add a redundant extra step. They impose a two-stage analysis (What is the default rule? Is a departure from the default justified?), but the

[39] *ITC* (n 1) [40] (Lord Reed).

[40] *Overseas Tankship (UK) Ltd v Miller Steamship Co Pty (The Wagon Mound (No 1))* [1961] AC 388 (HL).

[41] *Smith New Court Securities Ltd v Scrimgeour Vickers (Asset Management) Ltd* [1997] AC 254 (HL) 267 (Lord Browne-Wilkinson).

[42] *Depfa* (n 24) [122] (Aikens LJ).

[43] *Test Claimants in the FII Group Litigation v Revenue and Customs Commissioners* [2008] EWHC 2893 (Ch) [337]–[342]; *FII* (n 24) [309]–[315].

answers to both questions turn on the reason for the claim. It would be quicker and easier to cut to the chase and ask: what reasons justify this claim, and what rules do those reasons justify?

A good example of this approach is Chapter 9 in this collection, where William Day criticises the idea that there is a single default rule governing the interaction of unjust enrichment claims with contract. Instead, he identifies different reasons lying behind different unjust enrichment claims, and argues that these different reasons mandate different rules governing the interaction with the law of contract.

Nevertheless, one might defend the model of default rules by arguing that 'the untidy complexity'[44] of the reasons for a claim may underdetermine, or make it too difficult to determine, the rules which should apply. On this view, default rules work as an important stopgap. If it is clear that the reasons for the claim dictate certain rules, then the court should apply those rules (hence the change of position defence is inapplicable to *Woolwich* claims). But if the reasons for the claim fail to clearly dictate a rule, then the default rule fills the gap (hence the rebuttable presumption that the defence applies to all unjust enrichment claims). However, this amounts to the court applying a default rule simply because it cannot determine what rule to apply. This is arbitrary, and so the law fails to be a system of rules of how people should, for good reasons, behave. It is better for a judge to try their best to identify the reasons for the claim and the rules those reasons dictate, rather than applying an arbitrary default rule.

D. Four Questions

Summing up the argument so far, different unjust enrichment claims are justified by different reasons and so they are governed by different rules. Indeed, unjust enrichment should not even supply default rules.

If this is right, what is the point of classifying a claim as within or without the law of unjust enrichment? It is sometimes suggested that unjust enrichment claims are united by four questions.[45] On this view, a court should analyse an unjust enrichment claim by asking (1) is D enriched? (2) did that enrichment come at C's expense? (3) is D's enrichment unjust? and (4) does D have any defences?

This has its advantages. Birks originally proposed these four questions to:

> Overcome . . . the uncertainty which comes from there being no shared and stable pattern of reasoning . . . [The four questions] can provide the shared analytical

[44] Pablo Letelier, 'A Wrong Turn? Reconsidering the Unified Approach to Unjust Enrichment Claims' (2020) 136 LQR 121, 137.

[45] Burrows, *Restitution* (n 23) 27; Mitchell, Mitchell, and Watterson (10th edn) (n 2) para 1-08; Virgo (n 2) 9.

scheme which the subject lacks ... The intellectual difficulty and unpredictability of the subject can thus be reduced.[46]

As Lord Sales explains in Chapter 1 of this collection, a clear structure offers several advantages. Practitioners and judges have limited time and so need to know where to look in the books for material relevant to the case in front of them. Without the four questions to structure their inquiry, practitioners and judges may be stranded in a 'wilderness of single instances',[47] making it harder to find relevant material, and more likely that relevant authorities will be overlooked. Similarly, the structure offered by the four questions may make it easier for the public to consult the law (or at least easier for lawyers to explain the law to the public), allowing people to plan their lives accordingly, thus enabling the law to guide behaviour. By contrast, without the four questions, the Supreme Court in *ITC* warned of 'a risk that courts will resort to an unstructured approach driven by perceptions of fairness, with consequent uncertainty and unpredictability'.[48]

Despite offering these advantages, the four questions must be treated with caution in two ways. First, when different claims are analysed using the same four questions, it becomes easy to slip into to the error of applying the same rules to determine the answers. As this chapter has sought to explain, this is a mistake. Instead, as the Supreme Court explained in *ITC*, the 'four questions are no more than broad headings for ease of exposition ... [T]he questions are not themselves legal tests, but are signposts towards areas of inquiry involving a number of distinct legal requirements.'[49] Yet no sooner had the Court said this, it immediately fell into the trap of applying the same rules to different claims. The Court sought to squeeze different claims into conformity with a single legal test for determining whether an enrichment came at the claimant's expense, identifying dubious[50] 'equivalent[s] to a direct transfer'.[51]

Second, if the four questions are just headings for exposition, then they may not be the best headings for exposition. Enquiring into the reasons for a particular claim may reveal that it is best analysed without the four questions. For instance, if C and D both owe a debt to X and C pays that debt, then C may have a 'recoupment', 'contribution', or 'subrogation' claim against D.[52] The reason for these claims

[46] Birks, *Introduction* (n 31) 19–20. See also *Mann v Paterson Constructions Pty Ltd* [2019] HCA 32, (2019) 267 CLR 560 [199] (Nettle, Gordon, and Edelman JJ); Burrows, *Restitution* (n 23) 4; Virgo (n 2) 17–18; Burrows, 'In Defence of Unjust Enrichment' (n 2) 523; Helen Scott, 'Change and Continuity in the Law of Unjust Enrichment' [2019] Acta Juridica 469, 488–89; Mitchell, Mitchell, and Watterson (10th edn) (n 2) para 1–08.

[47] Alfred, Lord Tennyson, 'Aylmer's Field' (1793).

[48] *ITC* (n 1) [41] (Lord Reed).

[49] ibid (Lord Reed).

[50] Gregson, 'Is Subrogation a Remedy for Unjust Enrichment?' (n 20) 494–98.

[51] *ITC* (n 1) [50] (Lord Reed).

[52] eg *Brook's Wharf & Bull Wharf Ltd v Goodman Bros* [1937] 1 KB 534 (CA); Civil Liability (Contribution) Act 1978 s 1(1); *Niru Battery Manufacturing Co v Milestone Trading Ltd (No 2)* [2004] EWCA Civ 487, [2004] 1 CLC 882.

is that C has borne the burden of a debt which ought to have been borne by D.[53] Consequently, these claims can be disposed of by asking to what extent D ought to have borne the burden of C and D's debt to X. For these claims, the four unjust enrichment questions are at best superfluous and at worst a distraction.[54]

E. Summary

The law of unjust enrichment is like the law of torts, in that different unjust enrichment claims are justified by different reasons. Different reasons may justify different rules. As a result, classifying a claim as part of the law of unjust enrichment says nothing about what rules should apply to it. If unjust enrichment claims are unified by a high-level principle against unjust enrichment, then such a principle is too abstract to dictate the rules which should govern a particular case. Nor should unjust enrichment supply default rules. Instead, classifying a claim as part of the law of unjust enrichment merely supplies four headings for ease of exposition. But, even here, caution is needed to avoid two traps. The first trap is slipping from the exposition of different claims by asking the same four questions, to incorrectly assuming that the same rules govern the answers. The second trap is assuming without argument that the four unjust enrichment questions are indeed the best way to exposit a particular claim.

III. Correlativity

A. Two Changes in the Law

A second big idea which crosses the borderline between the law of torts and the law of unjust enrichment is that of correlativity, which states that a justification for a

[53] *Duncan Fox & Co v North & South Wales Bank* (1880) 6 App Cas 1 (HL) 11, 13 (Lord Selborne LC); *Brook's Wharf* (n 52) 544 (Lord Wright MR); *Re Downer Enterprises* [1974] 1 WLR 1460 (Ch) 1468–69 (Pennycuick VC); *Niru Battery Manufacturing Co v Milestone Trading Ltd (No 2)* [2003] EWHC 1032 (Comm), [2003] 2 All ER (Comm) 365 [31], [55] (Moore-Bick J); *Bofinger v Kingsway Group Ltd* [2009] HCA 44, (2009) 239 CLR 269 [7]–[8] (Gummow, Hayne, Heydon, Kiefel, and Bell JJ); Mitchell, *The Law of Contribution and Reimbursement* (n 38) paras 1.01, 1.09, 1.11, 3.28–3.29; Smith, 'Restitution' (n 7) 106–08; Stevens, *The Laws of Restitution* (n 2) ch 9.

[54] *Trades House of Glasgow v Ferguson* [1979] SLT 187 (IH) 192 (Lord Justice-Clerk Wheatley); Jonathan Hilliard, 'A Case for the Abolition of Legal Compulsion as a Ground of Restitution' (2002) 61 CLJ 551; Sonja Meier, 'No Basis: A Comparative View' in Andrew Burrows and Lord Rodger of Earlsferry (eds), *Mapping the Law: Essays in Memory of Peter Birks* (OUP 2006) 359–61; McBride, *The Humanity of Private Law* (n 6) 213; Sonja Meier, 'Enrichment "at the Expense of Another" and Incidental Benefits in German Law' [2019] Acta Juridica 453, 460–61; Rory Gregson, 'Subrogation, Marshalling, and Property' in Natalie Mrockova, Aruna Nair, and Luke Rostill (eds), *Modern Studies in Property Law Volume 12* (Hart 2023).

private law duty must link the parties, simultaneously justifying both why D owes a duty to C and why C has a right against D. Correlativity matters because it recently influenced two Supreme Court decisions which radically changed the law: *ITC* and *Prudential*.[55] However, this chapter argues that correlativity has been pushed too far, and it cannot justify the latter decision.

ITC and *Prudential* both concerned the requirement that, for an unjust enrichment claim to succeed, D's enrichment must come at C's expense. Before these cases, the test seemed to be whether there was a 'sufficient causal connection' between C's loss and D's gain.[56] These expansive tests were rejected in *ITC*. There, the customer bought services from the managers. As part of the price, the customer paid Value Added Tax (VAT) to the managers. The managers accounted to the Revenue for the VAT. It then transpired that the services ought to have been exempt from VAT. The customer sought to recover the VAT from the Revenue.

The Supreme Court denied the customer's claim. Giving the only judgment, Lord Reed held that D's enrichment is only at C's expense if 'there has been a transfer of value', which requires that C 'suffered a loss through his provision of the benefit' to D.[57] There was a transfer of value from the customer to the managers, and from the managers to the Revenue. However, these two transfers could not be 'collapsed into a single transfer of value' from the customer to the Revenue.[58] Therefore, the Revenue's enrichment was not at the customer's expense, so the customer had no claim against the Revenue.[59]

ITC led to another change in the law in *Prudential*,[60] which disapproved the earlier decision of *Sempra Metals Ltd v IRC*.[61] At their simplest, both of these cases concerned the Revenue breaching EU law by refusing to allow certain companies to defer their payment of tax. The tax was due, so the companies could not recover the capital sum of tax paid. However, the companies argued that the Revenue had been unjustly enriched by receiving the tax earlier than they should have done. The companies therefore sought compound interest for this period, representing the Revenue's opportunity to use the capital sum.

In *Sempra*, a majority of the House of Lords allowed the claim. Lord Nicholls said:

55 *ITC* (n 1); *Prudential* (n 1).

56 *Investment Trust Companies v Revenue and Customs Commissioners* [2012] EWHC 458 (Ch) [68] (Henderson J); *Menelaou v Bank of Cyprus plc* [2013] EWCA Civ 1960, [2014] 1 WLR 854 [42] (Floyd LJ); *TFL Management Ltd v Lloyds TSB Bank plc* [2013] EWCA Civ 1415, [2014] 1 WLR 2006 [57] (Floyd LJ), [61] (Moses LJ); *Relfo Ltd v Varsani* [2014] EWCA Civ 360 [83], [95]–[96] (Arden LJ), [103]–[104] (Gloster LJ), [115], [122] (Floyd LJ); *Investment Trust Companies v Revenue and Customs Commissioners* [2015] EWCA Civ 82 [67], [69] (Patten LJ); *Menelaou* (n 21) [27] (Lord Clarke).

57 *ITC* (n 1) [42]–[43].

58 ibid [71].

59 ibid [73]–[74].

60 *Prudential* (n 1).

61 *Sempra Metals Ltd v Inland Revenue Commissioners* [2007] UKHL 34, [2008] 1 AC 561.

> The benefits transferred by Sempra to the Inland Revenue comprised, in short, (1) the amounts of tax paid to the Inland Revenue and, consequentially, (2) the opportunity for the Inland Revenue, or the Government of which the Inland Revenue is a department, to use this money for the period of prematurity . . . Restitution, if it is to be complete, must encompass both heads. Restitution by the revenue requires (1) repayment of the amounts of tax paid prematurely (this claim became spent once set off occurred) and (2) payment for having the use of the money for the period of prematurity.[62]

However, the Supreme Court in *Prudential* disapproved *Sempra*.[63] Giving the Court's judgment, Lord Reed, Lord Hodge, and Lord Mance applied the 'direct transfer of value' test from *ITC*:[64]

> There has been only one direct transfer of value, namely the payment of the [principal sum]. The opportunity to use the money mistakenly paid can arise as a consequence of that transfer, but a causal link is not sufficient to constitute a further, independent, transfer of value. Contrary to the analysis of Lord Nicholls, the recipient's possession of the money mistakenly paid to him, and his consequent opportunity to use it, is not a distinct and additional transfer of value.[65]

The Court therefore denied the claim.

Prudential is a controversial decision. Some scholars have argued that there was in fact a direct transfer of value of both the capital sum and the opportunity to use that sum.[66] Mitchell, Mitchell, and Watterson criticise *Prudential*'s reliance on *ITC*:

> [*ITC*] and *Prudential Assurance* raised different questions. [*ITC*] immediately concerned whether, and if so, when unjust enrichment claims might be brought against indirect or remoter recipients. In contrast, *Prudential Assurance* concerned the extent of the restitutionary liability of a defendant who clearly qualified as a direct recipient . . . It is regrettable that Lord Reed . . . invoked the same concept—'direct transfer of value'—to resolve both issues.[67]

[62] ibid [102].
[63] *Prudential* (n 1) [79] (Lord Reed, Lord Hodge, and Lord Mance).
[64] ibid [68].
[65] ibid [71] (citation omitted).
[66] Charles Mitchell, 'End of the Road for the Overpaid Tax Litigation?' in Daniel Clarry (ed), *The UK Supreme Court Yearbook, Volume 9: 2017–2018 Legal Year* (Appellate Press 2019) 236–42; Burrows, 'In Defence of Unjust Enrichment' (n 2) 536–41; Alexander Georgiou, 'In Defence of *Sempra*' [2019] LMCLQ 38.
[67] Mitchell, Mitchell, and Watterson (10th edn) (n 2) para 6-102.

B. Correlativity

To evaluate the decision in *Prudential*, it is instructive to consider what motivated the Supreme Court to change the law. Before *ITC*, there was some difficulty in containing the boundaries of unjust enrichment claims. This is illustrated by Stevens' stamps:

> C and D each own one of only two examples of a rare collectible stamp worth thousands of pounds. C, by mistake, destroys his stamp, which causes D's stamp to more than double in value. D sells his stamp. C seeks restitution from D of the enrichment D has made at C's expense.[68]

Stevens says that 'all can see that no claim should succeed'. Yet this case seems to satisfy the pre-*ITC* causal test, and so some artificial exception was needed to exclude the claim.

A real-life example was *TFL Management Services Ltd v Lloyds TSB Bank plc*.[69] TFL brought an action in debt against Hesco Bastion Ltd. The court denied the claim, holding that Hesco's debt was in fact owed to Lloyds. TFL therefore sued Lloyds, arguing that Lloyds were unjustly enriched by TFL clarifying their right to recover from Hesco. A majority of the Court of Appeal refused to strike out the claim and allowed it to proceed to trial. In *ITC*, the Supreme Court took *TFL* as an indicator that the boundaries of liability had gone too far. Lord Reed said that the majority in *TFL* was 'wrong in not summarily dismissing the claim'.[70]

Consequently, unjust enrichment claims needed to be constrained. But how could they be constrained in a justified way? An answer was offered by an idea that Ernest Weinrib originally developed in relation to the law of torts: correlativity.[71] In a recent account, Weinrib explained correlativity as follows:

> The liability of a particular defendant is always a liability to a particular plaintiff. Accordingly, in holding the defendant liable to the plaintiff, the court is making not two separate judgments (one that awards something to the plaintiff and the other that coincidentally takes the same thing from the defendant), but a single judgment that embraces both parties in their interrelationship . . . The correlativity of the injustice means that the reasons for concluding that something is an injustice also have a correlative structure. Accordingly, the only considerations that matter for elucidating the injustice as between the parties are those that apply correlatively to both of them. Then the reasons that support liability render the

[68] Robert Stevens, 'The Unjust Enrichment Disaster' (2018) 134 LQR 574, 578. See also Smith, 'Restitution' (n 7) 99–100; Stevens, *The Laws of Restitution* (n 2) 30–32.

[69] *TFL* (n 56).

[70] *ITC* (n 1) [57] (Lord Reed).

[71] Ernest Weinrib, *The Idea of Private Law* (1st edn, Harvard University Press 1995).

> injustice for which the defendant is held liable the same as the injustice that the [claimant] has suffered.[72]

Weinrib argued that this has implications for both the law of torts and the law of unjust enrichment. In the law of torts, D's duty to pay damages to C cannot be justified by deterrence, as this can only explain why D owes the duty and not why D owes the duty to C. Nor can D's duty to pay damages to C be justified by compensating C's loss, as this can only explain why C has a right to compensation but not why C has that right against D. Combining these two unilateral reasons, by saying that D's duty to pay damages to C is justified by deterring wrongdoing and compensating loss, does not help. This can explain why D owes a duty and why C has a right, but not why D's duty and C's right are correlative.[73] This would equally justify a state compensation scheme, in which wrongdoers are deterred by being forced to pay into the scheme, and victims are compensated by being paid by the scheme.[74] Thus, unilateral reasons, says Weinrib, offer 'no reason to link any particular defendant to any particular plaintiff'.[75]

Instead, a private law duty can only be justified by a 'bipolar'[76] or correlative reason, which simultaneously explains why D owes a duty to C and why C has a right against D. Weinrib argues that D's duty to pay damages to C is justified by D breaching a primary duty owed to C.[77] D owes a duty to pay damages to C because D breached C's primary right; C has a right to damages from D because C's primary right was infringed by D.

Similarly, the duty to make restitution of a mistaken payment cannot be justified by C's impaired intention, as this can only explain why C has a right to restitution and not why D owes a duty to make restitution.[78] C's impaired intention would equally justify a state compensation scheme for mistaken payors.[79] Nor can the duty to make restitution be justified by D making a gain, as this does not explain why D ought to be under a duty to give up that gain,[80] still less why D must give up its gain to C rather than to the state.[81] Again, Weinrib argues that a private law duty can only be justified by a correlative reason. He argues that the duty to make

[72] Ernest Weinrib, 'The Corrective Justice of Liability for Unjust Enrichment' in Bant, Barker, and Degeling (eds), *Research Handbook on Unjust Enrichment and Restitution* (n 38) 168–69.

[73] Ernest Weinrib, *The Idea of Private Law* (rev edn, OUP 2012) 120–22; Weinrib, 'The Corrective Justice of Liability for Unjust Enrichment' (n 72) 170.

[74] Ernest Weinrib, *Corrective Justice* (OUP 2012) 6; Stevens, *The Laws of Restitution* (n 2) 20.

[75] Weinrib, 'The Corrective Justice of Liability for Unjust Enrichment' (n 72) 170.

[76] Weinrib, *The Idea of Private Law* (n 71) 120.

[77] ibid ch 6; Weinrib, *Corrective Justice* (n 74) ch 2. See also Robert Stevens, *Torts and Rights* (OUP 2007).

[78] Weinrib, *Corrective Justice* (n 74) 203; Weinrib, 'The Corrective Justice of Liability for Unjust Enrichment' (n 72) 176; Stevens, *The Laws of Restitution* (n 72) 46.

[79] Frederick Wilmot-Smith, 'Should the Payee Pay?' (2017) 37 OJLS 844, 845.

[80] Weinrib, *Corrective Justice* (n 74) 188.

[81] Nicholas McBride and Paul McGrath, 'The Nature of Restitution' (1995) 15 OJLS 33, 34.

restitution of a mistaken payment is justified by C making, and D accepting, a normatively defective transfer of value.[82]

Other unjust enrichment scholars have endorsed Weinrib's idea of correlativity.[83] In turn, these ideas influenced the Supreme Court's decisions in *ITC* and *Prudential*. Weinrib describes correlativity as the 'principal thesis of corrective justice'[84] and in *ITC* the Court described 'corrective justice' as 'the purpose of the law of unjust enrichment'.[85] Like Weinrib, the Court said that it 'follows' that an unjust enrichment claim requires a 'transfer of value'.[86] The Court said that this requires that C 'suffered a loss through his provision of the benefit' to D[87] so, consistent with the idea of correlativity, the Court articulated a test which embraced both parties.

Furthermore, Weinrib's idea of correlativity is foundational to Stevens' criticism of unjust enrichment,[88] and his argument that the duty to make restitution of a mistaken payment is instead justified by a performance, rendered by C and accepted by D, for no good reason.[89] In light of this, Stevens criticised *Sempra*. For Stevens, the only performance, rendered by C and accepted by D, was the payment of the capital sum. There was no performance, rendered by C and accepted by D, in respect of the opportunity to use the capital sum, so there could be no claim in respect of this use.[90] In *Prudential*, the Supreme Court adopted this analysis, and in one version of the judgment cited Stevens with approval.[91] Thus, one can trace a direct line from Weinrib's idea of correlativity, to Stevens' criticism of *Sempra*, to the Supreme Court's disapproval of *Sempra* in *Prudential*.

C. Two Justifications for Correlativity

In order to evaluate these developments, it is necessary to distinguish two justifications for correlativity: a formal justification and a moral justification. In turn, these two distinct justifications lead to different interpretations of what correlativity

[82] Weinrib, *Corrective Justice* (n 74) ch 6; Weinrib, 'The Corrective Justice of Liability for Unjust Enrichment' (n 72).

[83] Smith, 'Restitution' (n 7) 102, 111; Robert Stevens, 'Private Law and the Form of Reasons' in Andrew Robertson and James Goudkamp (eds), *Form and Substance in the Law of Obligations* (Hart 2019) 124; Stevens, *The Laws of Restitution* (n 2) 20–21; Helen Scott, 'What Mistake Can Do' in Nils Jansen and Sonja Meier (eds), *Iurium Itinera* (Mohr Siebeck 2022) 636–40.

[84] Weinrib, 'The Corrective Justice of Liability for Unjust Enrichment' (n 72) 169.

[85] *ITC* (n 1) [42]–[43] (Lord Reed).

[86] ibid [43] (Lord Reed).

[87] ibid (Lord Reed).

[88] Stevens, 'Private Law and the Form of Reasons' (n 83) 124; Stevens, *The Laws of Restitution* (n 2) 20–21.

[89] Stevens, 'The Unjust Enrichment Disaster' (n 68) 580–82; Stevens, 'Private Law and the Form of Reasons' (n 83) 130–46; Stevens, *The Laws of Restitution* (n 2) ch 3.

[90] Stevens, 'The Unjust Enrichment Disaster' (n 68) 596–97.

[91] Burrows, 'In Defence of Unjust Enrichment' (n 2) 538 fn 72.

requires, with the moral justification being more demanding. Crucially, it was this restrictive interpretation of correlativity which was adopted by Stevens, and ultimately the Court in *Prudential*. However, this chapter argues that the moral justification, the more demanding interpretation of correlativity, and in turn *Prudential* should be doubted. Instead, this chapter defends the formal justification and a more moderate interpretation of correlativity, and suggests how *Prudential* could have been decided differently in light of this.

The sound justification for correlativity is that justifying a duty requires justifying its form.[92] If D owes a duty to C, then justifying this duty entails justifying why D must act in a particular way in relation to C.[93] For instance, a good justification for D's duty to pay damages to C must justify why the duty is owed by D to C, as opposed to having a state compensation scheme in which D must pay the state and C has a claim against the state.[94] Similarly, a good justification for the duty to make restitution of a mistaken payment must justify why it is that D must pay C, rather than having a scheme in which the state compensates mistaken payors.[95] This formal justification for correlativity is, compared to the moral justification, relatively permissive. It demands some reason to link the parties—some reason why D must act in a particular way in relation to C—but it does not impose any limit on what that reason might be.

Sometimes Stevens endorses this formal justification for correlativity.[96] But at other times, he offers a different justification for correlativity, which appeals to morality:

> It is not the case, and cannot be, that the justification for recovery is wholly 'claimant sided'. Such an approach would be immoral. We would be using the defendant as a means to an end, requiring them to correct an injustice that was not of their doing.[97]

This argument faces three problems. First, not everyone accepts the Kantian[98] idea that it is immoral to use someone as a mere means and a utilitarian may disagree.[99]

[92] Weinrib, *The Idea of Private Law* (n 71) ch 2; Ben McFarlane, 'Form and Substance in Equity' in Robertson and Goudkamp (eds), *Form and Substance in the Law of Obligations* (n 83) 198; Ben McFarlane, 'Equity and the Justification of Private Rights' in Degeling, Crawford, and Tiverios (eds), *Justifying Private Rights* (n 2) 222–23.

[93] Weinrib, *Corrective Justice* (n 74) 338.

[94] ibid 6; Stevens, *The Laws of Restitution* (n 2) 20.

[95] McBride and McGrath (n 81) 34; Wilmot-Smith, 'Should the Payee Pay?' (n 79) 845.

[96] Stevens, 'Private Law and the Form of Reasons' (n 83) 124, 129–30; Stevens, *The Laws of Restitution* (n 2) 20.

[97] Stevens, 'The Unjust Enrichment Disaster' (n 68) 581–82; Stevens, 'Private Law and the Form of Reasons' (n 83) 132; Stevens, *The Laws of Restitution* (n 2) 46.

[98] Immanuel Kant, *Groundwork of the Metaphysics of Morals* (CUP 2012) 4:428–4:429.

[99] Rachel Leow and Timothy Liau, 'Birksian Themes and Their Impact in England and Singapore: Three Points of Divergence' [2021] LMCLQ 350, 378.

Second, even Kant did not claim that it was immoral to use someone as a means to an end. Instead, Kant's objection was to treating someone '*merely*' as a means to an end.[100] His explanation was that a 'rational nature exists as an end in itself . . . So act that you use humanity, in your own person as well as in the person of any other, always at the same time as an end, never merely as a means.'[101] Thus, even for a Kantian, it is permissible to treat a ticket-seller as a means to the end of obtaining a ticket,[102] or to treat a teacher as a means to the end of improving one's grades,[103] provided that one does not treat the ticket-seller or teacher as a *mere* means by denying their rationality or humanity. By the same token, imposing a duty on D to pay a sum of money to C does not deny D's humanity or rationality, and so it should not be immoral even for a Kantian.

Finally, Kant's objection was to using 'a human being' as a mere means to an end.[104] The argument does not work unless the defendant is human. A non-human legal person, such as a company or public authority, exists only to be a means to some end, whether that is to make money for humans or promote public good. As a result, it is not problematic to use a company or a public authority as a means to an end.[105] This is particularly significant because the defendant in *ITC* and *Prudential* was the Revenue: a public authority which exists to be merely a means to an end.

For these three reasons, the morality justification for correlativity should be doubted.

D. What Does Correlativity Demand?

However, this morality justification seems to have led to an overly restrictive interpretation of correlativity. Because Stevens is concerned with never using anyone as a means to any end, he ends up demanding D's acceptance to justify D's duty to make restitution of a mistaken payment.[106] Other writers have spotted that this is a misstep. In order to cover a decent range of cases, Weinrib and Stevens have to strain the meaning of acceptance, by saying that acceptance can be 'imputed'[107] or 'attributed'[108] to D. This dilutes the concept of acceptance to the point that it can

[100] Kant (n 98) 4:428 (original emphasis).
[101] ibid 4:429 (emphasis omitted).
[102] Gerald Cohen, *Self-Ownership, Freedom, and Equality* (CUP 1995) 239.
[103] Nicholas McBride, 'Must Private Law Be Private?' in Jodi Gardner and others (eds), *Politics, Policy and the Private Law* (Hart 2023) 12.
[104] Kant (n 98) 4:428.
[105] cf Peter French, 'The Corporation as a Moral Person' (1979) 16 Am Phil Q 207; Nick Friedman, 'Corporations as Moral Agents: Trade-Offs in Criminal Liability and Human Rights for Corporations' (2020) 83 MLR 255.
[106] Stevens, *The Laws of Restitution* (n 2) 46.
[107] Weinrib, *Corrective Justice* (n 74) 207–17.
[108] Stevens, *The Laws of Restitution* (n 2) 50.

no longer justify imposing a duty on D, defeating the point of requiring acceptance in the first place.[109]

On the other hand, if the morality justification is rejected, then the sound justification for correlativity is that justifying a duty requires justifying its form, so a correlative duty must be justified by a correlative reason. It is an error to jump from this to saying that D's duty to make restitution demands D's acceptance. Certainly, D's acceptance is one reason for imposing a duty on D. But it is not the only possible reason.

This might open the way to reviving the impaired intention justification for restitution. This account may be sold short when it is described as purely claimant-sided.[110] With a little more explanation, C's impaired intention may explain both why C has a right to restitution against D and why D owes a duty to make restitution to C. Helen Scott explains:

> Property passes by virtue of the transferor's intention to confer ownership on the recipient of the transfer and the recipient's corresponding intention to become owner; transfer is thus itself an exercise of the parties' autonomy . . . But where the intention of [C] in conferring the benefit is impaired, for example, because he is mistaken about his liability, that autonomy is only imperfectly expressed . . . It is this—the impairment of [C]'s autonomy in deciding to make the transfer—that provides the ethical justification for restitution.[111]

Similarly, Charlie Webb argues:

> (1) The claimant, as legal title holder of the relevant asset prior to its transfer, was authorized to determine who may receive and use that asset; (2) though the asset is now in the defendant's possession, it came into his hands only by virtue of a decision of the claimant's which was qualified or, in some way, impaired; (3) there is then good reason to treat the claimant as still the person authorized to determine the asset's use and disposition.[112]

[109] Zoë Sinel, 'The Place of Corrective Justice in Unjust Enrichment' (2011) 31 OJLS 551, 557–59; Sandy Steel, 'Private Law and Justice' (2013) 33 OJLS 607, 927–28; Dennis Klimchuk, 'The Normative Foundations of Unjust Enrichment' in Robert Chambers, Charles Mitchell, and James Penner (eds), *Philosophical Foundations of the Law of Unjust Enrichment* (OUP 2009) 89–93; Wilmot-Smith, 'Should the Payee Pay?' (n 79) 859–61; Burrows, 'In Defence of Unjust Enrichment' (n 2) 533–34; Tatiana Cutts, 'Unjust Enrichment: What We Owe to Each Other' (2021) 41 OJLS 114, 126–28; Alexander Waghorn, 'Book Review' (2021) 80 CLJ 187, 190.

[110] Burrows, *Restitution* (n 23) 86; Mitchell, Mitchell, and Watterson (10th edn) (n 2) para 1–25; Virgo (n 2) 121; Stevens, 'The Unjust Enrichment Disaster' (n 68) 577, 582; Stevens, 'Private Law and the Form of Reasons' (n 83) 129, 132.

[111] Helen Scott, *Unjust Enrichment in South African Law: Rethinking Enrichment by Transfer* (Hart 2013) 210 (footnotes omitted).

[112] Charlie Webb, *Reason and Restitution: A Theory of Unjust Enrichment* (OUP 2016) 75–76.

In other words, C's exercise of autonomy is the reason for D's entitlement. If that exercise of autonomy is defective, then so too is the reason for D's entitlement. If D seeks to keep C's payment, then D is seeking to claim the benefit of C's exercise of autonomy. If C's exercise of autonomy is defective, then so too is the benefit D takes from it.

These approaches fit with the intuition that there should be no restitution in *TFL* or Stevens' stamps example. In *TFL*, Hesco owed a debt to Lloyds all along. Lloyds' right to recover that debt was not dependent on TFL's exercise of autonomy, so the impairment of TFL's autonomy did not implicate Lloyds. Similarly, D is entitled to the value of their stamp because of their pre-existing property right to the stamp. D's entitlement to the value of their stamp was not dependent on the exercise of C's autonomy, and so any impairment to C's autonomy cannot impair D's entitlement.

However, there are also objections to these approaches. One objection is that they prove too much, since they seem to suggest that title should not pass from C to D.[113] Yet in the paradigm case of a mistaken payment, title does pass and C merely has a personal right to restitution of the value of the title.[114] However, as Webb observes, there may be countervailing reasons why the law should only give 'partial protection' to C's autonomy, by allowing title to pass and instead giving C right to restitution of its value.[115]

A more challenging objection is that these approaches prove too little. There are difficult questions over whether they can move beyond mistaken transfer of title to cash or property, and also justify restitution of mistaken bank transfers,[116] mistaken improvements of property,[117] and payments involving third parties.[118] For instance, suppose you repair my car, mistakenly thinking that it is your own.[119] You have increased the value of my title to the car but, all along, I had title to the car and the power to realise its value. My power to realise the car's value is not dependent on any exercise of your autonomy, and so any impairment of your autonomy does not impair my entitlement. As a result, these accounts seem unable to justify imposing an obligation on me to make restitution of the value of your repairs. One response is to concede that the justification for restitution of mistaken transfers of title to cash cannot justify restitution in these other cases. It may be that in these other cases restitution has a different justification or none.[120] Another response is to argue that these other cases are in some way sufficiently analogous to a mistaken payment for the same justification to apply.[121]

[113] Burrows, *Restitution* (n 23) 30; Sinel (n 109) 551–52.
[114] *Kelly* (n 22).
[115] Webb (n 112) 75.
[116] Wilmot-Smith, 'Reasons? For *Restitution*?' (n 28) 1131–34.
[117] Burrows, *Restitution* (n 23) 30; Wilmot-Smith, 'Reasons? For *Restitution*?' (n 28) 1131–34.
[118] Stevens, *The Laws of Restitution* (n 2) 33–34.
[119] cf *Greenwood v Bennett* [1973] 1 QB 195 (CA).
[120] Webb (n 112) 102–10.
[121] ibid 98–99.

Fully engaging with these issues and defending a justification for restitution of mistaken payments is not the goal of this chapter. This chapter has instead sought to raise some doubts about the morality justification for correlativity and the need for D's acceptance, and suggest that it might be possible to satisfy the formal demands of correlativity without D's acceptance.

E. *Prudential*

Retracing our steps, what does all this mean for *Prudential*? Stevens endorsed the morality justification for correlativity, arguing that correlativity is needed to avoid treating D as a means to an end. In light of this, Stevens argued that the correlative justification for restitution of a mistaken payment is that C rendered, and D accepted, a performance for no good reason. In *Sempra*, there was no performance, rendered by the taxpayer and accepted by the Revenue, in respect of the use of the capital sum, so the Revenue should not be under a duty to make restitution of the use of the capital sum. In *Prudential*, the Supreme Court adopted this analysis, citing Stevens in one version of the judgment.[122]

However, the second half of this chapter argued that the morality justification, and therefore the need for D's acceptance, should be doubted. Instead, this chapter endorsed the formal justification for correlativity. It was tentatively suggested that a vitiated intention approach may be able to satisfy the demands of correlativity without the need for D's acceptance.

What might this approach say about *Prudential*? In a typical mistaken payment case, the exercise of C's autonomy to pay D is the reason D becomes legally entitled to the capital sum. This exercise of C's autonomy is also the reason why D becomes entitled to use the capital sum.[123] If the exercise of C's autonomy was vitiated by a mistake, then so too is D's entitlement to the capital sum and its use. Accordingly, D ought to be under a duty to make restitution of the value of the use of the money. On this point, *Sempra* should be preferred to *Prudential*.

However, the complicating factor is that *Sempra* and *Prudential* were not typical mistaken payment cases. In both cases, there was a statutory obligation for the companies to pay Advanced Corporation Tax. UK-based companies could defer this obligation whereas EU-based companies could not, and this was contrary to EU law. Nevertheless, the statutory obligation to pay Advanced Corporation Tax remained valid until repealed in domestic law. Accordingly, the reason the Revenue was entitled to the capital sum (and its use) was not the exercise of the company's autonomy, but rather that statute said so. Any vitiation of the company's autonomy

[122] Burrows, 'In Defence of Unjust Enrichment' (n 2) 538 fn 72.
[123] Webb (n 112) 197–200.

did not vitiate the statute and the Revenue's entitlement to the capital sum (or its use), and so the claim for restitution ought to fail.[124]

To put this point into more familiar language, the Revenue was enriched at the claimant's expense, and on this point *Sempra* should be preferred to *Prudential*. The reason the claim ought to fail was that there was a 'lawful basis',[125] 'legal entitlement',[126] or 'justifying ground'[127] for D's enrichment. *Prudential* reached the right result but for the wrong reasons.

IV. Conclusion

This chapter considered two ideas which have crossed the borderline from the law of torts to the law of unjust enrichment. The first was the idea that the law of unjust enrichment is like the law of torts, in that it contains different claims justified by different reasons. Different reasons may justify different rules. Courts and commentators are therefore mistaken when they assume that the same rules apply to different claims, or even when they assume that there are default rules which apply to different claims. In other words, this first idea has not been followed through to its logical conclusion.

By contrast, the second idea, that of correlativity, has been pushed too far. This idea influenced the Supreme Court's decision in *Prudential* to disapprove *Sempra*. However, correlativity cannot support the Court's reasoning, which should be doubted.

[124] *Deutsche Morgan Grenfell Group plc v Inland Revenue Commissioners* [2006] UKHL 49, [2007] 1 AC 558 [81]–[90] (Lord Scott); Robert Stevens, 'Justified Enrichment' (2005) 5 OUCLJ 141; Stevens, *The Laws of Restitution* (n 2) 86–88. cf Burrows, *Restitution* (n 23) 90–91.

[125] Virgo (n 2) ch 7.

[126] Burrows, *Restitution* (n 23) 88–91.

[127] Mitchell, Mitchell, and Watterson (10th edn) (n 2) ch 2.

8

Unjust Enrichment's Borderlines

Mr Justice Foxton

Mapping the borderlines of the law of unjust enrichment presents a particularly challenging exercise in juridical cartography. Unjust enrichment is a newly emergent, and unstable, legal state, which took six hundred years to gain conceptual independence from the dominant categories of contract (in particular), but also tort and equity.[1] Robert Stevens, in Chapter 17, would refuse it recognition altogether, arguing that it is, at best, a collection of legal cantons rather than a sovereign state,[2] and, in the manner of the Macedonia controversy, challenge its right to its chosen name.[3] While Lord Rodger described Lord Goff and Gareth Jones as 'the Romulus and Remus of the English Law of Restitution' on the basis that 'out of a few weak and scattered settlements they founded a powerful city whose hegemony now extends far and wide',[4] the ruling council of that city state ceded vast swathes of its former territory to the law of tort, just as they were proclaiming its new identity.[5] That loss of territory is reflected in this collection by the location of Alexander Waghorn's chapter on restitution for wrongs in the context of the property/tort borderline.[6]

The four chapters tracing the contours of the law of unjust enrichment embrace a wide variety of topics: the role of conditional and defective intention in the law of unjust enrichment;[7] whether private law should be subject to a principle of correlativity such that there must be a single reason justifying the claimant's right and the defendant's liability;[8] the correctness of the test for lawful act duress;[9] and the theft of incorporeal money.[10] The ingenuity demonstrated by the contributors, in

[1] David Ibbetson, *A Historical Introduction to the Law of Obligations* (OUP 1999) ch 14.

[2] For particularly influential criticism of unjust enrichment as a 'failed state', see Robert Stevens, 'The Unjust Enrichment Disaster' (2018) 134 LQR 574.

[3] See also Robert Stevens, *The Laws of Restitution* (OUP 2023).

[4] Lord Rodger, 'Lord Goff of Chieveley, Senior Law Lord' *The Daily Telegraph* (London, 18 August 2016).

[5] Compare Gareth Jones (ed), *Goff and Jones: The Law of Restitution* (7th edn, Sweet & Maxwell 2007) and Charles Mitchell, Paul Mitchell, and Stephen Watterson (eds), *Goff and Jones: The Law of Unjust Enrichment* (8th edn, Sweet & Maxwell 2011) and following editions.

[6] See ch 15.

[7] See ch 9.

[8] See ch 7.

[9] See ch 10.

[10] See ch 16.

Mr Justice Foxton, *Unjust Enrichment's Borderlines* In: *Borderlines in Private Law.* Edited by: William Day and Julius Grower, Oxford University Press. © Mr Justice Foxton 2024. DOI: 10.1093/9780191995200.003.0008

fitting such a substantial and diverse range of topics within the 'borderlines' theme, may at times leave the reader wondering whether the conference was an exercise in legal taxonomy or one in legal taxidermy. No one can doubt, however, the insight and scholarship which the chapters offer, and the prospect of offering any form of commentary upon them is a daunting one. Unsure how a judge should approach the task of commenting on the work product of academics, and do so within around 3,000 words, I have taken inspiration from how academics set about the task of commenting on the work product of judges through the medium of case notes: a context which carries the privilege of identifying unanswered questions or possible further lines of enquiry, without any attendant responsibility for providing answers, or following those lines of enquiry to the point where their ultimate utility is known. Another form of power, without responsibility.

William Day[11] opens his chapter by describing 'the borderline between contact and unjust enrichment' as 'one of the most hotly argued boundary disputes in private law', noting the contribution to the marking out of that territory by Goff and Jones, the Lewis and Clark of this odyssey, and the subsequent consolidation of that nascent state by Peter Birks.[12] And yet such was the success of the Birksian project that the contract/unjust enrichment boundary has become the closest English private law comes to achieving the categorical neatness of the French law doctrine of *non-cumul*.[13] As Day notes, controversy around the borderline now centres on whether it is a completely closed frontier, or whether the conceptual iron curtain is punctured by the occasional checkpoint where the ingress of unjust enrichment would not undercut the recognition of the contractual right. Day rejects the notion that contract is sovereign and unjust enrichment the tributary state, arguing that the determining role of the terms of the contract in cases such as *Dargamo v Avonwick*,[14] and *Barton v Morris*,[15] lies not in the 'subsidiarity' of unjust enrichment as a conceptual category, but in the need for an objective agreement-based approach to identifying the basis of value transfer.

However, it is worthy of some note that, while it appears to be recognised that the transfer of a benefit may be subject to two conditions, the failure of either of which is in principle capable of giving rise to a claim in unjust enrichment,[16] it is clear from *Dargamo* that, as between parties to a subsisting contract, no 'second' condition not found in the contract can support such a claim. That does look like

[11] Who might be thought to disprove the example of conflicting goals given by Rory Gregson in ch 7.

[12] See ch 9.

[13] On this see Sir David Foxton, 'What Did the French Ever Do for Us? Historic and Prospective French Influences on English Private Law' (COMBAR Lecture in Memory of Edmund King KC, London, 8 March 2022).

[14] *Dargamo v Avonwick* [2021] EWCA Civ 1149, [2022] 1 All ER (Comm) 1244.

[15] *Barton v Morris* [2023] UKSC 3, [2023] AC 684.

[16] *School Facility Management Ltd v Governing Body of Christ the King School* [2020] EWHC 1118 (Comm), [2020] PTSR 1913 [421] (Foxton J); *Benzline Auto Pte Ltd v Supercars Lorinser Pte Ltd* [2018] SGCA 2, [2018] 1 SLR 239 [52] (Judith Prakash JA).

a principle of 'subsidiarity',[17] as does the fact that a contractual right to recover a payment would appear to preclude even a concurrent claim in unjust enrichment,[18] whatever benefits that might offer from the perspective of establishing jurisdiction or avoiding a limitation defence.[19] Indeed the dominance of the contractual analysis is such that the price payable if these steps necessary to accrue a contractual right to payment had been accomplished may well cap a claim in unjust enrichment where they have not,[20] and a contractual obligation to pay money which cannot be enforced because a procedural condition to bringing a claim has not been satisfied, will nonetheless provide an answer to any claim in unjust enrichment to recover that amount back.[21] The extent to which cases where benefits rendered under compulsion challenge a principle of the 'subsidiarity' of unjust enrichment claims in a contractual context is also open to debate. Where the compulsion in question comes from the contracting counterparty and induces the contract, whether duress or undue influence, a claim in unjust enrichment is only available if the contract is set aside.[22] Cases where the benefit is conferred under a legal duty owed to the recipient, and the benefactor then seeks to recover from a third party equally, or perhaps primarily, liable, do not raise 'subsidiarity' questions because there is no contract between the relevant parties.

Rory Gregson's chapter, on the torts/unjust enrichments borderlines,[23] is concerned not with the borderline itself, but with two cross-border concepts, only one of which finds favour.[24] Like Day and Stevens, Gregson's chapter reflects the spirit of cantonisation which characterises many of the discussions of unjust enrichment in this collection. He argues that, like the law of torts, the law of unjust enrichments recognises different types of claim for different kinds of reasons, with the consequence that different types of rules should apply to those different types of claim. That is an idea whose time has very much come, and which enjoys widespread academic support and approval from the Supreme Court in *Barnes v Eastenders Cash & Carry plc*.[25] However, there is nothing intrinsic in the law of tort(s) which requires it to take the form of a series of 'torticles'.[26] The French *Code civil* largely

[17] *Dargamo* (n 14) [67] and [70] (Carr LJ).

[18] *Pan Ocean Shipping Co Ltd v Creditcrop Ltd (The Trident Beauty)* [1994] 1 WLR 161 (HL) 164 (Lord Goff).

[19] As Janet O'Sullivan discusses in ch 3, this is one of the key pressure points on the contract/tort borderline.

[20] See the judgment of the majority in *Mann v Paterson Constructions Pty Ltd* [2019] HCA 32, (2019) 267 CLR 560.

[21] *Consulting Concepts International Inc v Consumer Protection Association* [2022] EWCA Civ 1699, [2023] 4 WLR 15 [47] (Andrews LJ) and cf *School Facility Management* (n 16) [262] (Foxton J).

[22] Charles Mitchell, Paul Mitchell, and Stephen Watterson (eds), *Goff and Jones: The Law of Unjust Enrichment* (10th edn, Sweet & Maxwell 2022) 10-10.

[23] The conference was one in which the placement of the letter 's' loomed large.

[24] See ch 7.

[25] *Barns v Eastenders Cash & Carry plc* [2014] UKSC 26, [2015] AC 1 [102] (Lord Toulson).

[26] Ibbetson (n 1) 97 (crediting the phrase to the late Bernard Rudden).

fits the law of delict into two articles, the divide depending on whether liability is fault-based or strict.[27] Rather than the result of rational choices that different reasons for imposing liability required torts with different rules, the rococo nature of English tort law is largely a product of its convoluted history.[28] In any event, not all torts are equal, the 'super-tort' of negligence having a conceptual reach which has come to condition our approach to other torts with different historical roots.[29]

Further, efforts to make sense of the mosaic of English tort law often focus on the nature of the interests the different torts protect: strict liability for certain interferences with bodily integrity, reputation, or property; something close to intention for most interferences with purely economic interests; and an objective fault-based liability for what lies between.[30] Viewed from that perspective, the fact that different torts have different rules may be justified, but it is not immediately clear what the equivalent organising principles might be in the law of unjust enrichment. To that extent at least, the law of unjust enrichment might be thought to bear some similarities with the law of contract, in having a single premise (unjust enrichments should be reversed, promises should be kept) the implementation of which varies in different contexts,[31] although Gregson is surely right to argue that the law of unjust enrichment encompasses a much greater diversity of context-specific rules than the law of contract(s). One of the principal criticisms made of 'unjust enrichment group think' is that it has led to the suggestion that a defence of change of position should be available to all unjust enrichment cases whereas its availability in failure of basis claims in particular is, as Gregson diplomatically puts it, 'controversial'. I will not further immerse myself in that controversy,[32] save to note that my own attempts to tease out answers were informed by concepts more often found in a contractual than a tortious context: the allocation risk and the importance of objective appearances. If unjust enrichment is structurally more similar to tort, substantively contract seems the closer relation, a view for which Day's chapter offers strong support.

The cross-border structure which Gregson criticises is the idea of correlativity: the idea that any duty that D owes to C must be justified by a single reason which simultaneously justifies both C's right and D's duty. Noting that the idea 'crosses the borderline between the law of torts and the law of unjust enrichment',

[27] Once arts 1382 and 1384, now arts 1240 and 1242.

[28] Ibbetson (n 1) 299–302.

[29] See in particular Tony Weir, 'The Staggering March of Negligence' in Tony Weir, Peter Cane, and Jane Stapleton, *The Law of Obligations: Essays in Celebration of John Fleming* (OUP 1998) 97–138.

[30] Tony Weir, *A Casebook on Tort* (10th edn, Sweet & Maxwell 2004) 146

[31] cf the oft-neglected volume two of H Beale (ed), *Chitty on Contracts* (34th edn, Sweet & Maxwell 2022), an early adopter of the 's'.

[32] I appear twice in Gregson's footnote summarising that controversy, *School Facility Management* (n 16) [455]–[500] and *Banca Intesa Sanpaolo SPA v Comune Di Venezia* [2022] EWHC 2586 (Comm), [2023] Bus LR 384 [393]–[402].

Gregson argues that it has contributed to two Supreme Court decisions which have developed the law of unjust enrichment in an unfortunate direction.[33]

Some concept of correlativity[34] is strongly entrenched in English private law: one by which the ambit of the right infringed (or of the legal obligation to which the defendant is subject) conditions the scope of the relief available to the claimant. It is seen in contract[35] in the doctrine of remoteness, perhaps most particularly in the controversial restatement of that doctrine in *The Achilleas*,[36] the rules restricting recovery for certain types of loss,[37] and, in some instances, the rules of causation,[38] and in both contract and tort in the concept of scope of duty,[39] and in the absence of any rule of remoteness in the tort of deceit.[40] Correlativity of this kind generally functions as a limit on the extent of court-ordered relief, and, at some level, gives effect to the idea that there should be some sense of proportion between what 'happened' to the claimant and the consequences of what the court orders the defendant to do. What Gregson interprets as the use of a concept of correlativity in *Prudential Assurance Co Ltd v Revenue and Customs Commissioners* to preclude a claim in unjust enrichment for the investment opportunity which arose from the payment of the capital sum appears to be animated by a very similar concern.[41]

Graham Virgo notes at the outset of his chapter that it is not meaningful to speak of a borderline between Equity and unjust enrichment, because one is a jurisdiction and the other an event.[42] He is concerned with cross-pollination, where the concepts used in one category have influenced the other,[43] and in particular the

[33] *Investment Trust Companies v Revenue & Customs Commissioners* [2017] UKSC 29, [2018] AC 275 and *Prudential Assurance Co Ltd v Revenue and Customs Commissioners* [2018] UKSC 39, [2019] AC 929.

[34] One different from, but with some relationship to, that articulated by Ernest Weinrib with which Gregson is concerned.

[35] See in particular Adam Kramer, 'An Agreement-Centred Approach to Remoteness and Contract Damages' in Nili Cohen and Ewan McKendrick (eds), *Comparative Remedies for Breach of Contract* (Hart 2005) 249.

[36] *Transfield Shipping Inc v Mercator Shipping Inc (The Achilleas)* [2008] UKHL 48, [2009] 1 AC 61.

[37] See generally Adam Kramer KC, *The Law of Contract Damages* (3rd edn, Hart 2022) ch 19.

[38] See, eg, *Financial Conduct Authority v Arch Insurance (UK) Ltd* [2021] UKSC 1, [2021] AC 649.

[39] *South Australia Asset Management Corp v York Montague Ltd* [1997] AC 191 (HL); *Manchester Building Society v Grant Thornton UK LLP* [2021] UKSC 20, [2022] AC 783 [2] (Lord Hodge and Lord Sales) and [179] (Lord Burrows).

[40] *Doyle v Olby (Ironmongers) Ltd* [1969] 2 QB 158 (CA).

[41] *Prudential* (n 33).

[42] See ch 10.

[43] These influences have not always been welcome. John Heydon, Mark Leeming, and Peter Turner (eds), *Meagher, Gummow & Lehane's Equity, Doctrines & Remedies* (4th edn, LexisNexis Australia 2002) refers, at *xi*, to the challenge to equity brought by 'proselytising members of the restitution industry (academic division)'. Scrutton LJ sought to repel boarders moving in the opposite direction, in his reference to a 'well-meaning sloppiness of thought' in *Holt v Markham* [1923] 1 KB 504 (CA) 513. Graham Virgo has a foot in both camps: see Graham Virgo, *The Principles of Equity and Trusts* (5th edn, OUP 2023) and Graham Virgo, *The Principles of the Law of Restitution* (3rd edn, OUP 2015).

influence (not always benign) of what he refers to as 'the equitable cathedral'[44] on the law of unjust enrichment.

One of the influences of equity (if not Equity) which Virgo identifies is the importance of the concept of conscience in the right to recover mistaken transfers of value in the law of unjust enrichment. As Virgo puts it, 'if you have received something from me in circumstances where I did not intend you to have it then it is only fair that you should pay for it'. If applied to the transfer of money or goods, this would recharacterise this part of the law(s) of restitution as a claim for unconscionable retention, because there can surely be nothing unconscionable in receiving a payment into one bank's account which has been sent there by mistake, or in spending that money, in the belief you are entitled to it.[45] While that characterisation has garnered support in Australia,[46] it has the effect of embracing within the definition of the claim something which is currently treated as a defence (change of position), with implications for the burden of proof. Further, while the concept of conscience may have relevance to unjust enrichment claims concerning payments or the transfer of goods, its relevance to claims for services rendered is less clear, as noted from Pollock CB's oft-quoted observation, 'One cleans another's shoes; what can the other do but put them on?'[47]

Virgo advances a compelling case as to the influence of equitable concepts on the recognition of the defence of change of position. That analysis provoked thought as to whether the machinery of Equity might provide a more nuanced basis for giving effect to the aims of fairness which the defence is meant to serve, when the precise effect of the value transfer on the recipient is not known.[48] If the defence of change of position results from the commencement of a claim or the assumption of an ongoing exposure, might an indemnity provide the answer? If it is work done by the defendant, what of an allowance, and is there more scope for protecting the interest of the recipient by imposing a lien on recovered property, as was done controversially in *Greenwood v Bennett*,[49] or protecting the position of the claimant by a lien pending sale?

The challenge tackled by Helen Scott in her chapter is how to provide a remedy for cases of 'indirect' value transfer under systems of law which have no doctrine

[44] Adopting Churchill's description of his relationship with the Church of England, I would regard myself as a buttress rather than a pillar of the equitable cathedral, supporting it from without.

[45] cf Lord Browne-Wilkinson's comment regarding a claim in equity in *Westdeutsche Landesbank Girozentrale v Islington London Borough Council* [1996] AC 669 (HL) 1020: 'Although the mere receipt of the moneys, in ignorance of the mistake, gives rise to no trust, the retention of the moneys after the recipient bank learned of the mistake may well have given rise to a constructive trust.'

[46] See, eg, *Ford v Perpetual Trustees Victoria Ltd* (2009) NSWCA 186, (2009) 75 NSWLR 42; *Heperu Pty Ltd v Belle* [2009] NSWCA 252, (2009) 258 ALR 727; *Roxborough v Rothmans of Pall Mall Australia Ltd* [2001] HCA 68, (2001) 208 CLR 516; *Equuscorp Pty Ltd v Haxton* [2012] HCA 7, (2012) 246 CLR 498.

[47] *Taylor v Laird* (1856) 25 LJ Ex 329, 332.

[48] Some of the difficulties are discussed in Mitchell, Mitchell, and Watterson (eds) (n 22) 27-25–27-31.

[49] *Greenwood v Bennett* [1973] QB 195 (CA).

of subsisting equitable title which can be 'traced' into subsequent assets.[50] The chapter was provoked by the decision of the South African Court of Appeal in *ASBA Bank Limited v Lombard Insurance Company Ltd*,[51] in which an employee (B) dishonestly procured the transfer of funds from her employer's (A's) bank account, and used those funds to reduce her debts to two banks (C and D). Scott suggests that one potential challenge to a claim by A against C and D under English law is the absence of any direct transfer of value, in the light of *Investment Trust Companies v HMRC*,[52] a decision whose reasoning is criticised by Gregson. Scott's answer to this difficulty is to suggest a differential test of what, as a matter of English law, would be the 'at the expense of' element of the four-stage analysis of the law of unjust enrichment, as between cases in which C voluntarily transfers value, albeit on mistaken or defective understanding (where the 'direct transfer' limitation would apply), and where money is taken by the defendant or where the claimant has conferred the money on the defendant but labours under a mistake so fundamental that he cannot be said to have intended the defendant to have it (where it would not).

English law is no stranger to cases which seek to protect the position of victims of dishonesty as against third parties who might otherwise look to the fruits of that fraud to meet their own claims. A particularly telling example is the apparent readiness to recognise a proprietary claim in some fraud cases even where the property in question was transferred pursuant to a contract which has not been set aside.[53] This exception is said to apply where a contract is not merely induced by fraudulent misrepresentation but is itself the instrument of fraud and no more than a vehicle for obtaining money by false pretences and where the position is akin to theft. The difficulty with special rules of this kind lies not simply in the conceptual certainty they erode, but in the uncertain scope of the exceptions. A rule which applies where the claimant has conferred the money on the defendant but labours under a mistake so fundamental that he cannot be said to have intended the defendant to have it might be thought to raise similar concerns. Further, by allowing the nature of the unjust factor as between the claimant and the initial recipient to condition the availability of indirect claims, Scott opens up the possibility of claims by indirect recipients of the initial recipient. Perhaps one justification of the

[50] See ch 16.
[51] *Absa Bank Ltd v Lombard Insurance Co Ltd* 2012 (6) SA 569 (SCA).
[52] *Investment Trust Companies* (n 33).
[53] See, eg, *National Crime Agency v Robb* [2014] EWHC 4384 (Ch), [2015] Ch 520 [41]–[44] (Etherton C); *Halley v Law Society* [2003] EWCA Civ 97, [2003] WTLR 845 [48] (Carnwath LJ); *Van Zuylen v Whiston-Dew* [2021] EWHC 2219 (Ch) [238] (Nicholas Thompsell sitting as a Deputy Judge of the High Court); *Global Currency Exchange Network Ltd v Osage 1 Ltd* [2019] EWHC 1375 (Comm), [2019] 1 WLR 5865 [41] (Andrew Henshaw QC sitting as a Deputy Judge of the High Court).

requirement of correlativity given effect in *Investment Trust Companies* is to avoid precisely that possibility.

We are told that good fences make good neighbours. Do clear borderlines make for more coherent categories of English private law? These analyses of the borderlines of unjust enrichment offer an interesting and diverse range of answers to that question.

9

Unjust Enrichment | Contract

William Day

I. Introduction

The borderline between contract and unjust enrichment matters in practice because of the difference in the remedies available to a claimant. The default remedy for breach of contract is compensatory damages, which seek to put the claimant in the position they would have been in but for the breach of contract.[1] The remedy is therefore loss-based but 'forward-looking', seeking to vindicate (in the broadest sense of that word) the transaction into which the parties have entered. In contrast, the remedy of restitution to reverse an unjust enrichment is gain-based and 'backwards-looking', seeking to restore the parties to the position they were in before transacting.[2] So a claimant who considers that their contract was a good deal will be incentivised to locate their claim in the law of contract, whereas a claimant who thinks that they entered a bad bargain will try to use the law of unjust enrichment to escape the contract altogether and recover what they have advanced under it.[3]

The borderline between contract and unjust enrichment has also become one of the most hotly argued private law boundary disputes in scholarship. The modern law of unjust enrichment can be traced back to the restitutionary land-grab of the first edition of *The Law of Restitution* in 1966. Robert Goff and Gareth Jones argued that quasi-contractual claims were 'founded on the principle of unjust enrichment' rather than having the 'special characteristic' of being 'founded on an implied contract'.[4] Peter Birks renamed most of the claimed territory the 'law of unjust enrichment' in contradistinction to the 'law of restitution' to focus on the causative event not the response.[5] This had the effect of ceding back to the law of contract the issue of restitution as a remedy for breach of contract, although that was in any event unfertile terrain,[6] and will not be considered further in this chapter.

[1] *Robinson v Harman* (1848) 1 Ex 850, 154 ER 363.

[2] See, eg, Andrew Burrows, *A Restatement of the English Law of Unjust Enrichment* (OUP 2012) 26.

[3] See also Paul Davies, 'Bad Bargains' (2019) 72 CLP 253.

[4] Robert Goff and Gareth Jones, *The Law of Restitution* (Sweet & Maxwell 1966) 4–5.

[5] Peter Birks, 'Misnomer' in William Cornish and others (eds), *Restitution: Past Present & Future* (Hart 1998).

[6] Negotiating damages are now seen as compensatory not restitutionary in nature: *Morris-Garner v One Step (Support) Ltd* [2018] UKSC 20, [2019] AC 649 [91] (Lord Reed). In principle, an account of profits for breach of contract is available pursuant to *Attorney General v Blake* [2001] AC 268 (HL), but it difficult to see how *Blake* will be applied in the future after the criticisms made of its reasoning in *One*

William Day, *Unjust Enrichment | Contract* In: *Borderlines in Private Law*. Edited by: William Day and Julius Grower, Oxford University Press. © William Day 2024. DOI: 10.1093/9780191995200.003.0009

Instead, the focus of this chapter is on the impact on claims in unjust enrichment of a contract between the parties. The Birksian project sought to give the law of unjust enrichment conceptual unity, and that has influenced the accounts then given to the relationship between contract and unjust enrichment in the modern law. The prevailing trend is to articulate a general rule about the effect of subsisting contracts which applies to all claims in unjust enrichment, no matter the ground for restitution. So, for example, although the current edition of *Goff & Jones* recognises that most of the leading cases are concerned with claims for failure of consideration (often now called failure of basis or failure of condition), it contends that 'there is no doubt that the principles developed in relation to failure of basis apply generally, whatever unjust factor is being relied upon'.[7] The same approach has been taken in recent leading cases. In *Dargamo Holdings Ltd v Avonwick Holdings Ltd*,[8] for instance, an argument was pursued by counsel that statements of principle in cases concerned with mistake-based claims should not be transplanted into claims for failure of basis. This was firmly rejected by Carr LJ, who said: 'I can see no good basis for not treating them as being of more general application.'[9]

This chapter begins by outlining the current understanding of the borderline between contract and unjust enrichment. The integrity of that borderline, as presently mapped, assumes that there is a unitary body of law known as *the* law of unjust enrichment which can be lined up alongside *the* law of contract to create a single borderline. But that is a view that no one now seems to defend. As Rory Gregson explores in Chapter 7 of this collection, unjust enrichment is like tort not contract in its internal diversity. Different types of claims in unjust enrichment (often described as 'unjust factors' or 'grounds for restitution') have different relationships with the law of contract and it is important, in this regard, to distinguish between (a) those unjust enrichment claims based on a claimant's conditional intention to enrich but where that condition has not materialised (namely failure of consideration or failure of basis); (b) those claims where the claimant's intention to enrich the defendant is juridically irrelevant (claims such as recoupment and for necessitous intervention); and (c) those claims where the claimant's intention to enrich was in some way defective (grounds of rescission such as mistake, duress, or undue influence).[10] This does not require the courts to engage in a normative search for the underlying reason for restitution in any given case;[11] the argument

Step. See further William Day, 'Restitution for Wrongs: One Step Forwards, Two Steps Back?' [2018] RLR 60.

[7] Charles Mitchell, Paul Mitchell, and Stephen Watterson, *Goff & Jones on Unjust Enrichment* (10th edn, Sweet & Maxwell 2022) 3-01.

[8] [2021] EWCA Civ 1149, [2022] 1 All ER (Comm) 1244.

[9] ibid [71].

[10] The argument pursued in this chapter is not dissimilar to that in Mat Campbell, 'Doubting the Subsidiarity of Unjust Enrichment' [2021] LMCLQ 535, 539–43, to which Rory Gregson kindly drew my attention at the conference.

[11] A concern raised at the conference and also expressed by Mrs Justice Cockerill in ch 2.

advanced in this chapter is simply that the courts can (and should) apply the existing ingredients of grounds for restitution in a way that avoids borderline controversies with contract law, such that there is no need to develop a generalised principle about the 'primacy' of contract or the 'subsidiarity' of unjust enrichment that applies to all grounds of restitution.

II. The Principle of Subsidiarity

A. Scholarship

The scope of the general rule governing the borderline between contract and all unjust enrichment claims is not free from doubt. However, the general consensus (challenged in this chapter) is that claims in unjust enrichment may not lie where there is a contractual basis for the enrichment. This is often framed in terms of a 'subsidiarity' principle, influenced by Ross Grantham and Charles Rickett, who wrote in the following terms:

> Subsidiarity describes the relationship between two claims or doctrines where the scope and operation of one claim are constrained by another claim, even where all the elements of the former claim are made out . . . Unjust enrichment . . . is subsidiary in the sense that the scope and operation of the principle of unjust enrichment are necessarily constrained by the scope and operation of the other core doctrines of the private law.[12]

According to Grantham and Rickett, this leaves unjust enrichment in a subordinate role, as a doctrine that supplements contract law but cannot contradict it, analogous to equity's relationship with contract law:[13]

> Unjust enrichment can be invoked only where there is at least some manifestation of (objective) consent, because, doctrinally, unjust enrichment is concerned with manifestations of consent that are subjectively defective. Quite simply, if there is no manifestation of (objective) consent at all (or no defect in subjective consent), and no prima facie effective transfer of wealth, there is nothing calling into play the objectives of unjust enrichment: there is neither an apparent consent to correct, nor a status quo ante to restore. This means that the law of unjust enrichment is, therefore, essentially modificatory in nature. It modifies the normal

[12] Ross Grantham and Charles Rickett, 'On the Subsidiarity of Unjust Enrichment' (2001) 117 LQR 273, 273.

[13] As to which see ch 4.

> consequences that would flow from the apparent manifestation of consent by the plaintiff to the transfer of the enrichment.
>
> As a doctrine supplementing or modifying the law of contract and the law of property, unjust enrichment fulfils a function similar to that historically attributed to equity. Like equity, unjust enrichment operates to mitigate the rigidities and short-sightedness of other doctrines, and to 'reverse' transactions that on closer inspection cannot be allowed to stand.[14]

As Mr Justice Foxton's contribution to this collection demonstrates,[15] the idea that unjust enrichment is subsidiary to contract is now a well-established and familiar rule in the practice of law. However, the *extent* of this subsidiarity rule is a matter of debate. Graham Virgo argues that the rule that contract bars unjust enrichment admits no exceptions:

> If the parties have entered into a valid agreement which is to regulate their relationship it is vital that the law of unjust enrichment does not undermine what they have decided. It is only where the agreement does not operate, or has ceased to operate, that the law of unjust enrichment should have a role to play in any dispute between the parties. Consequently, the law of restitution should be considered to be subsidiary to the law of contract.[16]

Andrew Burrows (as he then was) was more cautious in his *Restatement* of the law of unjust enrichment, positing in section 3(6) that '[i]n general, an enrichment is not unjust if the benefit was owed to the defendant by the claimant under a valid contractual ... obligation'.[17] While the unjust factor would normally be 'nullified' by existence of the contract, there are (he says) some 'limited exceptions':

> Where there is no underlying conflict between the reason for allowing restitution and the defendant's legal entitlement ... It might help to think of the legal entitlement as being easily outweighed by the unjust factor.[18]

B. Case Law

The case law has betrayed some ambiguity as to which of these two approaches is correct. In *Fairfield Sentry Ltd v Migani*, Lord Sumption followed Virgo's approach

[14] Grantham and Charles Rickett (n 12) 289–90.
[15] See ch 8.
[16] Graham Virgo, *The Principles of the Law of Restitution* (3rd edn, OUP 2015) 133–34. In similar terms, see James Edelman and Elise Bant, *Unjust Enrichment* (2nd edn, Hart 2016) 130–32.
[17] Burrows, *Restatement* (n 2) 31.
[18] ibid 33–34.

and said that the 'basic principle is not in dispute. The payee of money cannot be said to have been unjustly enriched if he was entitled to receive the sum paid to him.'[19] Similarly, in *DD Growth 2X Fund v RMF Market Neutral Strategies (Master) Ltd*, Lords Sumption and Briggs said that it was 'fundamental that a payment cannot amount to enrichment if it was made for full consideration; and that it cannot be unjust to receive or retain it if it was made in satisfaction of a legal right'.[20] Although this subsidiarity rule was stated in *Fairfield* and *DD Growth* without apparent qualification, the Burrows *Restatement* (with its reference to the existence of exceptions) was also cited with approval in both cases.

In *International Energy Group Ltd v Zurich Insurance plc*,[21] where there was an issue about the availability of a claim in recoupment, this tension became more obvious. Lord Sumption emphasised that a non-contractual right to recoupment could not 'mend men's bargains', continuing:

> It is I think beyond question that to require part of that amount to be repaid on the ground that its retention would be unjust is a reversal of the effect of the contract by operation of law, something which cannot be justified if the contract is valid, lawful and effective.[22]

However, Lord Mance disagreed, emphasising the exceptions identified in the *Restatement*, saying 'I do not accept that there is any absolute brightline principle', adding '[n]either jurisprudentially nor on authority is this so. There is a general rule to that effect, but it is subject to exceptions', those being where there was no 'policy inconsistency' between the contractual right and the right to restitution.[23]

Matters have not been made clearer by subsequent cases. *Dargamo* endorsed and applied the Burrows/Mance approach. Carr LJ recognised that a contract will normally leave no 'space' for the law of unjust enrichment but added that this was 'not absolute' and there were 'exceptions, albeit limited [ones]'.[24] Carr LJ went to consider and reject the proposition that any such exception might apply to the facts of that case, as considered later in this chapter.[25]

On the other hand, while the Supreme Court in *Barton v Morris* did not expressly take issue with the approach in *Dargamo*, a plurality appeared to lean more towards the Virgo/Sumption approach.[26] This is seen most clearly in Lord Leggatt's judgment:

[19] [2014] UKPC 9, [2014] 1 CLC 611 [18].
[20] [2017] UKPC 36, [2018] Bus LR [62].
[21] [2015] UKSC 33, [2016] AC 509.
[22] ibid [185].
[23] ibid [68] and [72] citing Andrew Burrows, *The Law of Restitution* (3rd edn, OUP 2011) 88–91.
[24] *Dargamo* (n 8) [72] and [76].
[25] ibid [128]. See further text to n 68.
[26] [2023] UKSC 3, [2023] 1 WLR 269. The exception was Lord Burrows at [237]–[240].

> There is also another broader reason why the existence of a contract precludes a claim based on the law of unjust enrichment. This is that there already exists a system of law for determining what rights and remedies contracting parties have in relation to the subject matter of their contract. It is called the law of contract. In relation to the subject matter of the contract, the law of contract determines, and governs the consequences of, not only the existence but also the absence of an obligation on one contracting party to confer a benefit on the other. To redistribute the allocation of benefits and losses provided for by the law of contract by applying another set of legal principles would undercut this regime.[27]

Subsidiarity was a central issue in the appeal to the Supreme Court in *Barton v Morris*. The Court of Appeal had determined that a claim in unjust enrichment could be made even where there was a valid commission contract for services between the parties.[28] That was on the basis that the claim for restitution representing the value of services rendered would not contradict any express term, the contract being silent on whether any commission would be payable in the circumstances that had transpired. As set out later in this chapter,[29] the majority (Lady Rose, Lord Briggs, and Lord Stephens) accepted that there should be no claim in unjust enrichment in those circumstances on the basis that the contract nonetheless represented a 'complete' bargain.[30] While Lord Leggatt dissented, this was on the basis that he considered that there was an implied contractual term that entitled the claimant to remuneration.[31] As the passage quoted above demonstrates, when it came to the claim in unjust enrichment, he appears to have adopted a harder attitude to the subsidiarity of unjust enrichment to contract than that envisaged in the Burrows/Mance approach; the logic of his position does not admit of exceptions.[32]

C. Underlying Assumptions

Lord Leggatt's *dictum* in *Barton v Morris* also underlines another point: that much of the debate about the borderline between contract and unjust enrichment assumes that a clear line can be drawn between, on the one hand, *the* law of contract and, on the other hand, *the* law of unjust enrichment. The same is true of the passage from Grantham and Rickett's foundational article set out earlier.[33] However,

[27] ibid [191].
[28] [2019] EWCA Civ 1999.
[29] See further text to n 69.
[30] *Barton* (n 26) [107].
[31] ibid [188].
[32] See generally ibid [189]–[193].
[33] See text to n 12.

the integrity of any borderline drawn between two different areas of the law is contingent on the internal coherence of the areas on either side of the line.

Contract law has a much more confident identity than the law of unjust enrichment. This may be a product of its intellectual maturity. The substantive law of contract escaped the 'medieval chains'[34] of the forms of action long before the law of unjust enrichment: 'by 1800 the law of contract could be treated as an abstract entity distinct from the forms of action.'[35] The same arguably did not happen for the law of unjust enrichment until 1966.[36] The confidence of contract law is also due to its clear conceptual focus on the legal effects of agreements.[37] Although plenty of academic ink is spilt over why agreements are given legal effect, there is at least normally common ground that this is what contract law is about, and that this gives it an internal unity and sets it apart from other branches of private law.[38] The same is not true for the law of unjust enrichment, even after the excision of restitution for wrongs.[39] The courts are currently content to treat the law of unjust enrichment as a coherent whole, the purpose of which is 'to correct normatively defective transfers of value',[40] but that view has come under sustained academic attack, most forcefully by Robert Stevens who argues that 'there is no unified area of law called "restitution" or "unjust enrichment" '.[41]

It is difficult to identify any academic currently working in the field who appears to defend the proposition that the law of unjust enrichment is *as* unified an area of the law as the law of contract. It is widely recognised that there are different reasons why a transfer of value may be normatively defective and should be reversed. Thus the current edition of *Goff & Jones* argues that the law of unjust enrichment is a legal category in the same way as tort law,[42] which is not in fact that far away from where the first edition began.[43] Burrows similarly has accepted that 'unjust enrichment is more like tort than contract'.[44] However, as Rory Gregson points out in Chapter 7 of this collection, these concessions have not been followed through to their logical conclusions. Like different tortious claims, different unjust factors are underpinned by different reasons for restitution. Furthermore, different reasons for restitution may interact in different ways with the law of contract. This should

[34] *United Australia Ltd v Barclays Bank Ltd* [1941] AC 1 (HL) 28.
[35] David Ibbetson, *A Historical Introduction to the Law of Obligations* (OUP 1999) 215.
[36] See text to n 4.
[37] See, eg, *One Step* (n 6) [21] (Lord Reed).
[38] Although other views are available: see, eg, Patrick Atiyah, 'Contracts, Promises and the Law of Obligations' in Patrick Atiyah, *Essays on Contract* (OUP 1986) and Grant Gilmore, *The Death of Contract* (2nd edn, Ohio State University Press 1995).
[39] See text to n 5.
[40] *Dargamo* (n 8) [54] (Carr LJ). See also *Investment Trust Companies v Revenue and Customs Commissioners* [2017] UKSC 29, [2018] AC 275 [42] (Lord Reed). cf *Patel v Mirza* [2016] UKSC 42, [2017] AC 467 [246] (Lord Sumption): 'English law does not have a unified theory of restitution.'
[41] Robert Stevens, *The Laws of Restitution* (OUP 2023) 3.
[42] Mitchell, Mitchell, and Watterson (n 7) 1-06–1-013.
[43] Goff and Jones, *The Law of Restitution* (n 4) 5.
[44] Andrew Burrows, 'In Defence of Unjust Enrichment' (2019) 78 CLJ 521, 530.

not be controversial; it is no different to the proposition that contracts can have different effects on different types of claims in tort.[45]

Nevertheless, as set out above, the orthodox approach in scholarship as adopted by the courts is still to contend for a rule (albeit arguably subject to limited exceptions) regulating the borderline between contract and all claims in unjust enrichment. This is a good example of the 'problem of overgeneralisation'[46] inherent in the Birksian approach. I have argued elsewhere that difficulties in the 'at the expense of' rule and as to the availability of proprietary restitution can be solved by dividing claims in unjust enrichment into different sub-categories.[47] The same approach could bring considerable clarity to the relationship between contract and unjust enrichment. In other words, the starting point should be that different claims in unjust enrichment have different relationships with contract law.

III. Conditional Intention Claims

As the current edition of *Goff & Jones* recognises,[48] most of the leading cases about the relationship between contract and unjust enrichment, including *Dargamo* and *Barton v Morris*, are concerned with the cause of action known as failure of consideration (or, with increasing regularity, as failure of basis).[49] This gives rise to an immediate oddity. On the one hand, the general rule typically derived from these cases is that there can be no valid contractual basis for the enrichment for a claim in unjust enrichment to succeed. On the other hand, an exception has to be created to accommodate this very category of claim. That apparent exception, as described by Burrows, is as follows:

> [Where a contract is] terminated for breach or frustration, contractual obligations accruing prior to the date of termination remain valid. Termination discharges contractual obligations for the future but not for the past. Nevertheless,

[45] To take one obvious example, a claim for damages in negligence in respect of a misrepresentation can be precluded or limited by a contractual term but a similar contractual defence is not available for a claim in deceit.

[46] Lionel Smith, 'Restitution: A New Start?' in Peter Devonshire and Rohan Havelock (eds), *The Impact of Equity and Restitution in Commerce* (Hart 2019) 97.

[47] William Day, '"At the Expense of" in Unjust Enrichment: Causal, Direct or Intentional Transfers of Value' [2017] LMCLQ 588, 602–05; William Day and Sarah Worthington, 'Proprietary Restitution' in William Day and Sarah Worthington (eds), *Challenging Private Law: Lord Sumption on the Supreme Court* (Hart 2020).

[48] Text to n 7.

[49] See, eg, *Attorney General of Trinidad and Tobago v Trinsalvage Enterprises Ltd* [2023] UKPC 26 [21]: 'Failure of basis[,] which used to be labelled failure of consideration', and [44]: 'Failure of consideration (or, as we would now say, failure of basis') (Lord Burrows). See also *Barton* (n 26) [78]: '"Failure of basis" . . . is generally preferred to "failure of consideration"' (Lady Rose) and [231]: 'Traditionally called failure of consideration but is now often referred to as failure of condition or failure of basis. The terminology of failure of consideration invites confusion' (Lord Burrows).

> there can be restitution of money paid or services rendered prior to discharge in respect of those past obligations that remain valid. The best explanation for this [exception] is that granting restitution does not conflict with the contractual allocation of risk given that the contract has been terminated.[50]

The better view, developed below, is that there is no need to create a general subsidiarity rule together with a 'termination exception'. By its nature, a claim based on failure of consideration cannot cut across the agreed allocation of risk because the consideration (or basis or condition) attaching to the enrichment must *also* be agreed between the parties. The agreement both as to conditionality and, more generally, as to the allocation of risk will be construed objectively and as a coherent whole.

A. Agreement-Based Claims in Contract and Unjust Enrichment

If a party pays for goods or services, and they are not delivered or (in the case of goods) title is not transferred by the counterparty, that party is entitled to recover the money paid by a claim in unjust enrichment.[51] This recognises that the money was paid subject to an agreed condition of receiving the goods (and title to the goods) or services, and that condition has not materialised, so the money ought to be returned. The opposite situation is where a party delivers goods or services on condition of being paid and is not paid: the creditor can bring a claim. However, the enforcement of this latter condition typically takes place in contract by way of a claim for a debt rather than in unjust enrichment.[52]

This distinction is demonstrated by *Taylor v Motability Finance Ltd*.[53] The former finance director of a company alleged that he was wrongfully dismissed and sued in unjust enrichment for the value of services rendered whilst in post. The claim was dismissed on the basis that all of the alleged work was within the scope of the claimant's contract of employment. There was therefore 'no room' for a concurrent remedy in restitution alongside any remedy in debt or damages.[54] Put another way, the claim failed because there was no agreed conditionality attaching to the services rendered beyond the terms recorded in the contract.

Although *Taylor* involved a claimant who was the innocent party, the same analysis arises where the claim is by the contract breaker. The cause of action involves strict liability; it is not interested in who was at fault or to blame for the lack of counter-performance. Authority in favour of the contract breaker obtaining

[50] Burrows, *The Law of Restitution* (n 23) 90.
[51] See, eg, *Rowland v Divall* [1923] 2 KB 500 (CA).
[52] This debt claim has been partly codified: Sale of Goods Act 1979, s 49.
[53] [2004] EWHC 2619 (Comm).
[54] ibid [23].

restitution for non-money benefits is in short supply,[55] which is probably a reflection of the likelihood that any relevant conditionality would be in the contract and so usually be seen as part of a contractual claim. However, the contract breaker can obtain restitution of money paid, subject to the agreed terms on which it was forwarded. For example, if the money was paid by way of deposit (and so by definition agreed not to have a conditional basis) it will not be recoverable.[56] But where the payment is simply paid on terms that counter-performance would be forthcoming, and it was not, that is treated as sufficient agreement for a claim for failure of consideration.[57]

The current state of the law has been criticised as drawing an 'illogical' and 'unjustifiable' distinction between money and non-money benefits.[58] The complaint is that this revives something like a distinction based on forms of action with restitution of money benefits belonging to the law of unjust enrichment and non-money benefits belonging to contract law, in circumstances where the substance of the claims is essentially the same.[59] Put another way, the criticism is that this borderline has been drawn in the wrong place: either contract law should be rolled back in favour of unjust enrichment, or vice versa, or there should be the possibility for concurrent claims in both contract and unjust enrichment.

Whether the claim sounds in contract or unjust enrichment appears to be a product of how the conditional agreement is characterised by the court. Where the agreed condition is a contractual condition, the claim will be in contract. When the agreed condition is a non-contractual condition (or 'consideration' in the traditional language), the claim will be in unjust enrichment.

This is illustrated by *Pan Ocean Shipping Co Ltd v Creditcorp Ltd (The Trident Beauty)*,[60] which was a claim for a money rather than a non-money benefit. The charterer failed in a claim to recover a hire instalment for a period when the ship was off-hire for repairs. The charterer had paid, and sought to recover from, the defendant, who was the assignee of the shipowner. However, the terms of the charterparty made it clear that the conditionality of those payments was as between the charterer and the shipowner, without regard to any assignment. Accordingly, any claim would need to be against the shipowner (who was considered not worth suing).

[55] At best there are *obiter* comments in *Hain Steamship Co Ltd v Tate and Lyle Ltd* [1936] 2 All ER 597 (HL) 612 (Lord Wright MR) and *Miles v Wakefield Metropolitan DC* [1987] AC 539 (HL) 553 (Lord Brightman) and 661 (Lord Templeman).

[56] Carmine Conte, 'Deposit Clauses' in Graham Virgo and Sarah Worthington, *Commercial Remedies: Resolving Controversies* (CUP 2017) 405.

[57] See, eg, *Palmer v Temple* (1839) 9 Ad & El 508, 112 ER 1304 and *Rover International Ltd v Cannon Film Sales* [1989] 1 WLR 912 (CA).

[58] Virgo (n 16) 334–36.

[59] Burrows, *The Law of Restitution* (n 23) 348–49.

[60] [1994] 1 WLR 161 (HL).

In *The Trident Beauty*, Lord Goff emphasised that, because the agreed mechanism for recovery of the hire was found in the contractual terms, that claim would be in contract not unjust enrichment: there is no room for concurrency of claims in this context.[61] But the better view is that there is no room for *inconsistent* concurrent claims in this context. As both the contractual claim and the unjust enrichment claim based on failure of consideration turn on the content of the objective agreement between the parties, they are incapable of yielding different answers. If the contract, properly construed, shows that there is no condition subsequent attaching to the conferral of the benefit that has been left unsatisfied, the same interpretative exercise in the law of unjust enrichment will lead to the same outcome.

It follows that this is a relatively thin borderline between contract and unjust enrichment.[62] Indeed, the historic label as applied to failure of consideration claims, quasi-contract, was not entirely inapt. The question of whether there is an agreed condition for the provision of the benefit requires for *both* types of claim, contractual and non-contractual, an objective assessment of the parties' shared intentions; in other words, this is an exercise in interpretation and implication.[63] Further, given that this is an exercise in construction, any alleged conditionality cannot contradict the contract terms or any other express basis on which the parties have dealt. So, for example, the value of services rendered pre-contract and expressly 'subject to contract' cannot be claimed by a claim alleging failure of consideration, because the person rendering those services has expressly agreed to do so at their own risk.[64]

The parties are free to agree to whatever condition or conditions that they consider to be in their interests. An enrichment may be on condition as to a particular state of affairs as well as, or instead of, by reference to some counter-performance. In *Westdeutsche Landesbanke Girozentrale v Islington BC*,[65] for example, payments under void interest rate swaps could be recovered because the payments had been made not just on the basis that payments would be received in return (subject to movements in the interest rate) but also on the basis that these payments were in discharge of contractual obligations. And that condition, so construed, had failed: the contract being void, there were no contractual obligations to

[61] ibid 164–65. For a different interpretation, see Campbell (n 10) 541.

[62] See also William Day, *Key Ideas in Commercial Law* (Hart 2023) 105–06.

[63] See, eg, *Giedo van der Garde BV v Force India Formula One Team Ltd* [2010] EWHC 2373 (QB) [285]–[286] (Stadlen J). Also Mitchell, Mitchell, and Watterson (n 7) 13-02–13-06; Virgo (n 16) 309–10; Stevens (n 41) 110–11.

[64] *Regalian Properties plc v London Docklands Development Corp* [1995] 1 WLR 212 (Ch) 231 (Rattee J). It might, of course, be different where the parties' conduct is such that they can be taken to have waived the 'subject to contract' restriction and agreed to some conditionality attaching to the pre-contractual performance rendered. Of course, when that occurs said waiver might be such as to lead to a contract rather than a claim for failure of consideration: *RTS Flexible Systems Ltd v Molkerei Alois Muller GmbH & Co KG* [2010] UKSC 14, [2010] 3 All ER 1.

[65] [1994] 4 All ER 890 (Com Ct and CA). The issue was not appealed to the House of Lords.

discharge.[66] This mattered because the 'Islington swap' (in contrast to some other swaps at issue in that litigation) had already seen payments going both ways, so it could not be said that the consideration had totally failed in terms of no counter-performance. Hobhouse J was at pains to emphasise that such a claim would be refused in circumstances where it was directly or indirectly enforcing an invalid contract.[67] However, since the restitutionary remedy is always backwards-looking, seeking to place the claimant in the position they were in before entering the contract, that is a concern which should never be realised.

B. Explaining Some Leading Cases

On an agreement-based account of failure of consideration claims, the leading cases on the borderline between unjust enrichment and contract are straightforward to analyse. They do not require any freestanding rule about the subsidiarity of this type of unjust enrichment claim to contract (or, indeed, for exceptions to be developed to such a rule to accommodate the ability to claim post-termination). This can be demonstrated by reference to five leading cases:

(1) *Dargamo Holdings Ltd v Avonwick Holdings Ltd* concerned a dispute as to the exercise of a share option for a company called Castlerose for $950 million. The buyers contended that approximately $200 million in fact related to the transfer of further assets, which were not transferred, such that they were entitled to restitution. As Carr LJ put it, the 'fundamental reason' why the claim in unjust enrichment failed was that the share purchase agreement expressly stated that the $950 million was consideration for the sale of shares in Castlerose.[68] It was not possible to construe some other agreed conditionality attaching to the purchase monies contrary to these unambiguous express terms. And the condition, so construed, had not failed.

(2) In *Barton v Morris*, the dispute arose out of an oral agreement by which a company promised to pay the claimant £1.2 million 'if' he introduced it to a purchaser for its property who bought it for £6.5 million (or more). The difficulty was that the trial judge had rejected the submission that the express term in the agreement should be construed on the basis that the claimant was to be paid 'if, and only if' the £6.5 million target was met. That meant that the express terms were silent on a sale for sub-£6.5 million. Nevertheless the natural interpretation of the company agreeing to pay

[66] As later put in *Guinness Mahon & Co Ltd v Kensington and Chelsea RLBC* [1999] QB 215 (CA) 227 (Morritt LJ): 'It is the very fact that the contract is ultra vires which constitutes the total failure of consideration justifying the remedy of money had and received or restitution for unjust enrichment.'

[67] *Westdeutsche* (n 65) 929.

[68] *Dargamo* (n 8) [115]–[116].

the claimant £*x* if the claimant procured *y* was that, if the claimant does not procure *y*, the company was under no obligation to pay the claimant anything (be it £*x* or any other sum). Adding 'but only if' emphasised the point but was ultimately surplusage. The parties' silence on the question of the company paying something less than £*x* for the claimant procuring something less than *y* was objectively unambiguous. A reasonable person would appreciate that the parties had turned their minds to what needed to be done in order to trigger the company's contingent payment obligation and that they had expressed their agreement in clear and comprehensive terms. Had the parties intended some smaller sum to be triggered for something other than *y*, they would have said so.[69] In other words, the parties had no shared objective intention that the services rendered would also be on condition of payment if the sale was under £6.5 million. The condition, so construed, had not failed.

(3) *Roxborough v Rothmans of Pall Mall Australia Ltd* is an earlier Australian authority and a focus of argument in both *Dargamo* and *Barton*. There, cigarettes were bought on the wholesale market for a price that included (as a distinct line item) tax in the form of a licence fee.[70] That tax was invalidated as unconstitutional. The buyer was held entitled to recover the licence fee. The obligation to pay the licence fee was, properly construed, a 'distinct and separate' part of the sales contract and only to be paid if it was in fact due to the revenue authorities.[71] Although not reasoned in this way, the case is best understood as turning on implied conditionality: simply put, on its proper construction the fee was paid on condition that the tax was due, and that condition had failed.[72]

(4) A more difficult Australian case is *Mann v Paterson Constructions Pty Ltd*.[73] A landowner contracted a builder to build two houses. The landowner agreed to pay the builder in instalments as construction progressed. The builder started construction but then the landowner repudiated the contract. The builder accepted that repudiation, terminating the contract, and sought restitution of the value of the work he had done. In respect of the instalments already earned, the builder was limited to the agreed rate for that work done.[74] But the High Court of Australia then divided over whether the builder could claim in failure of consideration in respect of the work done for the next instalment before being prevented from completing that phase

[69] William Day and Graham Virgo, 'Risks on the Contract/Unjust Enrichment Borderline' (2020) 136 LQR 349, 330–31, endorsed by the majority in *Barton* (n 26) [103] (Lady Rose).
[70] (2001) 208 CLR 516 (HCA).
[71] ibid [17] and [21] (Gleeson CJ, Gaudron and Hayne JJ).
[72] Stevens (n 41) 126.
[73] [2019] HCA 32, (2019) 373 ALR 1.
[74] But for different stated reasons. Contrast, eg, the reasoning at ibid [19] (Kiefel CJ, Bell and Keane JJ) with [62] (Gaegler J) and [169] (Nettle, Gordon, and Edelman JJ).

by the landowner's repudiation. The majority held that a claim in restitution was available even though the next milestone had not been reached.[75] Although this appears, at face value, to run against the agreed conditionality in the contract (that performance rendered by the builder was 'at risk' until the next stage for an instalment payment had been reached) the agreed conditionality was more nuanced than that. The implicit basis for the builder commencing the next stage of the work was that the landowner would not unlawfully deprive the builder of the opportunity to complete that stage.[76] That condition had failed and so triggered a right to claim in restitution.

(5) This agreement-based account also has explanatory power in three-party scenarios. In *MacDonald Dickens & Macklin v Costello*,[77] a couple acted through a company (of which they were the sole directors and shareholders) to contract with builders to build houses on their land. The builders were not paid by the company (who again was considered not worth suing) and so sued the couple in unjust enrichment. The claim was dismissed. Etherton LJ held that the claim failed because unjust enrichment could not be used to cut through the contractual arrangements.[78] But the better understanding of the case is that the requirements for the claim were simply not made out: the conditionality of the builder's services was agreed as between the builder and the company. It was not something to which the couple themselves were privy.[79]

C. A Residual Category

As has already been noted,[80] agreed conditionality can relate not to counter-performance but rather to a particular state of affairs. The state of affairs to which the condition is attached can be that a contract will be made between the parties, with that condition then failing when the contract fails to materialise. No distinction should be drawn between the approach to be taken in these cases and the others already discussed:[81] the focus should be a strict constructional analysis as to what conditionality was agreed as to the pre-contractual rendering of benefits and whether than conditionality has failed.

However, there is a line of case law at first instance which suggests that a fault-based analysis can sometimes be adopted. In *Countrywide Communications Ltd v*

[75] Nettle, Gordon, and Edelman JJ, supported by Gaegler J.
[76] David Winterton and Timothy Pilkington, 'Mann v Paterson Constructions Pty Ltd: The Intersection of Debt, Damages and Quantum Meruit' (2020) 44 Melbourne University LR 679, 704–06.
[77] [2011] EWCA Civ 930, [2012] QB 244.
[78] ibid [23].
[79] Day, 'At the Expense of' (n 47) 603.
[80] Text to n 65.
[81] *William Lacey (Hounslow) Ltd v Davis* [1957] 1 WLR 932 (QB) 935 (Barry J).

ICL Pathway Ltd,[82] it was held that the availability of a remedy would depend on a number of considerations including whether the benefit would normally be conferred gratuitously; whether the risk had been allocated in some way; the importance of the benefit to the defendant; and the extent to which it could be said that the failure of the contract to materialise was the 'fault' of the defendant, or beyond the risk as allocated between the parties. That analysis was followed subsequently in *MSM Consulting Ltd v United Republic of Tanzania*,[83] and then in *Benourad v Compass Group plc*.[84]

If these cases remain good law,[85] and are taken to recognise a ground for restitution within the law of unjust enrichment (as opposed to some other doctrine),[86] the claim is clearly not based on failure of consideration because it brings into play factors well beyond the usual test for that unjust factor. There is also no good reason to think that this other ground for restitution precludes the availability of a claim in failure of consideration when made out on the facts. At best, then, these cases recognise an *alternative* fault-based claim that can be brought concurrently with other non-contractual claims. However, it is not necessary to go beyond that observation for the purposes of this chapter: the *Countrywide* line of cases is not really concerned with the borderline between the law of unjust enrichment and contract law because, by definition, in this context no contract will have materialised.

IV. Intention Irrelevant Claims

A different analysis applies where the parties' intentions in transferring and accepting an enrichment are juridically irrelevant. Those unjust factors known as 'legal compulsion', 'necessity', and 'illegality' are typically justified by reference to some external policy rather than by reference to the parties' intentions.[87] In the case of necessity, the claim is said to exist to incentivise action to preserve another person or their property. Restitution for legal compulsion is said to ensure that losses are appropriately allocated between those primarily and secondarily liable. The purpose of the illegality ground for restitution is said to unwind the private law effects of illegal transactions. The characterisation of these claims, and their place in the law of unjust enrichment, has been questioned.[88] It suffices to say for present

[82] [2000] CLC 324 (Com Ct) 349 (Nicholas Strauss QC sitting as a Deputy High Court Judge).
[83] [2009] EWHC 121 (QB).
[84] [2010] EWHC 1882 (QB).
[85] cf Mitchell, Mitchell, and Watterson (n 7) 16-16.
[86] cf *Countrywide* (n 82) 349: 'Much of the difficulty is caused by attempting to categorise as an unjust enrichment of the defendant, for which an action in restitution is available, what is really a loss unfairly sustained by the plaintiff.'
[87] See, eg, Mitchell, Mitchell, and Watterson (n 7) chs 18–21 and 25.
[88] See, eg, Jonathan Hilliard, 'A Case for the Abolition of Legal Compulsion as a Ground of Restitution' (2002) 61 CLJ 551 and William Day 'Against Necessity as a Ground for Restitution' [2016] RLR 26.

purposes that, *if* they are unjust factors, then the relationship they have with contract must be conditioned by the nature of the policy underlying the claim rather than transplanting rules from other categories of unjust enrichment claim about the primacy of contract law.

The paradigm legal compulsion claim is where a guarantor makes a payment to a creditor in discharge of the primary obligor's debt. Having made payment to the creditor, the guarantor is then entitled to (1) rateable contribution from any co-guarantors, (2) recoupment of the entire amount from the primary debtor, and (3) subrogation to the rights of the creditor (such as any security) against the principal debtor. These claims in unjust enrichment (if that is what they are) exist *even though* there is a contractual basis for the primary debtor's enrichment. In making the payment that discharges the primary debtor's liability to the creditor, the guarantor has performed their own contractual obligations under the guarantee.[89] Indeed, if the guarantor were not contractually compelled to make payment to the creditor, there would be no right to contribution, recoupment, or subrogation as against the debtor. The contractual compulsion is therefore a necessary constituent of the claim.[90]

This is the very opposite of the general rule of subsidiarity as expressed in cases such as *Dargamo* and cannot be reconciled with it to the extent it is treated (per Virgo/Sumption) as an absolute general rule. And nor is it accurate to characterise this as some form of 'exception' (per Burrows/Mance): the alleged unjust enrichment in a claim for legal compulsion *only* exists if there was a contractual basis for the relevant enrichment: far from being exceptional, the existence of a valid and subsisting contract is foundational to the subsequent claim in unjust enrichment.

A similar point can be made in respect of many cases said to support restitutionary claims based on necessitous intervention. While most of the cases concern non-contractual relationships, where the claimants are bailees or fiduciaries such as agents and trustees (and may be so pursuant to a contract) the basic point is the same: the claims arise because the claimant has been required to act as a result of their existing relationship with the defendant. So, for example, a bailee is under a duty to take reasonable care of the bailed property.[91] That duty of care will always be engaged where circumstances require an intervention to protect or preserve the bailed property. The corollary is that the bailee has the right to recover any reasonable cost arising from complying with this duty. Again, the existence of a legal basis for the enrichment is foundational to the subsequent claim.

[89] This analysis received a mixed response from the judicial participants at the conference. Compare Lord Sales (ch 1) and Mr Justice Foxton (ch 8).

[90] See, eg, Mitchell, Mitchell, and Watterson (n 7) 20-02: 'The claimant must prove that he paid the third party pursuant to an existing legal obligation', adding by way of footnote that it 'is not enough for him to asset or concede the point'.

[91] See, eg, *Sutcliffe v Chief Constable of West Yorkshire* [1996] RTR 86 (CA) 90 (Otton LJ).

This is illustrated by *The Winson*.[92] That case concerned wheat on a ship stranded on a reef in the South China Sea that was rescued by salvors and stored at their cost in Manila. The salvors sought to recover that cost from the owners of the wheat. Lord Diplock found that a relationship of bailment existed and, referencing the core duty of care owed by the salvors *qua* bailees to the cargo owners *qua* bailors in relation to the wheat, held as follows:

> For any breach of such duty the bailee is liable to the bailor in damages for any diminution in the value of goods . . . and if he fulfils that duty he has, in my view, a correlative right to charge the owner of the goods with the expenses reasonably incurred in doing so.[93]

Lord Diplock found support for his view in *Great Northern Railway Co v Swaffield*.[94] There, the Court of Exchequer allowed the railway company to recover the cost of stabling the defendant's horse overnight. Pollock B held:

> It was the duty of the plaintiffs, as carriers, although the transit of the horse was at an end, to take such reasonable care of the horse as a reasonable owner would take of his own goods; and if they had turned him out on the highway, or allowed him to go loose, they would have been in default . . . If there were that duty without the correlative right [to charge the owner with the expenses reasonably incurred in so doing], it would be a manifest injustice.[95]

So, where there is a bailment relationship, the bailee is required to keep the bailed property out of harm's way and, correspondingly, the bailor is required to indemnify the bailee for his costs in so doing. Indeed, where the bailment relationship is for reward rather than gratuitous, this correlative right may even extend to remuneration for the services rendered and would likely be contractual in nature.[96] That should not preclude the claimant's ability to claim for the costs of intervention: the policy underpinning the claim still exists. Indeed, the existence of that obligation can be seen as essential for the subsequent claim in unjust enrichment.

V. Defective Intention Claims

The borderline between contract and claims in unjust enrichment reaches almost vanishing point when turning to 'defective intention' unjust enrichment claims.

92 [1982] AC 939 (HL).
93 ibid 960.
94 (1874) LR 9 Exch 132 (Ex).
95 ibid 137–38.
96 See, eg, *Guildford Borough Council v Hein* [2005] EWCA Civ 979 [51] (Clarke LJ).

These are cases which involve defendants precipitating a transaction by inducing a mistake in the claimant,[97] making an unlawful threat to the claimant,[98] or abusing their influence over the claimant.[99] In those circumstances, while there may be the appearance of an objective intention to effect the transaction, the law considers the claimant's actual intention to have been impaired and will not hold them to these transactions if they seek to undo them.[100] In these circumstances, defendants cannot seek to take advantage of the objective principle given their responsibility for the defective nature of the claimant's intention. In other words, these claims are available to ensure that parties' 'consent to the terms of the contract has been obtained fairly'.[101]

If the law of contract is defined to cover (as it normally is) not only the formation, content, and enforcement of contracts, but also the circumstances in which the contract can be set aside, these actions can simply be regarded as belonging to the law of contract. But even if these claims are kept on the unjust enrichment side of the borderline, there is no need for any freestanding rule barring the claim if there are subsisting contractual obligations. The very function of the unjust factor is to remove the contract: the ground for restitution is also a ground for rescission.

There are, however, two important ways in which these defective intention grounds for restitution and grounds for rescission are not entirely aligned. These are addressed in turn below.

A. Mistake Without Misrepresentation

A mistake-based claim does not always involve an *induced* mistake and, even if it were originally induced, the right to rescind for misrepresentation may have been lost in some way. This loss of ability (or inability) to set aside a contract for misrepresentation may not prevent a claim in restitution. Indeed, in the 'core case',[102] of a mistaken payment of a non-existent debt there is by definition no contract to set aside.

[97] cf *Hayward v Zurich Insurance Co plc* [2016] UKSC 48, [2017] AC 142 discussed further at text to n 107.

[98] cf lawful act duress as recognised in *Pakistan International Airlines Corp v Times Travel (UK) Ltd* [2021] UKSC 40, [2023] AC 101 criticised in William Day 'Duress and Uncertainty' (2022) 136 LQR 7.

[99] cf *Allcard v Skinner* (1887) 36 Ch D 145 (CA) where it is difficult to identify any abuse having taken place. However, the modern law of undue influence focuses on its abuse: *Royal Bank of Scotland v Etridge (No 2)* [2001] UKHL 44, [2002] 2 AC 773.

[100] See, eg, *Shogun Finance Ltd v Hudson* [2003] UKHL 62, [2004] 1 AC 919 [6]–[7]; *Cavendish Square Holding BV v Makdessi* [2015] UKSC 67, [2016] AC 1172 [13] (Lord Neuberger and Lord Sumption).

[101] *First Tower Trustees Ltd v CDS (Superstores International) Ltd* [2018] EWCA Civ 1396, [2019] 1 WLR 637 [104] (Leggatt LJ).

[102] Peter Birks, *Unjust Enrichment* (2nd edn, OUP 2005) ch 1.

On one view, it is the absence of a contractual (or other) entitlement to the payment in that core case that matters rather than fact of the mistake.[103] However, the better understanding of English law is that it is *combination* of both elements that matters: the absence of a legal basis is required in addition to, rather than instead of, any mistake. This is shown by the 'defence' of good consideration, which is available where the payment can be applied in discharge of some other debt.[104] Put another way, one person's mistake alone is not normally good enough to unwind contractual performance. This was recognised by Lord Hope in *Kleinwort Benson Ltd v Lincoln City Council*, where he said:

> Subject to any defences that may arise from the circumstances, a claim for restitution of money paid under a mistake raises three questions. (1) Was there a mistake? (2) Did the mistake cause the payment? And (3) did the payee have a right to receive the sum which was paid to him? . . . The third question arises because the payee cannot be said to have been unjustly enriched if he was entitled to receive the sum paid to him. The payer may have been mistaken as to the grounds on which the sum was due to the payee, but his mistake will not provide a ground for its recovery if the payee can show that he was entitled to it on some other ground.[105]

Thus, where there is a subsisting contract, and no misrepresentation, that lawful basis for the enrichment must then be removed through some other contractual doctrine, such as by successful invocation of the rules on common and unilateral mistake. However, unlike in the context of failure of consideration, terminating the contract will not suffice, because that does not remove the lawful basis of the performance already rendered. Although this has been expressed as the general rule that applies to all unjust enrichment claims, with an exception then developed for the availability of a failure of consideration claim brought after termination,[106] this exemplifies the over-generalisation of the Birksian approach. The more accurate and straightforward account of the law is that these defective intention claims simply have a different relationship with contracts than claims based on failure of consideration. Neither one provides a general rule for all claims in unjust enrichment, and neither one can fairly be described as the exception.

[103] See most recently Stevens (n 41) 71.

[104] *Barclays Bank Ltd v WJ Simms Son & Cooke (Southern) Ltd* [1980] QB 677 (Com Ct) 695 (Robert Goff J). See further Andrew Burrows, 'Is There a Defence of Good Consideration?' in Charles Mitchell and William Swadling (eds), *The Restatement Third: Restitution and Unjust Enrichment: Critical and Comparative Essays* (Hart 2013).

[105] [1999] 2 AC 349 (HL) 407–08.

[106] Text to n 50.

B. Misrepresentation Without Mistake

A claim to rescind for misrepresentation will not always involve a mistake, and so engage that orthodox ground for restitution. This is the effect of the Supreme Court's unfortunate decision in *Hayward v Zurich Insurance Co plc*.[107] Mr Hayward grossly and fraudulently exaggerated his injuries from a workplace accident. The employer's insurer, Zurich, never believed his claims.[108] However, concerned that the court would ultimately accept Mr Hayward's case at trial, it entered into a settlement with him. Later, Zurich obtained better evidence of Mr Hayward's true health, so it sought to rescind that agreement for misrepresentation.[109] In the Court of Appeal, the insurer's claim foundered. Briggs LJ concluded that:

> The authorities on rescission for misrepresentation speak with one voice. For a misstatement to be the basis for a claim to rescind a contract, the claimant must have given some credit to its truth, and been induced into making the contract by a perception that it was true rather than false.[110]

The Supreme Court reached the opposite conclusion. The Justices, led by Lord Clarke (Lord Toulson giving a concurring judgment), held that a mistaken belief was not 'necessary' as its own distinct requirement, but they accepted it could be 'very relevant' to causation, since the Court had to consider at that stage whether the misrepresentation had had an 'impact on the mind' of the claimant.[111] In *Zurich*, they said, it was sufficient for the insurer to show that the misrepresentation had impacted on its assessment of the risk in continuing with the litigation, and so had settled for £135,000 rather than something closer to £15,000. This meant that the misrepresentation claim could succeed, even though the insurer did not believe Hayward but merely thought there was a possibility that the judge at trial would accept his claims.[112] The Supreme Court was satisfied that the exaggerations regarding Mr Hayward's injuries had caused the insurer to settle for a much higher sum than otherwise would be the case. Accordingly, the settlement could be rescinded even though the misrepresentation had not been believed by the insurer.

In disagreeing with Briggs LJ, the Supreme Court placed considerable reliance on case law setting out the requirements for the tort of deceit, where mistake

[107] See also Paul Davies and William Day, 'A Mistaken Turn in the Law of Misrepresentation' [2019] LMCLQ 390.

[108] At first instance, it was found that 'neither' of the witnesses for Zurich Insurance 'can be said to have believed the representations complained of to be true': *Zurich Insurance Co plc v Hayward* (6 September 2013) [2.6] (HHJ Moloney QC).

[109] *Hayward* (n 97) [2]–[4], [9]–[10].

[110] [2015] EWCA Civ 327, [2015] 1 CLC 581 [28].

[111] *Hayward* (n 97) [18] and [29] (Lord Clarke).

[112] ibid [19] and [32] (Lord Clarke). See also [71] (Lord Toulson).

has never been a doctrinal requirement. There is nothing inherently wrong in reasoning by analogy with deceit, so long as care is taken,[113] but that is not what happened in *Zurich*. Instead, the Justices assumed (without explanation) that there should be no relevant difference on this point between a claim in tort and a claim for rescission.[114] In doing so, they did not engage with prior suggestions in the case law on rescission for misrepresentation that the latter claim was instead based on induced mistake.[115] As Lord Nicholls said in *Shogun Finance Ltd v Hudson*:

> The fact that [the claimant's] belief was induced by the other's fraudulent misrepresentation entitles him to repudiate the contract. His belief means there was a contract, but the fraudulent inducement of his belief means the contract is voidable.[116]

It is regrettable that the Supreme Court rejected the concept of misrepresentation as induced mistake. It provides the relevant bilateral justification for rescission.[117] The mistake explains why the claimant should be released, as the *dictum* from *Shogun Finance* quoted above makes clear. At the same time, the inducement of the mistake by the defendant explains why the defendant should be held responsible for the falsification of consent and so be disentitled to enforce the agreement. As Briggs LJ had recognised in the Court of Appeal in *Zurich*:

> The true principle is that the equitable remedy of rescission answers the affront to conscience occasioned by holding to a contract a party who has been influenced into making it by being misled or, worse still, defrauded by his counterparty.[118]

On this view, mistake is not just a *sufficient* condition for causation purposes but a *necessary* condition; it is by identifying a relevant mistake by the claimant for which the defendant is responsible that one can justify the departure from the usual position that contracts, once made, must be kept. The contrary decision of the Supreme Court in *Zurich* undermines this conceptual foundation for rescission for misrepresentation, without offering any alternative in its place.

The apparent relaxation of the requirements for misrepresentation in *Zurich* by removing mistake as a freestanding requirement also raises potentially significant implications for certainty and the security of contractual rights. However,

[113] *Derry v Peek* (1889) 14 App Cas 337 (HL) 359–60 (Lord Herschell).
[114] Davies and Day (n 107) 395–400.
[115] See, eg, *Edwards v M'Leay* (1818) 2 Swans 287, 289 (Lord Eldon LC); *Attwood v Small* (1838) 6 Cl & F 232 (HL); *Redgrave v Hurd* (1881) Ch D 1 (CA) 15–17, 21–22 (Sir George Jessell MR) and 23 (Baggallay LJ); *Peekay Intermark Ltd v Australia and New Zealand Banking Group Ltd* [2006] EWCA Civ 386, [2006] 2 Lloyd's Rep 511 [40] (Moore Bick LJ).
[116] *Shogun Finance* (n 100) [10].
[117] Davies and Day (n 107) 400–03.
[118] *Hayward* (n 97) [31].

its impact has been limited to 'three-party situations', where A contracts with B because of a concern that C will believe and act on B's misrepresentation. This distinction was first suggested by Nugee J in *Holyoake v Candy*,[119] and latterly by Foxton J in *School Facility Management Limited v Governing Body of Christ the King College*.[120] As put in the latter case, *Zurich* was 'a case in which the significance of the misrepresentation lay in the fact that the making of the misrepresentation might cause someone (in that case, a court) to believe that the matters asserted were true'. In 'paradigm'[121] two-party misrepresentation cases it therefore seems that induced mistake is still foundational for a claim for rescission, and so still aligned with the orthodox mistake-based ground for restitution.

VI. Conclusion

There is no single borderline or one general rule that governs the relationship between contract and unjust enrichment. The interaction between these two areas of the law varies depending on the particular reason for restitution invoked by the claim. Many of the leading cases on the boundary involve claims for failure of consideration or failure of basis but, once the ground for restitution is properly understood, there is no need for the subsidiarity rule that has been developed in that context: the process of construction avoids any border friction between contract and unjust enrichment. Nor should such a rule be transplanted to other contexts. For policy-motivated claims, any such read-across would be positively counterproductive: the relationship between such claims and contract should instead be informed by the policy underlying the claim. A subsidiarity rule is also probably unnecessary for defective intention claims, where grounds for rescission and restitution are nearly always coterminous and, subject to *Hayward*, should be so.

119 [2017] EWHC 3397 (Ch) [390]–[393].
120 [2020] EWHC 1118 (Comm) [400]–[401].
121 *Holyoake* (n 119) [390].

10
Unjust Enrichment | Equity

Graham Virgo

> By slow degrees the thoughts of our forefathers, their common thoughts about common things, will have become thinkable once more.[1]

I. Introduction: The Borderline between Equity and the Law of Unjust Enrichment

The notion of a borderline between Equity and the Law of Unjust Enrichment is fraught with conceptual difficulty, since like is not being compared with like. For, as Birks[2] correctly identified, it is logically impossible for there to be any friction between Equity and the Law of Unjust Enrichment, since, in his terms, unjust enrichment is an event and, not using his terms, Equity is a jurisdiction which ranks alongside the Common Law. The Law of Unjust Enrichment draws from both jurisdictional streams, albeit it is primarily a Common Law construct. Rather than there being a borderline between Equity and Unjust Enrichment, it is perhaps more accurate to analyse the relationship in terms of influence, one on the other.

But reflecting on the Equity/Unjust Enrichment borderline is useful, albeit artificial, since it enables old controversies to be approached in new ways. Unjust Enrichment can be used to explain and justify aspects of the equitable jurisdiction. For example, the court has an inherent equitable jurisdiction to authorise remuneration to trustees for exceptional services to the trust.[3] The legal basis for this jurisdiction has proved difficult to identify, both as regards its rationale and the method for assessing the award, but analysing it through the prism of Unjust Enrichment brings order and sense.[4] Unjust Enrichment can be used to provide

[1] Frederic Maitland, *Domesday: Domesday Book and Beyond* (CUP 1987) 520. These words are also inscribed on Maitland's memorial in Poets' Corner, Westminster Abbey.

[2] Peter Birks, 'Equity in the Modern Law: An Exercise in Taxonomy' (1996) 26 UWALR 1, 67.

[3] *Re Duke of Norfolk's Settlement Trust* [1982] Ch 61 (CA) 77 (Fox LJ).

[4] *Foster v Spencer* [1996] 2 All ER 672 (Ch). See Graham Virgo, *The Principles of Equity and Trusts* (5th edn, OUP 2023) 404.

Graham Virgo, *Unjust Enrichment | Equity* In: *Borderlines in Private Law*. Edited by: William Day and Julius Grower, Oxford University Press. © Graham Virgo 2024. DOI: 10.1093/9780191995200.003.0010

retrospective meaning to an established but incoherent jurisdiction, and can convert an uncertain discretion into a predictable right.[5]

Nevertheless, for some time there has been a sense amongst some judges and commentators that the young upstart 'Unjust Enrichment', created by the Common Law, is seeking to take over the long established principles of Equity and subvert them.[6] This has been expressed most powerfully by Gummow J, for example, in *Roxborough v Rothmans of Pall Mall Australia Ltd*,[7] a decision of the High Court of Australia, who said that the recognition of the unjust enrichment principle 'may distort well settled principles in other fields, including those respecting equitable doctrines and remedies, so that they answer the newly mandated order of things. Then various theories will compete, each to deny the others.'[8] In fact, the subjugation of Equity by Unjust Enrichment has not happened, either in Australia or in England. Much more concerning, since the formal recognition of Unjust Enrichment in England in 1991,[9] is a tendency to ignore the equitable influence on Unjust Enrichment, notably as regards the analysis of the justifications for recognising a distinct Law of Unjust Enrichment and the interpretation of reasons why an enrichment can be considered unjust: the grounds of restitution. Various explanations for this ignorance can be suggested, including: (1) poor scholarship, particularly as regards the origins of Equity and Unjust Enrichment; (2) desire for the assimilation of Equity into the Common Law; and (3) a failure to understand the capacity for the rich contribution of Equity to respond to contemporary legal problems.

The focus of this chapter will be on the actual and potential influence of Equity on the Law of Unjust Enrichment, as regards both the source of and rationale for its recognition and the interpretation of its constituent parts, notably the grounds of restitution (particularly lawful act duress), defences to claims, and available remedies. But at the heart of this chapter is a plea to both judge and commentator to reflect more carefully on the richness and complementarity of the Common Law and Equity jurisdictions. There should be no assumption that the way we did things in the past must be defended at all costs. We must be constantly aware of what value is being added by the way we think about private law. If Equity, or Unjust Enrichment for that matter, does not add value to our thinking about the law, we need to change what we think. But, as will be seen, after careful analysis the common thoughts of our forefathers should be thinkable once again.

[5] The language of unjust enrichment has also been used to justify the trustee's right to be indemnified by the trust fund for the discharge of liabilities incurred: *Equity Trust (Jersey) Ltd v Halabi* [2022] UKPC 36, [2023] AC 877 [69] (Lord Richards and Sir Nicholas Patten).

[6] In *Westdeutsche Landesbank Girozentrale v Islington LBC* [1996] AC 669 (HL) 685, Lord Goff acknowledged the tension between the aims and perceptions of 'restitution lawyers' and 'equity lawyers'.

[7] (2002) 185 ALR 335 (HCA).

[8] ibid 355.

[9] *Lipkin Gorman (a firm) v Karpnale Ltd* [1991] AC 548 (HL).

However, before these issues are examined, it is important to be clear as to what Unjust Enrichment and Equity are and are not.

II. What is Unjust Enrichment?

Unjust Enrichment is a category of different causes of action[10] which operate within the Law of Restitution, concerning the law of personal gain-based remedies. What connects these claims is the application of the formula[11] of the defendant being enriched, directly at the claimant's expense, in circumstances where a ground of restitution is recognised, where there is no lawful basis for the defendant's receipt, and where the defendant has no defence to the claim. Unjust Enrichment is distinct from other parts of the Law of Restitution, notably restitution for wrongs (where the wrong is the cause of action) and proprietary claims, regardless of whether the claimant seeks a proprietary[12] or personal remedy. Consequently, equitable claims for knowing receipt are not embraced by Unjust Enrichment, being proprietary in nature.[13]

Whilst the language of the old common counts continues to be used, such as money had and received and *quantum meruit*, these should not now be treated as distinct causes of action, but rather descriptors of the gain-based remedy available to reverse the defendant's unjust enrichment.

III. What is Equity?

It is appropriate to start with Maitland's underwhelming assessment:

> Equity is a certain position of our existing substantive law, and yet in order that we may describe this portion . . . we have to make reference to courts that are no longer in existence . . . The only alternative would be to make a list of the equitable rules and say that Equity consists of those rules . . . [However,] if we were to inquire what it is that all these rules have in common and what it is that makes them differ from all other rules administered by our courts, we should by way of answer

[10] *Attorney General of Trinidad and Tobago v Trinsalvage Enterprises Ltd* [2023] UKPC 26, [2023] 1 WLR 4045 [44] (Lord Burrows).

[11] *Banque Financière de la Cité v Parc (Battersea) Ltd* [1999] 1 AC 221 (HL) 227 (Lord Steyn). No lawful basis is implicit in that formula.

[12] *Foskett v McKeown* [2001] 1 AC 102 (HL). Whether the equitable remedy of subrogation should be explained by reference to unjust enrichment is considered in Section VIII. Compare the position in Canada where unjust enrichment can be reversed by means of a constructive trust: *Peters v Beblow* [1993] 1 SCR 980 (SCC).

[13] See *Byers v Saudi National Bank* [2023] UKSC 51, [2024] 2 WLR 237.

> find nothing but this, that these rules were until lately administered, and administered only, by our courts of equity.[14]

We can do better than this, and we can do so without needing to rely on the history of the old Equity courts which were abolished by the Judicature Act.

It is important first to distinguish between Equity and equity. The former is a body of substantive law which does derive from the old Equity courts. It is capitalised to distinguish it from the Common Law, with lower case common law referring to all judge-made law. But there is also a notion of (lower case) equity. This is not a body of substantive law, but a norm or a value originating from Roman law involving conceptions of justice.

Many jurists have sought to identify what Equity is. Lionel Smith[15] has correctly concluded that Equity does not have a single purpose, approach, philosophy, or norm, but provides 'an enduring conceptual toolkit': there is no single normative idea which underlies all of Equity.[16] Without seeking to be comprehensive, he has identified three norms of Equity relating to the performance of obligations, the depersonalisation of obligations, and elements of particular kinds of relationship which can generate new primary obligations. But none of these features seems particularly pertinent to the Law of Unjust Enrichment, where we are concerned with the creation of obligations in most cases regardless of the nature of the relationship between the parties. Smith's norms are particularly relevant to the trust and fiduciary duties, but neither has relevance to the imposition of liability for Unjust Enrichment.

But there is another view of the equitable cathedral, involving the identification of key attributes and values of Equity which may be of relevance to unjust enrichment.

A. Some Attributes of Equity

1. Supplementary flexibility

Equity exists to modify the harshness and rigidity of the Common Law,[17] so Equity depends on the existence of the Common Law to itself exist. Like mistletoe, it is parasitical, dependent on the existence of its host in order to survive. As Lord Briggs recognised in *Guest v Guest*:

[14] Frederic Maitland, *Equity: A Course of Lectures* (Alfred Chaytor and William Whittaker (eds), rev John Brunyate, 2nd edn, CUP 1936) 1.

[15] Lionel Smith, 'Equity is Not a Single Thing' in Dennis Klimchuk, Irit Samet, and Henry Smith (eds), *Philosophical Foundations of the Law of Equity* (OUP 2020) 144.

[16] ibid 146.

[17] *Vauxhall Motors Ltd v Manchester Ship Canal Co Ltd* [2019] UKSC 46, [2020] AC 1161 [63] (Lady Arden).

> One of the principal functions of equity is to put right injustice to which the law is otherwise blind, by restraining the rigid application of legal rules where their implementation would be unconscionable.[18]

Of course, this begs the questions as to why Equity is needed to do this and why the Common Law cannot cure the injustice itself.[19] The Common Law *can* do this. Indeed, the Law of Unjust Enrichment might itself be characterised as operating to modify the harshness and rigidity of the law of obligations, particularly the Law of Contract, by providing a remedy which is not otherwise available where justice demands one.[20]

Henry Smith has sought to justify the existence of Equity on the basis that it is 'Meta-law',[21] being 'Law about Law'[22] and having a second-order quality. However, there is nothing 'meta' about Equity. 'Meta' means 'beyond, above, [or] at a higher level'.[23] Yet Equity is not higher law.[24] A meta-discipline deals with ulterior issues in the same field. But that is most definitely not what Equity is about. Rather, it is an appendix to or a gloss on the Common Law.[25] It operates in parallel with rather than superior to the Common Law, and if we need to use a Greek prefix to describe Equity it would be better to call it 'para-law'.

However, despite his dubious use of Greek, Smith does provide an important defence of Equity as a supplement to the Common Law. Equity responds to problems of complexity and uncertainty and its existence enables the Common Law to be defined more simply and more generally.[26] The essence of Smith's thesis is that:

> Law provides general guidance over many cases in a simpler way. Equity bores in on specific problems and identified actors *ex post*, employing a great deal of contextual information. Law is a first cut at guiding behaviour, and equity is fine-tuning the *ex post* adjustment where the first cut doesn't work well.[27]

[18] [2022] UKSC 27, [2022] 3 WLR 911 [4].

[19] *Great Peace Shipping Ltd v Tsavliris Salvage Ltd* [2002] EWCA Civ 1407, [2003] QB 679 [156] (Lord Phillips).

[20] Which, in turn, raises the question of whether the recognition of Unjust Enrichment itself is an equitable response to Common Law injustice. This is examined in Section IV.

[21] Henry Smith, 'Equity as Meta-Law' (2021) 130 Yale LJ 1050. See also Robert Stevens, *The Laws of Restitution* (OUP 2023) 215.

[22] Smith, 'Equity as Meta-Law' (n 21) 1054.

[23] According to the entry in the Oxford English Dictionary.

[24] Even though, where there is a conflict between Law and Equity, the latter prevails: Senior Courts Act 1981, s 49(1). But this is a conflict-resolution mechanism which has rarely been deployed and, anyway, there should in principle be no conflict between the two, because Equity is a complementary jurisdiction. See generally Maitland, *Equity: A Course of Lectures* (n 14).

[25] Maitland, *Equity: A Course of Lectures* (n 14) 18; Jack Beatson, *The Use and Abuse of Unjust Enrichment* (OUP 1991) 246.

[26] Smith, 'Equity as Meta-Law' (n 21) 1071.

[27] ibid 1100.

A similar analysis has been advocated by Lady Arden in *Equity Trust (Jersey) Ltd v Halabi*:

> Equitable principles can apply flexibly because the function of equity is as a supplementary system of law, making exceptions and additions to the common law where equity considers it appropriate to do so.[28]

It is because of the existence of Equity, which is contextual and targeted in its operation, that the Common Law can be more formal and general which, as Smith recognises, is more efficient for creators and audiences of the legal rules,[29] especially since equitable intervention only occurs when Equity is needed. True, a homogeneous system would save 'the cost of toggling between the two modes, but it would tend towards some uniform level of formality'.[30]

2. Principled discretion

The key equitable attribute of flexibility of operation to secure justice has typically meant that the equitable jurisdiction is characterised as discretionary, but this does not mean that Equity is unprincipled. Discretion by its nature is guided by rational principles, so that a decision which is not susceptible to principled justification is not an exercise of discretion at all but involves the making of an arbitrary choice,[31] which would itself be a cause of injustice.[32] Modern Equity is founded on a framework of principles which purport to provide structure and predictability, but their application and the award of remedies can be tempered by the exercise of judicial discretion to secure a just and fair result.[33] A principle is a reason of general application.[34] These principles have emerged over time through the constant evolution of Equity and are continuing to develop. They typically constitute an external normative standard against which the defendant can be judged. The identification of principles is not unique to Equity, but it is the flexibility in their application which distinguishes the equitable regime. But this attribute does not describe all Equity; significant parts are rule-based without scope for flexible operation, particularly as regards the law of trusts and fiduciaries.[35]

In *Guest v Guest*,[36] Lord Leggatt identified three conditions for the recognition of judicial discretion in Equity, namely that the aim must be fixed in law and not

28 *Equity Trust* (n 5) [285].
29 Smith, 'Equity as Meta-Law' (n 21) 1100.
30 ibid.
31 Herbert Hart, 'Discretion' (2013) 127 Harv L Rev 652.
32 *Guest* (n 18) [161] (Lord Leggatt).
33 *Gavin Edmondson Solicitors Ltd v Haven Insurance Co Ltd* [2018] UKSC 21, [2018] 1 WLR 2052 [57] (Lord Briggs).
34 Simon Gardner, 'Ashworth on Principles' in Lucia Zedner and Julian Roberts (eds), *Principles and Values in Criminal Law and Criminal Justice: Essays in Honour of Andrew Ashworth* (OUP 2012) 9.
35 *Guest* (n 18) [164] (Lord Leggatt).
36 ibid [164]–[166].

left to the choice of the judge; the discretion must be necessary and structured; and the decision of the judge must be susceptible to audit, requiring reasons to be given for the exercise of the discretion. Framing the exercise of judicial discretion with reference to principles ensures that Equity is consistent with the rule of law.[37]

B. Some Values of Equity

The operation of Equity can be analysed in terms of 'aims'[38] or 'reasons',[39] but 'values' is more pertinent. There are a variety of values which can be identified, but two are of particular significance in the context of Unjust Enrichment claims.

1. Conscience

A vital value of Equity is that it responds to unconscionability; this is the 'universal talisman' that underpins Equity.[40] Gleeson CJ has said that the use of the word 'unconscionable' 'may be merely an emphatic method of expressing disapproval of someone's behavior, but its legal meaning is considerably more precise'.[41] However, identifying that precise legal meaning is not easy. Is unconscionability a state of mind or does it relate to a normative standard for evaluating conduct or is it simply what is morally or socially unacceptable?

The history of conscience in Equity is complex and uncertain.[42] Originally the conscience of the Chancellor was the measure of equity, referring to the individual moral judgement of the judge.[43] The focus then shifted to the assessment of the defendant's conscience, as determined by the court, but with reference to what the defendant knew or believed to be true, rather than what they believed to be morally right. Subsequently, through the development of a doctrine of precedent, categories of like cases were identified which were informed by past decisions and values, notably unconscionability. So, rather than seeking to identify unconscionability in each case, it was sufficient that a case fell within a particular category of liability, the existence of which could be justified by reference to the old language of conscience.[44] Here unconscionability operated as a matter of opinion, but one which had been 'formed and inferred by considered decisions in similar

[37] See generally Matthew Harding, 'Equity and the Rule of Law' (2016) 132 LQR 278.

[38] *Guest* (n 18) [164] (Lord Leggatt).

[39] *Equity Trust v Halabi* (n 5) [285] (Lady Arden).

[40] Anthony Mason, 'Themes and Prospects' in Paul Finn (ed), *Essays in Equity* (Thomson Reuters 1985) 44.

[41] *Australian Competition and Consumer Commission v CG Berbatis Holdings Pty Ltd* (2003) 214 CLR 51 (HCA) [7].

[42] See Dennis Klinck, 'The Unexamined "Conscience" of Contemporary Canadian Equity' (2001) 46 McGill LJ 571; Rohan Havelock, 'The Evolution of Equitable Conscience' (2014) 8 J Eq 128.

[43] Cristopher St German, *St German's Doctor and Student*, Theodore Plucknett and John Barton (eds) Selden Society, vol 91 (Selden Society 1974) 59.

[44] Chris Rossiter and Margaret Stone, 'The Chancellor's New Shoe' (1988) 11 UNSWLJ 11, 24.

but not identical cases, by the values of the community, that is by the palimpsest of past legal and community traditions'.[45]

Although unconscionability has been interpreted differently over the centuries, two different tests of conscience can be identified of significance today. First, conscience refers to the state of the defendant's mind, sometimes subjective but usually objectively assessed; it is a test of fault. This is consistent with the historical development of conscience in Equity: the court determines what the defendant's conscience should reasonably require them to do in light of the defendant's own awareness of the facts. Agnew considers that this use of the language of conscience explains how moral duties arise and identifies moral fault in the breach of these duties.[46] But the language of conscience can also relate to the judgment of the judge in assessing the defendant's conduct against a normative standard of behaviour; it is a construct of values and standards.[47] As Lord Sumption recognised: 'Good conscience . . . involves more than a judgment of the relative moral merits of the parties.'[48]

2. Responding to abuse

A core equitable value which is of particular relevance to the Law of Unjust Enrichment relates to Equity's concern to support claimants who have been taken advantage of by stronger defendants. Whether the advantage arises from abuse through fraud, through extortion, or the claimant being dependent on the defendant, Equity responds to exploitation by protecting the weaker party.[49]

C. The Assimilation of Law and Equity

Although the Judicature Acts 1873–75 fused the administration of Law and Equity into a single system, there was no assimilation of the substantive law. Yet are there still sufficient distinctive elements to justify the recognition of a separate body of substantive law which we can call Equity, or should it now be subsumed into the Common Law? Over the years many commentators have advocated some form of assimilation. Maitland,[50] for example, in the early twentieth century commended the Cambridge Law Tripos for not having Equity as a separate subject from real and personal property and contract and tort, noting that studying Equity as a

45 ibid 26. See also Paul Finn, 'Unconscionable Conduct' (1994) 8 JCL 37.

46 Sinead Agnew, 'The Meaning and Significance of Conscience in Private Law' (2018) 77 CLJ 479, 502.

47 William Gummow, *Change and Continuity: Statute, Equity, and Federalism* (OUP 1999) 44–51; Joachim Dietrich, 'Unjust Enrichment Versus Equitable Principles in England and Australia' in Jamie Glister and Pauline Ridge (eds), *Fault Lines in Equity* (Hart 2012) 10.

48 *Angove's Pty Ltd v Bailey* [2016] UKSC 47, [2016] 1 WLR 3179 [28] (Lord Sumption).

49 See Section VI.

50 Maitland, *Equity: A Course of Lectures* (n 14) 21.

system distinct from Law would have been 'a reactionary measure'. Having said that, it was the absence of Equity from the Law degree that motivated him to give his lectures on the subject and, subsequently, Equity was introduced as a distinct paper (which it still is).

The arguments for assimilation continue. Some have argued for significant assimilation,[51] others for a more pick and mix approach, either by preferring the perceived superior rule at Common Law or Equity, or blending the rules to develop a new set of hybrid rules.[52] There is, however, a danger that the rapid assimilation of rules which have existed for a long time will mean that the deep-rooted nuances and subtleties of the different parts of the law will be lost. Where there is no need for separate rules then assimilation is appropriate, but often the historical roots of the rules remain valid even today, and there may be other justifications for separate treatment.[53] Crucially, there is nothing inherently wrong with having dual systems,[54] and a proper understanding of Equity as a supplement to the Common Law, with specific attributes and values, justifies its continued recognition.

D. What Value Does Equity Add to Unjust Enrichment?

Why should it matter today whether a claim within the Law of Unjust Enrichment is equitable or is influenced by Equity? There has been a recent tendency to import equitable language into Common Law claims without obvious appreciation that this might also import other equitable apparatus, some of which might be unwelcome and require reconsideration of whether the initial equitable influence is appropriate. Five possible imports need to be considered.

1. Equitable principles

Recognising that an unjust enrichment claim is equitable means that the principles identified in Equity are applicable to determine the nature of the claim. The most significant of these to the Law of Unjust Enrichment will be the use of the language of conscience.

[51] Andrew Burrows, 'We Do This at Common Law but That in Equity' (2002) 22 OJLS 1; Sarah Worthington, *Equity* (2nd edn, OUP 2006) 4–6 and ch 10.

[52] Lusina Ho, 'Unjust Enrichment and Equity' in Elise Bant, Kit Barker, and Simone Degeling (eds), *Research Handbook on Unjust Enrichment and Restitution* (Edward Elgar 2020) 136.

[53] ibid 137. See further Graham Virgo, 'Restitution Through the Looking Glass: Restitution Within Equity and Equity Within Restitution' in J Getzler (ed), *Rationalizing Property, Equity and Trusts: Essays in Honour of Edward Burn* (LexisNexis 2003) 106.

[54] Lord Millett, 'Proprietary Restitution', in Simone Degeling and James Edelman (eds), *Equity in Commercial Law* (Law Book Co 2005) 309.

2. Equitable maxims

It is often forgotten that the equitable maxims will be applicable if the claim is characterised as equitable.[55] The identity and function of these maxims remains controversial, as is their purpose.[56] They can be regarded as a synthesis of a complex body of law and so could be treated as functioning as principles, but they tend to be more generalised in ambit and so should be kept distinct. Significant examples include: 'Those who seek equity must do equity', 'Those who come to Equity must come with clean hands', and 'Equity assists the diligent'.

3. Equitable defences and bars

If a claim is characterised as equitable it should follow that the defences which are peculiar to Equity will be applicable. This has long been recognised for the equitable remedy of rescission, which is defeated by bars which are interpreted differently in Equity than at Common Law. Further, the defence of laches will apply if the claim is equitable.[57]

4. Equitable remedies

As will be seen later,[58] the impact of Equity on restitutionary remedies to reverse unjust enrichment has been minimal. Equitable remedies, such as specific performance and injunctions, are generally available regardless of the nature of the claim, albeit their equitable foundation influences their operation. These remedies, however, have little impact in the context of unjust enrichment claims.

5. Equitable thinking

Lord Millett has described Equity as 'not a set of rules but a state of mind'.[59] This lays Equity open to the criticism that it is vague and incoherent. But there is some truth in what Lord Millett recognised. Equity is different from the Common Law because of both the mindset of Equity and the language that is used, language which constitutes a useful shorthand for particular ways of thinking about the operation of the law. As we will see, the shifting of equitable language into the Common Law without acknowledging its pedigree is more likely to result in charges of vagueness and inconsistency. This is not to argue that Equity has no role in traditional Common Law claims, but to emphasise that when Equity operates within those claims, and specifically within Unjust Enrichment, it is important to be aware that

[55] This is particularly significant in Smith's analysis of Equity: Smith, 'Equity as Meta-Law' (n 21).
[56] See William Swadling, 'The Mischief of Maxims' in S Elliott and B McFarlane (eds), *Equity Today* (Hart 2023) Ch 5.
[57] See Section VII.B.
[58] See Section VIII.
[59] Lord Millett, 'The Common Lawyer and the Equity Practitioner' in Daniel Clarry (ed), *The UK Supreme Court Yearbook*, vol 6: *2014–2015 Legal Year* (Appellate Press 2015) 175.

these claims might then be characterised as equitable such that the apparatus of Equity will also be imported.

IV. The Influence of Equity on the Recognition of Unjust Enrichment

The influence of Equity on what is now the Law of Unjust Enrichment can be traced back to the fifteenth century when the Chancery courts emerged.[60] As the writs of debt and detinue at Common Law became narrower, Equity provided a remedy where, for example, the purpose of a gift had failed and the transferor sought to recover it, and, even if an action for money had and received was available at Common Law, for property transferred by mistake, fraud, or duress.

In 1760, Lord Mansfield in *Moses v Macferlan*[61] sought to rationalise the action for money had and received to the use of the claimant with explicit reference to equitable language. Indeed, he called it an 'equitable action' which lay for 'money which, *ex aequo et bono*' the defendant was 'obliged by the ties of natural justice and equity' to refund. In *Clark v Shee*,[62] he described it as a 'liberal action in the nature of a bill in equity'. In *Straton v Rastall*,[63] Buller J went beyond merely drawing an analogy with Equity and recognised that the claimant had to show that he had 'equity and conscience on his side, and that he could recover it in a Court of Equity'. This would have had practical implications, such as the fact that the claim would not depend on written pleadings and that it would not have been necessary to state special circumstances to establish it. In the nineteenth century, whilst some cases considered that the action for money had and received involved technical Equity,[64] others recognised that the action was legal and that the notion that it was equitable had been exploded.[65] Subsequently, references to Equity emerged intermittently. For example, in *Banque Financière de la Cité v Parc (Battersea) Ltd*,[66] Lord Clyde described an unjust enrichment claim as equitable in the sense of seeking to secure a fair and just determination of the rights, but emphasised that it did not follow that it was entirely discretionary in its application.

Whether Lord Mansfield was referring to equity or Equity remains a matter of some controversy. At the turn of the twentieth century the general view was that

[60] See generally David Ibbetson, 'Development at Common Law' in Bant, Barker, and Degeling (eds), *Research Handbook on Unjust Enrichment and Restitution* (n 52) 30.

[61] (1760) 2 Burr 1005, 1012. The actual decision in the case, which set aside the judgment of a competent court otherwise than by appeal, was not followed later: *Marriott v Hampton* (1797) 7 Term Rep 269.

[62] (1774) 1 Cowp 197, 199–200. See also *Jestons v Brooke* (1778) 2 Cowp 793.

[63] (1788) 2 Term Rep 366, 370.

[64] *Rogers v Ingham* (1876) 3 Ch D 351 (CA) 355 (James LJ).

[65] *Miller v Atlee* (1849) 3 Ex 799 (Pollock CB), cited by Lord Sumner in *Sinclair v Brougham* [1914] AC 398 (HL) 456.

[66] [1999] 1 AC 221 (HL) 237.

the reference to 'equity' was not to that body of law administered in the Chancery Division[67] but to the *jus naturale* of Roman law and the idea of what was fair and reasonable.[68] This was even expressly identified as a Common Law principle of 'justice and equity'.[69] Ibbetson[70] considers that Lord Mansfield was unlikely to be seeking to replicate what was happening in Chancery and was influenced instead by Roman law as understood in the seventeenth and eighteenth centuries.[71] Kremer considers that Lord Mansfield was seeking to identify a rationale for the action for money had and received, which drew on equitable notions but was not intended to be equitable in the strict sense:[72] 'The result was very much an action at common law, but one whose determinant invoked principles analogous to those found in technical equity.'[73]

But whilst Lord Mansfield's use of 'equity' may not have been transplanted from the Chancery jurisdiction, the equitable influence is deeper, especially as regards the role of conscience. In various judgments, Lord Mansfield referred to the defendant's retention of a gain being against conscience,[74] and this plainly derived from Chancery.[75] The significance of conscience was emphasised subsequently. In *Fibrosa Spolka Akcyjna v Fairbairn Lawson Combe Barbour Ltd*,[76] Lord Wright, in an influential *dictum*, said of unjust enrichment that a civilised system of law should 'prevent a man from retaining the money of or some benefit derived from another which it is against conscience that he should keep'.

Even in *Lipkin Gorman (a firm) v Karpnale Ltd*[77] Lord Goff explicitly related the defendant's unjust enrichment to Lord Mansfield's contention that it would be against conscience for the defendant to retain the money in such circumstances. Since 1991 the language of conscience has been rarely[78] used in England when examining unjust enrichment,[79] and sometimes unconscionability has been specifically rejected as the basis for recognising unjust enrichment.[80] This can be

[67] *Sinclair* (n 65) 417 (Viscount Haldane LC), 454–56 (Lord Sumner).

[68] *Bradford Corporation v Ferrand* [1902] 2 Ch 655 (Ch) 662–63 (Farwell J); *Baylis v Bishop of London* [1913] 1 Ch 127 (CA) 137 (Farwell LJ).

[69] *Royal Bank of Canada v R* [1913] AC 283 (PC) 296 (Viscount Haldane LC).

[70] Ibbetson, 'Development at Common Law' (n 60) 34.

[71] David Ibbetson, 'Unjust Enrichment and Lord Mansfield' in Harry Dondorp, Martin Schermaier, and Boudewijn Sirks (eds), *De Rebus Divinis et Humanis: Essays in Honour of Jan Hallebeek* (V&R unipress 2019) 193. In 'An Essay on the Action for Money Had and Received' (1802) reprinted [1998] RLR 1, 4 Sir William Evans referred to the 'general principles of natural equity'.

[72] Ben Kremer, 'Equity and the Common Courts' in John Goldberg, Henry Smith, and Peter Turner (eds), *Equity and Law: Fusion and Fission* (CUP 2019) 203.

[73] ibid 205.

[74] *Moses v Macferlan* (1760) 2 Burr 1007, 1011; *Sadler v Evans* (1766) 4 Burr 1984, 1986; *Clarke v Shee* (1774) 1 Cowp 197, 199.

[75] Kremer, 'Equity and the Common Courts' (n 72) 223.

[76] [1943] AC 32 (HL) 61. See also *Kelly v Solari* (1841) 9 M and W 54, 58 (Parke B).

[77] *Lipkin Gorman* (n 9).

[78] See eg *Vedatech Corp v Crystal Decisions (UK) Ltd* [2002] EWHC 818 (Ch) [74] (Jacob J).

[79] It has been more common when defining particular grounds of restitution. See Sections V and VI.

[80] *Criterion Properties v Stratford UK Properties* [2004] UKHL 28, [2004] 1 WLR 1846 [4] (Lord Nicholls).

contrasted with Australia where 'legal principles of restitution or unjust enrichment can be equated with seminal notions of good conscience'.[81] In fact, the dominant view in Australia is to reject unjust enrichment as having a unifying role and instead justify restitutionary claims, for example for mistaken payments, specifically on the ground of unconscientious retention,[82] with unconscionability being assessed by reference to 'a construct of standards and values'.[83]

Where does this leave the Law of Unjust Enrichment in England? Whilst the justification for the recognition of this body of law appears to be equitable rather than Equitable, does the reference to conscience add any value? Since the recognition of unjust enrichment was first mooted, the justification for imposing strict liability has proved contentious. It is clear that, whilst unjust enrichment cannot constitute its own self-fulfilling justification for the award of a restitutionary remedy, perhaps the justification has been there all along in the form of conscience. Birks was particularly critical of the role of conscience within the Law of Unjust Enrichment. He said:

> There is no future for the gut reaction, nor for any form of mystical 'experience' which inarticulately claims the right to trump good intellectual order ... Conscience of the intuitive kind is ... antithetical to the rule of law.[84]

But the jurisprudence is only vague if justice is the sole criterion for determining liability; and it is not. Unjust enrichment provides the legal framework as to when liability will be imposed, but it is conscience which provides the justification. Fairness as a justification for restitution has been acknowledged by Priel,[85] who cites Kahneman and others who said: '[t]he cardinal rule of fair behavior is surely that one person should not achieve gain by simply imposing an equivalent loss on another'.[86]

This is far too vague to provide a structure for judicial reasoning and evaluation, but why cannot fairness provide the normative justification for the recognition of Unjust Enrichment? It is this notion of fairness which imbued the old language of conscience. If you have received something from me in circumstances where I did

[81] *Australian Financial Services and Leasing Pty Ltd v Hills Industries Ltd* [2014] HCA 14 (HCA) [16] (French CJ).

[82] Including *Roxborough v Rothmans of Pall Mall Australia Ltd* (2002) 185 ALR 335 (HCA) 355 (Gummow J); also *Australian Financial Services and Leasing Pty Ltd v Hills Industries Ltd* [2014] HCA 14. See also Joachim Dietrich, *Restitution: A New Perspective* (Federation Press 1998); Ian Jackman, *The Varieties of Restitution* (2nd edn, Federation Press 2017).

[83] *Australian Financial Services and Leasing* (n 82) [83]. Note also *Lampson (Australia) Ltd v Fortescue Metals Group (No 3)* [2014] WASC 2 [50], where Edelman J considered that unconscionability provided the normative basis for liability in unjust enrichment.

[84] Peter Birks, 'Equity, Conscience and Unjust Enrichment' (1999) 23 MULR 1, 21.

[85] Dan Priel, 'In Defence of Quasi-Contract' (2012) 75 MLR 54.

[86] Daniel Kahneman, Jack Knetsch, and Richard Thaler, 'Fairness as a Constraint on Profit Seeking: Entitlement in the Market' (1986) 76 Am Ec Rev 728, 731.

not intend you to have it then it is only fair that you should pay for it, save if your circumstances have changed as a consequence of the receipt of the enrichment. If you do not pay for it, then it is entirely appropriate for us to call that unconscionable.

But if we are going to rely on unconscionability to justify the award of a restitutionary remedy to reverse unjust enrichment, what do we mean by it? It is clear that unconscionability in the sense of fault on the part of the defendant has no role in unjust enrichment, but what about the other sense of a normative standard of behaviour? Where the elements of unjust enrichment can be established, we can conclude that it would be morally unacceptable for the defendant not to make restitution; a moral duty to make restitution is imposed.[87] But this is only acceptable as a rationale for restitution rather than having substantive effect. Where unconscionability is used instead as an element of the claim, as will be discussed in the next two sections, it is insufficient to rely on conscience without identifying the particular values and standards which underpin it.[88]

Whilst some commentators and judges are searching around for new normative justifications for the Law of Unjust Enrichment, the original foundations of that law have been ignored. It is consequently entirely appropriate to assert, as the Australians have done, that restitutionary liability is founded on unconscionable retention, but this is not sufficient in its own right to explain when liability will be imposed. The Law of Unjust Enrichment does that work. Birks said that conscience is like the fifth wheel on a coach[89] and can consequently be ignored. But the fifth wheel always served a purpose; it was needed if one of the wheels of the coach was broken. There is a danger that some of the wheels on the coach of unjust enrichment are broken, or at least are not strong enough to keep the coach moving. So now is the time to reinstate the language of conscience as the justification for the recognition of unjust enrichment. There are dangers in this, of course, since using the language of conscience and unconscionability might be treated as an invitation to the judge to determine liability in an arbitrary way. But that can be avoided by using the unjust enrichment formula to establish that the defendant's receipt and retention of the value of an enrichment is unconscionable. It is unjust enrichment which provides the beating heart of the claim, but it is conscience which justifies its existence. As Kremer recognised:[90]

> Conscience is used as a concept to underlie and structure the operation of an area of the law; it provides a generative, basal principle which is in turn used to construct rules . . . It is those rules which are applied judicially in determining a

[87] Agnew (n 46) 493.
[88] Ho, 'Unjust Enrichment and Equity' (n 52) 129.
[89] Peter Birks, 'Receipt' in Peter Birks and Arianna Pretto (eds), *Breach of Trust* (Hart 2002) 226.
[90] Ben Kremer, 'The Action for Money Had and Received' (2001) 17 JCL 93, 107.

> dispute. Conscience is thus not a determinant; it is a reference concept, a purpose, which is used to generate determinants.

Conscience is a value and by reinvigorating conscience as developed by Lord Mansfield, the thoughts of our forefathers will become thinkable once more.

V. Lawful Act Duress: A Case Study

In *Times Travel (UK) Ltd v Pakistan International Airlines Corp*,[91] the Supreme Court unanimously recognised the doctrine of lawful act economic duress as both a ground of restitution and reason for rescission. It also acknowledged that the doctrine would only apply in very exceptional circumstances. Lawful act duress was expressly identified as forming part of the Common Law doctrine of duress, yet the Court was influenced by equitable doctrines, notably undue influence, when formulating the criteria for lawful act duress, relied on the equitable language of conscience, and (in doing so) transplanted equitable values into a Common Law doctrine. Unfortunately, it ignored the need to be cognisant of the equitable apparatus which could be imported as well, and this has resulted in a weak and confusing doctrine. The Court's decision therefore provides a clear example of what happens when Equity is not respected.

The majority recognised that, exceptionally, a threat to perform a lawful act can be illegitimate if it involves reprehensible or unconscionable conduct which renders the enforcement of the contract unconscionable. But Lord Hodge, who gave the leading judgment, provided no definition of unconscionability, leaving it to be deduced from earlier decisions. The Justices[92] emphasised the importance of clarity and certainty in commercial law and for that reason they did not want the doctrine of lawful act duress to be drawn too widely. The majority acknowledged that unconscionability was an equitable concept[93] which involves a high standard of impropriety.[94] Indeed, a subsequent decision of the Supreme Court recognised that *Times Travel* had placed 'renewed emphasis on the link between duress and equitable doctrines, particularly the concept of unconscionability'.[95] It appears that what is needed is conduct which takes the matter outside of ordinary contractual dealings, such that the defendant is abusing rights through the dishonest assertion

[91] [2021] UKSC 40, [2023] AC 101.
[92] ibid [1(v)] (Lord Hodge), approving the approach of Lord Burrows.
[93] ibid [20].
[94] ibid [22] (Lord Hodge).
[95] *The Law Debenture Trust Corp plc v Ukraine* [2023] UKSC 11, [2023] 2 WLR 699 [141] (Lords Reed, Lloyd-Jones, and Kitchin). Note also ibid [166]: 'the relevant standard is one of unconscionability, drawing on the case law through which that concept has developed in the English law of equity'.

of entitlements, for example by asserting entitlements which the defendant knows do not exist.[96]

The majority were strongly influenced in their recognition of lawful act duress by the equitable jurisdiction where lawful threats have exceptionally been regarded as sufficient to establish a ground of restitution. This jurisdiction was analysed as forming part of the equitable doctrine of undue influence, but that doctrine depends on there being a relationship of influence, which is not necessarily a requirement for equitable intervention. For that reason, the equitable doctrine was preferably treated as distinct and characterised as relating to 'unconscionable bargains', although it is better described as 'undue pressure' to distinguish it from the distinct doctrine of 'unconscionable bargain'.[97] The Supreme Court correctly acknowledged that this equitable doctrine is reflected in a line of cases where the defendant threatened to report a crime or initiate a prosecution[98] against the claimant or a close family member of the claimant, and the claimant paid money to the defendant or entered into a contract with the defendant as a result; the money could be recovered or the contract set aside in Equity. This has been explicitly justified by virtue of Equity's response to unfair advantage being taken of inequality between the parties,[99] and as operating in Equity because lawful threats are not sufficient to establish duress at Common Law.[100] Now that such threats have been recognised as establishing duress, it appears that the equitable doctrine of undue pressure has been assimilated within the Common Law doctrine of duress.[101]

Was the Supreme Court right to recognise that threats of lawful acts should be sufficient to vitiate contracts or secure restitution and, if so, should this be done at Common Law or in Equity, or does it not matter? The reliance on unconscionability, with the explicit recognition that this was an equitable concept, is a cause for concern. Significantly, Lord Hodge said:[102]

> Unconscionability is not an overarching criterion to be applied across the board without regard to context. Were it so, judges would become arbiters of what is morally and socially acceptable. Equity takes account of the factual and legal context of a case and has identified specific contexts which call for judicial intervention to protect the weaker party.

[96] [2021] UKSC 40, [2023] AC 101 [44] (Lord Hodge).

[97] See Section VI. The phrase 'undue pressure' was used by Lord Chelmsford in *Williams v Bayley* (1866) LR 1 HL 200 (HL) 214 and by Lord Denning MR in *Lloyd's Bank Ltd v Bundy* [1975] QB 326 (CA) 338.

[98] *Williams* (n 97)); *Kaufman v Gerson* [1904] 1 KB 591 (CA); *Société des Hôtels Réunis v Hawker* (1913) 29 TLR 578 (KB).

[99] *Williams* (n 97) 216 (Lord Chelmsford).

[100] *Mutual Finance Ltd v John Wetton and Sons Ltd* [1937] 2 KB 389 (KB) 395 (Porter J).

[101] *Times Travel* (n 91) [9] (Lord Hodge).

[102] ibid [23].

But without providing any meat on the bones of unconscionability, there is a danger that judges will indeed become arbiters of what they consider to be morally and socially acceptable.

In fact, analysis of *Times Travel* and a small number of earlier cases indicates that there was a much more straightforward solution to this problem. In *Times Travel*, it was held that the defendant had not acted unconscionably, because it did not believe that it was liable for breach of contract as a result of its failure to pay commission.[103] Further, the defendant had not used reprehensible means to manoeuvre the claimant into a position of increased vulnerability in order to exploit that vulnerability. Rather, the defendant was engaged in hard-nosed commercial negotiations which legitimately exploited its position as a monopoly supplier.

In two earlier cases[104] where lawful act duress was established, there were findings of unlawful threats, or, at the very least, unlawful activity which contextualised the later lawful threats since they were part of the same chain of events,[105] which rendered the whole of the defendant's conduct unlawful. It should have been possible to recognise this as establishing unlawful act economic duress and without needing to rely on the language of unconscionability. The recognition of lawful act compulsion should have been confined to the equitable doctrine of undue pressure, where equitable principles and values legitimately operate to protect weaker parties from abuse by stronger ones. This would have enabled the Common Law to maintain its strict and rigid approach to duress, depending on proof of unlawful threats.[106] The Supreme Court has instead assimilated equitable principles and values into the Common Law, resulting in uncertainty as to when lawful threats should constitute duress. It is also unclear whether the incorporation of the language of conscience also brings in other parts of Equity, such as the maxims and defences. It is one thing to recognise equitable grounds of restitution as operating within the Law of Unjust Enrichment; it is a very different matter to characterise a ground of restitution as operating within the Common Law but use equitable language to define it. This blending results in confusion for all; it undermines the Justices' desire to ensure that the law is certain, especially in the commercial sphere,[107] and it was unnecessary.

The recognition of lawful act duress as a Common Law doctrine was an error. Rather, the Court should have recognised the distinct equitable doctrine of undue pressure which applies where the defendant has obtained a benefit as a result of

[103] ibid [58] (Lord Hodge).

[104] *Borelli v Ting* [2010] UKPC 21 and *Progress Bulk Carriers Ltd v Tube City IMS LCC* [2012] EWHC 273 (Comm).

[105] William Day, 'Duress and Uncertainty' (2022) 138 LQR 194, 196.

[106] As is the position in Australia: *Australia and New Zealand Banking Corp v Karam* [2005] NSWCA 344.

[107] Jonathan Morgan, 'The Thin Edge of the Wedge: Morality, Contract Law and Lawful Act Duress' (2022) 81 CLJ 17.

lawful threats,[108] but only where the defendant's conduct is characterised as unconscionable; this would have enabled the Common Law to hold firm. This is, after all, why we have Equity.

VI. Equitable Grounds of Restitution

Equity has had a significant influence on the development of grounds of restitution within the modern Law of Unjust Enrichment. Three types of influence can be identified.

A. Equity as Trailblazer

Equity sometimes led the Common Law in recognising reasons for restitution which were not accepted at Law until much later. For example, mistake of law relating to rights was a reason for restitution in Equity[109] long before mistake of law was recognised as a general ground of restitution.[110] Equity also led the way in providing a remedy despite the taint of illegality where the parties were not *in pari delicto*,[111] even where the basis for the underlying transaction had not failed.[112]

B. Equitable Grounds

There are established grounds of restitution which are creatures of Equity both in terms of origin and how they are interpreted today. In particular, undue influence is recognised as an equitable doctrine[113] which operates to prevent unjust enrichment,[114] where the defendant has abused a relationship of dependency with the claimant.[115] Whilst the recognition of this ground has been justified with reference to the defendant's unconscionable conduct,[116] it can also be justified as responding

[108] This doctrine applies beyond the cases recognised by the Supreme Court involving threats to invoke the criminal process, to encompass abuse of civil process (*Unwin v Leaper* (1840) 1 Man and G 747) and threats to publish information (*Norreys v Zeffert* [1939] 2 All ER 187 (KB)). These are all cases where Equity considered the defendant to have abused the claimant's weaker position by lawful threats.

[109] *Cooper v Phibbs* (1867) LR 2 HL 149 (HL) 164 (Lord Cranworth).

[110] *Kleinwort Benson Ltd v Lincoln City Council* [1999] 2 AC 349 (HL).

[111] *Osborne v Williams* (1811) 18 Ves Jun 379.

[112] *Cole v Gibson* (1750) 1 Ves Sen 503. See now *Patel v Mirza* [2016] UKSC 42, [2017] AC 467.

[113] *Dunbar Bank plc v Nadeem* [1998] 3 All ER 876 (Ch) 884 (Millett J).

[114] *Hart v Burbidge* [2014] EWCA Civ 992 [43] (Vos LJ). Undue influence has also been described as an 'equitable wrong': *Yorkshire Bank plc v Tinsley* [2004] EWCA Civ 816, [2004] 1 WLR 2380, 2389 (Peter Gibson LJ).

[115] *Royal Bank of Scotland plc v Etridge (No 2)* [2002] 2 AC 773 (HL) 795 (Lord Nicholls).

[116] *Dunbar Bank* (n 113) 884 (Millett J).

to the quality of the claimant's consent in transferring an enrichment to the defendant;[117] this is consistent with other Common Law grounds of restitution and raises the question as to whether the equitable origin of undue influence matters today. But the policy of protecting the vulnerable from exploitation by those who are in a stronger position[118] reflects equitable values, and the conditions for establishing this ground are such that the influence of Equity on the interpretation of the ground remains significant.[119] Consequently, this should be treated as an equitable claim operating within the Law of Unjust Enrichment.

Even clearer as an equitable ground of restitution is that of unconscionable bargain, which does not depend on the identification of a relationship of dependency between the parties, but applies where the defendant has unconscionably exploited their superior bargaining position to the detriment of the claimant who is in a weaker position.[120] Whilst unconscionability is at the core of this ground of restitution, clear criteria can be identified as to when it will be established, involving inequality between the parties such that the claimant is unable to exercise an independent judgement, unconscionable conduct on the part of the defendant involving bad faith,[121] and significant imbalance in the substance of the transaction to the disadvantage of the weaker party.

C. Equity Supplementing the Common Law

There is a final category of grounds of restitution which purports to operate within the structure of the Common Law of Unjust Enrichment, but where the ground is buttressed by the incorporation of equitable thinking and in circumstances where, at best, the use of equitable language does not add value, and, at worst, it creates significant confusion by not recognising what comes with the use of that language. Lawful act duress is one example, but so is restitution of mistaken gifts. The Common Law jurisdiction for restitution for mistake depends on proof that, but for the claimant's mistake, the enrichment would not have been transferred.[122] In parallel with this is an equitable jurisdiction to set aside mistaken voluntary dispositions to or from a trust.[123] The conditions for triggering the equitable jurisdiction are stricter than at Common Law, requiring proof of an operative mistake

[117] *Nature Resorts Ltd v First Citizen Bank Ltd* [2022] UKPC 10, [2022] 1 WLR 2788 [10] (Lords Briggs and Burrows).

[118] *Royal Bank of Scotland* (n 115) 795 (Lord Nicholls).

[119] *CIBC Mortgages plc v Pitt* [1994] 1 AC 200 (HL) 209 (Lord Browne-Wilkinson).

[120] *Earl of Chesterfield v Janssen* (1751) 2 Ves Sen 125, 157 (Lord Hardwicke); *Times Travel* (n 91) [77] (Lord Burrows). This is distinct from the doctrine of 'undue pressure' which requires proof of a lawful threat. See Section V.

[121] *Hart v O'Connor* [1985] AC 1000 (PC) 1028 (Lord Brightman).

[122] *Kleinwort Benson* (n 110).

[123] *Pitt v Holt* [2013] UKSC 26, [2013] 2 AC 108.

which was of sufficient gravity and, as Lord Walker recognised, this is 'to be assessed in terms of injustice—or, to use equity's cumbersome but familiar term, unconscionability'.[124]

However, this equitable jurisdiction is tentatively being extended to unjust enrichment claims which would otherwise be covered by the Common Law,[125] but without any consideration as to whether a stricter test is justified, or, assuming it is, whether and how the test of unconscionability should be applied. In *Fattal v Fattal*,[126] the equitable jurisdiction was even considered to be applicable where the claimant had transferred property to the defendant in the mistaken belief that the defendant had already paid for it. But this had not been intended to be a voluntary disposition since the mistake related to payment, and consequently *Pitt v Holt* should not have been applicable.[127] Further, in *Middleton v Middleton Enterprises (Holdings) Ltd*,[128] the equitable doctrine was extended to rescind a loan (albeit for no interest) on the ground that the making of the loan was motivated by a desire to avoid taxation but had actually incurred a significant inheritance tax liability. But a loan cannot sensibly be analysed as a voluntary transaction and this also involved an unnecessary extension of the equitable jurisdiction.

This is a mess, largely because of a failure to consider carefully the underlying policy objectives. It has sometimes[129] been acknowledged that something more than a causative mistake is required before a gift can be recovered, although the reasons for this have not been clearly articulated.[130] In *Pitt v Holt* itself, although Lord Walker was reluctant to commit to there being generally a narrower test of mistake for restitution of gifts,[131] the tenor of his analysis is at least consistent with the application of the serious mistake test to restitution of gifts at Common Law, perhaps because of the need to protect the security of the donee's receipt where the claimant has voluntarily transferred the benefit without thinking that they were under a liability to do so. But that is not a convincing reason for a distinct test of mistake for gifts. Stricter tests of mistake are adopted to set aside a contract for mistake or to rescind a deed. This can be justified on the ground that it should be more difficult to regard the claimant's intention to enter into such transactions as vitiated, because they are significant legal instruments which should only be set aside where the mistake is particularly potent. But this reason does not apply where the claimant has simply made a gift without using a deed. Further, no consideration

[124] ibid [124] (Lord Walker).

[125] *Pagel v Farman* [2013] EWHC 2210 (Comm), [2013] WTLR 1575; *Spaul v Spaul* [2014] EWCA Civ 679 [52] (Rimer LJ).

[126] [2022] EWHC 950 (Ch).

[127] Henderson J had earlier recognised that the equitable jurisdiction is not engaged where the transaction was not voluntary: *Mackay v Wesley* [2020] EWHC 1215 (Ch) [139].

[128] Unreported, Chancery Division, 20 March 2022.

[129] *Deutsche Morgan Grenfell v IRC* [2006] UKHL 49, [2007] 1 AC 558 [87] (Lord Scott).

[130] Although Hang Tang, 'Restitution for Mistaken Gifts' (2004) 20 JCL 1 sought to do so.

[131] [2013] UKSC 26, [2013] 2 AC 108 [126].

has been given to why the equitable test of unconscionability is appropriate when assessing whether a mistaken gift can be recovered, nor to how this would or should be applied. No equitable values are in play and, consequently, this is a context where there is no need for any equitable influence.

VII. Defences

It is in the context of defences that the influence of Equity on the Law of Unjust Enrichment is especially significant, both as regards the influence of equitable language and thinking on the formulation of defences to unjust enrichment claims, and as regards the identification of defences which are characterised as equitable and which will be applicable if the claim can likewise be characterised as equitable.

A. Equitable Influence on Unjust Enrichment Defences

In *Moses v Macferlan*,[132] Lord Mansfield recognised that '[the defendant] may defend himself by every thing which shews that the plaintiff, *ex aequo et bono*, is not entitled to the whole of the demand, or to any part of it'. The core principle which justifies the recognition of defences to a claim in unjust enrichment is that the justice of the defendant retaining a benefit outweighs the justice of the claimant recovering it.[133] This might be described as equitable, but not within the Equitable jurisdiction.

Nevertheless, the equitable influence on the formation of unjust enrichment defences is clear. Estoppel is a defence to unjust enrichment claims to which questions of equity and conscience have been identified to determine whether it is appropriate for the defence to bar the claim completely,[134] with unconscionability being used to enable Equity to mitigate the rigours of the Common Law.[135] This 'equitable' influence is especially apparent in the formulation of the defence of change of position. In *Lipkin Gorman v Karpnale Ltd*,[136] Lord Goff identified the essence of this defence as being that it is 'inequitable' for the defendant to make restitution.[137] This has generally been interpreted as meaning that the defence exists to secure practical justice,[138] so equity is used in the same sense as by Lord Mansfield

[132] (1760) 2 Burr 1005, 1010.
[133] *Baylis v Bishop of London* [1913] 1 Ch 127 (CA) 140 (Hamilton LJ).
[134] *Avon Country Council v Howlett* [1983] 1 WLR 605 (CA) 608 (Cumming-Bruce LJ) and 612 (Eveleigh LJ); *National Westminster Bank plc v Somer International (UK) Ltd* [2001] EWCA Civ 970, [2002] 1 All ER 198, 215 (Potter LJ) and 217 (Clarke LJ).
[135] *National Westminster Bank* (n 134) 217 (Clarke LJ).
[136] *Lipkin Gorman* (n 9).
[137] ibid 580.
[138] *Dextra Bank and Trust Co ltd v Bank of Jamaica* [2001] UKPC 50, [2002] 1 All ER (Comm) 193.

in *Moses v Macferlan*. Other cases have treated 'equitable' as incorporating a test of unconscionability.[139] Conscience is relevant to the defence in another way. The defence will be defeated if the claimant acted in bad faith. This has been interpreted in the same way as unconscionability for purposes of a claim for knowing receipt.[140] Here conscience is being used in its first substantive sense of fault, which here is interpreted as an objective test.

B. Equitable Defences

Where the claim is characterised as equitable, the Limitation Act 1980 is inapplicable[141] and so the equitable doctrine of laches applies. Consequently, where the claimant seeks a restitutionary remedy on the ground of undue influence or the defendant's unconscionable conduct, then, because such claims are equitable even though they are founded on the reversal of the defendant's unjust enrichment, it is the doctrine of laches rather than the statutory limitation period of six years which should be applicable.[142]

VIII. Restitutionary Remedies

Remedies to reverse unjust enrichment are almost always pecuniary and there is no obvious equitable influence on their formulation. The significant exception to this is the equitable remedy[143] of subrogation which is designed to ensure 'a transfer of rights from one person to another . . . by operation of law'[144] and which can have proprietary effect by giving the claimant priority over the defendant's creditors through subrogation to a security.[145] This remedy has been recognised as being available following a successful claim in unjust enrichment.[146]

In fact, Lord Sumption's analysis in *Lowick Rose LLP v Swynson Ltd*[147] of subrogation to a discharged security was more subtle. He recognised that equitable subrogation is a remedy which can give effect either to a proprietary right or 'to

139 *National Westminster Bank* (n 134) 210 (Potter LJ).

140 *Niru Battery Manufacturing Co v Milestone Trading Ltd* [2003] EWCA 1446 (Civ), [2004] QB 985; *Abou-Rahmah v Abacha* [2006] EWCA Civ 1492, [2007] 1 All ER (Comm) 827; *Armstrong DLW GmbH v Winnington Networks Ltd* [2012] EWHC 10 (Ch), [2013] Ch 156 [132] (Stephen Morris QC); *Re Hampton Capital Ltd* [2015] EWHC 1905 (Ch), [2016] 1 BCLC 374.

141 Limitation Act 1980, s 36(1).

142 *Allcard v Skinner* (1887) 36 Ch D 145 (CA).

143 *Sander v Pearson* [2013] EWCA Civ 1822, [15] (Arden LJ).

144 *Orakpo v Manson Investments Ltd* [1978] AC 95 (HL) 104 (Lord Diplock).

145 *Cheltenham and Gloucester plc v Appleyard* [2004] EWCA Civ 291.

146 *Banque Financière de la Cité* (n 11); *Bank of Cyprus UK Ltd v Menelaou* [2015] UKSC 66, [2016] AC 17; *Lowick Rose LLP v Swynson Ltd* [2017] UKSC 32, [2018] AC 313 [29] (Lord Sumption).

147 *Lowick Rose* (n 146) [29].

a cause of action',[148] and that unjust enrichment might be such a cause of action. He warned against trying to fit subrogation into 'any broader category of unjust enrichment'[149] and characterised the remedy as *sui generis*. He identified various differences between 'unjust enrichment' generally and 'unjust enrichment' triggering subrogation, including the fact that subrogation is not a restitutionary remedy as such, since it does not restore the parties to their pre-transfer position but enforces a defeated expectation, such as an expectation that the claimant will obtain a security. Further, establishing 'unjust enrichment' for the purposes of awarding equitable subrogation requires a significant adjustment of the elements of the claim, such as the basis for the enrichment not needing to be shared by the claimant and the defendant[150] and, implicitly, that the enrichment can be both incidental[151] and indirect.[152]

This is another example of established equitable principle being squeezed into a straitjacket of unjust enrichment thinking, when there is a perfectly serviceable equitable explanation of how the remedy operates, namely within Lord Sumption's first category of giving effect to a proprietary right rather than to 'a cause of action'. This analysis was adopted by Lord Carnwath in *Bank of Cyprus (UK) Ltd v Menelaou*,[153] and was one with which Lord Neuberger had considerable sympathy, with the former considering that subrogation could only be justified as a proprietary remedy to vindicate property rights, and the latter, although acknowledging the legitimacy of subrogation being awarded to reverse the defendant's unjust enrichment, preferring the vindication of property rights analysis, as being simpler and less controversial.[154]

Subrogation with reference to unjust enrichment is fraught with difficulty.[155] The better approach is to recognise that, where subrogation operates as a proprietary remedy, it is a remedy to vindicate the claimant's equitable proprietary right; an approach which has been endorsed by the High Court of Australia.[156] Indeed, in *Prudential Assurance Co Ltd v Revenue and Customs Commissioners*[157] the Supreme Court recognised that the award of subrogation might be based on a different principle to that of unjust enrichment. But, as Lord Sumption correctly acknowledged in *Lowick*, subrogation is also relevant as a remedy where a 'cause of action' can be established. An appropriate cause of action is unjust enrichment

[148] ibid [18].
[149] ibid [29].
[150] ibid [30]. Lord Sumption justified this on the ground that the 'windfall character of the benefit conferred on the defendant means that it is not unjust to give effect to the unilateral expectation of the claimant'.
[151] ibid [88] (Lord Mance) and [113] (Lord Neuberger).
[152] ibid [86] (Lord Mance) and [115] (Lord Neuberger).
[153] [2015] UKSC 66, [2016] AC 17.
[154] ibid [100].
[155] See Rory Gregson, 'Is Subrogation a Remedy for Unjust Enrichment?' (2020) 136 LQR 481.
[156] *Bofinger v Kingsway Group Ltd* [2009] HCA 44.
[157] [2018] UKSC 39, [2019] AC 929 [68].

for which subrogation might sometimes be an appropriate remedy, but only in its non-proprietary form to reverse a defective transfer of value.[158] Where the claimant seeks a proprietary form of subrogation, which gives the claimant a security interest in respect of the claim against the defendant, it is not appropriate to adopt a different interpretation of unjust enrichment; a different claim needs to be engaged.

IX. Conclusion

Whilst we would not normally consider there to be a borderline between the Law of Unjust Enrichment and Equity, since it is clear that Equity can operate within the Law of Unjust Enrichment, the analysis of the influence of Equity on the Law of Unjust Enrichment identifies some important truths. First, Equity continues to have a significant influence on the Law of Unjust Enrichment where the values of Equity are relevant, but it is always important to consider what might come with this equitable influence. Secondly, the recent tendency to incorporate equitable language, namely unconscionability, into unjust enrichment claims without careful consideration of the implications of this needs to be checked. Sometimes the use of such language is inappropriate, such as with the restitution of mistaken gifts; at other times the half-hearted transplantation into the Common Law is flawed, as has occurred with lawful act duress.

But the key lesson is that the analysis of the interface between the Law of Unjust Enrichment and Equity provides insight into the real function of Equity, generally as regards its relationship with the Common Law and specifically in providing the rationale for recognising the Law of Unjust Enrichment. None of this is new. It was observed by Maitland and particularly by Lord Mansfield. The thoughts of our legal forebears will genuinely become thinkable again, and in thinking this we need to give Equity the respect it continues to deserve.

[158] As in *Banque Financière de la Cité* (n 11).

11
Equity's Borderlines

Mr Justice Marcus Smith

I. Introduction

When considering the physical manifestation of a border, a border can either delineate vertically (where the plane is horizontal) as in a border between countries; or horizontally (where the plane is vertical) as in the layers of a trifle. Of course, the borders under consideration in this collection are *not* physical, but abstract and intangible. Nevertheless, the physical manifestation of borders is helpful when considering the borderline between the common law and equity. This is because the distinction between equitable rules and common law rules operates on *both* planes, albeit in different ways. A consideration of these two borderlines (the vertical and the horizontal) forms the bulk of the analysis in this chapter.

At the same time, it must be recognised that equitable rules and common law rules are now administered by the *same* courts in the *same* cases at the *same* time, often without differentiation. As a direct result, the question of the utility or purpose of *any* border existing between law and equity must be called into question in an altogether more fundamental way. That question is, hopefully, answered in the last part of this essay.

We begin with the more straightforward border, which is the vertical delineation. This occurs where equity supplements the rules of common law, without altering them or their essential function. There are many examples of such an auxiliary jurisdiction.[1] Often, these examples are purely remedial in nature (the injunction, specific performance), but at times they verge on the substantive (as in the case of rectification). To the student, or the lawyer not versed in the fine distinctions between the common law and equity, the distinction may not be apparent at all. For instance, in contract law books the equitable doctrine of rectification will often appear alongside legal rules regarding mistake, without any acknowledgment of its different juridical origin.

[1] Many terms are used to describe equity's relationship with the common law, and it is at the borderlines that this relationship becomes properly manifest. I am using the term auxiliary precisely because it implies a degree of subordination between common law and equity, with equity as the junior partner. I will use the term concurrent to describe the more muscular role that equity performs in the case of horizontal delineation. I accept, of course, that both these terms are loaded and controversial and that to a very considerable degree they betray where I am coming from.

Mr Justice Marcus Smith, *Equity's Borderlines* In: *Borderlines in Private Law.* Edited by: William Day and Julius Grower, Oxford University Press. © Mr Justice Marcus Smith 2024. DOI: 10.1093/9780191995200.003.0011

Horizontal delineation involves a degree of layering—concurrency, if you will—whereby the same case delivers—or appears to deliver—different responses. This is inherently (at least at first glance) pernicious. Sarah Worthington described the problem well by reference to the analogy of two teams playing the same game, but by different rules.

> The idea of coherence is critical. Different games may have different rules, but each set of rules must be designed to be internally coherent. Imagine what would happen if our five-year-olds were to have two sets of umpires monitoring their game, one applying red rules and red practices and delivering red responses to the events, the other applying green rules and green practices and delivering green responses to the events. The game would descend into chaos. The red umpire might recognise goals that the green umpire does not. Each team's score would then depend upon which umpire was in control at the appropriate time.[2] The same would be true of the assessment of infringements and the awarding of penalties: the red umpire would make her assessment on the basis of red practices and deliver decisions based on red rules; the green umpire would make his decisions on the basis of green practices and deliver decision based on green rules. Of course, the best way to bring order to such a bizarre game is simply to agree that only 'purple rules' are to apply.[3]

Coherence *is*, obviously, critical. And unless the borderlines that we are going to examine enhance, rather than erode, legal coherence they are to be deprecated and not lauded.

Of course, the question is a lot more nuanced than this. We have come a long way from the days when two legal systems operated in parallel, with courts of Common Law and courts of Equity, and one trumping the other through the use of different and uncoordinated powers and jurisdictions.[4] Although powers and jurisdictions were not themselves harmonised, the courts that administered them *were*.[5] Maitland justified the outcome in the following terms:

> We ought to think of equity as a supplementary law, a sort of appendix added on to our code, or a sort of gloss, which used to be administered by courts specially designed for that purpose, but which is now administered by the High Court of Justice as part of that code. The language which equity held to law, if we may

[2] This is an almost perfect description of the role of private international law in resolving which rules of what particular law district (by law district I mean the jurisdiction operating by a defined scheme of rules, usually a nation state, but often a geographic area within a station state such as New York or Wales) apply when two or more can plausibly be said to apply.

[3] Sarah Worthington, *Equity* (2nd edn, OUP 2006) 4–5.

[4] See the description in Marcus Smith and Nico Leslie, *The Law of Assignment* (3rd edn, OUP 2018) 10.19–10.23.

[5] ibid 10.25.

> personify the two, was not 'No, that is not so, you made a mistake, your rule is an absurd, and obsolete one'; but 'Yes of course that is so, but it is not the whole truth. You say that A is the owner of this land; no doubt that is so, but I must add that he is bound by one of those obligations which are known as trusts'.[6]

II. The First Borderline: Vertical Delineation

The equitable doctrine of rectification is often deployed to correct written contracts, although it can also apply to the rectification of other instruments, including in particular unilaterally created instruments.[7] In the textbooks, it appears seamlessly next to other devices for the correction of mistakes, whether common law or equitable.[8] This is as it should be: when considering a contractual question concerning (here) mistake, it would be both pointless and incoherent to have to have recourse to two different textbooks, one on equity and the other on common law.

Rectification is best seen as an equitable supplement to augment insufficient common law rules. To revert to Maitland again:

> We ought not to think of common law and equity as of two rival systems. Equity was not a self-sufficient system, at every point it presupposed the existence of common law. Common law was a self-sufficient system. I mean this: that if the legislature had passed a short act saying 'Equity is hereby abolished', we might still have got on fairly well; in some respects our law would have been barbarous, unjust, absurd, but still the great elementary rights, the right to immunity from violence, the right to one's good name, the rights of ownership and of possession would have been decently protected and contract would have been enforced. On the other hand had the legislature said 'Common law is hereby abolished', this decree if obeyed would have meant anarchy. At every point equity presupposed the existence of common law.[9]

When we come to the second borderline (the horizontal delineation) we will suggest that this passage rather understates the importance of equity as more than just a gap-filler of common law omissions. But it is a fair enough description of *this* borderline.

[6] Frederic Maitland, *Equity: A Course of Lectures* (Alfred Chaytor and William Whittaker (eds), rev John Brunyate, 2nd edn, CUP 1936) 18.

[7] Trust settlements, by way of example. There is a long line of cases dealing with mistake in this area, particularly in the context of pension funds.

[8] See, eg, Hugh Beale (ed), *Chitty on Contracts* (34th edn, Sweet & Maxwell 2022) ch 5 and in particular 5-057.

[9] Maitland (n 6) 19.

So, this borderline is characterised by two aspects: (1) jurisdictionally speaking, these different jurisdictions are administered by a unified court structure: there is no separate court of equity to which a case must go for equitable principles to be applied;[10] (2) in *this* case, equity has a limited, supplemental, role: auxiliary. There is, therefore, much to be said for seeking to ensure that the equitable gap-filling sits comfortably, consistently—coherently—with the common law mass to which it accretes.

For a long time, the textbooks spoke of two doctrines of common mistake: one equitable, one common law. Thus, earlier editions of *Chitty* rigorously differentiate between common law and equitable mistake.[11] That distinction has now, helpfully, been eroded. A later edition of *Chitty* notes:

> Until recently it could be argued that what has been said above about the circumstances in which the law takes account of a mistake by one party, or both parties, to a contract represented the position at common law; and that the rules of equity 'cut across this distinction'. This referred to the line of cases to the effect that in some circumstances a common mistake would give either party the right to avoid a contract that was not void for mistake at common law, based on a rule of equity. Now that these cases have been disapproved, and if the interpretation of certain cases of unilateral mistake that will be offered in this chapter is accepted, it seems that there is no inconsistency between common law and equity.[12]

Where equity is offering this sort of supplemental jurisdiction, the borderline where common law ends and equity begins ought to be seamless: there ought to be one coherent body of law, consistently applied irrespective of is historic provenance.

This, of course, begs a very large question. What, exactly, does coherence mean? At a minimum, in the case of this borderline, it should mean that equity ought only to offer a wider jurisdiction or intervention for good reason and (where it does) the rules of common law ought to fade away and wither, so there is only one rule. It is, to continue with the above example, difficult to justify two doctrines of mistake where (in the same case) common law and equity offer different, yet parallel, responses. This is incoherent and (as we have seen) in the area of mistake the distinction is being eroded. In short, the common law (using that term to refer to the case-by-case evolution of law in our legal system) must continue to evolve, but there is no reason why the same evolutionary thinking cannot affect the

[10] This is common to both borderlines and is a strong pointer towards coherence between the two jurisdictions.
[11] See, eg, Anthony Guest (ed), *Chitty on Contracts* (23rd edn, Sweet & Maxwell 1968) ch 5, which falls into two clear parts: 'mistake at common law' and 'mistake in equity'.
[12] Hugh Beale (ed), *Chitty on Contracts* (33rd edn, Sweet & Maxwell 2018) 3-010.

corpus of rules at common law and in equity at the same time, thereby bringing them together.

But does coherence go beyond this? Rectification is an excellent example, for it is a remedy or response that is not duplicative of common law rules. It is properly auxiliary. But ought the principles that inform the operation of this equitable jurisdiction be similar to—or made to be similar to—those of the common law? As is well known, the common law operates much more objectively than equity, which focuses rather more on the subjective. Indeed—as we will see—there is certainly room and a need for such overt differences. But is that the case where the rules of equity operate in an auxiliary fashion?

For a short period, this appeared to be the trend in the law of rectification: contracts were to be rectified in a manner much more closely analogous to the common law rules of offer and acceptance which—as is well known—operate objectively. The law of rectification deals with (amongst other things) those cases where a contract has been reduced to writing incorrectly. Where a common continuing intention between contracting parties is not manifested or correctly recorded in the written instrument, the written instrument may be rectified to accord with that common continuing intention. How is that common continuing intention to be determined or tested for? Is the test the usual, objective, test of the common law, manifest in its rules of offer and acceptance; or is the rule one based much more on the equitable notions of subjective states of mind and good conduct. In *Chartbrook Ltd v Persimmon Homes Ltd*,[13] Lord Hoffmann (*obiter*) expressed the opinion that:

> The judge and the Court of Appeal had been wrong in their assumption about what a party had to be mistaken about. Rectification required a mistake about whether the written instrument correctly reflected the prior consensus, not whether it accorded with what the party in question believed that consensus to have been. In accordance with the general approach of English law, the terms of the prior consensus were what a reasonable observer would have understood them to be and not what one or even both of the parties believed them to be.[14]

This rapprochement was short-lived. The *obiter* opinion of Lord Hoffmann was overruled by a strong Court of Appeal in *FSHC Group Holdings Ltd v GLAS Trust Corp Ltd*,[15] where it was held that the parties' common intention had to be determined by reference to subjective intentions, and not by reference to what an

[13] *Chartbrook Ltd v Persimmon Homes Ltd* [2009] UKHL 38, [2009] 1 AC 1101.

[14] ibid [57], quoting the submissions of counsel (Christopher Nugee QC), which Lord Hoffmann adopted. See also the academic debate in this regard, also cited by Lord Hoffmann at [57]: Marcus Smith, 'Rectification of Contracts for Common Mistake, Joscelyne v Nissen, and Subjective States of Mind' (2007) 123 LQR 116 and David McLaughlan, 'The "Drastic" Remedy of Rectification for Unilateral Mistake' (2008) 124 LQR 608.

[15] *FSHC Group Holdings Ltd v GLAS Trust Corp Ltd* [2019] EWCA Civ 1361, [2020] Ch 365.

objective observer would have understood in regard to the parties' pre-existing negotiations.

Whatever the respective merits of the two approaches (which is a matter beyond the scope of this chapter) there is now again something of a disconnect between what informs outcomes at common law in this area, and what informs outcomes in equity. The borderline is again very evident. From a purely coherence-focused point of view, and in the case of *this* borderline, that is unfortunate. If (and this itself is controversial) coherence is taken to mean not just the avoidance of different legal responses to the same case but actually ensuring that the same factors inform outcomes even where there is no overlap (but simply an auxiliary equitable jurisdiction) then we should be looking for more than a merely superficial harmony between the common law and equity. Instead we ought to be looking for harmony which is much more fundamental, and departed from only where there is good reason.

III. The Second Borderline: Horizontal Delineation

The horizontal delineation between the common law and equity is altogether more fundamental. How is it that a person can be the owner of a thing at common law, and yet *not* be its owner in equity. It is possible to say that equitable ownership is no such thing, in that the beneficial owner in equity does not have an *in rem* right, a right that is capable of vindication against the whole world. Yet that is to presuppose what ownership actually means, a difficult question if ever there was one. Nevertheless, it is true that the circumstances in which an owner at common law loses title to their property are different to the circumstances in which an owner in equity loses title to their property.

The differences between these legal and equitable rules arise out of the different rules of priority that exist within the two legal systems. Rules of priority determine when a later acquirer of a thing takes free from the prior claims of an earlier owner. English law has a very complex set of rules of priority—in the sense that there are arguably too many rules applicable in different cases—and space does not allow for their exposition.[16] Three of the rules will, however, be touched upon:

(1) *Competing legal claims.*[17] In the case of competing legal claims—by definition, claims to legal things—the general rule is that interests rank in the order in which they were created. This is a rule that seems entirely right, but try explaining to the bona fide purchaser for value of a second-hand car (call them C) why C must (as they do) return the car to the original owner

[16] The rules are stated in Smith and Leslie (n 4) [27.17] and described in detail in ch 27.
[17] This is Rule 2 in Smith and Leslie (n 4) 27.20ff.

A,[18] when to all intents and purposes B, who sold the car to C, looked like the owner, even after proper inquiry.

(2) *Competing equitable claims.*[19] As between competing equitable claims—claims, in effect, to choses in action—the rule is exactly the same.[20]

These first two rules of priority reflect a case of a right against property that is good against the whole world. Absent the *destruction* of the property, the later acquirer's rights will always be subject to those of the earlier owner. The earlier owner's interests are prioritised over those of the later (mere) acquirer of the thing. But that is one version of what constitutes ownership, which Honoré characterised as no more than the bundle of rights in a thing that represents the highest level of interest that can be.[21] There is no reason why the bundle of rights vesting in an owner cannot be more circumscribed so as to accord greater weight to the interests of later acquirers of property. In other words, there is no single, correct, definition of ownership.

We see a less protective rule of priority where the priority dispute is between competing legal and equitable claims:

(3) *Competing legal and equitable claims.*[22] In the case of competing claims to a thing, where the later claim is to a legal interest and the earlier claim is to an equitable interest, then the later claim takes free of the earlier claim provided that the later claimant is a bona fide purchaser of the legal estate for valuable consideration who obtained their legal interest at the time of their purchase without notice of the prior equitable right. Such a later claimant is often referred to as Equity's Darling and in this case the normal rule that an earlier interest takes priority over a later claim is displaced.[23]

There is thus a clear divergence between rules of priority, to the detriment of the holder of an equitable right. Unless one is very conscious of the rules in this area, which particularly underlie the law of assignment, mistakes in analysis (or, at least,

[18] Things are never as easy as this. A's claim will lie in the tort of conversion, and C will probably not have to specifically return the car: but C will certainly have to compensate A for interfering with A's property rights, and will have to pay an amount referable to the value of the car that A has been deprived of.

[19] This is Rule 3 in Smith and Leslie (n 4) 27.20ff.

[20] This implies that beneficial interests under a trust are merely personal rights. That, as will be seen, is not my position. Whilst the rights of a beneficiary under a trust are properly defined by the label 'chose in action', I see such rights (for reasons I give) as a form of ownership,

[21] Tony Honoré, 'Ownership' in Anthony Guest (ed), *Oxford Essays in Jurisprudence* (1st edn, OUP 1961).

[22] This is Rule 4 in Smith and Leslie (n 4) 27.27ff.

[23] As said above, I am *not* setting out all of the priority rules. The so-called rule in *Dearle v Hall*, obviously important in the case of assignments, is one I am deliberately not mentioning.

questions that go begging) will arise.[24] That, of course, is no justification for legal complexity: complexity ought only to exist where it is capable of justification, and even then the law ought to be no more complex than is absolutely necessary.

So the question is *not* whether equitable ownership is not ownership because the earlier owner's rights are defeasible in the case of Equity's Darling. Equitable ownership is a right good against the whole world except Equity's Darling, and it is a pointless matter to debate whether in some kind of Platonic ideal world this type of rule would not amount to ownership. We live in the real world, and the rights of an equitable owner are so extensive—so *in rem*—that to deprive these rights of the label ownership is pointless, confusing, and wrong.

Much more interesting is *why* this divergence exists. Here, Sarah Worthington's red rules versus green rules point arises with full force. We can agree that both rules of priority (first in time and Equity's Darling) are defensible formulations of the rights of an owner as against the subsequent acquirer of later property.[25] But to have both formulations subsisting at one and the same time in the same legal system (now administered by the same courts) *does* require a degree of justification.

What is it? The answer lies in the trust, which depends upon this distinction as between legal and equitable ownership. Take the express trust: the owner of legal property A may declare themselves trustee of that property in favour of B. The trusts so declared can be—and in Victorian times often were—used for the control of family fortunes. Even today, despite the prevalence of land registration, the legal regime cannot be understood without appreciating the significance of the trust. Much more to the point, nowadays, commercial structures of enormous economic importance and complexity exist, whose legal basis is the trust, and without which they would not work.

The beauty of the express trust is that A (the legal owner of trust property) sits in a schizophrenic state:

(1) As regards third parties, A protects the property as legal owner, and deals with it as legal owner, including in terms of disposing of it. Thus, A can transfer trust property (held on trust for X, Y, and Z) to B, and B takes free of the trusts, and holds the legal estate.
(2) The interests of X, Y, and Z in the cases of a lawful disposition are overreached: they transfer to that which A acquired in exchange for the property

[24] By way of example, the case law concerning the circumstances in which the assignor of a legal chose in action need not be joined to the proceedings is profoundly unsatisfactory, simply because the distinction between legal and equitable things is not borne in mind. See, eg, Smith and Leslie (n 4) 11.54 and (setting out the legal development in this area) 11.04ff. For a detailed examination, see also Marcus Smith, 'Locus Standi and the Enforcement of Legal Claims by Cestuis Que Trust and Assignees' (2008) 22 TLI 140.

[25] The acquirer of the second-hand car, C, in the example above, would doubtless be Equity's Darling, and would be an enthusiastic proponent of the notion that even at common law, the rights of the earlier owner ought to give way to those of the later owner.

they sold to B. Thus, the trust enables wealth and property to be both preserved and dealt with according to rules that can be as simple or as complex as commercial requirements dictate.

(3) Third parties to the trust (here, B) do not have to trouble themselves about the trust, unless they have conducted themselves in such a way as to trigger the equitable proprietary actions of knowing assistance and knowing receipt. Subject to that, it is only *A* that must account to *X*, *Y*, and *Z* for their conduct in regard to the trust property, and it is here that the notion of a trustee's duties originates.

So far, all that has been considered is the express trust. In addition to express trusts (and we include implied trusts with express trusts), there is the remedial trust (resulting and constructive) that provides remedies not merely in the case of where a claim in knowing assistance or knowing receipt might lie.[26]

This borderline between common law and equity really does matter, and consistency does not exist because of the very different functions of the two sets of rules. To repeat how Maitland put it:[27]

> You say A is the owner of this land; no doubt that is so, but I must add that he is bound by one of those obligations which are known as trusts.

Just so. Consistency of rule must give way to coherence and properly understood this borderline must, for the sake of the integrity of our law of property, be understood and observed most closely.

[26] I am trying, here, to steer away from controversy. Express and implied trusts all require an act of will, which is not so (or not the same) in the case of resulting and constructive trusts. Hence my use of the term remedial.

[27] Maitland (n 6) 19.

12
Property | Equity

*Ben McFarlane**

I. Introduction

Pursuing a project on borderlines in private law is, at least, consistent with a concern for the importance of taxonomy within private law. Such a concern was, of course, very clearly expressed in the influential work of Peter Birks. The approach in this chapter is not only consistent with, but in fact depends on, such an interest in the classification of private law concepts. As a result, it draws heavily on Birks' methodology. Its aim, however, is to argue that, even using that methodology, we can improve upon Birks' general analysis of the relationship between property and equity, including his view of the trust. As will be seen, the approach preferred in this chapter has important consequences for the practical operation of property and equity. It involves rejecting specific proposals, formulated by Birks but which have had a lasting influence throughout the common law world, on such matters as the operation of the bona fide purchaser defence,[1] the content of common law tracing rules,[2] the circumstances in which resulting and constructive trusts can arise,[3] and the liability of a recipient of misdirected trust assets.[4]

Those proposals of Birks can all be seen in his magisterial set of lectures on equity, published as 'Equity in the Modern Law: An Exercise in Taxonomy'.[5] A central aim of the analysis there, and of this chapter, is that 'like cases have to be decided alike';[6] this requires 'careful categorisation'.[7] Birks focused on equity in part 'because the bi-partition between law and equity exacerbates the problems caused

* I am grateful to Jordan English and for comments received at the conference.

[1] For the influence of Birks' analysis, see, eg, *Great Investments Ltd v Warner* [2016] FCAFC 85, (2016) 243 FCR 516 [106].

[2] For the influence of Birks' analysis, see, eg, *Trustee of the Property of FC Jones & Sons v Jones* [1997] Ch 159 (CA) discussed in Section IV.

[3] For the influence of Birks' analysis, see, eg, *Foskett v McKeown* [2001] 1 AC 102 (HL) 117 (Lord Hope).

[4] For the influence of Birks' analysis, see, eg, Lord Nicholls in *Criterion Properties plc v Stratford UK Properties LLC* [2004] UKHL 28, [2004] 1 WLR 1846 [4]; *Say-Dee Pty Ltd v Farah Constructions Pty Ltd* [2005] NSWCA 309 (later overturned by the High Court of Australia: [2007] HCA 22, (2007) 230 CLR 89); Charles Mitchell, Paul Mitchell, and Stephen Watterson, *Goff and Jones: The Law of Unjust Enrichment* (10th edn, Sweet and Maxwell 2019) 8-120ff. See the discussion in Section IV.

[5] Peter Birks, 'Equity in the Modern Law: An Exercise in Taxonomy' (1996) 26 UWAL Rev 1.

[6] ibid 5: see also 17, 27, 35, 38, and 95.

[7] ibid 17.

Ben McFarlane, *Property | Equity* In: *Borderlines in Private Law*. Edited by: William Day and Julius Grower, Oxford University Press. © Ben McFarlane 2024. DOI: 10.1093/9780191995200.003.0012

by the more general neglect of the essential exercise of classification, and also because some of the forms of equitable thought seem to pose insuperable obstacles to the would-be taxonomist'.[8] He also noted that a focus on taxonomy is needed to 'control the tendency to contradiction inherent in the duality of law and equity'.[9] Certainly, this chapter gladly accepts the need to treat like cases alike and two central arguments of Birks linked to that demand: first, that we should reject claims that equity, whether because of its distinctive historical development or otherwise, is inherently incapable of being classified and organised;[10] secondly, that differences between common law and equity cannot be justified *simply* by pointing to the jurisdictional origins of the conflicting rules or principles.[11]

In pointing out the many advantages of applying a taxonomical approach, Birks makes two points which are somewhat in tension:

> One advantage of a good classification is that it keeps all relevant possibilities in view and reduces the risk that one might be overlooked. Another is that it militates against the tricks that complex language can play in concealing similarities and unnecessarily proliferating entities.[12]

It is fair to say that, in those lectures, as in his work more generally, Birks' focus was on the latter of those two advantages, and in removing what he saw as unjustified barriers to the integration of principles separated only by their jurisdictional origin. In some cases, as with tracing rules, the effect of this would be to apply the equitable approach more generally;[13] more often, as with claims against recipients of misdirected property, the effect would be to give greater scope to the common law rules.[14] It seems that for Birks the point was not simply to bring consistency between common law and equity, but rather to adopt the solution which gave best effect to the particular underlying principle. So, for example, the equitable tracing rules were preferred as more effective in 'tracking the passage of value from one investment to another',[15] whereas the common law rules on claims against recipients of misdirected property were preferred as recognising a prima facie liability to

[8] ibid 3.
[9] ibid 4.
[10] At a number of points in his lectures, Birks cites work by John D Davies which is taken as making such a claim: see, eg, 'Restitution and Equitable Wrongs' in Francis Rose (ed), *Consensus ad Idem: Essays on Contract in Honour of Guenter Treitel* (Sweet & Maxwell 1996); 'The Re-Awakening of Equity's Conscience: Achievements and Problems' in Stephen Goldstein (ed) *Equity and Contemporary Legal Developments* (Jerusalem 1992).
[11] See too Andrew Burrows, 'We Do This at Common Law but That in Equity' (2002) 22 OJLS 1.
[12] Birks (n 5) 16.
[13] ibid 89.
[14] ibid 70.
[15] ibid 89.

return value received at the expense of another who did not intend the transfer of value.[16]

The aim of this chapter, however, is to focus on the first advantage of classification identified above: to keep all relevant possibilities in view and reduce the risk that some might be overlooked. In doing so, the chapter focuses first not on the events side of Birks' scheme, but on the rights to which such events give rise. For that scheme is built on the foundational assumption that:

> All rights are either (by jurisdictional origin) legal or equitable and (by the nature of their exigibility) proprietary or personal; and all such rights arise from wrongs, from consent, from unjust enrichment or from other causative events.[17]

The argument in this chapter is that in stating that rights must be either proprietary or personal, the scheme overlooks a relevant possibility: that there may be a third type of right, with a scope of exigibility that is distinct from both the prima facie *erga omnes* effect that Birks associated with a 'proprietary' right,[18] and from the defendant-specific effect of a personal right.[19] This third type of right, which will be examined in Section II, is a right that correlates to a particular type of duty owed by another: a duty in relation to a specific right held by that other party. This third type of right, which can be referred to as a 'persistent right'[20] or a 'right in relation to another right', is likely exclusive to, and certainly most prominent in, equity. The key feature of such a persistent right is that it is capable of having an effect on a *specific* group of third parties—essentially, successors in title to the party initially bound[21]—but is not prima facie binding on the rest of the world.

Certainly, unlike legal property rights, equitable property rights are *not* prima facie binding on the rest of the world[22] and, almost without exception,[23] are instead

[16] ibid 70, arguing that *Lipkin Gorman v Karpnale Ltd* [1991] 2 AC 548 (HL) 'seems to confirm that what is true of cases of mistake is also true of cases of ignorance'.

[17] Birks (n 5) 16.

[18] See, eg, Peter Birks, 'Before We Begin: Five Keys to Land Law' in Sue Bright and John Dewar (eds), *Land Law: Themes and Perspectives* (OUP 1998).

[19] For this argument, see, eg, Ben McFarlane, *The Structure of Property Law* (Hart 2009); Ben McFarlane and Robert Stevens, 'The Nature of Equitable Property' (2010) J Eq 1; Ben McFarlane and Robert Stevens, 'What's Special About Equity? Rights About Rights' in Dennis Klimchuk, Irit Samet, and Henry Smith (eds), *Philosophical Foundations of the Law of Equity* (OUP 2020); Robert Stevens, *The Laws of Restitution* (OUP 2022) ch 12.

[20] The term used by McFarlane, *The Structure of Property Law* (n 19) and by McFarlane and Stevens, 'The Nature of Equitable Property' (n 19).

[21] Where A holds a right subject to a duty to B, the group potentially bound by B's persistent right includes any party acquiring a right that depends on an exercise by A of a power arising along with the right A holds subject to the duty to B: so, if A holds a freehold on trust for B, the group potentially bound by B's equitable interest includes not only parties to whom A transfers the freehold, but also parties in whose favour A exercises A's power (which arises as part of A's freehold) to grant a lease over the land. See further McFarlane, *The Structure of Property Law* (n 19) 24.

[22] See, eg, *Leigh & Sillivan Ltd v Aliakmon Shipping Co Ltd* [1986] AC 785 (HL); *Parker-Tweedle v Dunbar plc (No 2)* [1991] Ch 12 (CA); *MCC Proceeds v Lehman Brothers* [1998] 4 All ER 675 (CA).

[23] The restrictive covenant forms an exception: whilst it is not prima facie binding on the rest of the world, it has been held to be capable of binding a squatter on the burdened land, and thus can bind a

best seen as persistent rights. A classificatory scheme, such as Birks', which does not have space for such a right therefore runs the risk of failing to appreciate a key contribution made by equity to our legal system, and of wrongly assuming that equitable property rights must operate in the same way as legal property rights. That is why, in this context, it is important to be able to count to three.

It will thus be argued that Birks' analysis provides an example of what Henry Smith[24] has referred to as a 'flattening' of private law, obscuring particular techniques, formerly most prominent in equity, which may have valuable applications, and overlooking differences between particular equitable doctrines and their supposed common law 'equivalents'.[25] In particular, the distinct formal nature of particular equitable rights means that cases where a party acquires such a right need not be 'like cases' to those where a legal right with the same, or a similar, name is acquired. Contrary to the analysis of Birks in some of these cases, there is no need for consistency in the events that give rise to these rights.

At the same time, as in any case where the term 'property' must appear in a title, there is a warning to be given as to the meaning of that term. This chapter makes the argument that the term 'property right', when applied to rights arising in equity, must, at the least, be used very carefully and, ideally, would not be used at all. This does not mean, however, that the term 'property' must necessarily be excluded from cases involving equitable intervention.

First, if property is defined widely, for example as 'subject to statute, anything of realisable commercial value',[26] then a wide range of equitable rights clearly fall within its scope. Indeed, on such a view, it can be said that a key contribution of equity has been in extending that scope,[27] for example by allowing a party to realise the value of a chose in action by means of an immediate equitable assignment. This chapter does not aim to deny the effects of that contribution, and its commercial importance, but rather argues that equity did not extend the existing concept of a property right beyond its common law limits, but instead recognised a distinct form of right. This means that, in this context, equity does not operate by correcting the common law, by extending it beyond an unjustified limit; rather, equity supplements the common law by recognising a new form of right which a party may acquire.

third party who has not acquired a right from the original covenantor: see *Re Nisbet and Potts' Contract* [1906] 1 Ch 386 (CA). See further Section II.

[24] See, eg, Henry Smith 'Equity as Meta-Law' (2021) 130 Yale LJ 1050 esp at 1096–97, 1136–38.

[25] See further Ben McFarlane, 'Equity and the Justification of Private Rights' in Simone Degeling, Michael Crawford, and Nicholas Tiverios (eds), *Justifying Private Rights* (Hart 2020).

[26] See Roy Goode, 'What is Property?' (2023) 139 LQR 1. This is not of course the only possible definition that may be given to the term: see, eg, Robert Stevens, 'Crypto is Not Property' (2023) 139 LQR 616 and McFarlane, *The Structure of Property Law* (n 19) pt I.

[27] As noted by, eg, Sarah Worthington, 'The Disappearing Divide Between Property and Obligation: The Impact of Aligning Legal Analysis and Commercial Expectation' (2007) 42 Tex Int'l LJ 917, 921.

For example, it has been persuasively argued that an equitable assignment of a legal chose in action does not challenge the common law prohibition on the transfer of such a right, as no transfer is involved:[28] rather, similar to the case of a self-declared trust, the equitable assignor retains the right against the debtor, and the equitable assignee instead acquires a right that relates to that retained right of the assignor. This is consistent with the historically supplementary nature of equity as a system: it accepts the existence of particular common law rights but provides a secondary set of rules which regulate dealings with those rights.[29]

Such an analysis has consequences for the operation not only of equitable property rights, and the events giving rise to such rights, but also for the operation of legal property rights, and the events giving rise to them. In particular, it may be that the existence of the equitable possibilities, whilst not contradicting the limits on the common law rules, makes it easier to justify those limits by mitigating some of their adverse practical effects. So, for example, the commercial inconvenience potentially arising from the inability to transfer a legal chose in action is reduced by the availability of equitable assignment.

Secondly, it is accepted here that some of the key concerns and tensions relevant to the operation of legal property rights, and which may be seen as characteristic of 'property', are also directly relevant to the consideration of equitable property rights. For example, to the extent that there is a 'basic tension' in property law between protecting prior users of a thing and instead protecting a party later acquiring a right in relation to that thing,[30] that tension is relevant to equitable property rights as well as to legal property rights. Yet the fact that the same general considerations may arise in considering two different disputes does not mean that the outcome at common law and in equity must be the same: as long as the basis of the claim is sufficiently different in each case, success in one system and failure in the other may be justifiable.

For example, in considering the relationship between claims in knowing receipt and the strict liability personal claim potentially available against the recipient of a mistakenly transferred asset, Birks correctly notes that in each case there is a tension between protecting the security of a claimant with an initial right and protecting the security of the defendant's receipt.[31] However, differing approaches as between common law and equity to the resolution of the tension are not necessarily inconsistent. As will be seen in Section II, where the claimant's initial right is an equitable interest, rather than a legal property right, then the difference in the formal nature of those rights justifies differing third party effects, so that

[28] See, eg, Chee Ho Tham, *Understanding the Law of Assignment* (CUP 2021).

[29] See Frederic Maitland, *Equity: A Course of Lectures* (Alfred Chaytor and William Whittaker (eds), rev John Brunyate, 2nd edn, CUP 1936) 19: 'At every point equity presupposed the existence of common law... Equity without common law would have been a castle in the air, an impossibility.'

[30] See McFarlane, *The Structure of Property Law* (n 19) ch 1.

[31] Birks (n 5) 68.

the apparent inconsistency between common law and equity disappears.[32] It will similarly be argued in Section III that, whilst Birks called for the unification of common law and equitable tracing rules, their divergence can be justified by the different forms of the rights arising where each form of tracing is successful.

II. A Third Type of Right

The argument made here rests on the view that equitable property rights are best seen as distinct in form from each of legal property rights and personal rights. This argument has been made in more detail elsewhere,[33] but it is useful to set out its basic features here.

Birks' definition of a property right, or right *in rem*, focuses on the exigibility of the right: 'rights *in rem* are those rights whose exigibility is determined by the location of a thing.' If, for example, O has ownership of a car, then the rest of the world is under a prima facie duty to O not physically to interfere, deliberately or carelessly, with the car.[34] The identity of the particular defendant is not relevant to the existence of the prima facie duty; the scope of the right is instead defined by the thing to which it relates. In contrast, for Birks, a personal right, or right *in personam*, is 'exigible against a particular person.' So if D makes a contractual promise to O to wash O's car, the duty to which O's right to performance of the promise correlates is a duty of D alone. Birks' scheme proceeds on the basis that 'there are two and only two categories of rights':[35] *in rem* and *in personam*.

We can, however, follow Birks in defining rights according to their exigibility, but identify a third type of right. Consider the standard case, such as a solicitor's client account, where A holds a bank account on trust for B.[36] A bank account in itself can be regarded as property in a general sense, as of realisable commercial value, but of course Birks' definition of a property *right* focuses on the exigibility of the right, and a bank account is simply an obligation owed to A by A's bank, and by no other party. A's right is therefore a personal right against A's bank, but, as in the case of a trust of that bank account, or an equitable charge over it, B can acquire an equitable property right in relation to that right of A.

The puzzle of the bank account example, for Birks' scheme, is that it is possible for B to have an equitable property right in relation to A's personal right against A's

[32] See, eg, Lionel Smith, 'Unjust Enrichment, Property and the Structure of Trusts' (2000) 116 LQR 412.

[33] See, eg, the work cited in n 19.

[34] See, eg, Simon Douglas and Ben McFarlane, 'Defining Property Rights' in James Penner and Henry Smith (eds), *Philosophical Foundations of the Law of Property* (OUP 2014).

[35] Birks (n 5) 8.

[36] See, eg, Briggs J (as he then was) in *Re Lehman Bros International (Europe) Ltd* [2010] EWHC 2914 (Ch) [241], noting that B can have a beneficial interest even where A holds a purely personal right, such as a bank account.

bank. B's right under the trust, like A's right against the bank itself, is clearly not prima facie binding on the rest of the world. The difference between B's position in relation to A, and that of A in relation to the bank, is that A's claim against the bank does not relate to any specific right held by the bank, whereas B's claim against A does relate to a specific right of A: the chose in action constituting the bank account. This technique of identifying the subject matter of a trust as a specific right held by the trustee holds true even where a specific thing can be identified: if, for example, there is a trust of land, then it is A's freehold or leasehold (a specific right) that is held on trust, and not the land itself; if there is a trust of a chattel, then it is A's title to the chattel that is held on trust, and not the chattel itself.

This relation of B's right to a specific right held by A distinguishes B's right both from a personal right but also from a legal property right arising where, for example, O has the best title to a car. In the case of a trust or equitable assignment, the subject matter of B's right is neither a specific thing, nor just a specific person, but is rather a specific right held by another person. This explains, for example, why, where title to a chattel is held by A on trust for B, any loss arising to B where X carelessly damages the chattel is regarded as pure economic loss,[37] and so, on an orthodox analysis,[38] a tort claim is not available to B against X.[39] In contrast, where A, without authority under the trust, transfers A's title to the chattel to C, it may be possible for B to bring a claim against C, as C now holds the specific right to which the trust related. As has been pointed out by, for example, Edelman[40] and Foster,[41] there is a long tradition of thinking of the subject matter of a trust as being specific rights, rather than a particular thing. Indeed, as noted in the joint judgment of Kiefel CJ, Keane, and Edelman JJ in *Carter Holt Harvey Woodproducts Australia Pty Ltd v Commonwealth of Australia*, the term 'trust property' is best understood as shorthand for the rights held on trust.[42] On this view, the scope of exigibility of B's equitable property right is closely related to the content of A's duty to B: just as A's duty to B relates to a specific right held by A, the third parties potentially subject to B's equitable property right are those third parties who acquire that same right,

[37] See, eg, *Shell UK Ltd v Total UK Ltd* [2010] EWCA Civ 180, [2011] QB 86.

[38] See, eg, *Lord Compton's case* (1587) 3 Leo 196; *Chudleigh's case* (1594) 1 Co Rep 120a, 122a; *Sir Moyle Finch's case* (1600) 4 Co Inst 85; *Leigh & Sillivan Ltd v Aliakmon Shipping Co Ltd* [1986] AC 785 (HL); *Parker-Tweedle v Dunbar* (n 22); *MCC Proceeds v Lehman Brothers* [1998] 4 All ER 675 (CA).

[39] The decision in *Shell UK* (n 37), whilst still requiring joinder of A where B brings a claim against X, does however recognise at least a liability of X to B in relation to loss caused to B by X's careless interference with the trust property. The reasoning however is fatally flawed as the finding of a special relationship of proximity between claimant and defendant is based on the relationship between the claimant and the trustee: ibid [135]–[136].

[40] James Edelman, 'Two Fundamental Questions for the Law of Trusts' (2013) 129 LQR 66, 72–73.

[41] David Foster, 'Historical Conceptions of the Express Trust, *c* 1600–1900' in Simone Degeling, Jessica Hudson, and Irit Samet (eds), *Philosophical Foundations of the Law of Express Trusts* (OUP 2023).

[42] [2019] HCA 20, (2019) 268 CLR 524 [24].

or a right that derives from it.[43] In other words, it is A's right, rather than anything to which it might relate, which determines the third parties potentially subject to B's equitable property right: B's right is therefore better seen not as a right relating to a thing, but as a right relating to A's right.

It is important to note that this analysis is consistent with the import, if not the terminology, of Lord Sumption's statement in *Akers v Samba Financial Group*[44] that B's equitable interest under a trust has:[45]

> The essential hallmark of any right in rem, namely that it is good against third parties into whose hands the property or its traceable proceeds may have come, subject to the rules of equity for the protection of bona fide purchasers for value without notice.

In the confidence with which it is made, as well as its content, this statement calls to mind Maitland's Englishman who, in his ordinary thinking,[46] regards B as the owner of the asset held on trust, subject only to the technical rule of bona fide purchase. There are two particularly telling points, drawn from Lord Sumption's own analysis in *Akers*, which make the use of the 'in rem' language particularly inapt. First, the specific focus is not on all third parties interacting with the trust property, but rather on a specific group of them: 'third parties into whose hands the property or its traceable proceeds may have come'. This is consistent with the point made above as to the limited exigibility of equitable interests. Secondly, even in those cases where C acquires the trust property (ie the rights held on trust) then, as Lord Sumption stated, 'the question becomes whether the conscience of the transferee is affected'.[47] This observation is consistent with the analysis above, as the extent of C's knowledge may be decisive in determining if C has come under a duty to B; but it again shows how B's initial right operates differently from a standard right *in rem*, where strict prima facie[48] liability is imposed on third parties, without

[43] In this context, a right deriving from A's right is a right arising because of A's exercise of a power arising with A's right, such as when A has a freehold of land and exercises a power to grant a third party a lease of that land: see n 21.

[44] [2017] UKSC 6, [2017] AC 424.

[45] ibid [82], citing Lord Browne-Wilkinson in *Westdeutsche Landesbank Girozentrale v Islington LBC* [1996] AC 669 (HL) 705.

[46] Frederic Maitland, 'Trust and Corporation' in David Runciman and Magnus Ryan (eds), *Maitland: State, Trust and Corporation* (CUP 2012) 75, 94.

[47] [2017] UKSC 6, [2017] AC 424 [89].

[48] The qualification 'prima facie' is important: contrary to the analysis of, eg, Christopher Langdell, 'A Brief Survey of the Equitable Jurisdiction' (1887) 1 Harv L Rev 55, 60, a right can be *in rem* in this sense even if it is subject to a defence such as the bona fide purchaser defence. It is not, therefore, the possibility of such a defence that prevents B's interest coming within this definition of a right *in rem*: it is rather the fact that the interest is not even prima facie binding on those third parties who do not acquire any right from A.

any examination of their conscience.[49] Lord Sumption's statement shows that it is of course possible, by adopting an idiosyncratic definition of a right *in rem*, to apply that label to a beneficiary's right. However, such a statement obscures an important difference in the nature, and practical operation, of equitable property rights as compared to legal property rights. It thus reminds us that, in Birks' words, 'one advantage of a good classification is that it keeps all relevant possibilities in view and reduces the risk that one might be overlooked'.[50]

III. Trusts and Other Equitable Interests

In his lectures on taxonomy in equity, Birks noted the difficulty caused by the trust for a classificatory scheme, exploring the then-recent House of Lords judgment in *Westdeutsche Landesbank Girozentrale v Islington LBC*.[51] The chief problem was seen as the trust's 'combination of proprietary rights and obligations', and Birks suggested that those two aspects of the trust should be treated differently within a scheme, so that the question of the location of 'equitable title' could be separated from that of the personal duties of a trustee.[52] Indeed, Birks proposed that:

> One way out of this problem would be to treat 'trust' as indicative only of an equitable proprietary interest (ie of a situation in which legal title was in one person and equitable title in another) and not to assume any linkage with any specific personal obligations.[53]

As Birks himself noted, such an approach 'would run counter to Lord Browne-Wilkinson's understanding of the matter' (in the *Westdeutsche* case);[54] there are however some hints of Birks' approach in parts of the analysis of the Supreme Court in *Akers*.[55] Nonetheless, the argument to be made here is that the distinct nature of an equitable property right as a right in relation to another right means that we should reject the notion of 'equitable title' and the idea that, like a legal property right, it can exist separately from a specific duty of another party. Indeed, the core parts of the decisions in each of *Westdeutsche* and *Akers* are inconsistent with any other approach.

[49] Note, eg, the strict liability in conversion: see eg Diplock LJ in *Marfani & Co Ltd v Midland Bank Ltd* [1968] 1 WLR 956 (CA) 970–71.
[50] Birks (n 5) 16.
[51] *Westdeutsche* (n 45).
[52] Birks (n 5) 19.
[53] Birks (n 5) 20.
[54] ibid.
[55] See, eg, *Akers* (n 44) [63]–[64] (Lord Neuberger) and [82] (Lord Sumption).

A. The Danger of 'Equitable Title'

First, as made very clear by Richard Nolan,[56] it is dangerous to talk of a third party being bound by 'the trust': where, for example, A has agreed to hold on trust for B, A may be under certain duties, arising as a result of that agreement, that will not bind C, even if C is, for example, a donee who still holds the trust property. A may have been, for example, under particular duties as to management and investment, whereas the basic liability of C is simply to give up the trust property, or its traceable proceeds. This may lie behind Lord Sumption's analysis in *Akers* that a beneficiary of a fixed trust has 'two main legal rights': a personal right against the trustee to have the trust administered according to its terms, and also a 'true proprietary right' capable of binding third party recipients of the trust property.[57]

Secondly, there are different ways of understanding this point about the extent of the duties of a third party, such as C, who is 'bound by the trust'. One way to understand it, which will be adopted in this chapter, is to distinguish between the core aspect of a trustee's duties, which is the duty not to use a particular right for the trustee's own benefit (unless and to the extent that the terms of the trust permit), and additional positive duties to which an express trustee may be subject as a result of consenting to such duties.[58] Where a recipient of the trust property, such as C, is 'bound' by the trust, without having agreed to act as trustee, then it is that core negative duty not to use the right for his or her own benefit that binds C. The crucial distinction is between a duty which is capable of persisting even when the trust property changes hands, and even if C has not consented to being subject to that duty, and duties which do not so persist. Contrary to Birks' analysis, the distinction is not between 'proprietary rights and obligations' but rather between different types of obligation. The 'equitable property right' of a beneficiary consists of a particular type of negative duty owed to the beneficiary by the trustee; other duties owed by the trustee to the beneficiary, such as those positive duties which bind a party only if they have consented to them, do not have the same third party effect and are thus not seen as proprietary.[59]

In *Akers*, Lord Sumption, in an echo of Birks' suggestion, states that the 'personal and proprietary rights of the beneficiary exist independently, and neither is dependent on the continued existence of the other'.[60] In its particular context, this

[56] Richard Nolan, 'Equitable Property' (2006) 122 LQR 232.

[57] *Akers* (n 44) [82].

[58] For discussion of the important role of a trustee's consent in the constitution of an express trust, see Ying Liew and Charles Mitchell, 'The Creation of Express Trusts' (2017) 11 J Eq 133, 133–34.

[59] This of course reflects the distinction made by Nolan (n 56) between positive and negative duties in this context. In *Williams v Central Bank of Nigeria* [2014] UKSC 10, [2014] AC 1189 [31], Lord Sumption wished to reserve the term 'trustee' to parties who have agreed to hold on trust: whether or not this is a plausible interpretation of the use of the term in the context of the Limitation Act 1980, it is contrary to the general usage that C, if bound by the core duty not to use a right for C's own benefit, is accountable to B as a 'constructive trustee'.

[60] [2017] UKSC 6, [2017] AC 424 [83].

statement can be justified: it merely reflects the fact that, even if B's potential claim against C is defeated by, for example, a bona fide purchaser defence, B may still have a personal claim against A, the trustee. However, it would be a mistake to insist on a full separation between the duties to which A is subject and the ability of B to bring a claim against C: this is one of the dangers of the use of the term 'equitable title' and of the separation suggested by Birks. As most famously argued by Maitland,[61] and underlying the analysis of Lord Browne-Wilkinson in *Westdeutsche*,[62] the fact of A's being under a particular type of duty to B is what generates B's ability to bring a claim against a third party and is thus the basis of B's having an equitable property right at all. The notion of 'equitable title' can mislead[63] as it may suggest that B's equitable right is based on a direct, unilateral connection between B and a particular resource, rather than on a relationship between A and B. A feature of legal title to a chattel is that it can be acquired unilaterally, as when B, on his own behalf, simply takes possession of a physical thing. In contrast, as Lionel Smith has argued, the acquisition of any equitable property right depends on there being at least two parties:[64] A must have a particular right, and A must be under a duty to B in relation to that right.

This point is in fact central to the decision of the House of Lords in *Westdeutsche*. The claimant bank had made a payment to a local authority under a contract which turned out to be void as *ultra vires* the local authority. The bank argued that the payment received by the local authority was held by it on trust for the bank. One of the arguments made by the bank was that, whilst the payment was effective to transfer legal title to the local authority, the bank, having acted under the mistake that the contract was valid, had retained its equitable title to the payment.[65] Lord Browne-Wilkinson's judgment exposes the fallacy in this argument. The bank had no separate legal and equitable titles to the money paid. For such an equitable right to arise, there would have to be a particular relationship between the bank and some other party; there was no such party, and the bank simply had the right to the money. For a trust to arise, therefore, the bank had to show a particular reason why the local authority should have come under a duty to it in relation to the specific right acquired by the local authority—or, in Birks' language, it had to point to an event giving rise to such a duty.

Thirdly, the notion of 'equitable title' is also misleading as it suggests that, where A has legal title and B has equitable title to an asset, competing claims are made by the parties, and common law and equity are disagreeing on the fundamental

[61] See, eg, Maitland, *Equity: A Course of Lectures* (n 29).
[62] *Westdeutsche* (n 45) 705.
[63] See further Ben McFarlane, 'The Persistence of Equity: Lessons from the Trust' in Ben McFarlane and Stephen Elliott (eds), *Equity Today: 150 Years after the Judicature Act* (Hart 2023).
[64] See, eg, Lionel Smith, 'Equity is Not a Single Thing', in Klimchuk, Samet, and Smith (eds), *Philosophical Foundations* (n 19) esp s V.
[65] *Westdeutsche* (n 45) 706.

issue of title to the asset. As Maitland memorably pointed out,[66] it would make little sense to have a legal system where two sets of courts take conflicting views on such a question. The view taken in this chapter avoids such 'civil war and utter anarchy'[67] as equity's recognition of a trust in B's favour does not deny A's title; indeed, the operation of the trust *depends* on A's having valuable claims against third parties, as it imposes a duty on A to B in relation to those claims.

A useful way of seeing this point as to the interrelation between equity and the common law of property is to consider the parallel question of the relationship between domestic and foreign law. It is striking that, in *Akers*, the Court was able to apply a law other than the *lex situs* of the shares to determine B's rights in relation to Saudi shares. As Lord Mance stated: 'in the eyes of English law, a trust may be created, exist and be enforceable in respect of assets located in a jurisdiction, the law of which does not recognise trusts in any form.'[68] Lord Mance drew on a long and consistent line of authorities in reaching that conclusion, and a significant part of the reasoning in those cases is that, in relation to each of jurisdiction and choice of law, the question of whether B has a right under a trust of, for example, land or shares is *not* governed by the same rules as the different question of whether a party has the right to the land itself, or to the shares themselves.[69] In claiming such a right under a trust, B is not claiming the asset held on trust, but is rather claiming that the holder of the asset is under a particular duty to B. This provides one reason why, in *Webb v Webb*, an English[70] and a European[71] court each held that, in claiming that A held title to French land on trust for him, B's claim did not have as its object a right *in rem* in immovable property, and so the French courts did not have exclusive jurisdiction under what is now Article 24(1) of the Recast Brussels Regulation.

One of the cases cited by Lord Mance in *Akers* was *British South Africa Co v De Beers Consolidated Mines Ltd*.[72] In applying to foreign land the equitable rule against clogging the equity of redemption, Cozens-Hardy MR stated that:

> If A by an English contract agreed to give a mortgage to secure an English debt upon land in a foreign country, the law of which country does not recognize the existence of what we call an equity of redemption, *which was the case of our common law*, and if a mortgage was given and duly perfected according to the lex situs, I feel no doubt that our courts would restrain the mortgagee from exercising the rights given by the foreign law and would treat the transaction as a mortgage

[66] Maitland, *Equity: A Course of Lectures* (n 29) 17. See too Jeffrey Hackney, *Understanding Equity and Trusts* (Fontana 1986) ch 1.

[67] Maitland, *Equity: A Course of Lectures* (n 29) 17.

[68] [2017] UKSC 6, [2017] AC 424 [34].

[69] See further Sinéad Agnew and Ben McFarlane, 'The Nature of Trusts and the Conflict of Laws' (2021) 137 LQR 405.

[70] [1991] 1 WLR 1410 (Ch D).

[71] (C-294/92) EU:C:1994:193, [1994] QB 696.

[72] [1910] 2 Ch 502 (CA).

> in the sense in which that word is used by us. In doing this our courts would not in any way interfere with the lex situs, but would by injunction, and if necessary by process of contempt, restrain the mortgagee from asserting those rights. Similar observations would apply to a trustee, if the lex situs does not recognize trusts.[73]

The passing reference, emphasised above, to the common law indicates that the analysis of the relationship between English law and foreign law may also apply to the relationship of common law and equity. Just as an English court taking jurisdiction, or enforcing a trust, in respect of foreign property, is not challenging the position that A holds the relevant property, so equity, in affording B an equitable interest, does not seek to undermine the common law position that A has title;[74] rather it regulates, in favour of B, A's use and enforcement of that right.

The fourth point to be made here relates to another confusion that may arise from the concept of 'equitable title' and from an attempt to separate too cleanly the personal and proprietary aspects of a trust. As made clear in some of his other writing, Birks regarded the bona fide purchaser defence potentially available to C against B's pre-existing equitable interest as an exception to the *nemo dat* principle,[75] and thus concerned with overcoming A's inability to pass a good title to C. This is consistent with an 'equitable title' analysis: A holds only legal title, and so for C to acquire both legal and equitable title, A must be able to give what A does not have to C.[76] The difficulty with such an analysis[77] is that, if A holds a right on trust for B, and then (without authority under the terms of the trust) transfers that right to C, it is not true to say that A does not have good title, so that C needs to invoke an exception to *nemo dat*. Instead, a crucial feature of the trust is precisely that the trustee *does* have the right to the trust property[78] and, as an incident of that, has the power to transfer that right to C.[79] As Jessica Hudson has

[73] ibid 514 (emphasis added).

[74] The analysis here thus accords with Maitland's view as to the peaceful coexistence of common law and equity (see, eg, Maitland, *Equity: A Course of Lectures* (n 29)) rather than with Hohfeld's criticisms of Maitland in Wesley Hohfeld, 'The Relations Between Equity and Law' (1913) 11 Mich L R 537: see further Ben McFarlane, 'Avoiding Anarchy? Common Law v Equity and Maitland v Hohfeld' in John Goldberg, Henry Smith, and Peter Turner (eds), *Equity and Law: Fusion and Fission* (CUP 2019) 331.

[75] Peter Birks, 'Notice and Onus in O'Brien' (1998) 12 TLI 2 (discussing the Court of Appeal's decision in *Barclays Bank v Boulter*, later overturned by the House of Lords: [1999] 1 WLR 1919 (HL)).

[76] See too Hanoch Dagan and Irit Samet, 'Express Trust as the Missing Piece in the Liberal Property Regime Jigsaw' in Degeling, Hudson, and Samet (eds), *Philosophical Foundations* (n 41).

[77] As discussed in Ben McFarlane and Andreas Televantos, 'As Complex as ABC? Bona Fide Purchasers of Equitable Interests' in Paul Davies and Tan Chen-Han (eds), *Intermediaries in Commercial Law* (Hart 2022).

[78] See further Ben McFarlane, 'Trusts, Property, and Rights' in Degeling, Hudson, and Samet (eds) *Philosophical Foundations* (n 41).

[79] See, eg, *Rolled Steel Products Ltd v British Steel Corp* [1986] Ch 246 (CA) 303 (Browne-Wilkinson LJ):

> If two trustees convey trust property in breach of trust, the conveyance is not void. As human beings they have the capacity to transfer the legal estate: their capacity to transfer flows from their status as human beings, not from the powers conferred on them as trustees. Even if their

observed,[80] the intervention of equity is required not in order to deny A's power to make the transfer to C, but to limit the practical effects of that transfer on B. The crucial point is that A does not have a liberty, *as against* B, to make the unauthorised transfer and cannot, for example, bring that transfer into account if a claim is made by B; but that does not alter A's general power, as an incident of A's having the right, to transfer that right to a party such as C.[81]

In fact, the outcome of *Akers* can be seen to depend on a rejection of an 'equitable title' analysis. It was held there that, even if C is not bound by B's pre-existing equitable interest, A's transfer of the trust property to C is not a 'disposition' of B's property for the purposes of section 127 of the Insolvency Act 1986.[82] If C's use of a defence, such as the bona fide purchaser defence, were seen as an exception to *nemo dat*, allowing C to acquire B's equitable title to the trust property, then surely a disposition of B's property *would* occur in such a case. The point is that, in a case such as *Akers*, A did have the rights constituted by the shares: as noted by Lord Sumption there, the general question after a transfer in breach of trust is not as to the rights C has acquired but is rather whether C's conscience is affected[83] in such a way that C comes under a duty, in relation to the rights acquired, to B. This means that rules protecting C's good faith acquisition of a right from an intermediary may have a significantly different form according to whether B's pre-existing right is legal or equitable.[84]

For example, consider the 'seller in possession' and 'buyer in possession' rules which can give C, a good faith purchaser from A, protection from a pre-existing but hidden legal title of B.[85] It is reasonable to see such rules as exceptions to the *nemo*

> powers under the trust instrument did not authorise the conveyance, the legal estate will vest in the transferee.

See too Aruna Nair and Irit Samet, 'What Can 'Equity's Darling' Tell Us About Equity?' in Klimchuk, Samet, and Smith (eds), *Philosophical Foundations* (n 19) 276–84.

80 Jessica Hudson, 'Equity's Gloss on Authority' in McFarlane and Elliott (eds), *Equity Today* (n 63).

81 On the difference between the general powers of a trustee, and their powers as against the beneficiaries, see too Jessica Hudson, 'One Thicket in Fraud on a Power' (2019) 39 OJLS 577; Jessica Hudson and Charles Mitchell, 'Trustee Recoupment: A Power Analysis' (2021) 35 TLI 3, 8.

82 See, eg, Lord Mance in *Akers* (n 44) [52], citing Lloyd LJ's analysis in *Independent Trustee Services Ltd v GP Noble Trustees Ltd* [2012] EWCA Civ 195, [2013] Ch 91 [106] that in such a case A 'cannot vest the beneficial interest in the property in [C]'. This analysis of the meaning of 'disposition' is also consistent with that of the House of Lords, in the context of s 53(1)(c) of the Law of Property Act 1925, in *Vandervell v IRC* [1967] 2 AC 291 (HL).

83 See, eg, Lord Sumption in *Akers* (n 44) [89].

84 See too Sinéad Agnew and Ben McFarlane, 'The Paradox of the Equitable Proprietary Claim' in Ben McFarlane and Sinead Agnew (eds), *Modern Studies in Property Law*, vol X (Hart 2019) 303, 311. Note too Maitland, *Equity: A Course of Lectures* (n 29) 142–43, noting the 'marked difference' between the *nemo dat* exceptions in the Factors Act 1889 and the bona fide purchaser defence in equity: whereas in the first cases, 'the buyer gets ownership, but we do not conceive that he gets it from the seller, for the seller never had ownership', in the latter cases 'the rule about the effect of a purchase in rendering equitable rights unenforceable is based on this: that the trustee has ownership, and transfers it to the purchaser, and that there is no reason for taking away from the purchaser the legal right which has thus been transferred to him'.

85 See Factors Act 1889, ss 8 and 9; Sale of Goods Act 1979, ss 24 and 25.

dat principle, as their statutory formulation makes clear that C is to be treated as though A had authority from B to transfer B's title to C. In contrast, where the bona fide purchaser defence applies to allow C to acquire trust property free from B's pre-existing equitable interest, there is no transfer of B's right to C. Rather, the circumstances of C's acquisition can be seen as giving C an immunity against B: B no longer has the power to make a claim against C, even if C later acquires knowledge that A held on trust and made the transfer without authority under that trust.[86]

B. A Non-Proprietary Explanation for Third Party Effect

Given the clear differences between the operation of B's interest under a trust and of a legal property right, why is it conventional to think of B's right as proprietary? The protection of B's right in A's insolvency, and the possibility of B's making a claim against a recipient from A, are of course central to this. However, it is clear that such features can arise even in a case where B's right is not conventionally thought of as proprietary. For example, Fox has recently shown how B's protection in A's insolvency (often said to depend on, and prove, the proprietary status of B's rights) was developed by the courts independently of any such classification of B's rights.[87]

This is not of merely historical interest, as it also shows that there is no necessary conceptual link between protection in insolvency and the holding of a right *in rem*. As Mitchell has pointed out,[88] for example, a legatee of an unadministered estate has no right in any specific property of the deceased, but this does not mean that general creditors of the personal representative have any access to the deceased estate to meet the debts of the personal representative.[89] Moreover, such a legatee may also make a claim against a third party to whom the personal representative makes an unauthorised disposition of assets in the estate.[90] Like such a legatee, an object of a discretionary trust also has the negative protection available to a beneficiary of a fixed trust, both in the insolvency of the trustee and against third party recipients of the trust property.

One way of understanding such protection is to see it as deriving from equity's treatment of the duty of due administration to which a trustee, like a personal

86 See, eg, Agnew and McFarlane, 'The Paradox of the Equitable Proprietary Claim' (n 84).
87 David Fox, 'Bankruptcy Protection for Trusts before the Judicature Acts' in McFarlane and Elliott (eds), *Equity Today* (n 63).
88 Charles Mitchell, '*Commissioner of Stamp Duties v Livingston* (1965)' in Brian Sloan (ed) *Landmark Cases in Succession Law* (Hart 2019).
89 See, eg, *Farr v Newman* (1792) 4 TR 620, 100 ER 1209.
90 See, eg, *Hill v Simpson* (1802) 7 Ves Jun 152, 32 ER 63; *Commissioner of Stamp Duties v Livingston* [1965] AC 694 (PC) 713–14.

representative, is subject.[91] To the extent that it relates to particular rights held by the defendant, the scope of the duty is extended to particular third parties,[92] and this need not depend on any proprietary entitlement of a particular claimant. The crucial point in explaining the third party effect of B's right, whether B is a beneficiary of a fixed trust, an object of a discretionary trust, or a legatee of an unadministered estate, is simply that A is under a duty, enforceable by B, in relation to specific rights held by A. There is no need to explain that third party effect by regarding B as in any way an 'owner' of, or having title to, the assets held by A.[93]

C. Beyond the Trust

Equity's contribution to the law of property, broadly defined, is not of course limited to the trust. The 'longer list of property rights'[94] arising from equity includes, in relation to land, estate contracts, equitable leases, and equitable easements, as well as the restrictive covenant and, more generally, the equitable charge. These types of rights will not be examined in detail here as the claim of the chapter is that such rights (with the exception of the restrictive covenant) can also be understood as related not to a thing, but rather to a right held by another.

The link between such rights and A's being under a duty to B is clear in the circumstances in which, for example, an equitable lease may arise. It is not the case that A can choose to give B a right with the content of an equitable lease as opposed to a legal lease.[95] Rather, the distinction is between the case where, either expressly or by implication, A does actually exercise A's power to grant B a lease (and B, subject to any registration requirements, thereby acquires a legal lease) and the case where A is instead under an enforceable duty to exercise that power (and B hence

[91] See, eg, Jessica Hudson, Charles Mitchell, and Ben McFarlane, *Hayton, McFarlane and Mitchell on Trusts and Equity* (15th edn, Sweet and Maxwell, 2022) 3.143–192. See too Hudson, 'Equity's Gloss on Authority' (n 80).

[92] For equity's extension of duties to third parties, where the duty relates to the benefit or use of a particular right, see, eg, Smith (n 64). Note, on this view, protection in insolvency can be seen simply as an application of the general rules on third party effect: this is why that protection arises even if, for example, there is no statutory provision specifying that assets held on trust are not available to the party acquiring or managing the insolvent estate: see, eg, Kiefel CJ, Keane and Edelman JJ in *Carter Holt* (n 42) [26].

[93] Indeed, the same third party effect arises in relation to a charitable trust, where there is clearly no party (other than the trustee) who can be identified as having a title to the assets. Note too that, even in the case where B is a beneficiary of a fixed trust, A's rights of indemnity demonstrate that it is dangerous to regard B as in any sense an owner of the trust assets: see further McFarlane, 'Trusts, Property, and Rights' (n 78). The view taken here is thus inconsistent with the analysis of the nature of an interest under a trust in, eg, Hanoch Dagan and Irit Samet, 'The Beneficiary's Ownership Rights in the Trust Res in a Liberal Property Regime' (2023) 86 MLR 701.

[94] See, eg, William Swadling, 'Property' in Andrew Burrows (ed), *English Private Law* (3rd edn, OUP 2013) 4.25.

[95] See, eg, *Alexander-David v Hammersmith and Fulham* [2009] EWCA Civ 259 [30]: 'a landlord does not elect to grant an equitable tenancy; such a tenancy arises in certain circumstances, recognised by equity.'

acquires an equitable lease).[96] The example of the equitable charge also clearly shows the difference between the transfer of a right (as occurs in a true mortgage) and A's retaining a right but coming under a duty to B in relation to that right (as occurs in an equitable charge). This helps to explain why it is possible for A to create such a charge, in favour of B Bank, over A's account with B Bank: it would not be possible for A to transfer such a right to B Bank, but there is no conceptual impossibility in A's being under a defeasible duty to B Bank in relation to a right that A has against B Bank.[97]

The restrictive covenant can be seen as the exception that proves the rule. Whilst clearly a creation of equity and based on a particular initial duty being owed by A to B, the right has a number of features which, on any view, make it anomalous amongst equitable property rights. First, and most importantly for present purposes, it can bind a third party, such as a squatter, who acquires title to land, even if that title does not derive from A.[98] As Maitland noted,[99] this is inconsistent with the general operation of equitable interests. However, it is required as a matter of policy if the restrictive covenant is to perform its important role of giving enduring protection to a party selling off part of its land.[100] Secondly, the restrictive covenant exists as an equitable property right only in relation to land: this suggests again that it meets a particular policy concern in relation to such property, as does the requirement that B has some land that benefits from the restrictive covenant. There is a strong argument that the restrictive covenant is an example of equity correcting the common law, of directly contradicting common law rules as to the scope of negative easements[101] and that, logically, such rights should be recognised by Parliament as capable of being legal interests.[102]

IV. Types of Event

As discussed in Section I, Birks' taxonomy can be seen as ultimately focused on identifying the events that give rise to particular types of right. Even if rights are divided only into proprietary and personal rights, there is a difficulty in Birks' use of wrongs, consent, unjust enrichment, and 'other events' as the four categories of events capable of giving rise to such rights. The formulation, as well as Birks'

96 See, eg, *Walsh v Lonsdale* (1882) 21 Ch D 9 (CA).

97 See *In Re BCCI (No 8) SA* [1998] AC 214 (HL); McFarlane and Stevens, 'The Nature of Equitable Property' (n 19) 25–26.

98 *Re Nisbet and Potts' Contract* (n 23).

99 Maitland, *Equity: A Course of Lectures* (n 29) ch 12, 169–70.

100 See Cozens-Hardy LJ in *Re Nisbet and Potts' Contract* (n 23) 409; Ben McFarlane, 'The Numerus Clausus Principle and Covenants Relating to Land' in Sue Bright (ed), *Modern Studies in Property Law*, vol VI (Hart 2011).

101 See, eg, Lord Jessel MR in *London & SW Rwy Co v Gomm* (1882) 20 Ch D 562 (CA) 580.

102 As recommended by the Law Commission, *Easements, Covenants and Profits à Prendre* (Law Com No 237, 2011)

discussion of sale,[103] may carry the implication that we should expect some continuity between the types of event giving rise to personal rights and those giving rise to proprietary rights. As a matter of principle, however, given the very different nature and effects of a legal property right on the one hand, and a personal right on the other, there is no reason to think that the same type of events should give rise to each type of right: the nature of the output (what type of right a party acquires) must affect the requirements of the input (what is sufficient for such a right to be acquired). As a matter of practice, the operation of English law certainly suggests that there are significant differences between the types of event capable of giving rise to legal property rights (such as taking possession, accession, or manufacture) and those which can give rise to personal rights. This point is partly hidden by the width of Birks' 'other' category, as well as by the ability of certain contracts of sale to pass title to goods without the need for any further acts.

Another factor hiding this problem in Birks' scheme is the failure to identify equitable property rights as a distinct category of right. It was argued in Section II that such rights depend on A's being under a particular type of duty to B. As such, there *is* a clear continuity between the events giving rise to *equitable* property rights and the events giving rise to personal rights, which are often also based on A's being under a duty to B (the difference being that, for a personal right, A's duty need not relate to any specific right of A). For example, one way of understanding the difference between a case where A, a fiduciary, receives a bribe to act contrary to the interests of the principal, B, and where A instead carelessly injures B is that, whilst in each case A commits a wrong against B, it is only in the former case that the courts have decided that addressing the wrong requires A to be under a duty to B in relation to a specific right held by A (the bribe).[104] Similarly, in a case such as *Westdeutsche*, were a trust to arise, it would not be based on a fundamentally different event from B's personal claim against A, arising as a result of B's payment to A under the void contract, but rather on the additional fact that B was able to enforce that duty against A at a point in time when A still held a right constituting the payment, or its traceable proceeds.[105]

The view adopted in this chapter, therefore, has two important consequences as regards the types of event giving rise to rights. The first concerns the grounds on which legal property rights may arise. The nature of such rights, as imposing prima facie duties on the rest of the world in relation to a specific thing, and thus relating their holder to that thing, differs clearly from the nature of equitable property rights or personal rights, which instead depend on a duty owed to their holder by another. As a result, we should not expect there to be continuity in the justifications

[103] Birks (n 5) 52.
[104] See *FHR European Ventures LLP v Cedar Capital Partners LLC* [2014] UKSC 45, [2015] AC 250.
[105] For such a case see, eg, *Wambo Coal Pty v Ariff* [2007] NSWSC 589.

for legal property rights on the one hand, and the justifications for equitable property rights and personal rights on the other.[106]

This is significant when considering Birks' discussion of tracing in his 1996 lectures.[107] Birks' argument that equitable tracing rules should be adopted by the common law depends on the view that the purpose of such rules is to support claims which depend on tracking the passage of value from claimant to defendant: the continuity of event demands adoption of the same rules. If, however, the common law rules can give rise to a right to a thing, and are based on identifying one *thing* as, to some extent at least, the product of an original thing to which the claimant had a right, whereas the equitable rules can give rise to a right to a right, and are based instead on identifying one *right* as, to some extent at least, the product of an original right to which the claimant had a right, then there is no requirement for such continuity. Hafeez-Baig and English, for example, make the case against common law tracing,[108] showing that its position in English law depends on an understanding of *Taylor v Plumer*[109] exposed as mistaken by Khurshid and Matthews,[110] and Smith.[111] Indeed, as Hafeez-Baig and English note,[112] Birks himself stated that '[c]ommon law never traced at all, and would perhaps never have done so but for a mistaken understanding of [*Taylor v Plumer*]'.[113]

A good example[114] of the confusion which Birks' approach can cause is provided by *Trustee of FC Jones & Sons v Jones*.[115] Dispositions of partnership assets made by Mr Jones, including payments to Mrs Jones, were void as made after an initial act of bankruptcy of the partnership. The proceeds from the payments were paid by Mrs Jones into her account with a firm of commodity brokers. Her trading was successful and the profits were paid into a deposit account with a bank. When the dispute arose, the bank interpleaded, seeking directions as to whether the sums credited to Mrs Jones' account should be paid to her or to the trustee in bankruptcy of the partnership. The decision depended on identifying one right (a bank account held by Mrs Jones) as the product of an earlier right (the partnership bank account) and the claim made by the trustee in bankruptcy should have been seen,

[106] The approach advocated in this chapter is thus consistent with the division adopted in Robert Stevens, *The Laws of Restitution* (OUP 2023) pt V, where events giving rise to legal property rights are considered separately from those giving rise to equitable property rights.

[107] Birks (n 5) 84–90.

[108] Mohammud Hafeez-Baig and Jordan English, 'Common Law Tracing: The Emperor's New Clothes?' (2018) 2 J Eq 260 and *The Law of Tracing* (Federation Press 2021) ch 3.

[109] (1816) 3 M & S 562, 105 ER 721.

[110] Salman Khurshid and Paul Matthews, 'Tracing Confusion' (1979) 95 LQR 78.

[111] Lionel Smith, 'Tracing in *Taylor v Plumer*: Equity in the Court of King's Bench' [1995] LMCLQ 240.

[112] Hafeez-Baig and English (n 108) 82.

[113] Peter Birks, 'The Necessity of a Unitary Law of Tracing' in Ross Cranston (ed), *Making Commercial Law* (OUP 1997) 239, 245.

[114] Used by, eg, Hafeez-Baig and English (n 108) 70–71 as well as by McFarlane and Stevens, 'The Nature of Equitable Property' (n 19) 21–22.

[115] *Jones* (n 2).

it is submitted, as a claim that Mrs Jones now held her bank account on trust for the partners. Millett LJ, relying in part on *Taylor v Plumer*, purported to apply common law tracing principles, but it cannot be said that the partners, at law, held the bank account which consisted of Mrs Jones' right against her bank. There is a similar difficulty with the use of common law tracing, and the conclusion that the claimant had a legal property right in cash received by the defendant, in *Lipkin Gorman v Karpnale*;[116] an alternative means of understanding the successful claim is to see it as dependent on the assertion of an equitable, rather than a legal, property right.[117] The key point in each case is that the holding of a right by a particular party,[118] whilst inconsistent with the claimant's having that very same right, is perfectly consistent with the claimant's having a right in relation to that right.

The second important consequence is in some ways the converse point: it should not be thought that limits on the recognition of legal property rights must also apply to equitable property rights. For example, the clear divergence between the events giving rise to legal property rights and those giving rise to equitable property rights can be seen in the Land Registration Act 2002. Whereas registration is often required for the acquisition of a legal estate or interest,[119] there is no case under the statute where the acquisition of an equitable interest depends on its registration.[120]

This point also shows the difficulties with another influential argument of Birks. He drew on an assumption as to when legal property rights may arise[121] when suggesting that, if B wishes to assert a legal or equitable property right in relation to assets 'in which, by substitutions and intermixtures, the original enrichment [of A] now survives', B must show a 'proprietary base': that is, 'the circumstances of the original receipt by the defendant must be such that, either in law or in equity, [B] retained or obtained the property matter received by the defendant, and then continued to retain it until the moment at which the substitution or intermixture took place'.[122] This argument has been influential,[123] but it is difficult to sustain in light

[116] *Lipkin Gorman* (n 16). The rogue partner, Cass, had withdrawn money from the partnership bank account for use in gambling. It was accepted that, as a partner, Cass had legal title to that money. It was held by Lord Goff (at 574) that the partnership nonetheless had some form of common law property right in relation to the money, such right based on tracing their 'property at common law' in the partnership bank account into the cash drawn out by Cass.

[117] See, eg, Ben McFarlane, 'Unjust Enrichment, Property Rights and Indirect Recipients' [2009] 17 RLR 37; Lionel Smith, 'Simplifying Claims to Traceable Proceeds' (2009) 125 LQR 338.

[118] Mrs Jones in *Jones* (n 2) and Cass in *Lipkin Gorman* (n 16).

[119] Land Registration Act 2002, ss 4 and 27.

[120] See McFarlane, *The Structure of Property Law* (n 19) 87–93 and 124–25; see further Aruna Nair, 'Equity and the Land Registration Act 2002: Form, Conscience, and the Judiciary' in McFarlane and Elliott (eds), *Equity Today* (n 63).

[121] Peter Birks, *An Introduction to the Law of Restitution* (rev edn, OUP 1989) 380: 'there has never been any doubt that this proprietary starting point is what the common law requires in order to raise a restitutionary interest *in rem* in the surviving enrichment.'

[122] ibid 378–79.

[123] See, eg, Roy Goode, 'Ownership and Obligation in the Commercial Transactions' (1987) 103 LQR 433; *Sinclair Investments (UK) Ltd v Versailles Trade Finance Ltd* [2011] EWCA Civ 347, [2012] Ch 453. See too the discussion below of *Byers v Saudi National Bank* [2023] UKSC 51, [2024] 2 WLR 237.

of, for example, the Supreme Court's recognition in *FHR European Ventures LLP v Cedar Capital Partners LLC*[124] that a constructive trust can arise in relation to a bribe received by a fiduciary.[125] In contrast, if an equitable property right, such as that arising under a constructive trust, is instead seen as arising where A is under a duty to B in relation to a specific right, then the relevant question in a case such as *FHR* can be answered directly: do the reasons which justify A's being under a duty to B also justify A's being under a duty to transfer to B *the very right* acquired as the bribe?[126]

The concept of a 'proprietary base' has also been used in relation to another equitable example discussed by Birks in his 1996 lectures: claims available against a recipient of trust property. *Byers v Saudi National Bank*,[127] which followed on from *Akers*,[128] considered a knowing receipt claim brought by the liquidators of SICL (B) against Samba (C). The issues to be considered by the Court were limited because procedural failures prevented C from making certain arguments: for example, C could not challenge the assumption that B's knowing receipt claim was governed by English or Cayman law. B's claim was nonetheless rejected. It was held that, as a matter of English or Cayman law, a knowing receipt claim could not be made against C where Saudi Arabian law, as the law governing the transfer of shares from A to C, prevented B from asserting its pre-existing interest under the trust of those shares against C. Influenced by the analysis of Millett J in *Macmillan v Bishopsgate (No 3)* that a knowing receipt claim is based on 'continuing equitable ownership',[129] both Fancourt J at first instance and the Court of Appeal adopted the requirement of a 'continuing proprietary base',[130] finding that a knowing receipt claim cannot arise if from the moment of receipt C has an 'unencumbered title'.[131] The Supreme Court agreed that, where the circumstances of the transfer to C extinguish or override B's 'proprietary interest', no knowing receipt claim can be made, justifying this conclusion by noting that the 'personal claim in knowing receipt against a transferee is closely linked to a proprietary claim for the return of the property'.[132] The language used in these analyses is thus inconsistent with that adopted in this chapter, and raises directly the question posed by Birks as to

[124] [2014] UKSC 45, [2015] AC 250.

[125] See too Robert Stevens, 'Proprietary Base Revisited' (forthcoming).

[126] See further McFarlane, *The Structure of Property Law* (n 29) 257–58, 560–61 and Ben McFarlane, 'The Centrality of Constructive and Resulting Trusts' in Charles Mitchell (ed) *Constructive and Resulting Trusts* (Hart 2012).

[127] [2023] UKSC 51, [2024] 2 WLR 237.

[128] *Akers* (n 44).

[129] [1995] 1 WLR 978 (Ch D) 988. An appeal against the judgment of Millett J was unsuccessful: [1996] 1 WLR 387 (CA).

[130] [2021] EWHC 60 (Ch) [205], [2022] EWCA Civ 43 [79]: 'In short, a continuing proprietary interest in the relevant property is required for a knowing receipt claim to be possible.'

[131] [2022] EWCA Civ 43 [49] and [76].

[132] See Lord Hodge (with whom Lord Leggatt and Lord Stephens agreed) [2023] UKSC 51 [4] and [5], referring to the detailed analyses of Lord Briggs at [23]–[24], [41]–[42], and [46] and Lord Burrows at [172], [201], and [145]–[149].

the relationship between a strict liability restitutionary claim and a knowing receipt claim: if the latter claim is based on B's assertion of a property right, why is C's liability not strict? Yet attempts to recognise such a strict liability in cases involving the protection of equitable property rights have been rejected by both the English[133] and Australian[134] courts.

This brings us back to the question discussed in Section I of the meaning to be given to terms such as 'property'. The first point is that a term such as 'proprietary' may be used to capture the fact that B's claim depends on B's having a particular type of pre-existing right, related either to a thing or another right, which is capable of binding a third party. In the case of knowing receipt of trust property, for example, B *does* need to show that C's conscience is affected,[135] but the particular means of doing so requires not only C's knowledge of the facts meaning that A's transfer to C was unauthorized, but also that C must have acquired a particular type of right. C's receipt of such a right is a fundamental part of B's claim.[136] Indeed, contrary to the analysis of Birks, it is the receipt of a *right*, and not just of a benefit or enrichment more generally, that is a requirement of liability.[137] This also shows how the effect of an equitable property right on a third party differs from that of a purely personal right: in the latter case, it is possible, for example, for a third party to be liable for procuring a breach of contract, but this liability does not depend on the receipt of any particular right. It also means that the circumstances in which C acquires the right may be relevant to the question of whether C's conscience is affected. So, the need for a 'proprietary base' may simply mean that, in a case such as *Byers*, where A initially holds a right on trust for B, the necessary (but not sufficient) elements of a knowing receipt claim following an unauthorised disposal of that right by A include: (1) C's having acquired a right in relation to which B has a pre-existing equitable property right; and (2) C's not having a defence based on the circumstances of C's acquisition of the right (such as, eg, a bona fide purchaser defence). If so, the 'proprietary base' requirement in knowing receipt is not inconsistent with the analysis in this chapter, and certainly does not mean that an equitable property right has the same effect on a third party as a legal property right.

The second point, consistent with the unity of approach in *Macmillan* and *Byers* is that, as Sinéad Agnew and I have previously argued,[138] a knowing receipt claim is based on exactly the relationship between B and C which must be demonstrated

[133] See, eg, *BCCI v Akindele* [2001] Ch 437 (CA).

[134] See, eg, *Farah Constructions Pty Ltd v Say-Dee Pty Ltd* [2007] HCA 22, (2007) 230 CLR 89.

[135] As argued by unsuccessful counsel in *Macmillan*: [1995] 1 WLR 978 (Ch D) 988.

[136] See Agnew and McFarlane, 'The Nature of Trusts and the Conflict of Laws' (n 69) 423–24.

[137] See *Byers* [2022] EWCA Civ 43 [22] (Newey LJ): 'A defendant must have received trust assets, not just benefitted from them.'

[138] Agnew and McFarlane, 'The Paradox of the Equitable Proprietary Claim' (n 84).

in order for B to succeed in an 'equitable proprietary claim'. That relationship depends on C's having held a right (to either the initial trust property or its traceable proceeds) with sufficient knowledge of A's earlier duty. A claim that C must give up that right, as in *Macmillan*, and a claim that C must account for its value, as in *Byers*, are simply different means of giving effect to the same duty of C. This can be seen as the particular sense in which B's knowing receipt claim is, as noted by Lord Briggs in *Byers*, 'ancillary'[139] to B's equitable proprietary claim. Logically, then, a rule which has as its purpose the protection of C from B's pre-existing right must also protect C from a knowing receipt claim.[140]

It is therefore possible to explain the approach adopted in *Macmillan* and *Byers* without needing to use the potentially misleading idea of B's needing to have 'continuing equitable ownership' of the assets acquired by C.[141] Certainly, it would be an error to think that B's having such a right is necessary for a knowing receipt claim: if so, such claims would then be unavailable where, for example, the rights received by C were held by A on a charitable trust, or on a discretionary trust. Contrary to the analysis of Lord Burrows in *Byers*,[142] a knowing receipt claim is not an 'equitable analogue' to a common law claim such as conversion, based on C's wrongful interference with B's property. Rather, like the 'equitable proprietary claim', a knowing receipt claim depends on a particular reason for which C's conscience is affected: C's receipt of a right which was initially held by A on trust[143] and was transferred by A without authority under that trust, where C acquires sufficient knowledge of that lack of authority whilst still holding that right or its traceable proceeds.[144] As in the case where C acquires a right from charitable trustees acting without authority, such liability can arise even if there is no specific beneficiary who can claim that their 'property' or 'equitable ownership' has been interfered with.

[139] [2023] UKSC 51, [2024] 2 WLR 237 [42].

[140] Note this is consistent with the analysis in Matthew Conaglen and Amy Goymour, 'Knowing Receipt and Registered Land' in Charles Mitchell (ed), *Constructive and Resulting Trusts* (n 126), arguing that where land registration provisions prevent B's asserting a pre-existing interest under a trust against C, no knowing receipt claim should be available against C.

[141] Note too there is also a point specific to the conflict of laws context in those cases: ie that the issue of whether C can invoke a defence against B's claim based on the circumstances of C's acquisition of a right (such as the bona fide purchase defence) should be determined by the *lex situs*: see Agnew and McFarlane, 'The Nature of Trusts and the Conflict of Laws' (n 69) 421.

[142] [2023] UKSC 51, [2024] 2 WLR 237 [148] and [151]–[153].

[143] The claim can also arise where the right acquired by C is the traceable product of a right A held on trust. More importantly for present purposes, the claim has also been recognised in cases where there is no initial trust, but A is subject to a fiduciary duty in relation to their exercise of a power to transfer a right (see eg *Belmont Finance Corpn v Williams Furniture Ltd (No 2)* [1980] 1 All ER 393). In such cases, there is no pre-existing 'equitable property right' of B. For consideration of these cases, see *Byers* at [56]–[62] and [177]–[188].

[144] Note C may also be liable to B where C acquires a right as a result of an exercise by A of a power arising along with a right A holds on trust: see n 21.

V. Conclusion

In his 1996 lectures, Birks stated that '[a] system which is indifferent to taxonomy will frequently fail to review all the possibilities, for it is the taxonomy which holds out the map upon which they can all be seen'.[145] Birks also noted there that the task of drawing an adequate map is an ongoing one, and any proposed taxonomies must be vigorously debated.[146]

The central claim of this chapter is that the scheme set out by Birks, by failing to accord sufficient weight to the distinctiveness of equitable property rights, overlooked the possibility of a third type of right, with an exigibility distinct from each of legal property rights and personal rights. The recognition of this type of right has significant consequences for Birks' key concern of treating like cases alike by identifying the events capable of giving rise to rights. As a result, it has implications for Birks' specific suggestions as to the operation of the law. For example, it allows us to defend differences between the approaches to tracing at common law and in equity, and also to defend the different operation of, on the one hand, the strict-liability restitutionary personal claim and, on the other hand, liability in knowing receipt.

As far as the relationship between property and equity is concerned, this chapter has thus rejected the (reasonably common) idea that equity has given flexibility to English property law by removing unjustified limits imposed by common law on the content, and means of acquisition, of property rights. Rather than *correcting* such limits on those rights relating to things which are prima facie binding on the rest of the world, equity has left them untouched,[147] and has instead *supplemented* the common law by recognising a different type of right. This has had the beneficial effect of increasing the options available to holders of rights and has thus played a key role both in extending the means by which a party can realise value from a right, and in extending the types of right from which parties can realise value. Equity's achievement has thus been to bypass, rather than to redraw, the crucial borderline between property rights and personal rights.

[145] Birks (n 5) 45.
[146] ibid 4.
[147] Subject to the anomalous, but limited, exception of the restrictive covenant, discussed in Section III.C.

13
Property | Contract

Sarah Worthington

I. Introduction: The Issues in Play

Borderlines mark distinctions. Things on one side of a border are not the same as things on the other. If the borderline is important, then the differences between the divided territories are profound. Such borderlines thus serve as valuable analytical tools: accurately allocating territories to one side of the borderline or the other will indicate a great deal about the consequences to follow.[1] Viewed in this context, property and obligation are commonly regarded as fundamentally different legal territories. Something is either one or the other; it cannot be both. Here the focus is on contract, not all obligations, but the distinction holds. A bicycle is property, a debt is contract. The assertion is made as confidently as distinguishing black from white. But how is that classification made, why is it important, and is it accurate?

The answer to the question of 'how to classify' depends profoundly on the answer to 'why we need to classify'. Choosing suitable plants for a Sissinghurst white garden demands one set of classificatory criteria; choosing suitable plants for the local vegetable allotment another. The lawyers' common answer to why we need to classify property and obligation or property and contract is that property is better protected than contract, especially on insolvency; property is more reliable and more useful than contract: it holds its value, and more can be done with it to advantage its owner; and, finally, the inherent characteristics of each are very different. Even if only some of this is true, then it is critical to establish where the borderline is, and what benefits accrue to being on one side or the other.

With that lead-in, it may be a surprise to find that this chapter seeks to advance two claims against this orthodoxy. First, and despite all suggestions to the contrary, we have no clear view of what territory lies on the property side of the boundary. All the markers we traditionally depend upon to describe property and distinguish it from contract fail. All the advantages we ascribe to property are found equally persistently in contract. It follows that we should desist from endeavours to divide up property and contract territories, since we cannot define any significant borderline between them. We should instead, so as to escape the shackles of 'property | contract' terminology, simply speak of a person's 'assets'. Secondly, and far more

[1] By way of illustration, consider the search to identify clear borderlines between leases and licences, or between fixed and floating charges.

Sarah Worthington, *Property | Contract* In: *Borderlines in Private Law*. Edited by: William Day and Julius Grower, Oxford University Press. © Sarah Worthington 2024. DOI: 10.1093/9780191995200.003.0013

significantly, insolvency protection is not an attribute of property which distinguishes it from contract. It is an attribute found in respect of *all* assets, although this attribute is legally significant only when those assets are *shared* between the insolvent and others. That sharing may be achieved by contract but may also arise in other ways.[2] Crucially, these various ways enable all assets to be shared, not simply some subset of assets already pre-ordained as 'property'.

These conclusions are not intended to shatter the deep intuition that there is a fundamental distinction between property and contract. What emerges, however, is that this intuitive distinction does not reflect a territorial boundary separating property from contract, but rather a difference in the *perspective* being adopted in relation to all of a person's assets. The property perspective examines the totality of the bundles of rights and liabilities a person has in relation to an asset, whatever the nature of that asset. The obligations perspective, by contrast, considers each of those rights and liabilities separately, and what they entail as between the parties concerned; and the contract perspective considers only that subset of obligations which are contractual. If an analogy is needed, the property perspective examines the wood; the obligations/contract perspective, the trees. If accepted, this analysis may help refocus attention on the proper place of distinctions between property and contract.[3] If that happens, then this borderlines project will have succeeded in its intended goal of testing commonly accepted thinking in different legal contexts and forcing increased analytical rigour in the use of our tools of the legal trade.

In successive sections, this chapter considers how borderlines are identified, the lack of such a borderline between property and contract, the alternative notion that what divides property and contract is a matter of perspective not borderline, and, finally, the all-important issue of how insolvency protection is delivered, since

[2] eg, by unilateral declaration (express trusts) and by operation of law (constructive and resulting trusts).

[3] There are innumerable articles addressing or touching on the issues considered in this chapter. The following list provides an abbreviated but informative selection: Roy Goode, 'Ownership and Obligation in Commercial Transactions' (1987) 103 LQR 433; Kevin Gray, 'Property in Thin Air' (1991) 50 CLJ 252; Bernard Rudden, 'Things as Thing and Things as Wealth' [1994] OJLS 81; Geoffrey Samuel, 'Property Notions in the Law of Obligations' (1994) 53 CLJ 524; George Gretton, 'Owning Rights and Things' (1997) 8 Stellenbosch L Rev 176; Kenneth Reid, 'Obligations and Property: Exploring the Border' [1997] Acta Juridica 225 (Reid's first sentence is a riveting 'Let us begin by excluding England'. Nevertheless, this article contains much that is exceptionally useful for English scholars); Robert Chambers, 'Integrating Property and Obligations' in Andrew Robertson (ed), *The Law of Obligations: Connections and Boundaries* (Routledge-Cavendish Publishing Ltd 2004); Ralph Cunnington, 'Contract Rights as Property Rights' in ibid; Jim Harris, 'Property: Rights *in Rem* or Wealth?' in Peter Birks and Arianna Pretto (eds), *Themes in Comparative Law* (OUP 2002); Henry Hansmann and Reinier Kraakman, 'Property, Contract, and Verification: The *Numerus Clausus* Problem and the Divisibility of Rights' (2002) 31 JLS 378; George Gretton, 'Ownership and Its Objects' (2007) 71 *Rabels Zeitschrift für ausländisches und internationales Privatrecht* (The Rabel Journal of Comparative and International Private Law) 803; Henry Smith, 'Property as the Law of Things' (2012) 125 Harv LR 1691; Lutz-Christian Wolff, 'The Relationship between Contract Law and Property Law' (2020) 49 CLWR 31.

this remains the linchpin in most definitions of property and the justification for its necessary segregation from contract.

II. Identifying Borderlines that Matter

Given pause for thought, it is evident that the borderline between property and contract is significant only if all the material on the property side of the line is property (and not contract), and all the material on the other side of the line is contract (and not property), and, further, that there is some important and interesting difference between the two that is worth our attention. Put another way, unless the two categories are mutually exclusive—unless 'X *and* not Y' and 'Y *and* not X' holds true for the two categories—the borderline between them is incapable of marking out some fundamental and legally significant difference between the territories on either side: it cannot possibly be a boundary that marks a cliff-edge distinction between the two territories. And if the distinction that is then in view is not interesting, we are simply wasting time examining it.[4]

Reliance on useful boundary distinctions is remarkably common. The borderlines between plants and animals or between France and Germany are examples. Obviously, the reasons for investigating a borderline will differ depending upon the objective in sight. Invariably, however, the two categories selected to face each other across a borderline must be defined so as to be free of category errors. There are no useful category markers to distinguish between animals and dogs, or between countries and Germany: these choices involve category errors because one selected category swallows the other whole. Similarly, there are category errors when the overlap is merely partial. 'Plants suitable for a Sissinghurst white garden' and 'plants suitable for a local vegetable allotment' are not mutually exclusive categories. These categories will not work if the objective is to mark out some fundamental and distinctive attribute of one category that is absent from the other category.

Rolling all this together, the first task in what follows is to determine whether there is a category error in the assumption that 'property' and 'contract' face each other across a distinctive borderline. As indicated already, the conclusion advanced here is that this selected opposition involves a category error, in that the two territories overlap in a way that renders the reliable allocation of distinctive attributes to one, and excluding those attributes from the other, simply impossible.

[4] Even if the categories are mutually exclusive, and thus free of category errors, the exercise is only worthwhile if the categories present distinctions worth examining in detail. We would not spend hours examining the mutually exclusive categories of dogs and spaceships, or white plants and stars. To be sure, there will some similarities and many differences, but the two categories are so unalike that it is meaningless to spend time on the answer since no useful analytical information is delivered by the exercise.

III. Identifying Borderlines between Property and Contract

Showing that property and contract are not separated by a useful borderline can be undertaken in a number of ways. The most obvious is to start with the reasons we deem such a borderline important, and check whether the attributes said to mark out the property category, but to be lacking in the contract category, do indeed follow that pattern. The common assumption (which this chapter seeks to displace)[5] is that there is a distinctive 'property' territory characterised first by inherent 'property-type' attributes, and also by greater practical usefulness and greater means of protection (especially rights to transfer and rights to exclude others, the latter delivered by 'rights against the world'[6]), and finally by insolvency protection.[7] By contrast, the 'contract' territory is seen to lack all these advantageous features.

Notice that the search for this version of a property/contract borderline imposes its own definition on the property category. It does so in a less transparent way than the overt delineation in a category labelled 'plants for a Sissinghurst white garden'. Nevertheless, the exercise serves as a reminder that the objectives in undertaking the classification implicitly define the categories themselves, even when the label suggests no element of choice is either needed or possible. To illustrate, if the objective were to separate property from contract when the crucial characteristic of property was seen as a right to possess, then the classification system would capture only tangible assets in the 'property' category, and only contracts in the 'contract' category. The categories would be mutually exclusive, clearly, but would also be so vastly different from each other that the exercise would reveal a boundary line that merited little detailed examination.[8] In labelling categories we are thus choosing meanings for words, whether we appreciate it or not.[9]

[5] The difficulties are roundly recognised by many others, but they have not gone so far as to dismiss the property/contract category allocation question as pointless: see the commentators noted at n 3. Also see Sarah Worthington, 'The Disappearing Divide Between Property and Obligation: The Impact of Aligning Legal Analysis and Commercial Expectation' in Simone Degeling and James Edelman (eds), *Equity in Commercial Law* (Thomson Reuters 2005) and the commentators cited there.

[6] These two aspects of property—the right to control allocation and access—are often seen as the key markers of property, even outclassing the two other important rights said to be associated with property and not with contract, those being insolvency protection and entitlement to the fruits derived from the property: see Gray (n 3). The truth, it is suggested here, is that all four are important, but all four are associated with 'bundles of rights', whether traditionally conceived of as property or as obligation.

[7] Abbreviating the attributes selectively, but for the detail see Tony Honoré, 'Ownership' in Anthony Guest (ed), *Oxford Essays in Jurisprudence* (1st edn, OUP 1961) esp at 107, providing a list of the attributes of property; and Gray (n 3). Both authors also note the importance of 'entitlement to the fruits' as a further characteristic of property, but this too is not an exclusive attribute of property, and one absent from contract: see the detail in Worthington, 'The Disappearing Divide' (n 5). This 2005 chapter also considers several other traditional markers of 'property' and finds them equally lacking in exclusiveness.

[8] See n 4. This particular system also suffers because the 'property' label is misleading: it does not convey the limited contents of the tin, either to a lay person or to a specialist: see n 9.

[9] Lewis Carroll, *Through the Looking-Glass* (Hayes Barton Press 1872) 72: '"When I use a word," Humpty Dumpty said in rather a scornful tone, "it means just what I choose it to mean—neither more

Adopting a property category marked out by the various characteristic 'property' attributes noted earlier, the next task is to determine whether these attributes apply only to property and not to contract. To anticipate, the conclusion is that they do not. In short, the existence or non-existence of these attributes is not grounded in a property–contract category opposition. Instead, these important characteristics are found in both categories. Further, no other features have been suggested by which property and contract might be marked out as occupying mutually exclusive territories with a solid borderline between them. The three sections which follow track this argument.

A. Inherent Attributes—The 'Thinginess' of Property and its Unique Association with Rights *in Rem*

One of the most intuitive reactions to the property/contract borderline is a deep-seated sense that property has an essential 'thinginess' about it. This is put in various ways: property exists regardless of the legal system, contracts do not; property exists separate from the person who owns it, contracts do not.[10] The suggestion is that land and cars meet this 'thinginess' test; contracts do not.

At its punchiest, this instinct would suggest that tangibles are property, but intangibles (choses in action, personal claims against another person) are not. The former deliver rights *in* an asset (rights *in rem*), the latter merely rights *to* an asset (rights *in personam*).[11] Even Reid, in his nuanced article on the issues, notes the power of this instinct.[12] This was also the distinction recognised by Goode when explaining the difference between property rights in an asset and personal rights to the delivery or transfer of an asset: 'I *own* property; I am *owed* performance of a transfer obligation'.[13] Gretton, too, has noted that it is extremely odd to speak of 'owning' contractual rights.[14]

nor less." "The question is," said Alice, "whether you can make words mean so many different things." "The question is," said Humpty Dumpty, "which is to be master—that's all"'.

[10] As Reid put it: 'The person (the legal subject) has a direct relationship with the thing (the legal object). This is the most important characteristic [of real rights, ie of property].' See Reid (n 3) 227.

[11] This seems to ignore that a chose in action may deliver rights to a service, rather than rights to an asset. On the general point, however, see the strict approach adopted in Arianna Pretto, 'Primary Rights and Rights *in Rem*' in Birks and Pretto (eds), *Themes in Comparative Law* (n 3) 65, 77–79, concluding that, 'supposing, as must be, that we do not intend to dissolve that distinction [between property and obligations], we have to say that property rights are only those rights which are *in rem* [and, in this context, meaning rights in tangible assets]'.

[12] Reid (n 3) 230: 'At the very core of ownership is the idea of possession.'

[13] Goode, 'Ownership and Obligation' (n 3) 433 (emphasis in the original). He then went on, at 438, to explain the dramatic impact of equity in specifically enforcing some contracts for the transfer of an asset, with the result that the underlying property is held by the seller on constructive trust for the buyer, thus creating one of the forms of property-sharing relationships discussed in Section V. This subtlety does not affect the key point being made here, however.

[14] Gretton, 'Owning Rights and Things' (n 3) 177.

But there is another way of looking at this, and in any event these various assertions do not address the core question. It is all very well to distinguish rights *in a thing* from rights *to a thing*, and to note that ownership of a car is very different from a contractual right to receive a car. But that is to focus on the car, and to avoid the real question. The proper focus should be on whether the bundles of *rights in respect of the car* are fundamentally different from the bundles of *rights in respect of the contract*. That is addressed further in what follows, but we must at least get the question right.

There might be protest that the previous paragraph has slipped improperly from 'the car' to 'rights in respect of the car' and from 'the contract' to 'rights in respect of the contract'. But that merely reflects the lawyers' perspective, written out in full.[15] It may well be true that land and cars can exist regardless of the legal system, but *legal rights* in relation to land and cars cannot exist independently of the legal system, and, as lawyers, it is the legal rights we are interested in. That move to a distinctively legal perspective seems to deliver, in one swoop, some damage to the instinctive reliance on the 'thinginess' of property. Legal rights are not separate things that can be possessed, even if the underlying asset is. That means there is a less obvious 'thinginess' to the bundle of legal rights which constitute ownership of a car than there was to the car itself. But in truth the 'thinginess' is still there. All the word serves to indicate is that the 'thing' (here, the bundle of rights) exists separately from the person who owns the thing. Penner put it this way: all property rights are rights to things that are only contingently connected to us and are not intrinsic aspects of ourselves. Viewed this way, the separability that is important is that these separate property rights can be transferred or lost or damaged separately from, and without harming, their owner's own bodily integrity.[16]

That would seem to go far enough to persuade that 'rights in respect of the car' and 'rights in respect of the contract' have the same essential 'thinginess' about them; both have this allegedly property-specific characteristic. Even accepting that, however, there is a challenge on another front. A further distinction between property and contract is that property rights are said to be rights *in rem* while contract rights are rights *in personam*. The idea has a distinguished lineage. It was recognised in Roman law, with its classification of law into categories dealing with persons, things, and actions.[17] The two categories, so described, appear suitably

[15] Frederick Lawson and Bernard Rudden, *The Law of Property* (3rd edn, OUP 2002) 5. And if it is also noticed that the focus is on rights, rather than the entire package of rights and obligations, that too is explicable: it is the potential transferability, use, and protection of the *rights* in issue that is in the sightlines in categorising 'property rights' and 'contract rights' and any borderline between them. By contrast, an assessment of *the entire package of rights and liabilities* associated with a single asset is what is done when *evaluating that particular asset from a property perspective*, as distinct from any property/contract boundary-identification. See Worthington, 'The Disappearing Divide' (n 5) 96–97.

[16] James Penner, *The Idea of Property in Law* (Clarendon Press 1997) ch 5 noting, however, that this is merely an attribute of property, not the sole determinant of whether something *is* property.

[17] Max Radin, 'Fundamental Concepts of the Roman Law' (1925) 13 CLR 208; Arnold Wajenberg and Danuta Gorecki, 'Classification of Roman Law: Problems and A Suggested Classification Scheme' (1981) 74 L Libr J 632. See also Reid (n 3) 244.

mutually exclusive. But despite that, this rights *in rem*/rights *in personam* category distinction does not stand up to scrutiny, either conceptually or practically. The conceptual problem is considered here, the practical problem later.[18]

The first conceptual criticism is that the rights *in rem*/rights *in personam* distinction involves a serious category error. We rarely notice this, but Reid put it plainly:

> It is to define by criteria which do not match. It is to compare apples with bananas.[19] One should either define by comparing relationships to things or by comparing enforceability against persons. To define real rights by reference to things and personal rights by reference to persons is helpful only if it can be taken as meaning (i) that a personal right is not about things, and (ii) that a real right is not enforceable against persons. But of course neither statement is true. If I lend you my pen I have given you a personal right (a contract of loan) in respect of a thing. And real rights—like all rights—are enforceable only against persons.[20]

There is no answer to this criticism. Reid makes plain what we all recognise. Even the bundles of rights associated with land or with cars consist largely[21] of rights which are *in personam*. Consider the familiar claims in trespass, conversion, nuisance, and negligence.[22]

But Reid does not go far enough on the contract side of this *in rem*/*in personam* division. It is one thing to say that a contract can be *about* an asset which is universally classed as property.[23] But the crucial point that can also be taken from this is that the contract holder too has rights *in rem*: she has rights in the 'thing' that is constituted by the bundle of rights under the contract. The courts have recognised this: the holder of contract rights has property rights, or rights *in rem*/rights in a thing,[24] which thing (ie the rights under the contract) can be held on trust,[25] or made the subject of a fixed or floating charge,[26] or

[18] See Section III.B.

[19] Worse, it seems: it is to compare apples with fruit farms.

[20] Reid (n 3) 225–26.

[21] Perhaps entirely, if equity is excluded. Further, what equity does, even when delivering a proprietary response, is not what the common law does. Equity imposes sharing arrangements: at its simplest, it gives the claimant an interest in property which the defendant owns at common law. See Sarah Worthington, 'Revolutions in Personal Property: Redrawing the Common Law's Conceptual Map' in Sarah Worthington, Andrew Robertson, and Graham Virgo (eds), *Revolution and Evolution in Private Law* (Hart 2018). More generally, see Sarah Worthington, *Equity* (2nd edn, OUP 2006) chs 3 and 4 and Sarah Worthington, *Proprietary Interests in Commercial Transactions* (OUP 1996).

[22] Even injunctions in these contexts are orders that a person act or desist from acting in certain ways.

[23] This too was the point Goode made, noting that these contracts give rights *ad rem* (ie rights *to* an asset) but also noting that equity may intervene: see n 3. See also Worthington, *Proprietary Interests in Commercial Transactions* (n 21).

[24] *Lipkin Gorman v Karpnale Ltd* [1991] 2 AC 548 (HL).

[25] *Foskett v McKeown* [2001] 1 AC 102 (HL).

[26] *Re Spectrum Plus Ltd (in Liquidation)* [2005] UKHL 41, [2005] 2 AC 680; *Re Brumark Investments Ltd* [2001] UKPC 28, [2001] 2 AC 710; *Bank of Credit and Commerce International SA (in Liquidation) (No 8)* [1998] AC 214 (HL).

assigned,[27] or protected from incursions by third parties.[28] This looks remarkably like the rights *in rem* that the owner of a car has in the bundle of rights that make up such ownership.

That final observation permits a further comment. The Cambridge Dictionary defines *in rem* as 'relating to a legal action that deals with property rather than a person'. This uses the slippery 'property' word, but the property/person opposition is clear. The Merriam-Webster Dictionary is similar: *in rem* means 'against a thing (such as a right, status, or property) without reference to the persons involved', explaining further that it is a term used especially of legal actions, judgments, or jurisdiction, and contrasting it with *in personam*, which means 'against a person for the purpose of imposing a liability or obligation to do or not do something'.

From that we can recognise that much litigation relating to land, cars, and contracts is *in personam*: the objective is to obtain a court order that requires someone pay a sum of money to someone else or requires someone to do or not do something. By contrast, we can also recognise that much litigation relating to land, cars, and contracts is not about this, but is about what particular rights make up the bundle of rights that some named holder has in relation to the land, the car, or the contract. This can be difficult; it can require a great deal of factual discovery of documents and uncovering of events. But in assessing the elements of a particular bundle of rights, the one thing we know is that the personal characteristics of the named individuals who hold those rights will not have a role to play. The interpretation of the underlying contract, the assessment of where ownership rights lie, the determination of the nature of any security interests, or the analysis delivering interests arising by operation of law can all be made without regard for the individuals who will then be affected by these conclusions. In making these judgments, the courts are determining the nature of the various bundles of rights which constitute the different assets held by the parties: they are determining rights *in rem*, in the dictionary sense of the term. This further reinforces the thinginess of 'bundles of rights'.

If all this is true, then for lawyers the 'thinginess' attribute is met by all manner of different bundles of rights: all these bundles of rights can be treated as 'things', and (as the succeeding sections show) all these things can be used productively by their owners, can be protected against third party incursions, and can entitle those with interests in the thing to insolvency protection. All that is as true of the bundle of rights associated with a car as it is of the bundle of rights associated with a debt. In this sense, the 'thing', or the legal object, can be a bundle of rights no matter how that bundle is created. The bundle may be derived from the combined effect

[27] Law of Property Act 1925, s 136 (assignments at law); *William Brandt's Sons & Co v Dunlop Rubber Co Ltd* [1905] AC 454 (HL) (assignments in equity). And see James Edelman and Steven Elliott, 'Two Conceptions of Equitable Assignment' (2015) 131 LQR 228.

[28] *Sevilleja v Marex Financial Ltd* [2020] UKSC 31, [2021] AC 39.

of common law and statutory rights of ownership of land or goods, or by statutory rights of ownership of intangible assets (intellectual property, carbon credits, milk quotas), or by contractual rights negotiated between parties (debts, shares, leases, licences, crypto assets), and so on. Each of these bundles of rights has the 'thinginess' intuitively associated with property.[29]

Although the lay perception of these contested legal issues is not material to their resolution, it is nevertheless reassuring to find that this expanded approach to the 'thinginess' of property accords with the common view of what a person 'owns': 'my licence' and 'my shares' are seen as no more inaccurate than 'my bicycle'; and various commentators have noted that it would be odd to say that a person's patrimony does not include his bank account, shares, pension fund, life assurance, and so forth.[30] As Harris put it, in criticising the competing narrow view of property:

> Wealth can be excluded from 'property' only if we adopt a static and fragmented understanding of the concept. My property would consist only of those tangible things that I own, or in respect of which I have lesser rights *in rem*. If I sell all my tangible assets and put the money in the bank, or use the proceeds for investment in intangibles, I become propertiless.[31]

That final sentence makes the point eloquently.

The end result, at least so far as this first attribute of the 'thinginess' of the 'property' category is concerned, is that the 'property' category swallows the contract category whole: things that might instinctively have been classed as property *plus* all those other bundles of rights arising from contract can all be regarded as having this first attribute commonly associated with property. This, as we will see, is the same for all the other attributes being considered.

Perhaps the conclusion should come as little surprise. Consider how we explain property to undergraduates. The typical common law classification *of property* (not property *and* obligation) suggests that property is divided into real and personal property; personal property is, in turn, divided into choses in possession and choses in action (tangible and intangible property respectively).[32]

[29] What has to be remembered, however, is that it is the bundle of rights which is the 'property': a contractual right to a royalty payment is 'property' in this sense, but that property right is not the same thing as a right to the *money* that may be received in the future: *Norman v Federal Commissioner of Taxation* (1963) 109 CLR 9 (HCA).

[30] Reid (n 3) 231. To the same effect, also see Roscoe Pound, *An Introduction to the Philosophy of Law* (1922) 236; Daniel Friedmann, 'Restitution of Benefits Obtained Through the Appropriation of Property or the Commission of a Wrong' (1980) 80 Col LR 504 (although arguably this takes the consequences too far); Rudden (n 3) 82.

[31] Harris (n 3) 56.

[32] It is possible to make the scheme even more specific by dividing personal property first into chattels real (leases) and chattels personal (other), and then dividing the latter into choses in possession and choses in action. Choses in action can then be further subdivided into documentary intangibles and pure intangibles, but neither of these complications affects the point being made.

And then comes the rub. We then insist that not all choses in action are property: put more starkly, not all obligations are property, but some are. Those 'choses' that are not property are merely personal rights, or personal obligations. The boundary is never defined. Indeed, it is often described as subject to revision according to social and political norms. And so we face head-on the dilemma of borderlines between property and contract which is the subject of this chapter. But perhaps we have finally reached the point where this is all far simpler, and all these rights *are* indeed property, as the initial headline in the classificatory structure suggests, and the subdivisions simply represent the different possible types or subsets of bundles of rights that might exist. Such sub-classification is useful, principally because the different sub-categories are subject to different legal rules determining how the asset can be transferred and protected from third party incursions. The rules on effective transfer of land, goods, shares, and debts are all different. The rules on protection from third party incursions are also different, especially as between tangible and intangible assets.

B. Rights to Benefits of Property and Rights to Protect Property

Next we turn to the practical benefits of property. There are a number of incidental practical characteristics also said to align with the property category and to be absent from the contract category. First, property has greater practical usefulness: it has exchange value and use value.[33] Secondly, property is afforded far greater protection, available against a far wider class of people (that is, delivered by 'rights against the world', this being a second and very different meaning attributed to rights *in rem*).[34] Taken together, property comes with rights to control *allocation* and *access*; contract, by contrast, is said to lack these attributes.

This section can be kept relatively brief, first because I have written about these issues at length elsewhere,[35] but secondly, and more importantly, because the claims being made seem no longer controversial.

[33] Rudden (n 3) 93. Note that property often has amenity value too: that aspect undoubtedly adds motivation to the housing, car, and art markets. Amenity value is not considered here, beyond noting that bundles of contract rights can be designed to lead to the delivery of land or cars, and also to the delivery of amenity value, and remedies are available when, via a breach of contract, they do not: on amenity value, see *Ruxley Electronics v Forsyth* [1996] AC 344 (HL); *Jackson v Horizon Holidays Ltd* [1975] 1 WLR 1468 (CA); *Jarvis v Swans Tours Ltd* [1973] QB 233 (CA).

[34] Two further benefits are associated with property, beyond these rights to control allocation and access. They are insolvency protection (dealt with later) and entitlement to the fruits derived from the property: Gray (n 3). See also n 7.

[35] See especially Worthington, 'The Disappearing Divide' (n 5) 99–113; and Worthington, 'Revolutions in Personal Property' (n 21) 230–35. Much of what follows here appears in expanded form in one or other of these two chapters, and the extended references to commentators are not repeated here, but should be consulted. In one way or another, a great deal of my other writing has also been concerned with these issues.

Things have changed relatively radically in this area. The early common law approach was to accord proprietary status to land and goods, but not to intangibles. Since intangibles were not assignable, they were not usable wealth. This restriction imposed a boundary between property and obligation that accords with the now outdated view of property as confined to tangible things, with everything else characterised as obligation and generating only personal rights against specific parties.

But equity changed all this. The judges effectively turned unusable obligation into usable property. They did this, first, by making intangibles assignable. Crucially, note the careful way they allowed for the bundle of *rights* (and only the rights) to be assigned, while maintaining the *obligation* side of the relationship between the original contracting parties.[36] They also expanded dramatically the types of interests that could be created in assets and allocated to others. This is the story of the evolution of trusts and charges and the like. This meant that no longer was it only possible (as at common law) to share ownership amongst several owners, or alternatively divide rights of ownership and rights of possession between different parties. It was also possible to share interests in assets by allocating trust interests or security interests (including securities by way of mortgage or charge, whether fixed or floating) to others. Moreover, these interests could arise intentionally between the parties or by operation of law in appropriate circumstances. Notice too that these sharing arrangements were available across the spectrum of assets: there was no need to distinguish between property and contract, or property and obligation. Assignment, trust, and security were possible across the board. The story is well known.[37]

In practice a qualification is needed here. All manner of constraints can be imposed on allocation decisions: the government may control transfers of assets (art works, currency, public utilities in times of national emergency); equally, the parties granting rights may impose conditions and constraints on those rights.[38] But that does not alter the general point being made here, which is simply that there is no principled division between the 'property' category and the 'contract' category which is marked by the presence of rights to allocate in one category and the absence in the other. There is no identifiable borderline that can be drawn on this basis.

Turning from allocation to access, or to protection from interference, we routinely assert that property is better protected than contract. This insight was famously articulated by Calabresi and Melamed over fifty years ago.[39] They suggested

[36] Worthington, 'Revolutions in Personal Property' (n 21): see the penultimate paragraph in pt III.

[37] See Worthington, *Equity* (n 21) ch 3. There the argument is simply that equity dramatically expanded the notion of property; nothing is made of the further point that there is no longer an effective borderline between property and obligation. All these new rights are uncontroversially regarded as assignable, and also as attracting some powers to exclude third parties. See too Worthington, 'The Disappearing Divide' (n 5) and Worthington, 'Revolutions in Personal Property' (n 21).

[38] See, eg, Roy Goode, 'Inalienable Rights?' (1979) 42 MLR 553.

[39] Guido Calabresi and Douglas Melamed, 'Property Rules, Liability Rules, and Inalienability: One View of the Cathedral' (1972) 85 Harv LR 1089.

that property rights are distinguishable because they are protected through 'property rules', not merely through 'liability rules'. Put in more familiar language, injunctions and specific performance are said to be the norm in protecting property rights, while compensation is the norm in protecting contract rights.[40] Once again, however, this preferential remedial approach no longer seems to track any meaningful property/contract divide. Property is protected by positive and negative injunctions, but even more frequently by compensation orders.[41] Contracts, too, are enforced using the full panoply of 'property' and 'liability' rules. This remains true even when the particular rights infringed appear to be *especially* personal rather than proprietary.[42] Generalising, it seems that contracts are sufficiently commonly protected by 'property rules', and vice versa, for this form of enhanced legal protection to be of little use in distinguishing property from contract.

Pursuing another aspect of access, or excludability, it is often said that property rights are 'good against the world'. But even here, notice that the degree of protection varies with the type of asset being protected, rather than with whether it is property or contract. Contrast the protection of land with the protection of ordinary goods. Notice too that the law increasingly protects all assets from external interference, regardless of whether they are categorised as property or contract.[43] For example, both intellectual property rights and pure contract rights may be subject to injunctive and compensatory rules protecting parties from third party interference with the underlying rights. This move alone has probably destroyed the argument that 'excludability' could provide a means of identifying a property/contract borderline.[44] There is perhaps a greater range of techniques in the courts' armoury in relation to tangible assets, whether land or goods, but that surely only reflects the greater range of infringements that are possible. Otherwise, however, the line between property and contract is blurred in the extreme.

Consider debts. A debt is simply a contract, and perhaps the purest example of contract not property. But a debt which is assignable, against which security can be granted, and which security then delivers insolvency protection, begins to look

[40] See the extended discussion of this issue in Robert Chambers, 'The Importance of Specific Performance' in Degeling and Edelman (eds), *Equity in Commercial Law* (n 5) ch 17, especially his consideration of *Semelhago v Paramadevan* 136 DLR (4th) 1 (SCC) and *Tanwar Enterprises Pty Ltd v Cauchi* [2003] HCA 57, (2003) 217 CLR 315.

[41] This is rendered especially stark when an owner whose goods have been converted is seen as generally entitled only to compensation rather than to specific recovery unless the court can be persuaded to exercise its statutory discretion to order the latter: Torts (Interference with Goods) Act 1977, s 3.

[42] See the discussion in *Co-operative Insurance Society Ltd v Argyll Stores (Holdings) Ltd* [1998] AC 1 (HL), and contrast *Lumley v Wagner* (1852) 1 De GM & G 604, 42 ER 687, where, despite the contract being one for personal services, the courts were prepared to order an injunction, although not specific performance.

[43] *OBG Ltd v Allan* [2007] UKHL 21, [2008] 1 AC 1. See also n 42.

[44] As Gray notes, 'the test of excludability throws into severe doubt the validity of any sharp dichotomy between contract and property': Gray (n 3) 302.

a lot like property, even if the financial value of the property is essentially determined by the solvency of the debtor.

C. Insolvency Protection

Finally, insolvency priority is widely regarded as the linchpin 'property' characteristic, and perhaps the one bright marker that might serve to distinguish 'property' from 'contract'. The assertion is that property rights are accorded insolvency protection; contract rights are not. This is usually illustrated by pointing out that if B is insolvent but has possession of A's car, then A can simply take her car:[45] she can remove *her property* from B's pool of assets; it will not be swept up along with B's assets to enhance the pool from which B's creditors will be paid. By contrast, if A's asset is a debt claim against B for £100, then A cannot simply remove £100 from B: she will instead be entitled to recover only what the insolvent estate can pay out when all the claims are met *pari passu*. It follows, so it is said, that A's property (her car) is protected on insolvency, but A's contract (her debt) is not.

But this assertion merits pause for thought. The first and all too obvious point is that having a debt claim for £100 is not the same as having £100. *A*'s debt asset in the example above is a bundle of rights with a value crucially dependent on the solvency of *A*'s debtor. That is the fatal risk with debts. Even more importantly, however, in the illustration above *A* is not endeavouring to 'remove her asset' (her debt) from *B*'s pool of assets to prevent her asset from being swept up with *B*'s assets to enhance the pool from which *B*'s creditors will be paid. She does not need that sort of insolvency protection. Her asset remains exclusively in her hands. She is in the same position as B's neighbour, who (bar B's theft) is not at risk of having B appropriate her gardening tools in order to meet B's debts. A is doing something quite different. She is merely endeavouring to realise the value of her asset by converting it to the performance promised by B. As Reid would say, this illustration of insolvency protection of A's car but not of her debt is comparing apples with bananas.

A better test is to consider what happens to cars and debts when both A and B have interests in them and B is insolvent. This was the case with the car in the earlier illustration: A had legal title; B had possession, but (so it must be assumed) a right to possession that terminated on B's insolvency. In those circumstances A could recover her car. If the facts had been different, so that B retained his right to possession despite his insolvency, then B's assets would include B's rights to possess, and those limited rights in the car would be an asset swept up into B's pool

[45] Note that this is true only if B does not have a continuing right to possession that survives his insolvency, and of course A will need to act legally. The point is, she will remain entitled to her car, not B.

of assets and available to B's creditors; the remaining interests in the car would remain with A.

But it is precisely the same with debts. Since debts are intangible, neither A nor B can have rights of possession. But the debt can be 'shared' if A owns the debt and B has a security interest or a trust interest in the debt asset. In those circumstances A will want to protect her own rights, while conceding that B too has rights in the asset, and those rights must be available to B's creditors.

In short, we are not typically concerned with 'insolvency protection' when *A* has the entire package of rights in her assets, whatever the type of asset. In those circumstances the assets are entirely A's, and B cannot take these assets to meet his own claims. If ownership is undisputed, the context is unlikely to generate disputes. But when A and B each have shared interests in the same asset, again whatever the type of asset, then the issue becomes important. In those circumstances it is essential to work out exactly what bundle of rights each has in relation to the asset (or what interests each has in the asset). There may well be dispute over the nature of the respective interests,[46] but once that is settled, A's interests will remain with A; they will be protected on B's insolvency, and B's interests (and only B's interests) will be available to B's creditors. This is considered in more detail below.

D. No Meaningful Borderline between Property and Contract

Taken together, the previous sections indicate that the task of locating a meaningful borderline between property and contract is impossible. If we wish to characterise the property territory as having certain particular attributes that are said to set it apart from contract, and to make it more valuable than contract, then what we find is that these same attributes apply generally to all assets, whether they would traditionally have been classified as property or contract. In short, we find that *all* assets display a certain 'thinginess' about them which renders each of them an asset separate from its owner; all assets come with the valuable practical rights of the owner being able to control allocation and access; and, finally, all assets deliver insolvency protection, preventing an owner's assets (or the owner's limited interests in those assets) being swept up in another's insolvency.

Put another way, the 'property' territory has swallowed the 'contract' territory whole; it has overrun it. This has happened over time, as both equity and tort law have developed to make these important attributes of 'property' available across the entire terrain. Of course, there are inherent limitations and differences, the

[46] See, eg, the long-fought disputes over whether the lender had a security interest by way of fixed or floating charge over the book debts offered by the borrower as security for a loan: *Spectrum Plus* (n 26); *Brumark Investments* (n 26).

clearest example being that intangibles cannot be possessed, and so there is then no need for rights which afford protection against interference with possession.

This exercise raises again a common question. Why do we attach so much importance to property? It is said to be necessary for successful societies to ensure greater productivity and commitment to effort: those who own property know that they, not others, will derive the benefits of their labour, so they are prepared to expend greater efforts. But it is immediately obvious that 'property' is surplus to this equation. Merely ensuring private ownership of *assets* of any type will deliver these benefits; there is no need to differentiate between rights in property and in contract. As the analysis in this chapter suggests, this is exactly the path the law has taken, evolving so that there is no longer a recognisable distinction between the property territory and the contract territory. We have, it seems, reached the point where there is no property-contract borderline.

One final comment is worth making in this context. In some quarters there is still significant resistance to the idea of someone 'owning' *rights*, especially contract rights. Put another way, there is resistance to the idea that a contract is property that can be owned by someone, just as a car can be owned by someone. But the point was made much earlier that, to lawyers, it is not the contract or the car that is in the sightlines, but the rights under the contract or the rights in the car. Just as we want to know what bundle of rights is available to the owner of the car, so too do we want to know what bundle of rights the contract entails; this is why contract interpretation can be such a fraught exercise. Both types of bundles of rights represent *property*, although it may take some time to adjust to that terminology.[47] In the meantime we might simply say that both types of bundles are *assets* belonging to someone.

E. Conclusion: Perspective Rather than Borderline

The previous sections advance the argument that there is no meaningful borderline between property and contract in modern English law, whatever was its history. Rather there is a difference of perspectives.[48] Contract describes how A and B are bound together by their agreed and voluntarily assumed obligations.[49] Property describes the total package of rights (and obligations) in each asset that an individual has under her dominium. These distinctive bundles of rights may

[47] This follows the scheme for property promulgated by Gaius: see Reid (n 3) 230–31, where the advantages and disadvantages of that approach are set out. It is not clear where Reid lands, but the advantages look to be far stronger than the disadvantages.

[48] ibid 233.

[49] And if instead of contract we looked to the broader category of 'obligations' as the territory under review, then we would be seeking to describe how *A* and *B* are bound together not simply by their agreed contracts, but also by externally imposed tort, unjust enrichment, and statutory obligations.

relate to land or cars or debts, but in every case they typically give A a wide variety of rights to use that asset for her own ends and advantages and to exclude others from similar enjoyment. Worded like this, the distinction or boundary between property and contract is not a borderline; it is not territorial or conceptual. It is instead a distinction based on perspective. Property examines A's 'wealth', asset by asset, bundle of rights by bundle of rights; contract examines *A*'s individual dealings with *B*. The former looks at the wood, the latter at the trees.

IV. Insolvency Protection—The Indispensible Element of Asset-Sharing

Before closing the discussion of borderlines between property and contract, it is important to return to insolvency protection. This protection was described earlier as the linchpin characteristic dividing property and contract. Yet the investigation so far has concluded that property and contract are not divided by a borderline: they are not differentiated by the existence of inherent property-type attributes, nor by rights to allocate or exclude, nor by insolvency protection.

Despite this, lawyers will not give up on the idea that insolvency protection is immensely valuable and has *something* to do with property. So it is, and so it does. It is therefore essential to ask what boundary or borderline this attribute marks out: what does *A* need to show so that *A* has insolvency protection on *B*'s insolvency? The easy assertion is that of course any assets owned absolutely by *A* will not be touched by *B*'s insolvency.[50] That needs no further consideration. The more subtle and important idea advanced here is that *A* will also have insolvency protection *if and only if, and only to the extent that,* A *can demonstrate a shared interest with* B in some underlying asset.[51] The underlying asset can be of any type: it can be land or a car or a debt; there is no need to characterise or confine it to property rather than contract.

Instead, the limiting factor is something quite different. It is that *A*'s shared interest in the underlying asset must be an interest *in the same asset* as the one in which *B* has an interest. Further, this is only possible if *A* or *B* has some form of *derivative interest* in the asset. In English law, derivative interests come in only four

[50] The question of whether *A* does indeed own an asset absolutely may need to be resolved as between *A* and *B* by the application of appropriate priorities rules: eg, is there a retention of title agreement or not? is *A* a bona fide purchaser for value or not? etc.

[51] This approach is considered in detail in Worthington, 'Revolutions in Personal Property' (n 21). This chapter explains that all derivative interests (ie possession, all other common law derivative interests, interests under a trust, security interests by way of mortgage or fixed or floating charge) are all analogous in that they all involve *both A* and *B* having proprietary interests in the *same* underlying asset, with the detailed aspects of those interests (ie the precise nature of *A* and *B*'s respective bundles of rights) set out in the documentation settling the sharing arrangement between them. Significantly for this chapter, it is immaterial whether the underlying asset in which *A* and *B* have shared interests is land, a car, or a contract; *any* type of asset will do.

distinctive forms,[52] although those four forms can be manipulated in endless ways. Starting with the simplest version, if *A* and *B* are to share interests in an asset, one may have legal title to the asset and the other may have a right to possession, or an interest under a trust, or an interest under a mortgage, or an interest under a charge (whether fixed or floating). Those four options cover the field. Such shared interests between *A* and *B* can be created consensually or by operation of law, and the precise terms of each sharing arrangement can be varied to suit the parties' or the courts' specific objectives. Each of these shared interests is then amenable to further sharing in the same way, creating sub-interests in the asset.

This can all be illustrated by considering a simple example. If *B* retains legal title but *A* has been given the right to possession, or an interest under a trust, or a security interest by way of mortgage or fixed or floating charge, then *A*'s interests in the underlying asset (whatever their extent) will be protected on *B*'s insolvency. Only *B*'s assets will be used to pay *B*'s creditors; *A*'s assets will be reserved to *A*. In this context, *A* and *B* have different bundles of rights which make up their different assets, with these bundles reflecting the fact that *B* no longer has absolute ownership of an asset but has shared his original bundle of rights with *A* in some chosen manner.

By contrast, if *A* merely has a contractual claim to have *B* hand over certain of *B*'s assets, this will not give *A* a shared interest in *B*'s assets unless the contract is specifically enforceable. *If* the contract is specifically enforceable, then *B* will hold the promised asset on constructive trust for *A*.[53] That will give *A* a shared interest in the underlying asset, and that interest will not be available to *B*'s creditors on *B*'s insolvency. By contrast, if the contract is not specifically enforceable, then all *A* has is her absolute ownership of her own contract claim, but that is a claim which will deliver little of value when *A* enforces it against *B*. Notice that the important question is what *interests* *A* has in *B*'s assets; it matters not whether *B*'s asset is a car or a debt.

Given that these important derivative interests are primarily equitable,[54] and may be delivered consensually or by operation of law,[55] this is all typically presented as a remarkable legal development by equity judges. At one level it is. But at another level these equitable interests merely represent different types of sharing arrangements by way of newly recognised forms of derivative proprietary interest in the underlying asset. Where the derivative interest is common law possession,

[52] To be comprehensive, this should also include some additional long-standing common law derivative interests which can exist in land: see n 54.

[53] In truth the issue is little more subtle. For an explanation and reference to different commentators, see Worthington, *Proprietary Interests in Commercial Transactions* (n 21); Sarah Worthington, 'Proprietary Remedies: The Nexus between Specific Performance and Constructive Trusts' (1996) 11 JCL 1.

[54] Other than the right to possession, and certain other common law derivative rights in land (not other tangibles), such as *profits à prendre* (which bear some similarities to a beneficiary's economic interest under a trust).

[55] eg, constructive trust, resulting trust, equitable lease, equitable mortgage, and equitable lien.

we barely pause to think of 'sharing'. Yet notice that all forms of property sharing, whatever the type of shared or derivative interest, follow the same model: the owner retains legal ownership, but that ownership is constrained by derivative rights given to another.[56] True, the trust beneficiary's rights are not the same types of rights as those arising under common law leases or equitable security arrangements, but the analogous sharing of the totality of the 'bundle of property rights' in any appropriate asset is evident.

The astonishing variety in the sharing arrangements that can be made is considered elsewhere.[57] For present purposes it is only the generality that matters: certain limited types[58] of agreed obligations between parties have, in English law, come to count as property of one sort or another when those obligations concern the sharing of benefits and burdens in an asset, with each party agreeing to have and hold different interests in the same asset. The diversity that can be built into these arrangements is vast, so careful analysis of the particular sharing terms is vital: simple identification of the broad family type will not reveal accurately the precise nature of the shared interests in issue.

In addition, special attention needs to be given to the question of whether the sharing arrangement is one which survives *B*'s insolvency. Many arrangements make explicit provisions for termination.[59] Consider the special fragility of *B*'s ownership of assets if those assets have been pledged or charged,[60] or of *B*'s trust interests if they are held under a protective trust,[61] or, similarly, the fragility of *B*'s possessory interests under a lease or hiring arrangement.[62] Moreover, note that the nature of the underlying asset is very much a secondary issue. And in all of this it does not matter that B may also be a trustee. The only change is then that *B*'s interests in those assets held by *B* on trust will be shared interests, not absolute interests, and so *B*'s insolvency pot will include *B*'s share but not the trust beneficiaries' share in the underlying asset.

Summing up, even when looking at insolvency protection in this distinctive way, there is still no borderline, no simple opposition between property and contract. Insolvency protection exists regardless of whether the underlying asset can

[56] And all these derivative interests are then amenable to the creation of sub-interests—sub-leases, sub-trusts, etc.

[57] Worthington, 'Revolutions in Personal Property' (n 21).

[58] Being possessory interests, trust interests, and security interests (by way of mortgage or charge), along with a small number of common law derivative interests in land.

[59] Although some care must be taken not to offend the provisions of the Insolvency Act 1986: see *British Eagle International Airlines Ltd v Compagnie Nationale Air France* [1975] 1 WLR 758 (HL); *Belmont Park Investments Pty Ltd v BNY Corporate Trustee Services Ltd* [2011] UKSC 38, [2012] 1 AC 383.

[60] Notice that the sharing here involves giving the security-holder either a possessory interest or an interest by way of equitable charge. The insolvency consequences do not depend especially on this, but on the particular terms of the sharing agreement itself (and, of course, any relevant legislation).

[61] Where rights to income from the trust assets will cease on *B*'s insolvency: Trustee Act 1925, s 33.

[62] Which may or may not include terms making the arrangement determinable on *B*'s insolvency.

somehow be classed as property or contract, which is an insurmountable challenge in itself. On *B*'s insolvency, all that matters is whether *A* or *B* owns the underlying asset absolutely (if so, and the asset is *B*'s, it falls into the insolvency pool; if it is *A*'s, it does not) or whether they 'share', with both having interests in the same asset (in which case *B*'s share falls into the insolvency pool, but *A*'s does not). That makes accurate analysis of the sharing arrangement absolutely critical. But it is irrelevant whether the shared asset is land, a car, or a debt.

V. Conclusion

The analysis in this chapter suggests there is no meaningful borderline between contract and property. All the characteristics typically associated with property are found to be equally associated with contract.[63] Both territories display the same sort of 'thinginess', or separability from their owner; both are associated with rights to enjoy the benefits and to control allocation and access; and both deliver insolvency protection, although not quite in the way that is often thought.

The significance of such a borderline-free territory depends on one's vantage point. If acknowledged to be true, it will end the search for this Holy Grail, and that in itself might liberate a significant amount of academic and judicial effort. It does not mean there is no longer a need to think about property and contract. It simply means that they should no longer be regarded as territories in opposition. Rather, they provide different and useful perspectives when examining and assessing the territory: the property perspective looks at *A*'s 'wealth', at all her assets and all their constituent bundles of rights; the contract perspective looks at *A*'s specific dealings with *B*. If an analogy is needed, property looks at the wood, contract at the trees.

Finally, there is one important positive finding set out in this chapter. Insolvency protection *is* delivered by property, but it is delivered by property regarded simply as 'bundles of rights' in all manner of underlying assets, without first classifying these underlying assets as property or contract. Once again, there is no opposition between property and contract. *A*'s absolute interests in any form of asset *and A*'s derivative interests in any form of asset (whether property or contract) are protected from *B*'s insolvency: *B* cannot access *A*'s property to pay *B*'s debts. The protection accorded to *A*'s absolute ownership is straightforward. The protection accorded to *A*'s derivative interests in assets in which *B* also has an interest delivers *A*'s share to *A*, untouched by *B*'s insolvency, and *B*'s share to *B* for the benefit of *B*'s creditors.

[63] Other than the right to possession, of course.

All the years of searching for a property-contract borderline can sometimes appear as fruitful as the search for the Holy Grail. Yet these endeavours invariably have the benefit of all rigorous journeys of exploration: with enough work, they each contribute to a ever-clearer understanding of the territory being mapped.

14
Property's Borderlines

Mr Justice Fancourt

The law of England and Wales accords great significance to property and proprietary rights, reflecting the precepts of life in a modern, liberal, Western democracy. What the law means by property is nowhere comprehensively defined, though as a matter of legal history it has always comprised realty and personality. The great property legislation of 1925 defines 'property' as including (subject to context) 'any thing in action and any interest in real or personal property'.[1]

As Robert Stevens explains elsewhere in Chapter 17, the word property is used by lawyers to mean different things. At a basic level, property may serve to identify physical things rather than legal rights, where possession is the indicium of ownership. In this sense, Mr Wemmick in *Great Expectations* adjured Pip to follow his guiding star and 'get hold of portable property'. This usage is of course legally inexact.[2] Most commonly in a legal context, property serves to identify those things rights in which are exigible against all the world, or *in rem* as it used to be said, as opposed to rights that are enforceable against a given person or persons only (*in personam*). This accords with Peter Birks' taxonomy of things being either legal or equitable and, by the nature of their exigibility, personal or proprietary.

An allied point is that particular remedies have traditionally been afforded to the enforcer of proprietary rights, remedies that go beyond mere compensation for loss. Indeed, it is the different remedy that once distinguished real property from other property. The proprietary interest is vindicated by granting specific remedies, whether specific performance or injunction upon an actual or intended wrong, reinstatement or delivery of possession, and even, in some cases, monetary compensation assessed on a different basis from compensation for losses actually incurred. I return to this point below.

This exigibility meaning does not portray a complete picture, however, as possessory rights are generally good against all the world except a person with better title, such as an earlier fee simple owner of unregistered land or the dispossessed owner of a chattel. Title at common law is relative, not absolute. A further different

[1] Law of Property Act 1925, s 205(1)(xx); Settled Land Act 1925, s 117(1)(xx); Administration of Estates Act 1925, s 55(1)(xvii). A more expansive (but still not exclusive) definition appears in Trustee Act 1925, s 68(1).

[2] cf real property and incorporeal property.

Mr Justice Fancourt, *Property's Borderlines* In: *Borderlines in Private Law.* Edited by: William Day and Julius Grower, Oxford University Press. © Mr Justice Fancourt 2024. DOI: 10.1093/9780191995200.003.0014

meaning serves to identify those rights that can be transferred, as a means of realising for their owner their exchange value. This is of paramount significance in insolvency law, distinguishing property from purely personal rights that cannot form part of a bankrupt estate. Property rights in this sense include rights in intangibles that do not fall within the other meanings of property, such as rights of action and shares, as well as intangible property that is exigible *in rem*, such as a patent.

Property being a matter of some considerable importance to life and the law, one may expect to find many points at which rights of or in property recognised by the common law connect with, butt up against, or even overlap other areas of law, such as family law, the law of torts, the law of contract, and statutory insolvency law, to name only a few. Equity is rather a special case, so far as the law of property is concerned, as it provides a very substantial overlay and supplement to the common law of property.

What matters to the law is not property as such but ownership of it or rights in it. Possession being, as is commonly said, nine-tenths of the law, it is usually possession rather than title that determines what claim a person may bring, or how their rights are affected by other legal rights and principles. A substantial statutory overlay providing for registration of rights serves to confirm title in many cases.

The torts of interference with goods, trespass to land, and nuisance can be taken as examples of claims that depend on possessory rights. In recent years, it has been established that a sufficiently exclusive right to make use of land is the minimum required for a claim to lie in trespass,[3] and that a person who merely has a licence to occupy, as opposed to a proprietary interest or exclusive possession, cannot bring a claim in the tort of nuisance.[4] Further, a person with only a licence to use property cannot sue for loss negligently caused to the property. The existence of these claims in the law of tort is therefore critically dependent on the existence of a proprietary interest, or something very close to it.

A lease is the example *par excellence* of a property interest that is as much dependent on the law of contract as it is on the law of property, and landlord and tenant law provides good examples of interplay at the borderline of property law. Prior to the 1925 property legislation, a lease was characterised as a chattel real rather than realty, and only became a legal estate in land at that time.[5] As such, it is (real) property both in giving rise to proprietary rights and as being transferrable for value.

A contractual stipulation that the lease be not assigned without permission of the landlord was ineffective to prevent a lease vesting in a transferee where no

[3] *Manchester Airport plc v Dutton* [2000] QB 133 (CA).

[4] *Hunter v Canary Wharf* [1997] AC 655 (HL). A quasi-exception was created by the decision of the Court of Appeal in *Pemberton v Southwark LBC* [2000] 1 WLR 1672 (CA), in which a so-called tolerated trespasser following a possession order was held to have *locus standi* in a nuisance claim, by reference to his previous (not wholly terminated) status as tenant.

[5] Law of Property Act 1925, s 1(1)(b).

permission was obtained, even though a forfeiture was incurred.[6] In this respect, the proprietary rights can be seen to have primacy over the contract, but in other respects the terms of the contract define the nature and extent of the proprietary rights,[7] and the House of Lords and Court of Appeal have repeatedly emphasised that the modern approach is to regard leases as primarily contracts rather than estates in land, and rent as something payable under a contract rather than reserved out of the land.[8]

As a matter of property law and in equity, the proviso for re-entry in the event of failure to pay rent reserved by a lease is regarded as 'security' for payment of the rent, such that the court has no real discretion to refuse relief against forfeiture in an ordinary case if the arrears, interests, and costs are tendered.[9] Following the Insolvency Act 1986, a question repeatedly arose whether by exercising its proprietary right a landlord was thereby enforcing security over the company's property, within the meaning of restrictions in the statute.[10] At first instance, the conclusion was initially reached that it was. In a later case, the House of Lords disagreed and held that a proviso for re-entry for unpaid rent did not secure the tenant's performance of its liability to pay rent.[11] Following that decision, another judge at first instance, considering whether there had been a valid re-entry, held that a right of forfeiture was a remedy against loss of rent, not security against the property of the debtor, and so was not a 'security' within the meaning of the Act.[12] The statute was amended in consequence. Whether the law of landlord and tenant should be regarded as similarly changed by the reasoning of the House of Lords is unclear, though it is probably not.[13]

Of course, registered title to land makes a significant difference to enforceability of proprietary rights, but it is not a complete code. The interface between the

[6] *Old Grovebury Manor Farm Ltd v W Seymour Plant Sales and Hire Ltd (No 2)* [1979] 1 WLR 1397 (CA) 1399 (Lord Russell of Killowen): 'It is of the nature of the creation of a term of years that the owner of the term is capable of dealing with it as a piece of property.'

[7] See, eg, *Goldmile Properties Ltd v Lechouritis* [2003] EWCA Civ 49, [2003] 2 P & CR 1.

[8] Following *dicta* of Lord Wilberforce in *United Scientific Holdings Ltd v Burnley Borough Council* [1978] AC 904 (HL) 935: 'The mediaeval concept of rent as a service rendered by the tenant to the landlord has been displaced by the modern concept of a payment which the tenant is bound by his contract to pay the landlord for the use of his land.' Note, however, that whether the contractual analysis extends to termination for repudiatory breach or breach of condition in place of re-entry is unclear: see Sir Timothy Fancourt, 'Forfeiture, Penalties and Damages in Property Law' (8th Annual Property Law Lecture at the School of Law and Social Justice, University of Liverpool, 21 February 2023).

[9] *Gill v Lewis* [1956] 2 QB 1 (CA).

[10] See, eg, *Exchange Travel Agency Ltd v Triton Property Trust plc* [1991] BCC 341 (Ch), *Re Olympia & York Canary Wharf Ltd* [1993] BCC 154 (Ch), and *Doorbar v Alltime Securities Ltd (No 2)* [1995] 2 BCLC 513 (Ch).

[11] *Re Park Air Services plc* [2000] 2 AC 172 (HL) 186 (Lord Millett): 'This is not a security interest subsisting in the tenant's property, nor is it capable of being realised by the landlord. It does not secure the performance of the tenant's liability to pay rent, which remains unsatisfied as well after re-entry as before. It cannot be valued or surrendered.'

[12] *Re Lomax Leisure Ltd* [2000] Ch 502 (Ch).

[13] The most recent authoritative decision on relief against forfeiture, *Keshwala v Bhalsod* [2021] EWCA Civ 492, [2021] 1 WLR 4004, implies no change to the approach in *Gill* (n 9).

principles of registration and fraudulent conduct remains an area of considerable difficulty, and the law of registered land is necessarily supplemented by the law of equity and equitable remedies where a contract has been made but not performed (constructive trust) or where a transfer has been executed and delivered but not registered (bare trust).

These few examples demonstrate, shortly, the point that the borders of property law and other areas of law are porous and sometimes unclear so far as concerns the effect of competing principles of law. As Sarah Worthington argues in Chapter 13, the conceptual borderline between property law and contract law is unclear, as rights to property and rights under contract are not mutually exclusive: all are assets, the critical question in all cases being whether they are solely owned or shared.

Some of the most challenging cases for judges arise where principles of property law, the law of contract, and insolvency law meet. A recent example is a case where the court had to decide whether a company voluntary arrangement was unfairly prejudicial to some creditors, where different categories of creditors (mainly landlords) were treated differently regarding restructuring rent due under leases and altering the landlords' other rights, which included proprietary rights.[14] The grant of varied or substituted rights was held to mitigate the prejudice, and differential treatment was held to be objectively justified on the facts. Clear principles of property law and the law of contract were made to cede to the principles underlying the statutory insolvency code.

A fascinating recent example of the interface between principles of property law and the law of tort is the decision of the Supreme Court in *Fearn v Board of Trustees of the Tate Gallery*.[15] By a bare majority, it was held that the Tate Gallery's use of a viewing platform that overlooked neighbouring flats was an actionable nuisance, owing to thousands of visitors daily peering into living rooms through the clear glass curtain walls of the block of flats, which were only some 30 metres distant at their closest point. Although the flat owners had no right to a view (having no proprietary right to protection in that regard) or right to protection against overlooking of their property (by reason of the Gallery's countervailing proprietary rights), the effect of the decision is that the owners did have, as appurtenant to their property, a right not to suffer visual intrusion caused by an abnormal use of the Gallery's land. Thus, the flat owners were owed a duty by the Gallery not to use its land in a particular way, even though the Gallery had the right to build on its land as it wished and the flat owners had no property-based right to be free from overlooking.

The law of nuisance can therefore, exceptionally, be seen as supplementing property rights, indeed as creating a quasi-proprietary right. That is because, as

[14] *Lazari Properties 2 Ltd v New Look Retailers Ltd* [2021] EWHC 1209 (Ch), [2021] Bus LR 915.

[15] *Fearn v Board of Trustees of the Tate Gallery* [2023] UKSC 4, [2023] 2 WLR 339.

firmly established previously by the House of Lords,[16] only a person with proprietary rights in land can bring a claim in nuisance, which is premised on loss of amenity value of property, not on personal discomfort suffered by occupants. The term 'nuisance' is 'properly applied only to such actionable user of land as interferes with the enjoyment by the plaintiff of rights in land'.[17]

There was no disagreement between the majority and the minority in *Fearn* that sufficiently intense viewing into the claimants' flats was capable in law of being a nuisance, as it was something different in principle from overlooking, which was not actionable. The difference was that the minority considered that, in view of the trial judge's unchallenged finding of fact that the flat owners too were making abnormal use of their flats, the principle of live and let live or reasonable reciprocity of compromise between neighbours required a balancing exercise of convenient use of each property, and this exercise entitled the judge to hold that the owners could be expected to take measures to mitigate the abnormal sensitivity of their flats. The majority considered that the use and sensitive nature of the claimants' property was irrelevant, given that the Gallery was itself making an exceptional use of its land that caused substantial diminution in the ordinary enjoyment of the flats. It was wrong in principle to throw the onus onto the claimants to seek to mitigate the impact of the Gallery's use. The sensitivity of the flats as used by the claimants would only have been relevant if the Gallery's use had been an ordinary use.

In its application, then, the reasoning of the majority does confer a right that is quasi-proprietary in character, in that it does not involve a balancing of competing rights to use land as each owner wishes but is an absolute right to object to an exceptional use that causes significant diminution in enjoyment, regardless of the nature of the owners' own use and the character of their flats. It would therefore appear to allow an owner to build an unusually sensitive building next to an established user (since coming to a nuisance is no defence) and object to it if the user is not common or ordinary for the locality. A defendant in such a case would not be able to rely on twenty years' use as of right because no nuisance existed until the sensitive building was built. These were approximately the facts of a famous old case, *Sturges v Bridgman*,[18] relied on by Lord Leggatt to support the majority decision. But in the twenty-first century it is perhaps questionable as a matter of policy whether use of property in densely occupied cities, in a way that society demands, should be actionable in private law in the absence of an enforceable contractual or proprietary right.

The tort of trespass is, similarly, firmly rooted in property law and the vindication of possessory rights. Alexander Waghorn considers in Chapter 15 whether a special remedy of user damages or disgorgement of profit, in cases of trespass to

[16] In *Hunter* (n 4).
[17] Francis Newark, 'The Boundaries of Nuisance' (1949) 65 LQR 480, 489.
[18] *Sturges v Bridgman* (1879) 11 Ch D 852 (CA).

land, is justified by the nature of the proprietary rights infringed. He uses the facts of a famous 1936 US case to consider what philosophical or juristic underpinning exists for an exceptional remedy. The entrance to a cave was on D's land but most of the cave lay underneath the surface of P's land. Without P's knowledge or consent, D charged visitors for entry to the cave. It is well established in English law that so-called negotiating or user damages are recoverable in principle, though more doubtful whether an account of profits is an available remedy, at least where there was no deliberate profiteering.

The remedy is in some ways exceptional but may be justified as orthodox on the basis that the actual loss suffered by P was the right to negotiate a fee for the use of his land. But what if in the counterfactual world P would have refused consent? The answer in English law appears to be that, exceptionally, P does not have to prove that he *would have* turned his property to account, only that he *could have* done so.[19] In that case, the actual loss seems not to be the benefit of the negotiation but the right to choose. Alexander Waghorn considers various possible justifications for the rule and finds them each unsatisfactory as a convincing explanation. He suggests that a proper explanation requires an analysis of why we accept that an owner of property owns the profits or fruits of exploiting the land,[20] which in turn depends on what benefits property rights secure or promote. The proper measure of damages should fairly reflect the extent to which those benefits are infringed in any given case.

Incorporeal property is, by definition, incapable of possession, except by a proxy or evidence of ownership such as a share certificate. Proof of creation and transfer are key to ownership of such property. In Chapter 16, Helen Scott considers incorporeal property of an everyday nature, a balance in a bank account, and considers the extent to which a proprietary or restitutionary claim should be available against someone who was not directly enriched at the expense of the claimant (A). The scenario is that B fraudulently obtains a credit from A's bank into his own bank account, and then further transfers the proceeds to C's account. Helen Scott asks, first, whether there is a pre-existing title to the debt owed to A that is capable of being followed as property into C's account at common law. Upon theft of a chattel, the law creates a trust that leaves A with an interest that can be asserted against anyone except a purchaser for value. But can part only of a debt owed by a bank to *A* be held on trust when the debt owed to A has been partially extinguished and a new debt is owed by C's bank to C? The question of whether a proprietary claim is available in such circumstances has an important bearing on the questions of

[19] *Ministry of Defence v Thompson* (1993) 25 HLR 552 (CA); *Ministry of Defence v Ashman* (1993) 25 HLR 513 (CA).

[20] What the late Tony Honoré called 'the right to the income of the land', see Tony Honoré, 'Ownership' in Anthony Guest (ed), *Oxford Essays in Jurisprudence* (1st edn, OUP 1961).

whether C has acquired that property and with what knowledge, and in the event of C's insolvency.

The difficulty with an unjust enrichment claim is that, on conventional analysis, there is no enrichment of C directly at the expense of A. However, if B is a mere conduit or agent rather than a recipient in their own right, should there not be an unjust enrichment claim as a corollary to the absence or loss of enrichment defence available to B?

The question of whether a claim is personal or proprietary is relevant also to Ben McFarlane's consideration in Chapter 12 of the boundary between property law and equity. He argues that, in presenting a simple dichotomy of personal and proprietary rights, the established taxonomy of legal rights is inadequate. The existing distinction between legal property rights and equitable property rights needs a correct understanding of the difference between them and leads to a conclusion that equitable rights are in the nature of rights over rights, with the equitable owner having rights against the legal owner's title to the property. Any equitable interest depends on there being a personal relationship with at least one other person.

So, where a bank account is held in trust, this creates an equitable property right in the beneficiary which is in the nature of a right against the account holder's rights. Ben McFarlane argues that the equitable rights are not just rights in property but specific rights that can be enforced against the trustee and others who stand in the shoes of the trustee, such as a trustee de son tort or a knowing recipient of the trustee's legal title to property. The rights of the beneficiary can be asserted as such against such a person, not just as equitable property but as a right to have the property dealt with in a particular way. For this reason, as the Supreme Court accepted in *Akers v Samba Financial Group*,[21] there can be an enforceable trust of property the *lex situs* of which does not recognise trusts. The beneficiary has rights against the legal owner, not ownership of the property in equity.

As Ben McFarlane explains, this analysis raises questions about the requirement for a proprietary base for a claim of knowing receipt of trust property.[22] Could it therefore be wrong in principle to speak of the beneficiary having a proprietary interest as opposed to the conscience of the recipient being affected by knowledge of the beneficiary's rights against the transferor? If so, it may be more accurate to recognise a new category of equitable property rights.

Sarah Worthington's chapter argues that there is no longer a recognisable distinction between the property territory and the contract territory, in terms of the nature of rights or protection of assets. Instead, the property/contract divide should be regarded as a difference of perspective, depending on whether one is looking at all the rights and obligations (if any) associated with the asset or just

[21] *Akers v Samba Financial Group* [2017] UKSC 6, [2017] AC 424.

[22] Accepted by the Court of Appeal in *Byers v Saudi National Bank* [2022] EWCA Civ 43, [2022] 4 WLR 22.

the rights and obligations in a particular contract. Property, as conventionally described, and the benefit of a contract are both bundles of rights. Critically, in terms of insolvency protection, it is not whether an asset is proprietary or contractual that matters but whether the asset is solely owned by A (the claimant) or by B (the debtor), or whether they each have shared rights of some description in the asset. A's solely-owned assets and her share of shared assets are protected from B's insolvency, whether the asset is property or the benefit of a contract, such as a debt. She concludes: 'all that matters is whether A or B owns the underlying asset absolutely.'

If, in this context, ownership is to be regarded as the benefit of rights in or over an asset, one pervasive difference between property and contract can be regarded as the means of enforcement of those rights. A property right can in principle be asserted against the world, whereas a contractual right has to be asserted against or through the contractual counterparty. This may underscore at least the greater value of proprietary rights, particularly in an insolvency context, where the value of the debt that A self-evidently owns outright is dependent on the ability of B to perform; but Sarah Worthington would doubtless answer that, rather than a difference in the nature or incidents of the rights in question, that point alone does not justify the hallowed divide between property and contract.

15
Property | Tort

*Alexander Waghorn**

I. Introduction

In the famous American case of *Edwards v Lee's Administrator*,[1] the defendant had charged tourists a fee to enter a cave, the entrance to which was on his land. However, it turned out that a large section of the cave extended underneath the land of the claimant, and so the defendant had been committing the tort of trespass in taking visitors into those parts of the cave to which the claimant had title.

What remedy, if any, should English law award to the claimant on these facts? In this chapter, I consider two plausible remedial responses, and ask whether either might be justified. The first is 'user damages',[2] a sum of money calculated at the amount which the claimant could reasonably have charged the defendant to permit him to act as he did. It seems to be tolerably clear that user damages would be available to the claimant here as a matter of positive law.[3] This is so even though the claimant has not suffered any obvious loss,[4] because they would not have been able to exploit the land themselves had the defendant not acted as he did, and because the market value of the claimant's land was unaffected by the defendant's activity.

The second remedy considered below is the disgorgement of profits made by the defendant as a result of their wrongdoing. Here, the positive law is far less clear. Disgorgement is certainly available under statute where a defendant profits by infringing a claimant's patent,[5] and there are some cases which could be rationalised as awarding disgorgement in other circumstances at common law.

* Thanks to Rory Gregson, Julius Grower, Joshua Pike, Nick Sage, Charlie Webb, and Yan Kai Zhou for helpful comments on earlier drafts of this chapter.

[1] 96 SW 2d 1028 (1936 CA Ken).

[2] I adopt the label used by Lord Reed in *Morris-Garner v One Step (Support) Ltd* [2018] UKSC 20, [2019] AC 649 [95].

[3] See the analysis of Lord Reed, *Morris-Garner* (n 2) [25]–[30].

[4] Hence Lord Shaw's famous example:

> If A, being a liveryman, keeps his horse standing idle in the stable, and B, against his wish or without his knowledge, rides or drives it out, it is no answer to A for B to say: 'Against what loss do you want to be restored? I restore the horse. There is no loss. The horse is none the worse; it is the better for the exercise.'

Watson, Laidlaw & Co Ltd v Pott, Cassels & Williamson 1914 SC (HL) 18, 31.

[5] Patents Act 1977, s 61(1)(d).

Alexander Waghorn, *Property | Tort* In: *Borderlines in Private Law.* Edited by: William Day and Julius Grower, Oxford University Press. © Alexander Waghorn 2024. DOI: 10.1093/9780191995200.003.0015

In *Oughton v Seppings*,[6] for example, the defendant sold off a horse belonging to the claimant, who was able to recover the proceeds of sale. Despite this, it is not at all clear whether there is a rule of English law which would govern the facts of *Edwards*. In what follows, I do not attempt a doctrinal analysis of those cases which might be marshalled in support of any particular view. Those cases have been ably recounted elsewhere,[7] and so I do not consider there to be much value in running through them in this chapter. All that would achieve would be to confirm what textbook writers have already demonstrated: there is some support for the view that disgorgement is sometimes available as a remedial response to some torts. In part because of the confused state of English law, my concern below is to consider what the law ought to be; fit with the decided cases is not crucial for the success of such a project.

Before setting out the structure of the chapter, I should explain why I have chosen to limit my inquiry to such a narrow set of facts. It seems to be accepted, by both legal commentators and judges, that there is something special about property in relation to both user damages and disgorgement. If we can pin down what that something special is, then we should be on firmer territory when we consider whether similar remedies should be available elsewhere. So, leading commentators claim that, if disgorgement as a response to a tort should be available anywhere,[8] it is where the tort involves interference with another's property.[9] A similar point goes for user damages, which are just one instance where English law might award a claimant damages calculated to represent the amount that the claimant could have demanded from the defendant to permit them to act as they did. Such damages—'negotiating' damages—are also available after a breach of contract, if that contract 'created or protected' a 'valuable asset' which could have been exploited for economic gain.[10] In formulating this rule, the Supreme Court began with user damages, considering them to be the central case where damages of this sort are appropriate, and purported to use their rationale to explain and to limit negotiating damages more generally. This is an approach popular with legal theorists, many of whom have sought to determine the proper role for negotiating damages by starting with what they consider to be the central case of interference with

[6] *Oughton v Seppings* (1830) 1 B & Ad 241.

[7] See, eg, Graham Virgo, *The Principles of the Law of Restitution* (3rd edn, OUP 2015) ch 17; Andrew Burrows, *Remedies for Torts, Breach of Contract, and Equitable Wrongs* (4th edn, OUP 2019) ch 19; James Edelman, Jason Varuhas, and Simon Colton (eds), *McGregor on Damages* (21st edn, Sweet & Maxwell 2020) ch 15.

[8] Although some commentators, including Steve Hedley, doubt that disgorgement for torts should be possible at all: Steve Hedley, *A Critical Introduction to Restitution* (Butterworths 2001) 248; Steve Hedley, *Restitution: Its Division and Ordering* (Sweet & Maxwell 2001) 108.

[9] See, eg, Burrows, *Remedies* (n 7) 351; Virgo (n 7) 453. Other writers claim that disgorgement should be available for *all* deliberate wrongs, and so implicitly reject the claim that proprietary wrongs are the central case where disgorgement is most easily justified: see, eg, *McGregor on Damages* (n 7) 15.007.

[10] *Morris-Garner* (n 2) [92] (Lord Reed).

property, and then by working out from that central case to see whether other cases are sufficiently similar to it such that negotiating damages should be available.[11]

The rest of this chapter is made up of three sections. The first sets out the methodology I adopt and explains why my approach differs from much of the existing literature on this topic. The second focuses on the thought, which strikes many as intuitively attractive, that the concept of 'property' itself can do some work in justifying either or both of our two remedies. I flesh out different forms of that argument and argue that none is convincing. In the final section, I say something more positive. If we are to work out how a wrong should be remedied, we should first know why the duty which the defendant breached should exist. In the present context, that requires a justification of a claimant's right to exclude others from their property. I sketch out four such justifications and consider what they might have to say about whether user damages and/or disgorgement can be justified.

II. Method

My aim is to consider whether user damages and/or disgorgement might be justified in response to a case like *Edwards*, or—to put the same thing in another way—to ask whether there are any good reasons for the law to award these remedies. This is a prescriptive exercise; fit with the positive law is not decisive. In this, I make quite a radical departure from most of the literature on these remedies, which tends to be written with an 'interpretive' approach.[12] I hope to say enough in this section to explain why I do not follow that trend.

First, however, an explanation of interpretive theory is necessary.[13] When doing interpretive work, the commentator seeks out 'normative commitments' which are immanent within and which explain existing law.[14] This is done through an iterative process of reasoning: we start with the legal materials (ie the outcomes and

[11] For examples of this approach, see Daniel Friedmann, 'Restitution of Benefits Obtained through the Appropriation of Property or the Commission of a Wrong' (1980) 80 Colum L Rev 504; Lionel Smith, 'Disgorgement of the Profits of Breach of Contract: Property, Contract and Efficient Breach' (1994) 24 Can Bus LJ 121, 129–32; Ernest Weinrib, 'Restitutionary Damages as Corrective Justice' (2000) 1 Theo Inq L 1; Hanoch Dagan, 'Restitutionary Damages for Breach of Contract: An Exercise in Private Law Theory' (2000) 1 Theo Inq L 115, 132–39; Nicholas Sage, 'Disgorgement: From Property to Contract' (2016) 66 U Toronto LJ 244.

[12] Recent works which consider user damages, negotiating damages, or disgorgement, and which are explicitly labelled by their authors as 'interpretive' include: Andrew Burrows, *The Law of Restitution* (3rd edn, OUP 2011); Katy Barnett, *Accounting for Profit for Breach of Contract: Theory and Practice* (Hart 2012); David Winterton, *Money Awards in Contract Law* (Hart 2015); Burrows, *Remedies* (n 7); Stephen Smith, *Rights, Wrongs, and Injustices: The Structure of Remedial Law* (OUP 2019).

[13] The most influential recounting of interpretive theory remains that in Stephen Smith, *Contract Theory* (OUP 2004). See too Allan Beever and Charles Rickett, 'Interpretive Legal Theory and the Academic Lawyer' (2005) 68 MLR 320; Jason Varuhas, 'Mapping Doctrinal Methods' in Paul Daly and Joe Tomlinson (eds), *Researching Public Law in Common Law Systems* (Edward Elgar 2023).

[14] I take this phrase from Varuhas, 'Mapping Doctrinal Methods' (n 13).

reasoning of decided cases) and suggest some candidate explanatory principles of those materials, which are then assessed against a number of criteria to determine their plausibility. Some principles will be more normatively appealing than others; some will fit the materials better. In order to determine which principle is the best one to adopt, we must weigh these criteria against one another. When we have done this exercise, we are then in a position to say that some cases may have been wrongly decided because they do not cohere with the preferred explanatory principle.

Like many but by no means all interpretivists, the general aim which motivates my work in this chapter is to consider what decisions judges and legislatures ought to make.[15] Two classes of decision are particularly important here: (1) decisions as to what legal rules govern those issues on which existing law is unclear; and (2) decisions to remove, to retain, or to change existing legal rules. In the rest of this section, I argue that this aim is not most usefully served by interpretive theory. To be clear, I do not claim that interpretive theory is valueless, nor that it cannot ever be useful in pursuit of my aim. To the contrary, interpretive theory is obviously valuable. It can point out plausible inconsistencies in the law which call for our attention and it can reveal reasons in support of legal rules which are genuinely good reasons. What I hope to do is push against the thought that interpretive theories should influence decision-makers.

To see the limits of interpretive theory, it is useful to contrast it with an alternative sort of account, which we can term a purely prescriptive account. Purely prescriptive accounts come in two forms.[16] They could be directed at the question of what the law ideally should be, as if starting from scratch, from a completely blank slate. Or they could instead ask what the law should be now, given that we have been doing things a particular way for a period of time. That courts have decided certain cases certain ways in the past plausibly has some normative force, even if those decisions were unjustified when they were first made. If that is right, then this second sort of purely prescriptive account accepts that we may have good reasons not to adopt the prescriptions of a purely prescriptive account of the first sort.

The question for interpretive theories is what rational purchase they can have on decision-makers, when contrasted with purely prescriptive accounts. Obviously, decision-makers should be interested in purely prescriptive accounts; they might, for example, purport to tell a judge how they should decide a novel case. But there is nothing left here for interpretive theory to do.[17] To see the point most clearly,

[15] For examples of interpretivists explicitly stating that they intend to guide future decisions in relation to negotiating damages, see Barnett (n 12) 5 and Winterton (n 12) 20. Other interpretivists claim that their aim is only to 'enhance understanding' of the law, and do not claim to be evaluating the law or suggesting how it should develop: see, eg, Smith, *Rights, Wrongs, and Injustices* (n 12) 25–27.

[16] Charlie Webb, 'Property, Unjust Enrichment, and Defective Transfers' in Robert Chambers, Charles Mitchell, and James Penner (eds), *Philosophical Foundations of the Law of Unjust Enrichment* (OUP 2009) 337.

[17] For much the same point, see Charlie Webb, 'The Double Lives of Property' (2011) 2 Juris 205, 215.

imagine that a judge is confronted with a novel case, and that an interpretive theory suggests a solution which is different to one suggested by a (sound) purely prescriptive account of the second sort. It is implausible to think that the judge could be justified in ignoring the prescriptions of the latter, so that they might give effect to the former. If the prescriptive account is sound, then it *must* follow by the nature of purely prescriptive accounts that the suggestion of the interpretive theory should not be adopted. The same point holds for the case where a judge or legislature is called on to remove, retain, or alter an existing rule. It makes no sense to think that the suggestions generated by an interpretive theory ought to be preferred to those generated by a sound prescriptive one.

So, there looks to be no useful role here for interpretive theory to play. But there is a deeper issue with interpretive theory that should be highlighted: it is not a form of argument that, taken in isolation, has the means to make claims about how anyone—including decision-makers—ought to behave. Recall that interpretive theories purport to explain the law by revealing its normative commitments. However, simply setting out the law's normative commitments does nothing to establish that those commitments should continue to be adopted. What is required is a further argumentative step, either claiming that those commitments are good, or claiming that those commitments ought to be followed regardless of their merit. In other words, we need to end up with some sort of purely prescriptive account.

An example makes this point clear. Consider Nicholas McBride's avowedly interpretive account of user damages.[18] He distinguishes between 'welfare-oriented' and 'liberty-oriented' legal rights. The law recognises the former, he argues, to protect an 'interest we have in things going well for us', while the latter are recognised to protect an 'interest we have in being allowed to determine for ourselves how things go for us'.[19] User damages, McBride argues, respond to infringements of rights which the law considers to be liberty-oriented:

> When a liberty-oriented right is violated, it would be inappropriate to confine the plaintiff to suing the defendant for welfare-oriented compensation. As the right that was violated in the plaintiff's case was geared towards protecting his liberty, then he may well not have suffered any material harm to his welfare as a result of that right being violated. However, the plaintiff will still have lost something—a liberty—that *the law thinks he was entitled to have* . . . For example, where A goes for a ride on B's horse without B's permission, he deprives B of a freedom that *the law sought to grant him*—the freedom to decide for himself who gets to ride on the horse and who doesn't. By allowing B to sue A for [user] damages, *the law seeks to compensate B* for the loss of this freedom by giving him an amount of money that

[18] Nicholas McBride, 'Restitution for Wrongs' in Charles Mitchell and William Swadling (eds), *The Restatement Third: Restitution and Unjust Enrichment* (Hart 2013).

[19] ibid 273.

reflects the value of being able to say whether or not A could go for a ride on his horse.[20]

The italicised words emphasise that McBride's account is about how to understand existing practices. But claims about what people have done are claims of a different order to those about what people should do. The former, taken alone, tells us nothing about the latter. Suppose, for example, that A calls on the courts or the legislature to remove the rule that holds A liable to pay user damages to B. It misses A's point to respond by telling him that the law considers B's right to be liberty-oriented, and that the law is seeking to compensate B for the loss of some freedom the law sought to grant him. A might fairly respond that he knows full well what the law is trying to do, but that he is challenging it. For example, he may argue that the law should not think of B's right in this way, or that the law should not respond to all infringements of liberty-oriented rights with negotiating damages.

Alternatively, suppose that D invades a right of C's, and that C then brings a claim against D for negotiating damages. Suppose further that no case has yet recognised that such damages are available after that particular wrong. The law is unclear. We do not know that it considers C's right to be liberty-oriented and, even if it does, we do not know that it always responds to infringements of liberty-oriented rights with negotiating damages. The best a judge might do with McBride's account here is ask whether they should consider C's right to be liberty-oriented and ask what remedies should follow. When read without any added prescriptive elements, McBride's account simply does not have the tools to tell a judge what they should decide.

Of course, it might be argued that interpretive theories can be recast as a kind of purely prescriptive account when we factor in the force of the principle that like cases ought to be treated alike. Thus, an argumentative step is added to the claim that some theory reveals the normative commitments of an area of law—the claim that decisions ought to be made in line with those commitments, so that all legal decisions are made on the same grounds as any other.

If one endorses this position, then there is no true objection here; on this view, interpretive theory collapses into the second sort of prescriptive account mentioned above. It may be that a full prescriptive theory concerned with determining the proper role for negotiating damages and/or for disgorgement would need to take the law's pre-existing normative commitments into account.[21] If so, then we

[20] ibid 273–74 (emphasis added).

[21] However, I strongly doubt that this thought, if true, could plausibly justify the claim that judges should make decisions to cohere with some interpretive theory. When taking account of the principle that like cases should be treated alike, our concern is primarily with consistency of outcome (who wins or loses the case, and the remedial consequences) rather than with consistency of the normative commitments which explain that outcome. If a judge decides a case in a way which is consistent with the outcome of an earlier one, but does so by adopting some new rationale, it seems implausible to think that any serious injustice is done to the participants in the earlier case. Alternatively, if the thought is that judges should not act in a way that might disrupt the settled expectations of citizens who need to

do need some answer to the question of what those commitments are. However, in this chapter I shall ask what I consider to be a more important question—whether there are good reasons for the law to have these remedies at all. It is worth briefly explaining this prioritisation. No one seriously believes that the law's normative commitments should continue to be followed whatever they may be. Those commitments could be sufficiently unjust such that they should be changed. Where this is done, it may follow that some past disputes were decided inconsistently with how disputes of the same sort will be decided in future; the principle that like cases must be treated alike has its limits.

The interpretive method gives us no tools to work out when these changes can be justified. In order to do so, we must weigh the reasons in favour of the other possible positions against the reasons in favour of departing from them given to us by existing practice. This exercise can only be done if we know what both those sets of reasons are. So, if interpretive theory is collapsed into prescriptive theory, and if the theorist aims to guide decision-makers, then at some stage the interpretivist must engage with the question of what the law should be, even if it is only to demonstrate that their account of it is not too radical a departure from more attractive positions. And in order to do that, they must also be able to tell us what good reasons we have to stick with the commitments or the rules which we already have. On any view, then, an inquiry into the genuine values which may be promoted by disgorgement or by user damages is needed. As the following two sections make clear, I do not think that this is an inquiry which has yet received sufficient attention.

III. Property

It follows from the previous section that what I am looking for are good reasons for the law to award either user damages or disgorgement following facts like those of *Edwards*, where one person makes unauthorised use of property belonging to another. To keep things manageable, I consider things in this chapter as if working from a blank slate; I leave consideration of how the weight of history might change my conclusions to another time.

As a starting point, I want to examine the intuitively attractive thought that the very idea of property can justify either or both of these remedies.[22] Justifications which seek to build on that thought come in two forms in the existing literature.

plan their affairs, then it is bizarre to think that they should do so by developing the law in accordance with some normative commitment hidden within it. If that commitment required academic interpretation to be discovered, then presumably no citizen will have based any of their affairs on it.

[22] Although writers disagree about whether the arguments considered in this section are persuasive only in relation to one of disgorgement or user damages, or in relation to both, I shall take the two together. My criticisms bite no matter which remedies these arguments are intended to cover.

First, there are accounts which invoke the supposed need to protect the institution of private property as a whole. Typical of accounts of this sort is that of Ian Jackman, who argues that user damages in particular are awarded because the law's 'facilitative institutions'—including private property—'require protection against those who seek to take the benefit of an institution without submitting to the burdens thereof'.[23] Although offered in relation to user damages, it seems to me that this argument would also strike many as plausible in relation to disgorgement.

However, exactly what this argument is supposed to mean is not entirely clear to me. On one view, it amounts to no more than the claim that user damages or disgorgement can be justified because they deter wrongful interferences with property.[24] If this interpretation is correct, then the account is open to the objection that neither user damages nor disgorgement work very well as a deterrent.[25] Although they remove some incentive to commit a wrong, they encourage the thought that wrongdoing may be worth the risk: the worst that can happen to the wrongdoer is either that they pay a reasonable fee for what they have done, or that they are returned to the position they were already in before their wrong. Since that wrong may never be discovered or litigated, neither remedy does much to deter. Taken seriously, the sensible inference to draw from the argument is that the law should not recognise either remedy, and our debate should be about the proper role for punitive damages.

When read in any other way, institutional accounts look circular. The institution of private property is just the sum of the rules which govern our dealings with items of property. But our debate is about what those rules should be, and so about what the institution of private property should be. We are constructing an institution, not protecting an existing one from harm. This account is therefore of little help for my purposes in this chapter.

More useful then may be the second kind of account which builds upon the intuition that 'property' can be helpful in constructing a justification of user damages or disgorgement. These accounts focus on a concern for the individual property rights of particular people, rather than on broader institutional or societal concerns. Typical is the following argument made by Ernest Weinrib, which has proved very influential:

[23] Ian Jackman, 'Restitution for Wrongs' (1989) 48 CLJ 302, 302. See too Ian Jackman, *The Varieties of Restitution* (2nd edn, Federation Press 2017) ch 8. For arguments along similar lines, see, eg, Peter Cane, *The Anatomy of Tort Law* (Hart 1997) 116–17 and Mitchell McInnes, 'Gain, Loss and the User Principle' (2006) 14 RLR 76, 81.

[24] For explicitly deterrence-focused defences of disgorgement, see James Edelman, *Gain-Based Damages* (Hart 2002); Barnett (n 12); *McGregor on Damages* (n 7) 15.005.

[25] McBride, 'Restitution for Wrongs' (n 18) 263–66. See too Lionel Smith, 'Fiduciary Relationships: Ensuring the Loyal Exercise of Judgment on Behalf of Another' (2014) 130 LQR 608, 627 and Robert Stevens, *The Laws of Restitution* (OUP 2023) 300–01.

> Because property rights give proprietors the exclusive right to deal with the thing owned, including the right to profit from such dealings, any gains resulting from the misappropriation of property are necessarily subject to restitution. Gains from dealings in property are as much within the entitlement of the proprietor as the property itself.[26]

Weinrib goes on to endorse the view that user damages remove the value of a gain taken by the defendant,[27] and so his argument is intended to cover both user damages and disgorgement. However, it is only Weinrib's formulation of his preferred principle—as one allocating gains to an owner—that makes this a central feature of his account. Other writers have claimed that user damages respond to a 'loss', but still endorse much the same underlying idea. For example, Francesco Giglio claims that user damages respond in part to the claimant's loss, because they restore to them an 'element of a property or property-like right' which the defendant has taken away from them.[28] For present purposes, the important underlying claim here is that property rights bring with them an exclusive right to determine the property's use, and user damages serve to give the claimant something to which they are entitled by virtue of their prior right over the property used by the defendant.

Many writers endorse these arguments, but state them in different terms. Perhaps the most prominent advocate of this view is Daniel Friedmann,[29] but similar views have been expressed by Peter Birks,[30] William Day,[31] Ross Grantham and Charles Rickett,[32] Sirko

26 Weinrib, 'Restitutionary Damages' (n 11) 12.

27 ibid 16.

28 Francesco Giglio, 'Restitution for Wrongs: A Structural Analysis' (2007) 20 CJLJ 5, 17.

29 See, eg, Friedmann, 'Restitution of Benefits' (n 11) 507: 'the defendant acquires a benefit that belongs, under principles of property law, to the owner; he is, therefore, unjustly enriched at the owner's expense.' See too Daniel Friedmann, 'Restitution for Wrongs: The Basis of Liability' in William Cornish and others (eds), *Restitution: Past, Present and Future* (Hart 1998).

30 Peter Birks, 'Unjust Enrichment and Wrongful Enrichment' (2001) 79 Tex L Rev 1767, 1785: 'Economic assets are meant to earn, and it makes perfectly good sense to say that the earning opportunities inherent in such an asset are all attributed to its owner.' See too Peter Birks, *Unjust Enrichment* (2nd edn, OUP 2005) 82–86.

31 William Day, 'Restitutions for Wrongs: One Step Forwards, Two Steps Back?' (2018) 26 RLR 60, 62: 'There is a convincing argument that restitution should be a remedy for causes of action protecting (per se) property rights because property rights carry with them an exclusive entitlement to profit from the asset in question—or at least to control who does profit from the asset.'

32 Ross Grantham and Charles Rickett, 'Tracing and Property Rights: The Categorical Truth' (2000) 63 MLR 905, 909:

> The right to protection from interference and the right to exclusive benefit of the asset are central rights which in large measure define property rights. The plaintiff's right to recover the value of the asset, and indeed any incidental benefits obtained from the use of the asset, are, therefore, already present at the moment of interference by virtue of his property right.

See too Ross Grantham and Charles Rickett, *Enrichment and Restitution in New Zealand* (Hart 2000) 484–85; Ross Grantham and Charles Rickett, 'Disgorgement for Unjust Enrichment?' (2003) 62 CLJ 159.

Harder,[33] Peter Jaffey,[34] and Graham Virgo.[35] Although each one differs in some details,[36] all agree that user damages and/or disgorgement are available after interference with the claimant's property because the defendant either presently has, or previously had, something which belongs to the claimant. The law makes the defendant give that something—or perhaps only its value—over to the claimant. Following Friedmann, I shall call this the 'property theory'.

Despite its popularity, the property theory looks circular; it is little more than a restatement of whatever candidate rule we are trying to justify. To use Weinrib's language, how do we know that an owner of property has a right to all of the gains or profits derived from that property? The answer is that we know this because we award gains or profits derived from that property to the owner. But then if we did not make such awards, it would not be the case that the owner of property has a right to all of those gains. The property theory therefore looks like little more than an assertion that disgorgement and/or user damages should be available because they should be available.

To some extent, this apparent circularity is explicable because not all of the authors who endorse the property theory intend it to provide an external framework against which we might criticise or defend the law. Instead, it is said to be an interpretive principle drawn out from the cases which the law adopts, whether it should or not. Weinrib is clearest here; his aim is 'to *understand* the particulars of private law in the light of its general and pervasive ideas'.[37] But this is not true of all authors. Harder, for example, believes the property theory to address the issue of 'when gain-based relief in this area *ought* to be available',[38] and expressly begins his study by drawing a sharp distinction between the description of the law and the evaluation of that law.[39] Other writers are far less clear on their methodology. They label the property theory the 'underlying principle',[40] the

[33] Sirko Harder, *Measuring Damages in the Law of Obligations* (Hart 2010) ch 13. Harder claims (at 216) that user/negotiating damages and disgorgement should follow the 'unauthorised use of an exclusive entitlement'—defined (at 216) as an asset 'the exploitation of which is exclusively reserved' for a specific person—and (at 219) that ownership of tangible or intangible property is the 'prime example' of an exclusive entitlement.

[34] Peter Jaffey, 'Licence Fee Damages' (2011) 19 RLR 95, 107: 'The remedial right to [user damages] arises directly from, and in vindication of, the primary right of property—the right to the property and its value, including the value realisable through use.' See too Peter Jaffey, *Private Law and Property Claims* (Hart 2007) 99–103.

[35] Virgo (n 7) 422:

> Since the profits derived from the use of the claimant's asset, it is appropriate that the defendant makes restitution of the value of that benefit to the claimant. So, for example, where the defendant takes the claimant's car and hires it out without permission, it is appropriate that the money received by the defendant should be paid to the claimant since it constitutes the fruits of the claimant's asset.

[36] In particular, there is disagreement about how the claims should be classified. Some argue that user damages and disgorgement are an instance of 'unjust enrichment', others do not.

[37] Weinrib, 'Restitutionary Damages' (n 11) 5 (emphasis added).

[38] Harder (n 33) 209 (emphasis in original).

[39] ibid 12–13.

[40] Friedmann, 'Restitution of Benefits' (n 11) 504.

'justification',[41] the 'explanation',[42] the 'concern',[43] and/or the 'basis'[44] of the law, but rarely, if ever, do they explain what those terms are intended to mean. Nonetheless, the theory is invariably used to generate prescriptions for decision-makers. Some writers have claimed that particular cases are incorrectly decided because they do not cohere with the theory,[45] while others claim that novel cases should be decided in accordance with it.[46] Therefore, with apologies to those writers who did not mean to endorse the theory in this way, I shall treat the property theory as an attempt to answer the question of whether there are good reasons for the law to make user damages and/or disgorgement available.

There are, I think, two ways in which we might try to flesh out the property theory such that it becomes more like an argument in defence of a candidate rule, and less like a restatement of that rule. Those ways track a useful distinction that Charlie Webb has drawn between two senses in which one might use the concept of 'property'.[47]

A. The Analytical Concept

First, we can take 'property' in its analytical sense: as a descriptive label to attach to certain legal rights or interests. This is the sense in which theorists use the term when they debate what property *is*, what it means to say that someone has a property right, or whether certain legal rights properly count as property rights. Birks used 'property' in its analytical sense when he claimed that property rights, in contrast to personal rights, are those rights 'whose exigibility is defined by reference to the existence and location of a thing'.[48] Similarly, when Wesley Hohfeld argued that

[41] Virgo claims that the property theory is one idea which 'justifies' user damages and disgorgement, and that the theory explains why these remedies are 'appropriate' after interference with another's property: Virgo (n 7) 422.

[42] Jaffey, 'Licence Fee Damages' (n 34) 104.

[43] Grantham and Rickett, 'Disgorgement' (n 32) 162.

[44] Jaffey, 'Licence Fee Damages' (n 34) 105.

[45] A few examples will suffice. Jaffey argues that *Wrotham Park Estate Co Ltd v Parkside Homes Ltd* [1974] 1 WLR 798 (Ch) was wrongly decided on the basis of his theory: ibid 108 fn 56. Virgo suggests that both *Stoke-on-Trent City Council v W and J Wass Ltd* [1988] 1 WLR 1406 (CA) and *Forsyth-Grant v Allen* [2008] EWCA Civ 505, [2008] Env LR 41 may be incorrect, because they refused to award negotiating damages or disgorgement in response to private nuisance, a tort which protects property rights: Virgo (n 7) 461–62.

[46] Again, a few examples make the point. Grantham and Rickett argue that it follows from the property theory that disgorgement of the defendant's gains should be available on the facts of *Edwards*, even though no English case clearly establishes this: Grantham and Rickett, 'Disgorgement' (n 32) 173–75. Birks too claims that disgorgement should be awarded on the facts of *Edwards* by English courts: Birks, *Unjust Enrichment* (n 30) 84–85. Friedmann, Jaffey, and Weinrib all finish their analyses by considering whether the property theory suggests that similar remedies should be available in a wide range of cases which do not obviously involve unauthorised interference with property, including after a breach of contract or an invasion of privacy.

[47] Charlie Webb, 'Three Concepts of Rights, Two of Property' (2018) 38 OJLS 246.

[48] Peter Birks, *An Introduction to the Law of Restitution* (rev edn, Clarendon Press 1989) 49.

a property right is a 'complex aggregate of rights (or claims), privileges, powers, and immunities' held against other people, he was seeking to flesh out the analytical concept of property.[49]

The important point here is not whether Birks or Hohfeld were correct. Rather, to bring the discussion back to user damages and disgorgement, the thought is that if these remedies are not available to a claimant in a case like *Edwards*, then it might follow that that claimant does not truly have a property right in their land. However, this conclusion seems absurd; the fee simple absolute in possession is surely a property right if anything is. Some writers seem to endorse this argument when they formulate a version of the property theory. For example, Friedmann considers the 'right of exclusive enjoyment' of a thing which is owned to be the '*essential* attribute of property'.[50] Similarly, Grantham and Rickett claim that the 'right to protection from interference and the right to exclusive benefit of the asset are central rights which in large measure *define* proprietary rights'.[51] The worries here are analytic rather than normative: user damages and/or disgorgement should follow as a matter of logic from the recognition that the claimant has a property right.

The problem with all this is that it is not clear why we should care about whether the English legal system is one which recognises 'true' property rights. What we care about is whether the substantive rules of the system are justified. It may be true that if English law removed user damages and refused to recognise disgorgement then it would not have, or would have only some watered-down version of, private property. However, it does not follow that this would be a substantive flaw. At most, this form of the property theory could only prove that the label 'property right' would not accurately describe our legal titles to tangible things.

B. The Normative Concept

The second sense in which we might use the notion of 'property' is as a normative concept, ie as a ground of, or explanation for, reasons or duties which govern our actions. If a thing which you own is in my possession, without your consent, most people would ordinarily be happy to say that I should give it back to you, at least if and when you demand it from me. And the idea of property plays an important part in my reasoning: I have a reason to hand possession over to you, or I have a duty to do so, *because* that thing is yours and not mine. Here, to say that 'property'

[49] Wesley Hohfeld, 'Fundamental Legal Conceptions as Applied in Judicial Reasoning' (1916) 26 Yale LJ 710, 746.

[50] Friedmann, 'Restitution of Benefits' (n 11) 507 (emphasis added).

[51] Grantham and Rickett, 'Categorical Truth' (n 32) 909 (emphasis added).

is an explanation for my action is not to state that I am subject to a duty to keep off the thing but is rather to say why I am under such a duty.

Can this normative concept of property help us to rehabilitate the property theory? It is hard to see how it can. If we ask why the defendant should hand their gains over to the claimant in *Edwards*, it is hardly satisfying to argue that they should do so because those gains belong to the claimant. The next question we would have to ask is why they do, and so here the notion of property is not in fact doing any real justificatory work.

One way in which a property theorist might seek to get around this concern is to deny that it is a problem at all. They might accept that their argument looks circular in this way but claim that it is nevertheless true—that we cannot point to some further value served by a legal rule is not always a mark against that rule. Indeed, it is a feature of some rules that they appear to be justifiable in this way. That everyone is under a legal duty not to interfere with another's body is probably the most intuitively plausible example. It seems odd to ask someone to point to the goods brought about by this rule in order that they can justify it; the rule is justified, one might think, because our bodies are not means at another's disposal. That strikes many as sufficient, even though it looks like little more than a restatement of the rule which we are trying to justify.

Moves along these lines are familiar in property law scholarship. In particular, some writers have made similar arguments in debates about whether rights to exclude others from things can be justified. Arthur Ripstein is the clearest exponent of a view of this sort.[52] Property rights, he argues, are amenable to the same arguments as those which justify our bodily rights:

> If we ask why what others do with or to your body is up to you, there seems to be only two possible types of answers: one says that you have such authority because giving people authority in this way is likely to promote happiness, autonomy, or something else in the long run. The other type of answer says that you are not available for other people to use; the reason what others do to or with your body is up to you is because it is not up to them . . . My claim is only that in looking for the point or purpose of 'giving' someone the right to exclude others from their property, the form of the answer can be the same, just as the form of the right is the same. It is up to the owner to decide what happens because it is not up to any other person—the owner is entitled to be independent of others with respect to the use of the things in question.[53]

[52] Arthur Ripstein, 'Possession and Use' in James Penner and Henry Smith (eds), *Philosophical Foundations of Property Law* (OUP 2013).
[53] ibid 175.

Thus, on this view, property rights can be justified without pointing to some good consequences that those rights bring about. Their existence need not serve some further purpose. Instead, our rights are constitutive of our normative relationship with others. This captures, says Ripstein, the sense in which it seems wrong to interfere with someone else's property even if it could be demonstrated that the interference has brought about some valuable state of affairs that would otherwise not exist.

If arguments of this sort seem persuasive, then it may be that user damages or disgorgement could be justified in similar terms. Perhaps profits derived from the use of an owner's property *are* means which belong to that owner. If so, that could be reason enough to endorse the property theory. One could say that it is up to the claimant to decide how those profits are to be used because it is not up to any other person. Certainly, the analogy to bodily rights seems to me to weaken the claim that the property theory is circular in a problematic way. If circularity of this sort is endemic to the justifications of legal rules, then it is not such a strong mark against the property theory.

Ultimately, I suspect that your intuitions either go along with this theory or demand that you roundly reject it. There is not the space in this chapter to consider fully whether the theory can be defended. However, I can try to weaken whatever intuitive force it has, with two points. First, writers disagree quite profoundly about whether and when disgorgement can be justified. Although many writers do endorse the property theory, others claim that there is no reason to allow disgorgement,[54] that it is justified after *any* wrong,[55] or that it is justified only after any *deliberate* wrong.[56] If the first of these views is right, then the property theory must be wrong; if the second is right, then the property theory is redundant because disgorgement could be justified without reliance on the theory. This sort of disagreement about the property theory's force suggests that we should be resistant to the claim that the theory is amenable to arguments of the sort made by this version of the property theory.

Secondly, I suspect that some of the intuitive strength of the theory comes from an analogy with the fruits doctrine. That doctrine holds that a person who owns a thing is automatically entitled to the physical fruits of that thing when they are produced, simply in virtue of their owning the first (principal) thing.[57] If I own an apple tree, I own its apples. A person who deliberately interferes with those apples commits a tort against me in doing so, whether they were blown off by the wind

[54] See n 8.

[55] This was the position adopted in earlier editions of *Goff and Jones*: eg Gareth Jones, *The Law of Restitution* (7th edn, Sweet & Maxwell 2007) 36.006.

[56] See, eg, *McGregor on Damages* (n 7) 15.007.

[57] For textbook discussion see, eg, William Swadling, 'Property: General Principles' in Andrew Burrows (ed), *English Private Law* (3rd edn, OUP 2013) 4.434; Duncan Sheehan, *The Principles of Personal Property Law* (2nd edn, Hart 2017) 25; Michael Bridge and others (eds), *The Law of Personal Property* (3rd edn, Sweet & Maxwell 2022) 17.033.

and lying on the ground, or whether they were plucked from the branches of my tree.[58] Here, we are on firmer territory than in relation to user damages and/or disgorgement. It has been said that the fruits doctrine is one recognised in all known systems of property law,[59] and writers sometimes claim that the doctrine follows self-evidently from the recognition of ownership of the principal.[60] In his classic work on ownership, Tony Honoré grouped an owner's rights to fruits, to rent, and to profits derived from their property together under a single incident of ownership, which he labelled the 'right to the income'.[61]

However, the analogy to the fruits doctrine is weak. In the case of fruits, the profit is the best title to a tangible chattel which has been physically and newly produced. This is not the profit made in cases where user damages and/or disgorgement are claimed, which is whatever the defendant happens to have acquired in the process of making use of the property. This difference also seems to be of normative significance. That fruit has come physically from the principal goes some way in explaining why the fruit should be owned by the owner of the principal.[62] Where an apple falls from a tree, that apple was previously a part of the tree, and so the owner of it had rights over the apple while it was on the tree.[63] To say that the owner of the tree does not own the apple is not to prevent them gaining a right over that apple; it is to extinguish a right over it which they previously held.[64] To reject the fruits doctrine is akin to claiming that, when I rip a page out of your book, you lose your rights over the page but retain your rights over the rest of the book.

Thus, I consider the property theory to be unsatisfying, whatever precise form it takes. The theory can be fleshed out in different ways, but every iteration of it seems to be incomplete. If we are to find a full justification of either of our two remedies, we should look elsewhere.

[58] *Mills v Brooker* [1919] 1 KB 555 (KB).

[59] Felix Cohen, 'Dialogue on Private Property' (1954) 9 Rutgers L Rev 357, 366.

[60] See, eg, Andrew Burrows, 'Proprietary Restitution: Unmasking Unjust Enrichment' (2001) 117 LQR 412, 418; Sarah Worthington, 'Revolutions in Personal Property: Redrawing the Common Law's Conceptual Map' in Sarah Worthington, Andrew Robertson, and Graham Virgo (eds), *Revolution and Evolution in Private Law* (Hart 2018) 231.

[61] Tony Honoré, 'Ownership' in Anthony Guest (ed), *Oxford Essays in Jurisprudence* (1st edn, OUP 1961) 117–18.

[62] Samuel Pufendorf, *De Jure Naturae et Gentium Libri Octo* (Charles Oldfather and William Oldfather tr, Clarendon Press 1934) bk IV, ch 7, §4. See similarly Stevens, *Restitution* (n 25) 302. My argument differs from Stevens in that I do not mean to suggest that the fruits doctrine is *required* in virtue of this fact. For a fuller analysis of the merits of the fruits doctrine, see Alexander Waghorn, *The Goals of Property Law* (PhD thesis, University of Cambridge 2021) ch 5.

[63] Although this point seems to me to be uncontroversial, Lionel Smith must doubt it because he insists on drawing a distinction between the production of fruit and the 'subdivision' of a thing: Lionel Smith, *The Law of Tracing* (OUP 1997) 21–22.

[64] For the same point in the context of rights over things, such as hair or sperm, separated from our bodies, see Muireann Quigley, *Self-Ownership, Property Rights and the Human Body* (CUP 2018) 239.

IV. Property, Again

In this section, I build on a different intuitively attractive thought in order to consider whether user damages or disgorgement might be justified. That thought is that the remedy which should follow an infringement of a given right should be determined by reference to the reasons which justified the infringed right. If that thought is correct, then it follows that our answer depends on an account of the reasons which might justify the recognition of an owner's right to exclude others from their property.[65]

I do not have the space in this chapter to fully defend that starting thought.[66] However, I can instead demonstrate its plausibility by showing that an alternative strand of theorisation of user damages is incomplete as a justification of those damages, and that this strand of thought is incomplete precisely because it is missing an account of the reasons which justify an owner's right to exclude others. According to this view, user damages respond to the mere fact that a duty has been breached. The central point has been put in different ways. Some argue that user damages 'vindicate' an infringed right;[67] others argue that user damages provide a 'substitute' for that right.[68] If these arguments are correct, then my starting point looks out of place. What matters under these accounts is not *why* a right should exist. Rather, what matters is that a right *does* exist and that it has been infringed. If those facts are made out, user damages follow.

However, to be plausible, such accounts must incorporate some explanation of what it is that makes particular right-infringements more or less serious than other infringements of the same right.[69] I might drive your car around town, or I might instead spend that time touching it with my little finger. In both cases, I have infringed the same right: your right to exclude me from the car.[70] In both cases, the

[65] I am not the first to make this argument in this context: see James Gordley, 'The Purpose of Awarding Restitutionary Damages: A Reply to Professor Weinrib' (2000) 1 Theo Inq L 39 and James Gordley, *Foundations of Private Law* (OUP 2006) ch 21. I discuss Gordley's substantive arguments in Section IV.C.

[66] The thought obviously owes much to John Gardner's 'continuity thesis', set out in John Gardner, *Torts and Other Wrongs* (OUP 2019) ch 2 and explored in Sandy Steel, 'Compensation and Continuity' (2020) 26 Leg 250. The continuity thesis has its doubters: see, eg, Charlie Webb, 'Duties and Damages' in Paul Miller and John Oberdiek (eds), *Oxford Studies in Private Law Theory*, vol I (OUP 2020) and John Goldberg and Benjamin Zipursky, *Recognizing Wrongs* (Belknap Press 2020) 159–63.

[67] See, eg, Jason Varuhas, 'The Concept of "Vindication" in the Law of Torts: Rights, Interests and Damages' (2014) 34 OJLS 253, 284–89; Smith, *Rights, Wrongs, and Injustices* (n 12) 202–06.

[68] See, eg, Robert Stevens, *Torts and Rights* (OUP 2007) ch 4 and Stevens, *Restitution* (n 25) ch 17.

[69] For variations of this criticism levelled at the substitutive account, see James Edelman, 'The Meaning of Loss and Enrichment' in Chambers, Mitchell, and Penner (eds) (n 16) 219 and Burrows, *Remedies* (n 7) 48. Both Edelman and Burrows claim that the way to determine an infringement's seriousness is in reference to its consequences. Although I do not doubt that consequences must be important, my example shows that they are not the only issue at play here.

[70] One might object at this point that we can disaggregate your right to exclude me from the car into many different rights, including two separate rights: the right that I not touch the car with my little finger, and the right that I not drive the car around town. But this objection simply kicks the can down the road. Why is the latter right more significant than the former? And, just as importantly, why is your

vindicatory and substitutionary accounts therefore appear to call for the same response. But this result is implausible; it ignores the relative significance of the two right-infringements. What is being vindicated or substituted cannot be the right itself, but rather it is something like the extent of the infringement of the right.

It follows that these accounts are incomplete without a further account which can explain whether a given right-infringement is more or less significant than another.[71] An account which attempts to justify user damages as a response to the mere fact of a breach of duty alone cannot succeed. What is needed is reliance on the reasons which justify the infringed right: the more a given wrongdoer acts contrary to the reasons which justify the right that they infringe, the more significant is their infringement.

Like the property theory, the vindicatory and substitutionary accounts lack an analysis of the reasons which might justify an owner's right to exclude others from their property. It may be that these accounts can be made convincing once such an analysis is added to the accounts; I will not attempt a rehabilitation in what follows. Nor do I have the space to consider each and every justificatory approach towards private property. There is a huge literature on that topic, written from many different perspectives. Instead, I shall sketch out four justificatory accounts of private property, which I have selected either because of their popularity among private law theorists or because they appear most obviously relevant to the problem at hand. I then consider whether each one suggests, taken on their own terms, a plausible justification for user damages or for disgorgement in the core case, analogous to the facts of *Edwards*.

A. Kantian Accounts

The first is the 'Kantian' account, which has been most clearly expounded by Ripstein.[72] The account begins by considering a pre-legal state of nature, where all people are subject to duties which dictate that they must act consistently with each other's independence. To be an independent person is to be in a relationship

right that I not touch the car with my little finger equally as significant as your right that I not touch the car with my thumb?

[71] Smith makes a brief attempt to set out such an account: Smith, *Rights, Wrongs, and Injustices* (n 12) 207–08. On Smith's (interpretive) account, the law considers three factors to determine a wrong's seriousness: the importance of the right infringed; the defendant's state of mind when committing the wrong; and the wrong's consequences. However, Smith's factors suggest that the same remedy should follow in both examples in relation to the car.

[72] Arthur Ripstein, *Force and Freedom: Kant's Legal and Political Philosophy* (Harvard UP 2009). In this chapter, I focus only on Ripstein's account. However, there are a number of alternative interpretations of Kant available in the literature. See, eg, Sharon Byrd and Joachim Hruschka, 'The Natural Law Duty to Recognize Private Property Ownership: Kant's Theory of Property and his Doctrine of Right' (2006) 56 UTLJ 217; Ernest J Weinrib, *Corrective Justice* (OUP 2012) ch 8.

with others whereby those others do not make choices about your means.[73] In the pre-legal state, independence first requires that people do not interfere with each other's bodies. Kant then considers how one might justify shifting from that normative position to one in which independence includes a respect for people's rights over items of property. That move is a morally demanding one. It entails that people's freedom to act is reduced, because they become subject to duties to keep off items of property which would otherwise be available for them to take and use.

Kant's solution is to invoke a 'postulate of practical reason', that is, a principle that is true but 'incapable of further proof'.[74] The postulate means that all people must will a system of private property into existence, lest they act contrary to the postulate, and so contrary to reason. This is so because to deny such a system would mean that we would not be able to set or pursue plans to the same degree that we otherwise would. Suppose you are making an omelette.[75] If you have no right to the eggs that you earlier gathered while you cook the mushrooms, you have no right to stop another taking those eggs; your ability to set and pursue purposes would depend on the choices of another. To avoid this state of affairs, Kant argues, rights to exclude others from the eggs are needed.

For present purposes, this account is unhelpful because it cannot justify why, in a case like *Edwards*, the claimant should have an *absolute* right to exclude people from their land, rather than simply a right that others not interfere with the uses to which the claimant is putting the land. A system of usufruct, which only recognises much more limited rights of that sort, would be sufficient to address the concern which motivates Kant to endorse the postulate.[76] In fact, such a system appears superior under Kantian premises, because it would leave more projects open to non-right-holders which they might pursue without committing legal wrongs. Thus, I do not think that a Kantian account can help us to justify user damages or disgorgement in *Edwards*. In fact, it rather does the opposite. If the defendant's actions should not be wrongful, then presumably no remedy should follow them.

B. Use-Value Accounts

A second sort of justification attempts to avoid the flaws of the Kantian account by invoking instrumental concerns. It begins from a similar premise to that which underlay Kant's postulate: people should not interfere with those valuable projects being pursued by others, and private property is best justified because it allows people to pursue those projects free from interference. On such an account, it is

[73] Ripstein, *Force and Freedom* (n 72) 15.
[74] ibid 61.
[75] The example is Ripstein's: ibid 91–92.
[76] I am here adopting an argument made by James Penner in response to Ripstein's interpretation of Kant: James Penner, *Property Rights: A Re-Examination* (OUP 2020) 177–80.

our (non-legal) interest in *using* items of property which is central,[77] and property rights imperfectly promote and protect that interest.

At first blush, this account, again, cannot help us to justify user damages or disgorgement, because it suggests that a mere trespasser commits no wrong; if the claimant's legal right serves their interest in making use of land, then others should be free to act, so long as they do not interfere with that use. In response, we can invoke some or all of the following instrumental concerns. First, to permit trespasses increases the risk that an owner's uses for their property are interfered with. Secondly, an absolute right of exclusion is cheap for courts to enforce.[78] They need not inquire into the mental state of the right-holder to determine what projects the property was planned to be used for, but instead need only ask whether the purported wrongdoer physically interfered with it. Thirdly, for similar reasons, an absolute duty of non-interference is a relatively easy norm for citizens to follow. They need not work out to what uses property is being put to know whether their actions are non-wrongful, but rather need only know to keep off those things which are not theirs.[79] Fourthly, even supposedly harmless trespasses may cause some kind of psychological harm which the law has reason to prevent.[80]

Do these four arguments have any implications for *Edwards*? The first and third concerns suggest that the law has reason to draw a distinction between cases where the defendant acts innocently and cases where they act knowing that they are creating a risk that they might interfere with the claimant's use of their property. If they could not reasonably be expected to know of that risk, then they could not take steps to avoid it. So, a legal rule holding innocent defendants liable to pay user damages or disgorgement would not promote the values identified by the first or third concern. In contrast, if one knowingly risks interference with an owner's uses, these concerns do bite and suggest that a substantial remedy may do some good.

However, these concerns do not map onto user damages or disgorgement. In the case where the defendant acts knowingly, there seem to be two plausible underlying thoughts which might justify the award of a substantial remedy. First, one might argue that a remedy is needed to act as a deterrent—to ensure that people do not go about risking interference with the uses to which others are putting their property. But, as we have seen, neither user damages nor disgorgement help very

[77] See, eg, James Penner, *The Idea of Property in Law* (OUP 1997) 70–71: 'The right to property is grounded by the interest we have in using things in the broader sense. No one has any interest in merely excluding others from things, for any reason or no reason at all. The interest that underpins the right to property is the interest we have in purposefully dealing with things.'

[78] Thomas Merrill and Henry Smith in particular have emphasised the importance to property law of minimising costs for courts and citizens. See, eg, Thomas Merrill and Henry Smith, 'Optimal Standardization in the Law of Property: The *Numerus Clausus* Principle' (2000) 110 Yale LJ 1.

[79] Penner, *Re-Examination* (n 76) 198–99.

[80] For instance, it may be that a harmless trespasser to land causes the wronged person to fear for their personal safety, and that this fear disrupts their ability to live their life as they did before the wrong. For an example of a rationalisation of the wrongfulness of (some) supposedly harmless trespasses along these lines, see Colin Bird, 'Harm Versus Sovereignty: A Reply to Ripstein' (2007) 35 Phil & Pub Aff 179.

much to deter anything. The worry here would be much better addressed via punitive sanction. Secondly, one might argue that a remedy is needed to communicate disapproval at the fact that the defendant has exposed the claimant to a risk that their use-interest be set back. Again, user damages and/or disgorgement would be remarkably ineffective ways to achieve this putative aim. Neither remedy takes any account at all of the severity of the setback risked by the defendant, nor of the likelihood of that setback materialising. Yet these concerns would be important if we took seriously a desire to communicate disapproval about the defendant's risk-taking behaviour. Although these remedies may bring about some desirable consequences, it is implausible to claim that those consequences can satisfyingly justify either user damages or disgorgement.

The second and fourth concerns identified above are of even less help. If our aim is to keep costs on courts down, then it is odd to encourage litigation via legal rules which give claimants a financial incentive to litigate.[81] And if our concern is to respond to psychological harm, then the sensible thing to do would be to compensate for that harm whenever it is actually suffered. Neither a reasonable fee for the use of the claimant's property nor the amount of the defendant's gain bear any relation at all to the claimant's psychological harm.

C. Aristotelian Accounts

A third kind of justification of private property rights takes its inspiration from Aristotle, who argued that property rights are justifiable primarily as a means of providing incentives to work, and to resolve quarrels over the allocation of resources.[82] In an alternative system of common property, the thought goes, some would receive benefits despite putting in little work to care for what is owned in common, while others would receive little relative to their efforts.

Writing explicitly under this Aristotelian framework, James Gordley has argued that user damages are justified because they discourage disputes and encourage parties to bargain with each other and to come to agreements.[83] Suppose that D wants to use C's property for some commercial venture. There are two incompatible interests pulling in different directions: C's interest in securing a high price

[81] In comparison to, eg, a rule which said that the claimant could recover only nominal damages in *Edwards*. An argument might be made that permitting the claimant a choice between user damages and orthodox compensation for loss would reduce costs in that it would save courts from determining counterfactual loss. Although this argument seems to me to have some merit, it is surely insufficient to justify user damages. It seems wrong to think that this concern could make permissible a legal rule which allows a claimant to recover substantially more than their actual loss. In the same way, it would be absurd to allow claimants to choose between their losses and being paid £1,000,000. This is so even though that rule would have plenty of cost-saving merit.

[82] *Politics* bk II, pt V.

[83] Gordley, 'Restitutionary Damages' (n 65) 48–52.

and D's interest in securing a low one. When C and D enter negotiations, Gordley argues, having user damages as a default background legal rule helps to balance these interests. So, D is unlikely simply to press ahead and use C's property without authorisation, because D knows that they will incur a substantial liability if they do so. If, instead, D would only be liable for, say, damage done to the property, D would be incentivised to ignore C's rights, so long as D was confident that they would be able to use the property without damaging it. Moreover, the default rule of user damages means that C cannot demand an exorbitant fee to permit D to make use of their property. If C did so, D would be incentivised to press ahead and then pay the legally mandated reasonable fee.

I doubt that Gordley accurately describes the incentives created by user damages in this example. He claims that C is incentivised not to demand an exorbitant fee from D. However, there seems to be a plausible argument that this is exactly what C is incentivised to do. If they make such a demand, there is a chance that D will agree to it. Given the default user damages rule, C can make that demand safe in the knowledge that a reasonable fee will act as a safety net, a fixed minimum sum from which they can move upwards. We can raise similar doubts in relation to the incentives placed on D, who is plausibly incentivised to make unauthorised use of C's property. If they do so, the worst that might happen is that they are ordered to pay the going rate for what they have done, while the best that could happen is that C does not bring a claim against them. User damages seem to encourage disputes here if they do anything.

Leaving Gordley's arguments to one side, I doubt that there are good reasons for user damages under the Aristotelian premises. Any sufficiently clear rule should avoid quarrels,[84] and it is difficult to see why compensation for counterfactual loss would be insufficient to reassure those who labour on property that they will be secure in reaping what they have sown. On this view of things, user damages give claimants an undeserved windfall. Consider *Edwards* as an example. On its facts, the claimant had not sown anything. Had they done so—for example, had the defendant's tourist business drawn customers away from a rival business run by the claimant—they could have recovered compensation for their lost profits. That award would be sufficient to ensure that people are secure in reaping what they have sown.

The same point holds in relation to disgorgement. To award the claimant the profits made by the defendant does nothing to protect the claimant in their

[84] Or at least any rule which is not so out of line with ordinary reflections about how a dispute should be resolved that the rule would simply be disregarded. However, even where this is the case, it is open to doubt to what extent the law should take citizens' reflections into account. A sufficiently unjust law ought not to be kept simply because ordinary citizens generally take it to be a justified law. As I mentioned above, I am approaching things in this chapter as if working from a blank slate. In part, this is so I can look at the problem free from arguments of this sort, which turn in part on empirical facts about what people generally do (or do not) believe to be justified.

labouring or to incentivise them to work. Instead, it confers on them the benefits of work which they have not in fact done.

D. Authority-Value Accounts

A final sort of justification of property rights argues that they serve the interest people have in determining the normative situation of others. An example of this sort of account is that of David Owens, who argues that property rights may be justifiable, in part at least, because they serve an interest that people have in 'having authority over things', by which he means an ability to shape the obligations, powers, and liberties of others.[85] The legal rights recognised by a system of private property promote that interest because they give the holder of the right the authority to shape the norms to which others are subjected. For example, as an owner of land, I am able to confer liberties to use that land on others who would otherwise be under a duty to keep themselves off it.

According to Owens, authority in this sense is worth having for its own sake. Consider the case where my painting has been stolen.[86] Even if the painting is irretrievable, it still seems to make some rational sense for me to value the fact that I have rights over it. I might give those rights to my child or grant a liberty to use the painting to a friend, and it is at least plausible that both I and my child or friend have reason to value the change to our normative position. My child and the friend would prefer to have these rights than not. This is so, Owens argues, even if none of us will ever use, possess, or control the painting.

If this authority interest exists, then it does seem to be able to help us to make sense of a case like *Edwards*. Under this account, even if the claimant had no interest in using his land, he did have an interest in 'determining who is forbidden or permitted to come onto [his] land'.[87] That interest was set back by the defendant when they trespassed on the land.

I should here raise a point about the argument's scope. It has nothing in particular to say about why an absolute right to exclude others from property should be permissible. Owens' point is rather that, once such a right has been recognised, the authority interest kicks in and can be used to help to explain certain further features of property.[88] So, if I only had, say, a right that others not interfere with my use of my land, then the authority interest would still be in play. I could grant someone a liberty to interfere with my use; the ability to do this would be valuable because it changes the normative situation of others. Thus, this fourth account of

[85] David Owens, 'Property and Authority' (2019) 27 J Political Philos 271. See too David Owens, *Shaping the Normative Landscape* (OUP 2012).
[86] Owens, 'Property and Authority' (n 85) 284.
[87] ibid 286.
[88] ibid 288.

property is not truly an alternative to the others but is rather an addition to them. It depends for its force on the attractiveness of some prior justification of absolute rights to exclude.

If Owens' argument is correct, can it help us with *Edwards*? I struggle to see how it could lead us to disgorgement. One might think that we could remedy the defendant's invasion of the claimant's authority by allowing them to 'adopt' that invasion as their own, to make it as if the defendant had been acting on the claimant's behalf.[89] However, as Sandy Steel has argued, this argument is incomplete.[90] We could remedy the invasion of the claimant's authority by making it as if the defendant had had permission to act as he did on the condition that he pay a fee, or on the basis that the claimant permitted him to act free of charge. How can we choose between these alternatives, without question begging?

Here is one argument: allowing the claimant to select between the alternatives would appear consistent with Owens' authority-based account. If a reason in favour of the claimant's right to exclude is that the right gives them authority over others, then perhaps that reason suggests that the claimant having authority in relation to the remedy would be appropriate as a means to make up for the initial setback to their authority interest. However, this argument strikes me as rather weak. It cannot be right that the claimant is able to choose *any* remedy they might want, because that would permit them to inflict wildly disproportionate harm onto the defendant. The remedial options from which the claimant can choose must be limited. Whether disgorgement should be one of those available options is a question which is left unanswered.

Under something like Owens' account, user damages look more palatable. It makes some sense to award the claimant whatever they would have agreed to permit the defendant to act as they did, because that sum reflects the value which they place on the infringement to their authority interest.[91] However, this is not (yet) an argument in defence of user damages, which are quantified at an objectively reasonable amount. If the claimant would only have agreed to allow the wrong at an extravagantly high price, the implication of the argument is that there is a *pro tanto* reason to award the claimant that extravagant sum. If such a reason exists, then the award of a reasonable sum can be justified, on this view, as an approximate figure which works rough justice and is easier to administer than a rule which requires courts to discover the sum at which the claimant would have agreed to permit the defendant's wrong.

[89] This is similar to a justification of disgorgement offered by Ripstein: Arthur Ripstein, 'As if it Never Happened' (2007) 48 Wm & Mary L Rev 1957, 1993 fn 84.

[90] Sandy Steel, 'Damages Without Loss' (2023) 139 LQR 219, 233–34.

[91] This argument is similar to those adopted in McBride, 'Restitution for Wrongs' (n 18) 272–74, in Charlie Webb, *Reason and Restitution: A Theory of Unjust Enrichment* (OUP 2016) 197–200, and in Steel, 'Damages Without Loss' (n 90) 240–42.

V. Conclusion

John Gardner once wrote that propositions which are widely accepted to be obvious should put us on our guard. A philosopher's job, Gardner thought, is to 'expose the difficulties with what most people . . . take to be obvious' in case it turns out that the supposedly obvious is not in fact true.[92] A similar thought motivated this chapter. In the existing academic literature, no one has seriously doubted that user damages should exist, and only very few have not accepted that disgorgement should follow the wrongful use of another's property. Instead of examining their possible justifications, commentators have been on a quest to find the Holy Grail: the one explanatory theory that can reconcile as many decided cases as possible while managing to paint them in an attractive light. In doing so, I fear that we have missed out on asking more important questions. Although I have not done enough to show that neither user damages nor disgorgement can be justified, I have argued that almost all of the existing attempts to do so fall short. Or, more accurately, I have argued that whatever normative commitments the law adopts may well not be commitments worth having. If so, that is an issue which more obviously calls for our attention.

[92] John Gardner, 'As Inconclusive as Ever' (2019) 19 Jerusalem Rev Leg Stud 204, 209.

16

Property | Unjust Enrichment

Helen Scott[*]

I. Introduction: Some Borderlines

A chapter concerning the borderline between property and unjust enrichment could plausibly deal with a number of quite different subjects. Which one comes first to mind depends largely on one's primary legal culture.

Asked to consider the borderline between property and unjustified enrichment, a Scots or South African lawyer would immediately think of enrichment through either the unauthorised expenditure on, or the improvement of, another's property, a body of law that has its roots in a group of cases set out in Book II of Justinian's *Institutes*: that of the man who builds a house with his own bricks on another's land in the belief that it is his own,[1] that of the man who mistakenly sows corn in another's field,[2] and that of the man who writes in golden characters on another's papyrus or parchment thinking it is his.[3] In all three cases, the mistaken improver loses ownership of his property: the bricks or corn or gold leaf accede to the land or paper. In all three cases, however, if the improver is in possession of the principal, he can resist the owner's *vindicatio* to the extent that the owner refuses to pay the price of the materials or the wages of his workmen.[4] In the modern civil law, this defence—the *exceptio doli*—becomes an action. There is considerable diversity across legal systems regarding the scope of the category of unjustified enrichment by unauthorised expenditure and the place of these cases within it.[5]

* I would like to thank Professor Wolfgang Ernst, Regius Professor of Civil Law at the University of Oxford, for his invaluable help with the German law set out in Section II.A. All remaining errors are mine.

[1] Justinian, *Institutes* II.1.30.

[2] ibid II.1.32.

[3] ibid II.1.33.

[4] ibid II.1.30, 32, 33.

[5] For Scottish and South African lawyers, these cases are central to the category. In both systems the rules regulating these cases vary according to whether the improvements in question are necessary or useful and whether the improver is bona fide or mala fide. See Daniel Visser, *Unjustified Enrichment* (Juta & Co 2008) 590–642; Jacques du Plessis, *The South African Law of Unjustified Enrichment* (Juta & Co 2012) ch 9; Robin Evans-Jones, *Unjustified Enrichment: Enrichment Acquired in any Other Manner*, vol II (W Green & Son 2013) ch 5; Niall Whitty, *Stair Memorial Encyclopaedia: Unjustified Enrichment Reissue* (Law Society of Scotland Edinburgh 2021) ch 10. Germany retains the systematic distinction between possessing and non-possessing improvers seen in the original Roman law. Only cases not covered by the specific provisions set out in §994 and §996 BGB (the owner-possessor model) fall inside the scope of unjustified enrichment; specifically, these are seen as instances of the claim in respect of

Helen Scott, *Property | Unjust Enrichment* In: *Borderlines in Private Law*. Edited by: William Day and Julius Grower, Oxford University Press. © Helen Scott 2024. DOI: 10.1093/9780191995200.003.0016

This category barely features in the common law of unjust enrichment.[6] Although the approach to the mistaken improvement of chattels adopted in *Greenwood v Bennett*[7] bears a remarkable resemblance to the Roman one, the common law understanding of title to land as distinct from title to chattels has perhaps impeded the emergence of a general doctrine applicable to both movable and immovable property. Competition from alternative bodies of law (specifically, the equitable doctrine of proprietary estoppel in the case of land) has also inhibited its development. Most fundamentally, the common law simply prefers the robust individualism of Pollock CB's approach in *Taylor v Laird*, even where the claimant is no risk-taker.[8] In fact, for the common lawyer asked to reflect on the relationship between property and unjust enrichment, the subject most likely to occur is proprietary restitution: specifically, newly generated rights or interests *in rem* arising as a response to unjust enrichment.[9] Insofar as it entails the creation of proprietary rights in response to events in the law of unjust enrichment, it seems the quintessential borderline.

But, here again, there is striking asymmetry as between the common law and civilian traditions. In the common law world, proprietary restitution is certainly controversial: its scope is disputed,[10] and there is at least a respectable minority view that it does not or should not exist.[11] In the civilian world, on the other hand, the concept of proprietary restitution is unknown. German law may in fact recognise instances of proprietary restitution outside the technical confines of unjustified enrichment,[12] and certain features of the civilian law of unjustified enrichment can be understood as the functional equivalents of proprietary restitution.[13]

unauthorised expenditure, the *Verwendungskondiktion*, instantiated in §812 I 1 and §951 BGB. For details (in English) see Reinhard Zimmermann and Jacques du Plessis, 'Basic Features of the German Law of Unjustified Enrichment' (1994) 2 RLR 14, 30; Gerhard Dannemann, *The German Law of Unjustified Enrichment and Restitution* (OUP 2009) 107–16.

[6] cf Andrew Burrows, '"At the Expense of the Claimant": A Fresh Look' (2017) 25 RLR 167, 176–77; Robert Stevens, *The Laws of Restitution* (OUP 2023) ch 14. For a recent comparative survey, see Daniel Visser 'Unrequested Improvements in English Law' in Nils Jansen and Sonja Meier, *Iurium Itinera: Historical Comparative Law and Comparative Legal History* (Mohr Siebeck 2022) 651.

[7] [1973] QB 195 (CA).

[8] *Taylor v Laird* (1856) SC 25 LJ Ex 329, 332: 'One cleans another's shoes; what can the other do but put them on?'

[9] The definition is Birke Häcker's: see Birke Häcker, *Consequences of Impaired Consent Transfers: A Structural Comparison of English and German Law* (Hart 2013) 125.

[10] See Charles Mitchell, Paul Mitchell, and Stephen Watterson, *Goff & Jones: The Law of Unjust Enrichment* (10th edn, Sweet & Maxwell 2022) 37-08–37-30 and the secondary literature referred to there.

[11] See in particular the work of William Swadling: most recently, William Swadling 'Unjust Enrichment, Value, Rights, and Trusts' (2021) 137 LQR 56 and the other sources collected in Mitchell, Mitchell, and Watterson (n 10) 967 fn 10.

[12] See in particular §119 BGB (rescission of contract on grounds of error), discussed in Häcker (n 9) 171–74.

[13] cf the right to specific restitution (*jus in personam ad rem acquirendam*) recognised in §812 I and §816 I 1 BGB (Section II.A) and in Scottish and South African law (Section II.B).

Nevertheless, German law 'return[s] an empty box at the intersection of the event "unjust enrichment" and the response "rights *in rem*"',[14] and whereas Scots law, under the influence of English law, has accorded some limited recognition to the constructive trust as a response to unjustified enrichment,[15] recent attempts to persuade South African judges to incorporate the doctrine of restitutionary subrogation into South African law have been met with incredulity.[16]

There is, however, a third potential borderline between property and unjust enrichment: namely, enrichment by interference with the claimant's right. The *Eingriffskondiktion* or 'encroachment *condictio*' features prominently in the Wilburg-von Caemmerer taxonomy of German unjustified enrichment: enrichment by virtue of interference with or encroachment on the claimant's wealth-allocating right is an important sub-species of enrichment claim.[17]

For civilian legal systems such as Scotland and South Africa that have been strongly influenced by German scholarship, this category enables the grouping together and rationalising of a number of isolated fragments of the uncodified civil law: for example, the claim said to be available to the owner of goods incorporated by another into his own property via *accessio* or transformed via *specificatio*.[18] Moreover, it is this category which seems to offer the best hope of explaining recent developments in South African law in terms of which the victim of the theft of incorporeal money is able to proceed against the third party recipient of that money (or rather its proceeds).[19]

As for the common law, the 2017 decision of the Supreme Court in *Investment Trust Companies v Revenue and Customs Commissioners*,[20] as well as recent shifts in academic opinion regarding the nature and justification of claims in unjust enrichment,[21] oblige enrichment lawyers to reflect carefully on the scope of the 'at the expense of' element. Insofar as 'situations in which the defendant has received a benefit from the claimant, and the claimant has incurred a loss through the provision of that benefit, usually arise where the parties have dealt directly with one

[14] Häcker (n 9) 125.

[15] See the comprehensive account in Whitty (n 5) paras 882–901 and the authorities cited there, esp George Gretton, 'Constructive Trusts: I' (1996–97) 1 Edin LR 281.

[16] By the South African Constitutional Court in *Absa Bank Ltd v Moore* 2017 (1) SA 255 (CC). For details, see Helen Scott, 'Interference without Ownership: The Theft of Incorporeal Money in the South African Law of Unjustified Enrichment' [2021] Acta Juridica 343, esp 365–70.

[17] Although interference with the claimant's property right does not exhaust this category, it is certainly the central instance of *Eingriff*: see further Section II.A.

[18] The original instance of this claim appears in Justinian's *Institutes* II.1.26. On Scottish law see Evans-Jones, *Unjustified Enrichment* (n 5) 4.78–4.92; Whitty (n 5) paras 523–25. On South African law, see Visser, *Unjustified Enrichment* (n 5) 655–59; du Plessis, *The South African Law of Unjustified Enrichment* (n 5) 359–60.

[19] Scott (n 16) as well as Helen Scott and Daniel Visser, 'Unjust Enrichment in South Africa' [2023] LMCLQ 656.

[20] *Investment Trust Companies v Revenue and Customs Commissioners* [2017] UKSC 29, [2018] AC 275.

[21] In particular Stevens (n 6).

another, or with one another's property',[22] it seems important to understand not only what is meant by 'dealing' and 'property', but also the reasons why dealing with another's property satisfies the 'at the expense of' element.

II. Enrichment by Interference with the Claimant's Right in the Civilian Tradition

A. German Law

Again, the origin of the category 'enrichment by interference with the claimant's right' is to be found in German law: specifically, in the so-called Wilburg-von Caemmerer taxonomy of enrichment claims developed by the scholars Walter Wilburg (in the 1920s) and Ernst von Caemmerer (in the 1950s).[23] According to this taxonomy, it is important to distinguish two modes of enrichment: enrichment by performance (*Leistung*), that is enrichment deliberately and purposefully conferred by the claimant on the defendant, and enrichment 'in another way'. This latter category can then be further divided into the claim arising from interference by the defendant with the claimant's right, or *Eingriffskondiktion*, and claims arising from the imposition of a benefit on the defendant by the claimant, a category which comprises both enrichment through unauthorised improvements to the defendant's property (giving rise to the *Verwendungskondiktion*)[24] and enrichment through the payment of the defendant's debt (giving rise to the *Rückgriffsko ndiktion*).[25] Importantly, where enrichment has been obtained by performance, non-performance-based claims are usually barred.

Performance-based claims are recognised not only by virtue of the first alternative in the first sentence of §812 I of the German Civil Code (Bürgerliches Gesetzbuch or 'BGB')—the so-called 'general clause', according to which 'a person who, without legal cause, obtains something by way of another person's performance or in some other way at another's expense, is obliged to surrender to that person what he has so obtained'[26]—but also in the more specific provisions

[22] *Investment Trust Companies* (n 20) [46].

[23] Walter Wilburg, *Die Lehre von der ungerechtfertigten Bereicherung nach österreichischem und deutschem Recht* (Leuschner & Lubensky 1934); Ernst von Caemmerer, 'Bereicherung und unerlaubte Handlung' in Hans Dölle, Max Rheinstein, and Konrad Zweigert (eds), *Festschrift für Ernst Rabel*, vol I: *Rechtsvergleichung und Internationales Privatrecht* (Mohr Siebeck 1954) 333. Fortunately, there is now also a substantial English-language literature: see, eg, Zimmermann and du Plessis (n 5); Visser, *Unjustified Enrichment* (n 5) 122–29; Dannemann (n 5); Häcker (n 9); Sonja Meier, 'Enrichment "at the Expense of Another" and Incidental Benefits in German Law' [2019] Acta Juridica 453.

[24] cf n 5.

[25] For a summary of these principles in English, see Häcker (n 9) 25–28. Also Zimmermann and du Plessis (n 5) 24–30; Dannemann (n 5) ch 1; Meier, 'Enrichment' (n 23) 454–61.

[26] Translation from Häcker (n 9) 338.

contained in the second sentence of §812 I and in the first sentence of §817. It is striking that this is in the first instance a claim for specific recovery of what was transferred, along with any secondary benefits received,[27] although it does not confer any protection on the claimant in the event of the transferee's insolvency.[28] It is only if the transferee is unable to make specific restitution of the benefit received that they come under an obligation to make restitution of its value.[29]

Like performance claims, claims arising from interference with the claimant's right are recognised not only by virtue of the second alternative in the first sentence of §812 ('in another way'), but also in a number of other provisions scattered throughout the BGB. Where B eats A's lunch, A will have a claim for the value of the food under §812 I.[30] Also included within §812 I are claims arising from the infringement of intellectual property rights and personality rights capable of commercialisation:[31] in the case of intellectual property rights in particular, the claimant is usually awarded an appropriate licence fee.[32] On the other hand, a special instance of the *Eingriffskondiktion* is contained in the first sentence of §816 I: 'If an unauthorised person disposes of an object in such a way that the disposition is effective vis-à-vis the person entitled, he is obliged to surrender to the person entitled what he has obtained by virtue of the disposition.'[33]

A simple example of such an unauthorised disposition is the case in which B sells A's bicycle to C for £100. According to German law, such an unauthorised disposition of movable property is effective where C is in good faith (defined in §932 II)[34] and where the bicycle has not been stolen, lost, or otherwise separated from A without her consent (§935 I),[35] meaning that C becomes owner of the bicycle for all purposes.[36] A, however, acquires an unjust enrichment claim against B. On one view, this claim is limited to the value of the bicycle, but for others it is a personal right to acquire the substitute asset received by B, a *jus in personam ad rem acquirendam*.[37] It takes the place of A's lost

[27] §818 I BGB.

[28] See, eg, Häcker (n 9) 65.

[29] §818 II BGB.

[30] eg, Zimmermann and du Plessis (n 5) 29.

[31] Dannemann (n 5) 93–96. According to the 'doctrine of attribution' developed by Wilburg and von Caemmerer, if the legal order attributes the gain in question to the holder of the right, restitution is granted, but if the right in question was not bestowed on the claimant so that they could make or retain this particular gain, no claim arises. See, eg, Dannemann (n 5) 94.

[32] See, eg, Dannemann (n 5) 95.

[33] Translation from Häcker (n 9) 338.

[34] According to §932 II BGB, 'the purchaser is not in good faith if he is either aware, or, as a result of gross negligence, unaware, that the thing does not belong to the transferor'. Translation from Häcker (n 9) 341.

[35] Even where the circumstances described in §935 I BGB apply, it is open to A to ratify B's disposition: see §185 II. This allows the victim of theft to proceed against B or C in unjustified enrichment (under §816 I 1 or 2) in circumstances where the stolen property cannot be located and where the *vindicatio* is therefore practically unavailable.

[36] See §932 BGB, explained by Häcker (n 9) 216–19.

[37] Häcker (n 9) 298–305.

vindicatio.[38] Where B has acted wrongfully and with fault, a delictual claim against him may also arise. Where B makes the disposition gratuitously (for example, where B gives A's bike to C as a gift) B's act is once again effective to make C owner of the bike, despite the fact that C has not given value for it.[39] But in this case, C (as the person who obtains an immediate legal advantage through the disposition) is obliged to surrender to A what he has obtained by virtue of B's unauthorised disposition.[40] This claim, enshrined in the second sentence of §816 I, arises from C's unjustified enrichment at A's expense.[41] Importantly, where B disposes of money or bearer instruments[42] belonging to A, the restrictions set out in §935 I do not apply: according to §935 II, C acquires ownership of the money even if it has been stolen, lost, or otherwise separated from A without her consent. So whereas ownership of a stolen chattel, like a bike, persists even where the bike is transferred to a good faith third party, where money is concerned, A has only an unjustified enrichment remedy.

A further specific instance of enrichment through interference with the claimant's right can be found in §951 I, according to which one who has lost ownership of movable property by virtue of *accessio*, mixture, or *specificatio* 'can demand reparation in money from the person who benefits from the re-allocation of rights in accordance with the provisions about the surrender of an unjustified enrichment'.[43] Unlike in the case of §816 I 2, here the law takes no account of whether or not the defendant gave value for the claimant's property to a third party.[44] Certain provisions set out in §§985–1003 (Claims Derived from Ownership) seem also to concern enrichment by virtue of interference with the claimant's rights: for example, §988 imposes on the gratuitous possessor of another's property a duty to surrender to the owner any secondary benefits[45] he has reaped before the action becomes pending 'in accordance with the provisions about the surrender of an unjustified enrichment', whereas §993 I limits this duty in the case of bona fide possessors for value to the surrender of fruits that do not fall within the ordinary yield of the thing.[46] These claims are not, however, seen as instances of enrichment by interference with the claimant's rights but are rather aspects of the specific regime

[38] Sonja Meier, 'Bona Fide Purchase as a Defence in Unjust Enrichment' in Andrew Dyson, James Goudkamp, and Frederick Wilmot-Smith (eds), *Defences in Unjust Enrichment* (Hart 2016) 255, 264.

[39] See again §932 BGB, explained by Häcker (n 9) 216–19.

[40] Häcker (n 9) 222–25.

[41] ibid 222 fn 33.

[42] See Gerhard Dannemann and Reiner Schulze (eds), *German Civil Code*, vol 1 (CH Beck 2020) 1818 (commentary on §935 II) for an explanation of what is understood by 'bearer instruments'.

[43] Translation from Häcker (n 9) 342. To the extent that enrichment occurs through the act of the defendant, this can be described as a special case of the *Eingriffskondiktion*: see Häcker (n 9) 44–45.

[44] Meier, 'Bona Fide Purchase' (n 38) 270.

[45] According to §100 BGB, 'secondary benefits are the fruits of a thing or of a right as well as the benefits which are afforded by the use of the thing or of the right'. Translation from Häcker (n 9) 329.

[46] In both cases the possessor can claim reimbursement from the owner for any necessary expenditure on the thing: see §994 BGB. cf n 5.

that regulates illegitimate possession, the owner/possessor model.[47] Insofar as it deals with the unauthorised use of another's property, this specific regime ousts the general clause in §812 I. Nor is the *rei vindicatio* set out in §985 generally treated as part of the law of unjustified enrichment.[48]

B. South Africa and Scotland

As long ago as the 1980s, Reinhard Zimmermann suggested that the Wilburg-von Caemmerer taxonomy developed in respect of German law offered 'a way through the forest' of South African unjustified enrichment.[49] More recently, textbooks such as Daniel Visser's *Unjustified Enrichment*, Jacques du Plessis' *South African Law of Unjustified Enrichment* (in South Africa), Robin Evans-Jones' *Enrichment by Deliberate Conferral: Condictio* and *Enrichment Acquired in any Other Manner*, and Niall Whitty's *Stair Memorial Encyclopaedia: Unjustified Enrichment Reissue* (in Scotland) have made explicit use of the Wilburg-von Caemmerer categories and of the category of enrichment by interference with the claimant's right in particular.[50] Although their laws of unjustified enrichment have developed from different strands of the civilian tradition, both Scotland and South Africa have seized on the German categories as a way of systematising this inherited material.

Like Germany, both Scotland and South Africa treat enrichment by deliberate conferral as the central instance of unjustified enrichment. Here too, in cases involving the transfer of movable property, the claimant is entitled in the first instance to the return of that specific thing, along with its fruits and accessions, but this personal right confers no protection in the event of the defendant's insolvency.[51] As for enrichment by interference with the claimant's right, at least in South African law its scope is drastically curtailed by the rule that unjustified enrichment claims are capped by the claimant's impoverishment.[52] While A can

[47] See, eg, Zimmermann and du Plessis (n 5) 29; Dannemann (n 5) 89–91; Häcker (n 9) 45–46.

[48] See, eg, Dannemann (n 5) 89–91.

[49] Reinhard Zimmermann, 'A Road Through the Enrichment-Forest? Experiences with a General Enrichment Action' (1985) 18 CILSA 1.

[50] Visser, *Unjustified Enrichment* (n 5) ch 11 ('Enrichment by Invasion of Rights or Enrichment by Act of the Party Enriched'); du Plessis, *The South African Law of Unjustified Enrichment* (n 5) chs 11–12 ('Enrichment by Taking from Another or Infringement of Another's Rights'); Evans-Jones, *Unjustified Enrichment* (n 5) ch 4 ('Interference with Another's Property Rights Without a Legal Ground and Analogous Rights'); Whitty (n 5) ch 9 ('Enrichment by Interference with Another's Rights').

[51] In Scottish law this has traditionally been the provenance of the remedy of restitution (as opposed to repetition—money—or recompense—services, etc): see Robin Evans-Jones, *Unjustified Enrichment: Enrichment by Deliberate Conferral: Condictio*, vol I (W Green & Son 2003) 9-05–9-09. The position in South African law is contested: see Visser, *Unjustified Enrichment* (n 5) 162–63.

[52] See Wouter de Vos, *Verrykingsaanspreeklikheid in die Suid-Afrikaanse Reg* (3rd edn, Juta & Co 1987) ch 7, in particular 180, and more recently, Visser, *Unjustified Enrichment* (n 5) 115–16; du Plessis, *The South African Law of Unjustified Enrichment* (n 5) 41–48. Scottish law does not insist on this requirement in the context of enrichment by interference: see in particular Whitty (n 5) para 1021.

sue B in unjustified enrichment for eating her lunch, South African law admits no equivalent to the *Eingriffskondiktion* that arises where B infringes A's intellectual property right[53] or (in certain instances) personality right.[54] Both Scots and South African law lack German law's sophisticated general regime regarding unauthorised dispositions.[55] Where A's movable property is handed by B to C without A's authorisation, this disposition is in principle ineffective. Thus, A's *vindicatio* survives against C; these legal systems do not therefore recognise any direct equivalent to the *Eingriffskondiktion* available to A against B set out in §816 I 1 BGB (where B receives goods or money in exchange for A's property) or the claim available to A against C set out in §816 I 2 BGB (where the disposition is gratuitous). Nor does South African law protect the gratuitous good-faith recipient of stolen money against the owner's *vindicatio*: provided that the money remains identifiable, its original owner can vindicate it.[56] Where, however, C gives value for the stolen money, it seems that A's *vindicatio* fails.[57]

As in German law, where the claimant's movable property has been consumed or their right of ownership extinguished by virtue of *accessio*, mixture, or *specificatio*, both legal systems recognise an unjustified enrichment claim against the person who benefits from the legal order's reallocation of the claimant's right (cf §951 I BGB).[58] In South Africa at least, these rules apply to money as well as other corporeal things.[59] Thus where A steals B's cash and hands it to C, and C becomes owner of the cash by virtue of the mixture of A's money with C's own,[60] A can sue C in unjustified enrichment; this claim is described as a *condictio sine causa specialis*.[61] It lies only where the defendant receives the money gratuitously,

[53] Visser, *Unjustified Enrichment* (n 5) 685–90; du Plessis, *The South African Law of Unjustified Enrichment* (n 5) 364.

[54] Visser, *Unjustified Enrichment* (n 5) 680–85; du Plessis, *The South African Law of Unjustified Enrichment* (n 5) 365.

[55] But cf Visser, *Unjustified Enrichment* (n 5) 657–59; du Plessis, *The South African Law of Unjustified Enrichment* (n 5) 350–57; Evans-Jones, *Unjustified Enrichment* (n 5) 4-62–4-77; Whitty (n 5) paras 519–21.

[56] In this respect Justinian's Digest 46.3.78 (Javolenus) appears to state the modern South African law. On the vindication of money in Scots law, see in particular *Crawfurd v The Royal Bank* (1749) Mor 875, discussed by Whitty (n 5) para 910.

[57] Johannes Voet, *Commentarius ad Pandectas* (Abraham de Hondt, 1707) 6.1 fn 8 seems also to require that the good-faith purchaser for value has either spent or mixed the money. In *Woodhead Plant & Co v Gunn* 1894 (11) SC 4, esp 8, De Villiers CJ did not require this additional step, treating good-faith receipt of cash as sufficient to extinguish the original owner's *vindicatio*. The earlier decision in *York v Van der Lingen* Roscoe 1 (1866) 337 is similar. cf Scott (n 16) 348–49.

[58] Visser, *Unjustified Enrichment* (n 5) 657–59; du Plessis, *The South African Law of Unjustified Enrichment* (n 5) 357–63; Evans-Jones, *Unjustified Enrichment* (n 5) 4-60–4-61; 4-78–4-92; Whitty (n 5) paras 522–25.

[59] In theory Scots law recognises an enrichment claim arising from the unauthorised appropriation of another's money. However, such claims seldom arise. One reason for this, as Whitty speculates, may be the availability of the constructive trust in Scottish law. See Evans-Jones, *Unjustified Enrichment* (n 5) 4-37–4-39; Whitty (n 5) paras 526–29.

[60] On loss of title to money through mixture, see again Digest 46.3.78.

[61] *Trahair v Webb & Co* 1924 WLD 227. See further Visser, *Unjustified Enrichment* (n 5) 659; Jacques du Plessis, 'The Cause of Action in *Nissan South African (Pty) Ltd v Marnitz NO*' in Hanri Mostert

ex causa lucrativa, rather than for value, *ex causa onerosa*.[62] This claim appears to be similar in function to the claim set out in §816 I 2 BGB, according to which C is obliged to surrender to A what he has obtained gratuitously by virtue of B's unauthorised (but effective) disposition. Moreover, over the course of the last twenty years, South African courts have upheld this claim also in cases involving the theft of incorporeal money. Where funds have been stolen from one bank account and deposited into another, the courts have afforded the victim of such theft a claim in unjustified enrichment against the receiving bank, allowing the victim to side-step the thief's insolvency.[63] Similarly, where money has been paid by the claimant into the bank account of a third party under the influence of a fundamental mistake,[64] or where the claimant has been powerless to stop funds to which they are entitled from flowing into a third party's account,[65] the bank at which the third party's account is held has been found to be liable in unjustified enrichment.[66] It seems that these cases are best understood as falling within the scope of enrichment by interference.[67] But in fact the right interfered with is nothing more than the claimant's contractual right against their own bank: that is, a personal right rather than a real one.

Both Scots and South African law recognise claims dealt with in German law under the owner/possessor model: for example, the claim available to the true owner against the possessor of land in respect of the use of that land. This claim is treated by both Scots and South African writers as an instance of enrichment by interference with the claimant's right.[68] Like German law, neither South African nor Scots law regards the *rei vindicatio* (the action for compelling the restitution of property belonging to the claimant) as part of the law of unjustified enrichment.

and Marius de Waal (eds), *Essays in Honour of CG van der Merwe* (LexisNexis 2011) 1, 14–17; Scott (n 16) 349.

[62] See here the final sentence of Voet (n 57) 6.1 fn 8: 'Coins belonging to another which have been used up in good faith by a creditor can neither be vindicated nor claimed in a personal action [*condictio*].' A more recent authority is *Govender v Standard Bank of South Africa Ltd* 1984 (4) SA 392 (C).

[63] *First National Bank of Southern Africa Ltd v Perry* 2001 (3) SA 960 (SCA); *Absa Bank Ltd v Lombard Insurance Co Ltd* 2012 (6) SA 569 (SCA).

[64] *Nissan South Africa (Pty) Ltd v Marnitz NO* 2005 (1) SA 441 (SCA).

[65] *Firstrand Bank Ltd v Spar Group Ltd* 2021 (5) SA 511 (SCA), discussed by Scott and Visser, 'Unjust Enrichment' (n 19) 658–60.

[66] It is unclear whether this claim is excluded where the stolen money has been used to satisfy debts owed to the bank by its customer (overdraft, mortgage debt, etc): contrast the decision in *Absa Bank v Lombard* (n 63) with that in *Firstrand Bank* (n 65) (in which the former was not considered).

[67] As argued in Scott (n 16).

[68] Insofar as such a claim exists in South African law: see Visser, *Unjustified Enrichment* (n 5) 665–73; du Plessis, *The South African Law of Unjustified Enrichment* (n 5) 346–48. On Scottish law, see Evans-Jones, *Unjustified Enrichment* (n 5) 4-40–4-59; Whitty (n 5) paras 506–17.

III. Enrichment by Interference with the Claimant's Right in English Law

In the third edition of his *Law of Restitution* in 2011, Andrew (now Lord) Burrows treated 'title and tracing' as an exception to the general rule that only direct providers are able to satisfy the 'at the expense of' requirement: '[a] defendant's enrichment is at the claimant's expense where it was the claimant's property that was transferred by the third party to the defendant.'[69] His *Restatement* of the following year is similar:

> (1) The defendant's enrichment is at the claimant's expense if the benefit obtained by the defendant is—
> (a) from the claimant, and
> (b) directly from the claimant rather than by way of another person.
> (2) In any of the following cases, it does not matter that the benefit obtained by the defendant (D) is from the claimant (C) by way of another person (X)—
> (a) where X transfers an asset to D but C has a better right to that asset than X.[70]

It was essentially this approach that was adopted by the Supreme Court when it addressed the 'at the expense of' question in the *Investment Trust Companies* case in 2017.[71] According to Lord Reed, the 'at the expense of' element would be present where there had been a normatively defective 'transfer of value' from claimant to defendant: specifically, where the defendant had received a benefit from the claimant, and the claimant had suffered a loss[72] through her provision of the benefit.[73] Such a normatively defective transfer would usually be present where either the parties had dealt directly with one another or where the defendant had dealt with the claimant's property.[74]

Lord Reed then went on to list a number of situations which the law considered equivalent to the direct provision of a benefit:[75] these included cases in which the defendant received property from a third party into which the claimant could trace an interest.[76] Like Lord Burrows, then, Lord Reed treated the case where the defendant had dealt with the claimant's property and the case where the claimant

[69] Andrew Burrows, *The Law of Restitution* (3rd edn, OUP 2011) 75–76. This issue is distinct from the 'correspondence question': whether a loss to the claimant equivalent to the defendant's gain is also required.
[70] Andrew Burrows, *Restatement of the English Law of Unjust Enrichment* (OUP 2012) s 8(2)(a).
[71] *Investment Trust Companies* (n 20) esp [46]ff and [52]ff.
[72] ibid [44]–[45].
[73] ibid [43].
[74] ibid [46].
[75] ibid [47]–[50].
[76] ibid [48].

could trace an interest into property received by the defendant as instances where the 'at the expense of' element would be present even in the absence of any direct provision of the benefit to the defendant by the claimant. The claims arising in such cases were, however, to be understood as expressions of the same principles of corrective justice that underlie restitution where the parties have dealt directly with one another, rather than as exceptions to a general 'direct providers' rule.[77] In an article published more or less contemporaneously with the *Investment Trust Companies* decision, Lord Burrows argued that 'at the expense of' in English law should follow the German pattern, with *Eingriff* (rendered as 'taking') recognised as one of several clearly defined instances in which enrichment could be characterised as having occurred at the claimant's expense, the most important of these being *Leistung* or deliberate conferral.[78] 'Taking' is here understood by Lord Burrows explicitly in terms of the infringement of rights, with 'rights' apparently limited to legal or equitable title, but understood to include rights obtained by operation of tracing.[79]

It can be plausibly argued, then, that English law recognises a category of enrichment by interference with the claimant's right roughly equivalent to the *Eingriff* of German, Scots, and South African law. But what does this category contain?

If B takes A's sandwich out of A's bag and eats it, A can sue B in conversion for the market value of the sandwich. This is true even if B believes the sandwich to be his. A's conversion claim is the functional equivalent of the *Eingriffskondiktion* inherent in §812 I BGB (second alternative). If B takes A's bike, again, A can sue B in conversion: here, the courts may order B specifically to hand over the bike; otherwise, again, B is liable to A for the market value of the bike.[80] If B gives the bike to C, A can sue C, regardless of whether C is aware of B's theft, and regardless of the fact that there has been no interaction between them.[81] A's conversion claim is proof against either B or C's insolvency: it lies also against their trustee in bankruptcy. A's action in tort in respect of the bike is the functional equivalent of the civilian *vindicatio*.

If B picks A's pocket, taking her £10 note, A can again sue B in conversion for the same amount.[82] If B hands the money to C, A can sue C.[83] Where, however, C is a good faith purchaser for value—for example, where B uses the money to buy a

[77] See, eg, ibid [47] and [50].
[78] Burrows, '"At the Expense of the Claimant"' (n 6) esp 170–71. Under these limited circumstances it would be possible to sue even a remote defendant: see 174, 'The Third Party Issue'. Note also the express reference to the Wilburg-von Caemmerer taxonomy at 170–71.
[79] ibid 170, 171, and 174, esp fn 41.
[80] Torts (Interference with Goods) Act 1977, s 3(2)(a).
[81] A cannot, however, recover damages from both B and C: see Torts (Interference with Goods) Act 1977, s 5.
[82] *Holiday v Sigil* (1826) 2 C & P 176.
[83] It should be noted that, in German law, C would acquire ownership of the money, bona fide purchase not being limited to purchasers for value, and would be liable not to a *vindicatio* but rather to a specialised *Eingriffskondiktion* under 816 I 2 BGB. See further Section II.A and Section IV.

sandwich from C—C acquires good title to the money.[84] Whether A can, in the alternative, bring a claim against B or C in unjust enrichment is moot. To the extent that A's title in the money survives, it is unclear whether B or C can accurately be described as 'enriched' at A's expense.[85] And on facts such as those at issue here, it makes little difference how the claim is framed: the damages awarded are the same in either case, and bona fide purchase by C is said to afford C a defence also against A's unjust enrichment claim.[86]

What if B steals A's cow and gives it to C, who turns it into mince, steak, and sausages? As we have seen, in the law of Germany, Scotland, and South Africa, where title to a chattel belonging to A is extinguished by virtue of accession, specification, or mixture, A can sue C for the value of the cow. But whereas civilian legal systems are obliged to analyse A's claim against C in terms of unjustified enrichment, A's right of ownership having been extinguished, this factual variation makes little difference in English law: C's specification of the cow is comprised within the scope of conversion,[87] and A's success in that action does not depend on the persistence of their title to the chattel at the time of suit; since C is unable to return the cow *in specie*, they must pay damages amounting to its market value at the moment that it was converted.[88]

As for cases in which B derives some benefit from the unauthorised use of A's property, whether personal or real, to the extent that A's damages take the form of the disgorgement of profits, such cases are now generally assigned to the law of restitution for wrongs, rather than the law of unjust enrichment. Net profits obtained by B by virtue of his charging tourists to enter a cave running under A's property do not appear to be 'from' A in the required sense;[89] and it is difficult to discover on these facts any 'loss' in the sense required in the *Investment Trust Companies* case. The argument for the inclusion of such cases within 'autonomous' unjust enrichment is stronger where damages are calculated relative to the notional rent payable by B to A for the use of his property.[90] Here, it is possible to conceptualise B's use of A's property in terms of a transfer of value from A to B, as in the uncontroversial

[84] *Miller v Race* (1758) 1 Burr 452; *Clarke v Shee & Johnson* (1774) 1 Cowp 197. In English law, as in Scots and South African law, bona fide purchase is limited to money: see, eg, Mitchell, Mitchell, and Watterson (n 10) ch 29, esp 29-04.

[85] See William Swadling, 'A Claim in Restitution?' [1996] LMCLQ 63; William Swadling, 'Ignorance and Unjust Enrichment: The Problem of Title' (2008) 28 OJLS 627. See also Stevens (n 6) ch 15.

[86] See, eg, Mitchell, Mitchell, and Watterson (n 10) 29-12–29-17.

[87] See, eg, Sarah Green and John Randall, *The Tort of Conversion* (Hart 2009) ch 3; Nicholas McBride and Roderick Bagshaw, *Tort Law* (6th edn, Pearson 2018) 482.

[88] See, eg, McBride and Bagshaw (n 87) 495.

[89] The facts are those in *Edwards v Lee's Administrators* 96 SW 2d 1028 (1936 CA Ken). But cf Peter Birks, *Unjust Enrichment* (2nd edn, OUP 2005) 83–86, as well as Peter Birks, '"At the Expense of the Claimant": Direct and Indirect Enrichment in English Law' in David Johnston and Reinhard Zimmermann (eds), *Unjustified Enrichment: Key Issues in Comparative Perspective* (CUP 2002) 493, 509–12.

[90] The damages of US$25 per month awarded in *Olwell v Nye & Nissen Co* 173 P 2d 652 (1946) were said to represent the reasonable value of the defendant's use (of the claimant's machine).

cases where A deliberately renders services to B.[91] This appears to be the approach taken in Scots law.[92] It should, however, be noted that cases where the defendant is in possession of the claimant's property[93] are dealt with in German law according to the owner/possessor model, rather than as instances of enrichment by interference with the claimant's right.[94]

What if B steals £100 from A and uses it to buy a bike from C? Provided that C is in good faith, she acquires good title to the £100, thus precluding a claim against her by A. As we have seen, B is undoubtedly liable to A in conversion or (perhaps) unjust enrichment. But does A acquire title to the bike? The answer depends on whether A is able to trace her title to the money into the bike by virtue of B's unauthorised substitution of the bike for A's money.

The decision in *Taylor v Plumer*[95] was long understood to enable the tracing of common law title.[96] Where Walsh, Plumer's stockbroker, used cash drawn on Plumer's bank with Plumer's authority to buy American stock and bullion and then absconded, it was held that Walsh's assignees in bankruptcy did not have title to the stock and bullion and that Plumer (who had taken possession of the assets) was therefore entitled to retain them, resisting the assignees' action in trover. This was understood to mean that Plumer had acquired legal title to the assets received by Walsh in substitution for Plumer's cash. Thus, in *Sinclair v Brougham*, Viscount Haldane LC expressed the principle in *Taylor v Plumer* in the following terms:

> If money in a bag is stolen, and can be identified in the form in which it was stolen, it can be recovered in specie. Even if it has been expended by the person who has wrongfully taken it in purchasing some particular asset, that asset if capable of being earmarked as purchased with the money can be claimed by the true owner of the money.[97]

The principle in *Taylor v Plumer* has been relied on to justify common law tracing even where the asset appropriated consists not of notes or coins but rather funds held in the claimant's bank account: a mere chose in action. Shortly after the decision in *Sinclair v Brougham*, in *Banque Belge pour l'Étranger v Hambrouck*,[98] where H had obtained by fraud two cheques in his favour purporting to be drawn by his employer, P, on the claimant bank; had paid them into his account at a

[91] As in *Benedetti v Sawiris* [2013] UKSC 50; [2014] AC 938.

[92] See the Scottish materials cited in n 68.

[93] As was the case in both *Edwards* (n 89) and *Olwell* (n 90).

[94] See text to nn 45, 46, and 47.

[95] *Taylor v Plumer* (1815) 3 M & S 562; 105 ER 721.

[96] For a recent, comprehensive treatment of *Taylor v Plumer* and those cases purporting to apply it, see Mohammud Hafeez-Baig and Jordan English, *The Law of Tracing* (Federation Press 2021) ch 3. The definitive account remains that of Lionel Smith, 'Tracing in *Taylor v Plumer*: Equity in the Court of King's Bench' [1995] LMCLQ 240.

[97] *Sinclair v Brougham* [1914] AC 398 (HL).

[98] *Banque Belge pour l'Etranger v Hambrouck* [1921] 1 KB 321 (CA).

different bank, which collected the cheques and credited H with the amounts; and had then drawn those amounts out of this account and paid some of the money to S, his mistress, who paid some of what she had received into her account with a different bank, the claimant bank was able to recover in interpleader proceedings the funds remaining in S's account. For the majority, this claim was explicable as an action for money had and received: those funds were identifiable as the proceeds of the fraudulently obtained cheques and no valid defence of bona fide purchase was available to S.[99] The money paid out by the claimant bank when the cheques were presented to them for payment was said to belong to the claimant.[100]

In *Lipkin Gorman v Karpnale*,[101] Cass, a partner at the claimant firm of solicitors, used various methods to withdraw money from the firm's client account. Principally, cash cheques were made out by the firm's cashier, signed by Cass, and cashed at the bank, the cash then being handed to Cass.[102] On one occasion he procured the issue of a banker's draft in favour of the firm which was handed to him by the cashier. Cass used most of the stolen money to buy chips from the defendant club and place bets at the club's roulette tables. All in all, £323,222 was withdrawn by him from the firm's account, of which £100,313 was replaced, recovered, or accounted for, leaving a balance of £222,908 outstanding. Approximately £561,014 was staked by Cass at the roulette tables operated by the defendant club, while Cass won £378,294.

The claimant's claim in respect of the money paid by Cass to the club was understood by both Lord Templeman and Lord Goff to be a personal one arising in unjust enrichment.[103] Because the gaming contract between Cass and the club was void according to the law then in force,[104] these payments were said to constitute in law a gift to the club.[105] No defence of bona fide purchase was therefore available to it.[106] However, the club was held by Lord Goff (with whom Lord Ackner and Lord Bridge agreed) to have changed its position insofar as it had paid out substantial sums in winnings to Cass.[107] After certain adjustments were made, the club agreed that it had won £174,745 overall over a period of about ten months, of which £154,695 was derived from money stolen from the solicitors' client account. The amount recoverable in unjust enrichment was therefore limited to

[99] ibid (Bankes and Atkin LJJ). Scrutton LJ took the view, at 330, that the funds could not be traced at common law.
[100] See in particular the judgment of Bankes LJ: ibid 325.
[101] *Lipkin Gorman v Karpnale Ltd* [1991] 2 AC 548 (HL).
[102] The facts and figures set out here are taken from the speeches of Lord Templeman and Lord Goff.
[103] See in particular the speech of Lord Goff in *Lipkin Gorman* (n 101) 572. Lord Bridge and Lord Ackner also took this view.
[104] Gaming Act 1845, s 18.
[105] See *Lipkin Gorman* (n 101) 562, 565 (Lord Templeman); 575, 577 (Lord Goff).
[106] This point was controversial: ibid 575–77 (Lord Goff).
[107] See Lord Goff at ibid 578–81 (on the recognition of the change of position defence in principle) and 581–83 (on the application of the defence to the facts of the case).

£150,960,[108] with a further £3,735 recoverable as damages for the conversion of the banker's draft.[109]

It is a striking feature of this decision that the claimant firm was able to proceed against the club despite the absence of any direct dealings between them. Lord Templeman described Cass straightforwardly as a 'thief' who had handed 'stolen money' to the club.[110] This suggested that the firm remained the owner of the money that Cass handed to the club in exactly the same way as A remains owner of cash stolen out of her back pocket by B and handed to C. But the obvious difficulty with this approach was the fact that, as an authorised signatory, Cass (and Cass alone) was held to have acquired title to the money which he withdrew from the partnership account.[111] In order to circumvent this obstacle, Lord Goff relied on *Taylor v Plumer*: 'It is well established that a legal owner is entitled to trace his property into its product, provided that the latter is indeed identifiable as the product of his property.'[112] The cash drawn out of the firm's bank account was the 'direct product' of the firm's original chose in action, which was itself 'a species of... legal property belonging to the solicitors at common law.'[113]

Both *Banque Belge* and *Lipkin Gorman* were subsequently relied on by the Court of Appeal in *Trustee of the Property of FC Jones & Sons v Jones*[114] in holding that the trustee in bankruptcy of a firm could trace his property—money held in the firm's joint account—into cheques drawn by one of its partners and from there into the proceeds of those cheques which his wife, the defendant, had deposited into her bank account. Furthermore, the trustee could also trace into the profits made by her through dealings on the potato futures market. The defendant had 'no title at all' to the money, which was recoverable by means of a claim described as 'exclusively proprietary',[115] an instance of 'following'.[116]

The reasoning of the House of Lords in *Lipkin Gorman* has long been regarded as problematic. Troubled by Lord Goff's treatment of the firm's chose in action as legal property capable of being traced into the cash drawn from the client account,

[108] ibid 583 (Lord Goff), taking a generous approach to the application of the defence (cf his discussion of other possible approaches at 581–83).

[109] See in particular ibid 583–88 (Lord Goff). cf the approach of Lord Templeman, who at 567 treated the entire £154,695 as recoverable in unjust enrichment.

[110] ibid 559–63 (Lord Templeman). See also 558 (Lord Bridge).

[111] Lord Goff relied on *Union Bank of Australia Ltd v McClintock* [1922] 1 AC 240 (PC) and *Commercial Banking Co of Sydney Ltd v Mann* [1961] AC 1 (PC) in reaching this decision. See *Lipkin Gorman* (n 101) 573. But cf Stevens (n 6) 208, who argues that the facts at issue in *Lipkin Gorman* were different to those considered in *McClintock* and *Mann*, where the bank issued drafts payable by itself to named payees. Instead, he argues, Cass held the money under a joint tenancy with the other partners such that the firm had title to the cash received by the club.

[112] *Lipkin Gorman* (n 101) 573.

[113] ibid 574. Critically, the club conceded that if the solicitors were able to establish legal title to the money withdrawn by Cass from the firm's account, 'that title was not defeated by mixing of the money with other money of Cass while in his hands.' See *Lipkin Gorman* (n 101) 572 (Lord Goff).

[114] *Trustee of the Property of FC Jones & Sons v Jones* [1997] Ch 159 (CA).

[115] ibid 167–68.

[116] See in particular ibid 169.

commentators have justified the decision instead in terms of the firm's unexercised power *in rem* to revest in itself that chose in action at the moment when the club received the funds.[117] This seems to be what Lord Goff meant when he said that, '"tracing" or "following" property into its product involves a decision by the owner of the original property to assert his title to the product in place of his original property'.[118] But an unexercised power seems a fragile basis on which to found such a far-reaching claim,[119] and this reading of the decision is difficult to reconcile with the rest of Lord Goff's speech. In fact, as is now widely appreciated, the understanding of *Taylor v Plumer* adopted in *Sinclair v Brougham* and relied on in *Banque Belge*, *Lipkin Gorman*, and *Jones* was wrong. Walsh was probably the legal owner of the cheque handed to him by Plumer, and certainly the legal owner of the bank notes drawn by him at Plumer's bank.[120] But these notes were held on trust for Plumer, as were the bullion and securities that Walsh purchased.[121] *Taylor v Plumer* involved instead equitable tracing, despite being decided by a common law court,[122] and has no application outside that context. Thus, the common law claim to substitute assets appears to have been built on sand. Indeed, it is difficult to see how A's original legal title could somehow persist in a new asset acquired by B.[123]

However, it is striking that the claim envisaged in *Sinclair v Brougham*—again, 'if money in a bag is stolen [then] even if it has been expended by the person who has wrongfully taken it in purchasing some particular asset, that asset if capable of being earmarked as purchased with the money can be claimed by the true owner of the money'—does appear to align closely with the *Eingriffskondiktion* set out in §816 I 1 BGB—again, 'if an unauthorised person disposes of an object in such a way that the disposition is effective vis-à-vis the person entitled, he is obliged to surrender to the person entitled what he has obtained by virtue of the disposition'.[124] At least according to one view, the German claim lies in respect of the

[117] Most prominently, Peter Birks 'The English Recognition of Unjust Enrichment' [1991] LMCLQ 472 and Peter Birks '"At the Expense of the Claimant"' (n 89) 514–16. Other explanations are available: in addition to the argument of Stevens referred to in n 111, see Lionel Smith, 'Simplifying Claims to Traceable Proceeds' (2009) 125 LQR 338, esp 346:

> The fact is that all of the cases in which the action for money had and received is deployed in relation to the surviving proceeds of an unauthorised disposition can be understood as allowing a common law claim in respect of a determined sum of money held in trust for the claimant, being the traceable proceeds of an unauthorised disposition of trust property or of the claimant's legal property.

[118] *Lipkin Gorman* (n 101) 573.

[119] cf the critique offered by Stevens (n 6) 207.

[120] Smith, 'Tracing in *Taylor v Plumer*' (n 96) 257, relying on Salman Khurshid and Paul Matthews, 'Tracing Confusion' (1979) 95 LQR 78.

[121] Smith, 'Tracing in *Taylor v Plumer*' (n 96).

[122] ibid. This interpretation of *Taylor v Plumer* was accepted in *Jones* (n 114) 169.

[123] As argued by Graham Virgo, *The Principles of the Law of Restitution* (3rd edn, OUP 2015) ch 21, esp 560–61.

[124] 'The nearest functional equivalent to the broad English principles of tracing and claiming is constituted by the *Eingriffskondiktion* in 816 I 1 BGB': Häcker (n 9) summary to ch 8 at 320.

substitute asset received by B, even if the value of that asset exceeds the value of the original object.[125] This suggests that a claim to substitute assets need not be explained either in terms of the vindication of the claimant's persistent legal title or in terms of a newly created equitable property right. In fact, it can be explained as a personal claim arising from the unjust enrichment of the defendant by virtue of his unauthorised but effective disposal of the claimant's property. Equally, where B does not spend the stolen money but hands it to C as a gift, A's claim against C need not be analysed in proprietary terms but can be understood as arising from C's unjust enrichment at A's expense.[126]

It is not suggested here that English law should simply follow German law.[127] Nor is it suggested that an *Eingriffskondktion* would arise in German law on the facts of *Banque Belge*, *Lipkin Gorman*, or *Jones*.[128] Where A's asset takes the form not of cash but of a personal right against A's bank, it is difficult to describe A's cause of action against either B or C in terms of *Eingriff*.[129] Thus, the claim in §816 I 1 BGB appears to be confined to cases involving the unauthorised disposition by B of cash or other corporeal property belonging to A.[130] The claim against the good faith third party recipient—C in our scenario—set out in §816 I 2 BGB likewise appears to be confined to cases in which C receives cash or other corporeal property disposed of by B.[131] Nor can §816 I 1 BGB advance beyond a single substitution.[132] And these difficulties are compounded where, as in *Lipkin Gorman*, B obtains good title to cash that he withdraws from A's bank account: insofar as B makes C owner of the cash by virtue of his performance, this is a case of *Leistung*, not *Eingriff*. Rather, the argument made here is that the norms that justify the claims set out in §816 I 1 and 2 BGB justify also claims in the English law of unjust enrichment against one who disposes of another's assets without their consent and against the good faith third party recipient of the proceeds of those assets. In particular, it is

[125] On the implications for this claim of B's insolvency, see Häcker (n 9) 314–19.

[126] cf Burrows' analysis of this claim in terms of ignorance (the unjust factor) and 'title and tracing' (an exception to the general rule that only direct providers are able to satisfy the 'at the expense of' requirement) in Burrows, *The Law of Restitution* (n 69) ch 16, esp 404–08, and 75–76.

[127] An immediate objection to such a transplant would be that the default remedy in the English law of unjust enrichment is damages rather than restitution of a specific asset: see, eg, Mitchell, Mitchell, and Watterson (n 10) ch 36, esp 36-03, 36-05. Speaking more generally, deep structural differences between the two systems preclude it: see Häcker (n 9) in its entirety for a masterful exposition of these.

[128] cf the brief discussion of §816 I 1 BGB by Birks, '"At the Expense of the Claimant"' (n 89) 511–12 in the context of his defence of 'interceptive subtraction', with reference to both *Edwards* (n 89) and *Jones* (n 114), as well as the implicit reference to §816 I 2 at 517–18, in support of the claim that the facts of *Lipkin Gorman* (n 101) disclosed 'a sufficient proprietary connection'.

[129] cf Birks, '"At the Expense of the Claimant"' (n 89) 517–18, discussing *Lipkin Gorman* (n 101) in light of §816 I 2 BGB. Regarding the closely related question of whether conversion is possible in respect of contractual rights, see *OBG Ltd v Allan* [2007] UKHL 21, [2008] 1 AC 1, discussed by Amy Goymour, 'Conversion of Contractual Rights' [2011] LMCLQ 67.

[130] See, eg, *Münchener Kommentar zum Bürgerlichen Gesetzbuch, Band 7* (8th edn, Beck 2020) regarding §§812–22 (Title 26) as well as *Band 8* (9th edn, Beck 2023) regarding §§929–36. See also Häcker (n 9) 222–25, 298–305.

[131] Häcker (n 9) 222–25.

[132] ibid 313.

suggested, they are capable of justifying the unjust enrichment claim recognised by the House of Lords in *Lipkin Gorman*.[133]

IV. Taking Without Title

As we have seen, German law accords extensive protection to the security of third party receipts through its treatment of unauthorised dispositions.[134] According to §932 BGB, where B transfers A's property to C, C acquires good title to it. This is true even where B gives a chattel to C, ie where there is no bona fide purchase for value. However, this rule is disapplied where that chattel has been stolen, lost, or otherwise separated from A without her consent (§935 I BGB). In that case, German law's commitment to the security of third party receipts is trumped by the need to protect A's rights as owner. The protection afforded to third party recipients is stronger still in the case of money or bearer instruments. Even where money has been stolen from A (or has otherwise left her possession without her consent), C acquires good title to it by virtue of B's unauthorised disposition (§935 II BGB). This is true even where B gives the money to C. However, the fact that A lost possession of the money without her consent remains morally and legally significant. Whereas the bona fide purchaser for value of cash is proof against both the *rei vindicatio* and any claim in unjustified enrichment, where C is a gratuitous recipient the law of property and the law of obligations diverge: although C becomes owner of the money, she is liable to A's *Eingriffskondiktion* under §816 I 2 BGB. Like the claim set out in §816 I 1 BGB, this is a species of substitute *vindicatio*.[135] In other words, although the security of C's receipt is protected by the law of property, the law of unjustified enrichment recognises the non-consensual nature of the shift of wealth inherent in the theft (or other non-consensual loss of possession), giving expression to the same norm that usually—according to the general rule in §935 I BGB—prevents the passing of ownership in stolen property. Indeed, something similar can be said of the admittedly much less sophisticated South African rules regarding the good faith gratuitous recipient of stolen cash in whose hands coins are mixed: while the law on mixtures dictates that A loses ownership in the original coins, the fact that the coins were stolen from A (or otherwise separated from

[133] cf Carsten Zülch, '*Bona Fide* Purchase, Property and Restitution: *Lipkin Gorman v. Karpnale* in German Law' in William Swadling (ed), *The Limits of Restitutionary Claims: A Comparative Analysis* (UKNCCL 1997) 106, in which the approach of the House of Lords in *Lipkin Gorman* (n 101) is contrasted with that of the German Federal Court in two similar cases. Zülch examines in detail the applicability of §816 I BGB to the facts of *Lipkin Gorman*. However, his acceptance of the House of Lords' common law tracing analysis leads him down a different path to the one followed here: see in particular 136–40, 'Conclusions and Comparative Remarks'.

[134] As emphasised by Häcker (n 9) ch 6. See Section II.A.

[135] Text to n 38.

A without her consent) explains the *condictio sine causa specialis* for the value of the coins available to A against C.

The successful claim in *Lipkin Gorman* can be understood in the same way. Again, according to the authorities as interpreted by Lord Goff, Cass became owner of the cash that he withdrew from the partnership account. This meant, among other things, that any third party who received the money from Cass did not become liable in conversion and could, if sued in unjust enrichment, plead change of position. But as German law shows us, the law's decision to give good title to Cass did not exhaust the significance of the fact that the withdrawal had happened without the firm's consent (indeed, it amounted to theft for the purposes of the criminal law).[136] In recognising a claim in unjust enrichment in favour of the firm against the club on the basis that it had received the assets substituted by Cass for the firm's original chose in action, the common law was able to balance the considerations underlying the *McClintock* and *Mann* decisions as interpreted—in particular, the need to allow partners to deal freely with partnership assets—against the right of the other partners to determine how the money in the firm's bank account was disposed of.

It is widely assumed that *Lipkin Gorman* recognised that bona fide purchase could in principle be a defence to unjust enrichment, although on the facts of the case that defence was not available (again, because the gaming contract between Cass and the club was void).[137] On this understanding of the decision, had the contract between Cass and the club been valid (as it would be today), the defence of bona fide purchase available in respect of the firm's claim in unjust enrichment would have prevented the stultification of the law of property insofar as it worked to confer title on the club, as a good faith purchaser for value without notice, to the money paid over by Cass.[138] However, on the view of the case presented here there was no danger of such stultification, as it was not possible for the firm to trace its property into the money received by the club. Nor should we necessarily expect the laws of property and unjust enrichment to pull together in cases of this kind. In fact, to the extent that bona fide purchase featured in *Lipkin Gorman*, it may be that it was not a potential defence to a claim in unjust enrichment at all. Rather, it was perhaps the gratuitous nature of Cass's disposition—the fact that the club had given no value for the money received—in addition to the firm's lack of consent to the initial shift of wealth to Cass that substantiated the firm's claim.

The thesis presented here is able to account for a puzzling feature of the decision in *Lipkin Gorman*. As we have seen, the club was said to benefit from the defence of change of position insofar as it was able to reduce its liability to the extent that it had paid out substantial winnings to Cass. But the amount ultimately

[136] See *Lipkin Gorman* (n 101) 569 (Lord Goff).
[137] See, eg, Mitchell, Mitchell, and Watterson (n 10) 29-12–29-17.
[138] ibid 29-12–29-17 and the secondary literature there cited.

awarded under the head of unjust enrichment—namely £150,960[139]—represented that portion of the net sum received by the club from Cass that was found to have derived from money stolen from the firm's client account. There is no suggestion in the judgment that, in calculating the club's liability, Lord Goff started from the total amount staked at the club's roulette tables by Cass, some £561,014, and then subtracted from that sum the amounts paid out by the club to Cass, found to be £378,294. Indeed, since that higher amount included the considerable sums restaked by Cass from his winnings, it would have been absurd to do so. There is thus a disconnect between the approach that Lord Goff purported to apply and the way he actually approached the calculation of the club's enrichment at the firm's expense. This difficulty falls away once it is appreciated that the sum awarded in respect of the club's unjust enrichment (£150,960) was calculated neither relative to the amounts paid by Cass to the club nor with reference to the traceable proceeds of the firm's property surviving in the club's hands.[140] Instead, the claim was a receipt-based claim, arising in unjust enrichment, in respect of that portion of the funds paid by Cass to the club that were found to have derived from the non-consensual shift of wealth from the firm to Cass.

V. In Defence of Ignorance

In the law of property, theft and fundamental mistake—factors excluding consent—typically prevent the passing of ownership. According to the thesis presented here, however, in *Lipkin Gorman* these factors served to justify a claim in unjust enrichment. How is this thesis to be integrated into existing accounts of the normative foundations of the subject? Only a preliminary answer can be given here.

In English law, as we have seen, the requirement of a 'normatively defective transfer' is usually satisfied either where the parties have dealt directly with one another or where the defendant has dealt with the claimant's property. Likewise, in the civilian jurisdictions canvassed here, enrichment liability is generally limited to cases in which there has been some *Leistung* (German law) or *negotium* (Scots and South African law) between the parties. There are good reasons for the prominence of performance cases in the law of unjust enrichment.[141] Similarly, where the claimant has deliberately conferred a benefit, there are sound reasons to restrict the range of possible defendants to one, namely, the immediate recipient of

[139] cf Lord Templeman, who believed the whole amount of £154,695 to be recoverable on the basis of the club's unjust enrichment.

[140] Again, the club's concession made it unnecessary for the firm to identify such a fund. See n 113.

[141] Not least the fact that where the defendant has either accepted or requested the benefit in question, the moral case for restitution becomes relatively straightforward: see Lionel Smith 'Restitution: A New Start?' in Peter Devonshire and Rohan Havelock (eds), *The Impact of Equity and Restitution in Commerce* (Hart 2019) 91.

the benefit.[142] When A deliberately confers a benefit on B, she takes the risk of B's insolvency should an unjust enrichment claim arise. No further shift in wealth (for example, a gift by B to C caused by the receipt of the benefit from A, a gift from B to C of something exchanged for property received from A, or even the conferral by B on C of the very same object received from A) can give A rights against that remote recipient.[143]

Where, however, the shift in wealth from A to B is non-consensual, no such limitation is in place. The absence of A's consent means that she cannot be said to have assumed the risk of B's insolvency. And insofar as it is possible to identify A's asset or its proceeds in the hands of a third party, C, there is no reason why C should not also be liable to A on grounds of his enrichment at A's expense. The absence of A's consent is salient in respect of C also: there was no deliberate conferral of the benefit on B or anyone else. It is this that explains the real character of the unjust enrichment claim at issue in *Lipkin Gorman*: the fact that it lay even against the club, a remote party. Where B acquires wealth from A without A's consent, A's mental state is salient not insofar as it establishes an unjust factor of ignorance or powerlessness[144] but rather insofar as it precludes the limitation on claims against third parties inherent in deliberate conferral cases.

The arguments advanced here in support of the unjust enrichment claim recognised in *Lipkin Gorman* are capable also of justifying claims against the gratuitous third party recipients of incorporeal money: for example, where B is able to direct funds from A's bank account into his own, and then transfers part of or all of the stolen funds into the account of C as a gift. Here, the civilian law of property runs out entirely; nor is it easy to see how incorporeal money can be treated as property at common law.[145] Nevertheless, that the proceeds of stolen money move freely through bank accounts implies a strong commitment to the security of receipts similar to that expressed in the provisions on unauthorised disposition set out in §932 and §935 BGB: not only the good faith third party recipients for value of incorporeal money but also the gratuitous recipients of such money acquire 'title' to it, in the sense that they generally acquire a valid claim in respect of those funds

[142] Thus, in German law, *Leistung* usually excludes liability for enrichment 'in another way'.

[143] It is difficult for this thesis to account for §822 BGB: 'If the recipient gratuitously bestows what he has obtained upon a third party, then, to the extent that the recipient's liability to make restitution is in consequence excluded, the third party is obliged to surrender what he has received as if he had, without legal cause, received it from the creditor.' Translation from Häcker (n 9) 339. As Häcker explains, this provision applies only to cases where ownership of the asset in question passes from A to B by virtue of deliberate conferral (*Leistung*), and where B's gift of the asset to C affords him a good defence against A's *Leistungskondiktion*: Häcker (n 9) 225–26. In *Unjust Enrichment* (n 89), Birks attempted to defend a purely causal account of the 'at the expense of' element of the claim in *Lipkin Gorman* (n 101) with reference to §822 BGB. But in '"At the Expense of the Claimant"' (n 89) Birks relied instead on §816 I 2 in order to support this argument: see 518ff.

[144] As per Peter Birks, *An Introduction to the Law of Restitution* (Clarendon Press 1985) 140–46, and, more recently, Burrows, *The Law of Restitution* (n 69) ch 16.

[145] On the persistence or otherwise of title to incorporeal money, see David Fox, *Property Rights in Money* (OUP 2008) ch 5. cf also *OBG* (n 129).

against their own bank.[146] However, according to the thesis presented here, such a gratuitous third party recipient remains vulnerable to a claim in unjustified enrichment. Factors that generally preclude the passing of title in movable property—again, theft, fundamental mistake etc—have continuing relevance insofar as they are capable of justifying such an unjust enrichment claim.

VI. Conclusion

English law undoubtedly recognises enrichment by interference with the claimant's right as a category of claims within unjust enrichment. But comparison with certain civilian legal systems, principally German law, reveals that much of the work done by the *Eingriffskondiktion* is performed in English law by the law of tort, specifically the tort of conversion. Conversely, claims that could plausibly be dealt with as instances of unjust enrichment in English law are dealt with in the German law of property. The exclusion of restitution for wrongs from common law unjust enrichment diminishes the scope of the category still further. However, it has been argued here that the claim recognised in *Lipkin Gorman* is explicable as an instance of the English *Eingriffskondiktion*. This argument is justified not by arguing that the firm's chose in action against their bank was property or was like property,[147] nor by arguing for the wholesale reception of German rules into English law, but rather by drawing attention to the norms underlying the claims set out in §816 I BGB. B's acquisition of title to money taken from A without her consent, and the effective transfer of title to the money from B to C, does not preclude the recognition of an unjust enrichment claim by A against C where C is a gratuitous recipient. The norms that usually prevent the passing of title to movable property in cases where the owner does not consent—cases involving theft, fundamental mistake, etc—also justify A's unjust enrichment claim. It is the continuing relevance of these norms that explains the claim's real character. More work remains to be done in order to situate this claim within the wider theoretical framework of contemporary unjust enrichment.

[146] cf the decisions of the South African Supreme Court of Appeal in *First National Bank* (n 63); *Nissan* (n 64); *Absa Bank v Lombard* (n 63); *Firstrand Bank* (n 65). In these cases, the proceeds of money flowing from the claimant's bank account into the defendant's as a result of theft, fundamental mistake, or powerlessness were held to enrich the bank at which the account was held, rather than the account holder, and to be recoverable by the victim of the theft from the bank in unjust enrichment (although in *Absa Bank v Lombard* the bank was found to have a good defence). cf *Jeremy D Stone Consultants Ltd v National Westminster Bank plc* [2013] EWHC 208 (Ch).

[147] cf Ben McFarlane and Simon Douglas, 'Property, Analogy and Variety' (2022) 42 OJLS 161, esp 170–73.

17

Borderlines in Private Law: A Response

Robert Stevens

I. Introduction: Types

As others have pointed out,[1] Peter Birks would have considered this project misconceived. The various categories selected are not all of the same kind. There can be no borders between mammals, carnivores, and aquatic animals. Some animals fall into one or other of these categories, sometimes into two, or even all three (for example, dolphins). By contrast, there can, even for categories which really are of the same kind, be boundary difficulties of classification at their edges. Mammals evolved from reptilian proto-mammals, and so at their margins classification between the two groups can be challenging. In law, when we are dealing with legal categories of the same type, the same can be true, but it is not so for the categories of contract, torts, property, equity, and 'unjust enrichment', each of which is of a fundamentally different type (save, Birks would have argued, the first and last).

Legal concepts are not historically contingent or dependent upon context. Like concepts generally, they are not tied to any particular time or place. What types of legal category are those selected?

Contracts are a source of, or *reason* for, primary enforceable duties between persons. The antique French word torts, by contrast, refers to species of wrong, breaches of primary duties owed to others that create secondary duties (ordinarily to pay compensatory damages). Within the genus of wrongs are also breaches of contract, and these are only not labelled as torts by stipulation. There is a boundary between torts and breach of contract, but none between contract and torts, although there is a boundary between contract and various contract-like primary duties, the breach of which may constitute a tort.

The category 'property', unlike contract, is not given unity by the reason why rights arise any definition. One sense in which common lawyers use property, following Austin's corruption of Roman usage,[2] is to distinguish between rights *in rem* (rights exigible against the rest of the world in relation to physical things external to ourselves, for example, title to Blackacre) and rights *in personam* (rights exigible against particular individuals, for example, the right to be paid a contractual debt). The former may be said to be property rights, whereas the latter are personal rights.

[1] See, eg, chs 7 and 12.
[2] John Austin, *Lectures on Jurisprudence* (3rd edn, John Murray 1869) 380.

Robert Stevens, *Borderlines in Private Law: A Response* In: *Borderlines in Private Law*. Edited by: William Day and Julius Grower, Oxford University Press. © Robert Stevens 2024. DOI: 10.1093/9780191995200.003.0017

They are rights distinguished by their *form*. Contractual and tortious obligations also share a particular form (they are species of rights *in personam*) but there is no border between them and property any more than there could be a boundary between the species dogs and the genus reptiles.

Birks would have strongly endorsed Maitland's view[3] that equity is a body of rules only distinguished by its historical *source*: the Courts of Chancery in England, the ancestor of the Chancery Division of the High Court in our current legal order. Equity is a species of judge-made law, alongside the common law, and this wider genus of judge-made law is a source of law in the same way that legislation is. In one sense there is no meaningful border between the judge-made law of the common law and equity; we can always tell which judgment came from which corner of the south end of Westminster Hall. The boundary, in a sense, was the short walk between the two, but we can always tell which case comes from which court.

If, however, there were no more to it than that, we might expect to find contracts and torts arising in equity. But we do not. Nor is equity ever a source of property rights, in the sense of rights in relation to physical things exigible against the rest of the world. All of our first three categories of rights are, properly, sourced only in the common law.

On these definitions, a vendor-purchaser constructive trust is a form of dolphin. It arises because of a contract. The contractual duty to convey is specifically enforceable, and in equity that gives rise to a trust. The beneficiary's interest under a trust is, in a sense that we shall discuss, a property right.

The joker in the pack, or perhaps more accurately the cuckoo in the nest, is so-called 'unjust enrichment'. Birks saw this too as a source of primary personal rights, in the same way as contract is. The recipient of a payment to which they are not entitled, exemplified by a payment made under a mistake as to the obligation to do so, is under a duty to make restitution of the payment made. Whether such cases and the many others (including the right to contribution between co-tortfeasors) which Birks and other commentators conceived of as covered by 'unjust enrichment' are usefully understood as governed by any such omnibus principle[4] is, to say the least, very doubtful.[5] Still more questionable is Birks' claim that 'unjust enrichment' could be a source of property rights in the sense of rights in relation to things. However, that there are a large number of other reasons why rights, that are both personal and primary, arise which are also a species of the genus to which contractual rights belong—quasi-contracts if you will—may be readily accepted.

[3] Quoted disapprovingly in ch 10.

[4] Advocates of 'unjust enrichment', other than Birks in his final work, are often guilty of wanting to eat their cake but still have it afterwards. They therefore claim that it is governed by a four-stage test, with each stage independent of the others. Yet we are also commonly told that 'unjust enrichment' is not a cause of action, but instead encompasses many different reasons for restitution. If, however, the latter is true, then why would it ever be safe to analogise across from one entirely different kind of claim to another, as the four-stage test presupposes is possible? See ch 7.

[5] Explored (at tedious length) in Robert Stevens, *The Laws of Restitution* (OUP 2023).

II. Contract

The law of contract may be defined as the law of enforceable *promises* that have been *agreed* by the parties. As such, the law of contract is a subset of two larger categories. First is the law of promises. The category of promises with some legal effects is wider than the law of contract, including, for example, promises made in deeds, which are not dependent upon any agreement (that is to say, an offer and an acceptance) between the parties. Second is the law of agreement, which also includes, for example, the law of gifts. If I wish to make a gift to you of the title to my somewhat difficult terrier, I cannot do so unilaterally. You must accept what is offered in order for there to be a valid gift.

III. Torts

The law of promissory or voluntarily assumed obligations outside of the law of contract has not been given a satisfactory general label. An obvious example is that of a gratuitous bailment. If I bail my horse to you, you come under a positive duty that care will be taken of it that persons generally are not under. Similarly, persons generally are under no obligations to care for or cure their neighbours. If, however, you put up a large sign saying 'Hospital' and accept patients, you come under a non-delegable positive duty that care will be taken of those admitted, unlike strangers to those people.

If the horse is lost or the patient dies, when care would have ensured that neither happened, the party who entrusted the animal or the estate of the deceased, respectively, will potentially have a claim for damages for the wrong they have suffered. It is, however, a serious mistake to think that their claim is one for 'property damage' or 'personal injury' as it would be against a stranger who had killed or injured another's horse or their person. We do not have rights generally that others take care of our things or cure our bodies of illness. Rather the claim against the bailee or the hospital is for breach of the voluntarily assumed duty.

Such duties are not contractual because, in England but not in some other jurisdictions, the provision of consideration is a necessary condition of an enforceable contract. That the breach of such non-contractual voluntary undertakings is actionable does not undermine, but rather makes more readily justifiable, the doctrine of consideration.

First, the remedies available are different from those available in contract. By far the most common contractual action is one for the agreed sum, not damages. Specific remedies of this kind are not available to enforce gratuitous undertakings. Secondly, the defences are different. For example, contributory negligence will apply to a claim based upon a gratuitous voluntary undertaking, when it clearly will not where what is claimed is a contractual debt. Thirdly, the default standard of the duty imposed may in many cases be different. Where consideration has been provided it is legitimate to conclude that the duty is one to achieve a result, not merely that care is taken to deliver on time, but to deliver on time. Fourthly, consequential loss is required. Breach of contract is actionable per se, the breach of a gratuitous undertaking of care is not. Fifthly, and most importantly, gratuitous promises are revocable up until the time where this is no longer fair. The promisor can change his mind, the bailed horse can be returned. However, it may be impossible to any longer so revoke for two reasons. First, the passage of time may make it too late. Once the horse is lost, or the patient is dead, it is too late for the bailor or surgeon to turn around and say: 'Actually, I don't want to undertake to be careful after all'. Secondly, the claimant may have relied upon the undertaking, so that it is no longer fair to allow the promisor to revoke it. Reliance is one way, but not the only way, of demonstrating that revocation is no longer possible.

In this light, the decision of the House of Lords in *Hedley Byrne & Co Ltd v Heller & Partners Ltd* becomes readily explicable.[6] The key to understanding that case is the result. The claim failed. Why? The claimants were advertising agents who had placed advertisements on behalf of a client on terms that they were personally obliged to meet. Having become concerned about the financial viability of their client, they made enquiries of the defendant bank as to the financial position of the client who banked with them. The bank replied that the client was 'considered good for its normal business engagements'. The statement was made 'without responsibility'. In reliance on this reassurance, the claimants placed orders which their client defaulted on, resulting in losses of £17,000. The House of Lords accepted that, absent the fact that the statement was made 'without responsibility', the bank would have been liable. If I put a big neon sign on the top of my car disclaiming all responsibility to others who may be injured, with speakers on the side loudly broadcasting the same, this will not assist me if I do negligently injure a pedestrian. That the duty in *Hedley Byrne* could be disclaimed, whilst our general duties not to injure others cannot be, shows that the basis of the decision was that the only possible duty that arose was one based upon an assumption of responsibility. There is no general right not to suffer loss through another's negligence and speaking of an exclusionary rule in cases of pure economic loss is (very) misleading.

As Janet O'Sullivan discusses, problems sometimes arise in the law of limitation because of the different conditions for actionability of a breach of contract and of breaches of contract-lite gratuitous undertakings.[7] Because the latter are only actionable upon proof of consequential loss, time will only start to run at the point at which such loss is suffered. By contrast, because a breach of contract is actionable per se, time will run from the moment of breach without more ado. As the latter will commonly come first, and claims for breach of contract and torts are both subject to a six-year limitation rule, the tortious claim is more advantageous.

[6] [1964] AC 465 (HL).
[7] See ch 3.

It makes no sense to treat the party who has provided consideration worse than the party who has not. In *Henderson v Merrett Syndicates Ltd*,[8] the House of Lords correctly concluded that it is possible for a claimant to disclaim any reliance upon their provision of consideration, and to be treated on the same basis as a party to whom a gratuitous undertaking had been given. That does not mean that where a solicitor has undertaken to advise a client, or a builder to repair your house, that there are two voluntarily undertaken duties, one in contract and another 'in tort' (*sic*). There is just one undertaking, and so one wrong. However, it should be and is open to the claimant not to rely upon their provision of consideration but instead upon the later moment at which they suffer consequential loss as the moment from which their action accrues. The authority stating that this is untrue in the context of building work will have to be revisited.

IV. Property

Common lawyers often use a single word to cover different concepts.[9] As discussed, one usage of property is to refer to rights in relation to things exigible against all others. Having such a right is, of course, often determinative of whether you have suffered a tort. For example:

> *C* leases a bridge from *X* in order to operate a tram service. *D*, a lorry driver, negligently crashes into the bridge rendering it unsafe to use. *C*'s business is forced to stop operating, causing him large consequential economic losses.

The lease gives C a right in relation to the bridge exigible against the rest of the world (a property right). D infringed that right when he negligently crashed into the bridge, a tort. C can claim not only for the damage to the bridge, but also, subject to remoteness, for her consequential economic loss.

By contrast, if C merely had a contractual licence to use the bridge the analysis would be quite different. Such a licence would give C only a personal right against X, and without more no property right in relation to the bridge exigible against D or anyone else. (C might have such a right through occupation, but in the context of intermittent crossing, probably does not in this case.) If C has no right to the bridge itself exigible against anyone other than X, D has committed no tort with respect to her. C's loss is purely economic (that is to say, not consequent on the violation of any right), in Latin it is *damnum sine injuria*. As such, it is irrecoverable directly by C against D. Again, speaking of an exclusionary rule is misleading; there is no general entitlement to recover for losses caused by another's blameworthiness.[10]

[8] [1995] 2 AC 145 (HL).
[9] Such as consideration or rescission.
[10] Robert Stevens, *Torts and Rights* (OUP 2007) is a book-length labouring of the point.

It may be that C has a contractual claim against X if the bridge is shut. And X will have a claim against D for the tort he has suffered as a result of the damage to the bridge he has title to. X's claim against D may therefore include a claim to recover the damages X must pay to C. It may therefore be that C's consequential loss will still fall upon D, but this is dependent upon the terms of the contract between C and X.

Commercial lawyers often use property in a quite different sense. If a corporation goes into liquidation, what is its property? In this context, what we are interested in are those rights that are capable of transfer. Such rights will usually have an exchange value, and so be realisable in money. Such money can then be distributed to creditors. Receivables, equitable interests, and shares in companies are not rights that have as their subject matter physical things. Such rights need not relate to an identifiable separate subject matter, such as a thing, at all. They are also not exigible *erga omnes.* They are, however, property in the different sense that they are transferable rights, and hence realisable in money.

Not all rights are so transferable of course. My rights not to be defamed or not to be punched on the nose cannot be transferred away. If I go into bankruptcy, these will not form part of the estate that is acquired by my trustee in bankruptcy.[11] Even some rights in relation to tangible things exigible against the world may not be transferable, such as a lease of land that is by its terms non-assignable. Civilian lawyers helpfully refer to the category of transferable rights as patrimonial rights, so as to differentiate them from property rights in our first sense and also from those rights that are personal to us. Unfortunately, common lawyers often simply muddle the two concepts.

V. Equity

As Maitland warned, making incautious general claims about the nature of equity, other than as to its historical source, is foolish. If we claim that equity is based upon unconscionability, it is possible to identify successful claims where the defendant's behaviour *ex ante* was, from a moral standpoint, beyond reproach, as in *Boardman v Phipps.*[12] Indeed, equity's hard-hearted approach towards the liability of trustees led to statutory intervention to protect the blameless.[13] At best, it is possible to speak of certain features being characteristic of, if not definitional features of, equitable rules.

It was, and is, the common law that determined rights to tangible things (areas of land, pieces of paper, lumps of coal). Equity did not. There was and is no room

[11] Insolvency Act 1986, s 283.
[12] [1967] 2 AC 46 (HL).
[13] Trustee Act 1925, s 61.

for it to do so. The common law had already determined who was entitled to which things, and it would have been flatly contradictory for equity to give a different answer to the same question. Where then was and is the room for equity?

Two related answers are plausible. The first is that Equitable rules operate at a different level from common law rules. The nature of equity is a product of its history. Equity was, and primarily still is, a system of rules relating to those common law rules. Again, it is a body of law distinguished by its form. This second order, or supplemental nature, takes a number of different forms.

Sometimes, equity will restrain the enforcement of rights that the common law recognises. Examples of this include equitable estoppel in its legitimate form, equitable relief against forfeiture, rescission for innocent misrepresentation and undue influence, and equitable set-off.[14] The common law, by contrast, never overrode or prevented the enforcement of equitable rights. The Judicature Acts' proposition that in cases of conflict between the rules of law and equity, the rules of equity shall prevail, stated what was already the position. Equity may accurately[15] be described as a form of meta-law, not parallel.[16]

A central example of this form of law is, of course, the trust.[17] Trustees hold rights on trust, not physical things. If a right to land is held on trust, and another trespasses upon that land, it is the trustee who may sue, not the beneficiaries.[18] This is not simply a matter of standing. If a beneficiary personally suffers consequential loss, this is not recoverable. [19]

The trust is obligational, a duty to another not to use identifiable rights for the trustee's own benefit. Where there is a duty to transfer a particular right to another, as there is in the context of a contractual duty to convey title to land, a trust will arise because that is what a trust is. Again, there is no border here as contract and equity are different types of categories. The vendor-purchaser constructive trust arises because of the contractual duty, and the form of right created is a trust. The beneficiary's right is not however *in rem* in the sense of giving an entitlement to the

[14] See Robert Stevens, 'Set-off and the Nature of Equity' in Paul S Davies, Simon Douglas, and James Goudkamp (eds) *Defences in Equity* (Hart 2018) 42.

[15] For a contrary view, see ch 10.

[16] Ben McFarlane and Robert Stevens, 'What's Special About Equity? Rights About Rights' in Dennis Klimchuk, Irit Samet, and Henry Smith (eds), *Philosophical Foundations of the Law of Equity* (OUP 2020); Henry Smith, 'Equity as Meta-Law' (2021) 130 Yale LJ 1050.

[17] See ch 12.

[18] *MCC Proceeds v Lehman Brothers* [1998] 4 All ER 675 (CA). See, eg, *Schalit v Joseph Nadler Ltd* [1933] 2 KB 79 (Div); *Parker-Tweedle v Dunbar plc (No 2)* [1991] Ch 12 (CA); *Atlasview Ltd v Brightview Ltd* [2004] EWHC 1056 (Ch), [2004] 2 BCLC 191. But see *Shell UK Ltd v Total UK Ltd* [2010] EWCA Civ 180, [2011] QB 86, [132], where the distinction between legal title and the beneficial interest under a trust was considered 'legalistic'. The result in *Shell* is probably *per incuriam* as the earlier decision of the Court of Appeal in *Parker-Tweedle* was not cited to the court. See also James Edelman, 'Two Fundamental Questions for the Law of Trusts' (2013) 129 LQR 66; William Swadling, 'In Defence of Formalism' in Andrew Robertson and James Goudkamp (eds), *Form and Substance in the Law of Obligations* (Hart 2019) 95.

[19] *Hayim v Citibank NA* [1987] AC 730 (PC) 747–48; *Parker-Tweedale v Dunbar Bank plc (No 1)* [1991] Ch 12 (CA) 19–20; *Nimmo v Westpac Banking Corp* [1993] 3 NZLR 218 (NZHC) 236–37.

land, the physical space, exigible against all others. Rather the beneficiary's right is a property right in the patrimonial sense, but one that gives them protection upon the trustee's bankruptcy.[20] A trust will also arise where there is an obligation to reconvey, as where a fully executed contract for the sale of land is rescinded by the seller because of the buyer's fraud. Here, however, the obligation is restitutionary, not contractual.

A second distinguishing feature is that equity is a subset of the law of court orders. It is meaningful to speak of an unenforceable contract, such that its performance cannot, without more, be reversed. Similarly, an obligation to pay damages for a tort is not extinguished because it ceases to be actionable because of the expiry of a limitation period, and its payment will not be recoverable even if made by mistake after the lapse of the ability to sue. It is, however, meaningless to speak of an 'unenforceable' trust or to conceive of rectification or rescission in equity or equitable relief against forfeiture as operating outside of the courtroom. If we closed all the courts, our common law duties owed one to another would not disappear, but equity would no longer exist. Obviously, the availability of specific performance or injunctions for the enforcement of common law duties would cease, but so too would the other equitable doctrines.

It is probably this second feature that leads to the view that equity is in some way more flexible or discretionary than the common law. Although much of equity consists of fine-grained, hard-edged rules that a court cannot disapply, as a cursory reading of a trusts textbook should tell anyone, at the stage of making court orders a range of considerations come into play that are not relevant when determining the substantive rights and obligations between parties *inter se*. At the stage of applying the threat of the force of the State, and its resources, to compelling the compliance with judicial orders, the court may refuse to make an order for reasons that do not need to conform with the bilateral reasons that justify rights as between persons.[21] It may deny specific performance of a contract because one party was making a mistake,[22] or because one party made an exceptionally poor bargain,[23] or because complying with their contractual obligation may be extremely difficult for a defendant in dire personal circumstances.[24] None of these constitute good reasons why a contract may be invalid as a matter of the parties' rights *inter se*. Similarly, an injunction may be refused because an activity, although constituting

[20] Rights held on trust are not transferred to a trustee in bankruptcy upon a trustee's insolvency, and so are not realisable and distributable to creditors: Insolvency Act 1986, s 283(3)(b). Where the trustee is a corporation, if it goes into an insolvency proceeding, the corporation remains under a duty not to use the rights held on trust for the corporation's own benefit, and so they are also not realisable and distributable to creditors.

[21] Whilst accepting that legal duties that *A* owes to *B* must be justified by reasons why *A* must act in a particular way in relation to *B*, Gregson denies that such reasons are also constrained by the need not to use *A* as a mere means to an end: see ch 7.

[22] *Malins v Freeman* (1837) 2 Keen 25.

[23] *Falcke v Grey* [1859] ER 710, (159) 4 Drew 651, (1851) 62 ER 250.

[24] *Patel v Ali* [1984] Ch 283 (Ch).

a nuisance and therefore a wrong to the claimant, is in the public interest, such as the defence of the realm.[25] Again, none of these reasons entails that damages are not payable (a proof that the obligation to pay damages arises independently of the making of any court order). Because of this wider range of reasons that need to be taken into account in deciding whether to make a court order compelling compliance with our primary duties, equity can appear more discretionary.

The above two features of equity became confused in the difficult-to-defend decision of the Supreme Court in *Guest v Guest*.[26] This is, at present, the culmination of the sorry history of what is called proprietary estoppel since the beginnings of its cancerous growth in the decision of the Court of Appeal in *Crabb v Arun DC*.[27] The modern history of this doctrine is well told in Lord Leggatt's dissenting judgment.[28]

The proper role of estoppel is that of estopping. It is possible to estop the assertion of two things: facts and rights. When estoppel bars the assertion of facts it is operating as a rule of evidence, and there is historically nothing peculiarly equitable about estoppel in this form. Equitable estoppel, properly so called, involves the barring of the assertion of rights. Such rights need not be proprietary, but where they *are* proprietary estoppel is an accurate label. Similarly, promissory estoppel correctly concerns the barring of the assertion of promissory rights. Equitable estoppel in these legitimate forms is a classic example of a rule concerning another rule.

A good illustration is provided by *Inwards v Baker*.[29] Old Mr Baker had title to six acres of land. His son lived nearby and wished to purchase another area of land on which to build a bungalow. His father said to him: 'Why not put the bungalow on my land and make the bungalow a little bigger', which is what the son did. The son then lived there for thirty years. The father died, leaving the title to the land to others in his will, who then sought to evict the son. The Court of Appeal concluded that it would be inequitable to allow the assertion of the right to exclude from possession against the son. The court did not enquire into the value of the work the son had put into erecting the property. Estoppel in this form is also a digital matter: the rightholder is estopped from asserting the right relied upon. Its degree does not vary according to the quantum of reliance.

Since 1976, however, a form of estoppel has arisen that is a misnomer.[30] It is a freestanding cause of action travelling under that name. That something has gone wrong is apparent from the fact that the label does not reflect the true nature of the rule, the fact that the rule is relatively recent in origin, and the fact that the rule is

[25] *Dennis v Ministry of Defence* [2003] EWHC 793 (QB), [2003] 2 EGLR 121.
[26] *Guest v Guest* [2022] UKSC 27, [2022] 3 WLR 911.
[27] *Crabb v Arun DC* [1976] Ch 179 (CA).
[28] *Guest* (n 26) [138]–[159]. See also Stevens, *The Laws of Restitution* (n 5) ch 14.
[29] *Inwards v Baker* [1965] 2 QB 29 (CA). See also *Bibby v Stirling* (1998) 76 P & CR D36 (CA).
[30] *Guest* (n 26) [167] (Lord Leggatt).

not reflected in the laws of other jurisdictions (for example, Scotland or the United States). Indeed, it is possible to identify the source of the mistake which generated it.

Guest v Guest involved the frequent fact pattern of a son working as a farmer for many years on pay at below the market rate based upon an assurance from his father that he would eventually inherit the farm, a promise unenforceable as a matter of contract. The parties fell out, and the son sought redress. The court ordered either that the title to the farm be held on trust, or that the father pay compensation to the son for its value now, but with a reduction to reflect its earlier than anticipated receipt, at the defendant father's option. (That the defendant has this unusual choice as to the order he complies with is also an indication that something has gone awry in the analysis.)

What, as a matter of principle, should the position be? The correct answer is that such a case should have nothing to do with estoppel properly so called. The father is not being estopped from asserting anything. He asserts nothing at all. Rather the son wishes to bring a claim against him. A contractual action is ruled out for one of a number of reasons: the promise is too uncertain to be enforced, in a family context there may be no intention to create legal relations, and the promise is to convey title to land and because it is not in writing is unenforceable as not compliant with the statutory formality requirements.

The correct analysis was adopted by the Supreme Court of Canada in 1954 in *Deglman v Guaranty Trust Co of Canada and Constantineau*.[31] The claimant lived with his aunt in Ottawa. She owned two houses and agreed that if he was good to her and did such chores as she requested from time to time, she would leave him one of them in her will. The nephew performed his side, taking her on pleasure drives, doing odd jobs, and running errands. The aunt died intestate. The agreement between them, being one to convey land, was unenforceable under section 4 of the Statute of Frauds 1677. Because the house was not conveyed to him, the claimant was held entitled to the value of the service he had provided over the years. The agreed condition under which the work was done had failed. Restitution of the value of the work was ordered.

This award is properly calculated by reference to the value of the work done, and not according to any loss suffered by the claimant in reliance upon the undertaking by the defendant.[32] We are also uninterested in the extent to which the defendant has been left enriched, if at all, by the work. It should not matter if the father in *Guest v Guest* had employed his son uselessly painting coal white for forty years in a way that left the father in no sense better off because he could personally have

[31] [1954] SCR 725, [1954] 3 DLR 785 (SCC). See also *Grey v Hill* (1826) Ry & M 420, 171 ER 1070; *Scott v Pattison* [1923] 2 KB 723 (KB); *Pavey & Matthew Pty Ltd v Paul* (1987) 162 CLR 221 (HCA). But see in Scotland *Gray v Johnston* 1928 SC 659, 1928 SLT 499 (IHCS).

[32] cf *Davies v Davies* [2016] EWCA Civ 463, [2016] 2 P & CR 10 [38].

obtained the same pointless labour elsewhere for nothing. The award is also not concerned to make good the claimant's expectation. The Supreme Court in *Guest v Guest* was correct that the father should not be compelled to convey the title to the farm, the condition precedent expressed in the promise (the father's death) not having been satisfied, but there should be no such enforcement even were that condition to have been met (unless we are to ignore the statute prohibiting such enforcement). At one time English law recognised a doctrine of part performance as an alternative to the formality requirement for the enforcement of contracts for the sale of land.[33] However, the part performance doctrine was (foolishly) abolished in England in 1989,[34] and the courts cannot legitimately reintroduce it under the different label of estoppel.

The claimant in *Guest v Guest* should have been entitled to the market value of the work that he had done over the years, with a deduction for whatever he had been paid, but that is all. This claim for restitution is how other jurisdictions outside of the common law deal with such a common fact pattern, rather than through a peculiar 'estoppel' doctrine, which in our jurisdiction has jumped its rails. Lord Briggs' judgment for the majority in *Guest v Guest* states:

> One of the principal functions of equity is to put right injustice to which the law is otherwise blind, by restraining the rigid application of legal rules where their implementation would be unconscionable.[35]

This (correctly) describes the traditional rules-about-other-rules conception of equity in general, and equitable estoppel in particular. However, so-called proprietary estoppel as a cause of action has nothing whatsoever to do with the restraining or restricting of common law rights or powers. Lord Briggs continues:

> Equity may in such circumstances provide the promisee ... with a remedy if a promise has been made to confer property upon him in the future, (or an informal assurance that the property is already his) in reliance upon which he has acted to his detriment... The equitable remedy is to restrain, or stop or 'estop' the promisor from reneging on the promise.[36]

This muddles up different senses of right. Equitable estoppel, properly so called, concerns the barring of the assertion of claim-rights,[37] powers,[38] or immunities.[39]

[33] *Maddison v Alderson* (1883) 8 App Cas 467 (HL); *Steadman v Steadman* [1976] AC 536 (HL).
[34] Law of Property (Miscellaneous Provisions) Act 1989, s 2(8).
[35] *Guest* (26) [4].
[36] ibid [4].
[37] As above in *Inwards* (n 29).
[38] See, eg, *Hughes v Metropolitan Rly* (1877) 2 App Cas 439 (HL).
[39] See, eg, *Commonwealth of Australia v Verwayen* (1990) 170 CLR 394 (HCA).

It is not, accurately speaking, either a cause of action or a defence, but may be essential to either a cause of action or a defence succeeding. By contrast, Lord Briggs is using the idea of estoppel (*sic*) to bar the assertion of *a liberty*: to create a free-standing new obligation on the defendant. The defendant is barred from not fulfilling his promise. A new form of promissory obligation that does not fulfil the necessary conditions for enforceable contractual promises is thereby created.[40] Lord Briggs then states:

> Equitable remedies are generally more flexible than those afforded by the common law and they are always discretionary.[41]

However, in recognising a new kind of right that promisors must keep their promises, we are not in the realm of remedies (that is to say, of court orders). Rather, we are concerned with the substantive primary rights that the parties have one against another before they enter the courtroom. That must be ascertained first before determining what order to give. As we have seen, in deciding *not* to specifically enforce such rights, equity does indeed take into account a wide range of sometimes incommensurable factors. It does not follow that the judges have a discretion to create primary rights from whole cloth by way of court order.

The primary foundational authority relied upon by the majority for such a power is the decision of Lord Westbury LC in *Dillwyn v Llewelyn*.[42] However, the judgment in that case does not mention estoppel, unsurprisingly as it did not involve estopping the assertion of anything. A father placed land in the possession of his son, signing a memorandum that he gave the son the title to the land in order to enable him to build a home. The son then built the expected home and took up residence. There had not, however, been any deed of conveyance, meaning that the legal title to the property remained in the father at the time of his death.

Although, for the protection of third parties, there are good reasons why we require formality requirements to be fulfilled before title to land is transferred (third parties need to be able to ascertain who has the power to give them permission to enter the land, or who can give them good title to the land), as between the father and the son *inter se*, the son had the better entitlement to the land. As a result, the father held the legal title to the land for his son, and the court ordered the conveyance of that title to be made upon the father's death. This did not undermine the reasons for the formality requirements, which still needed to be satisfied for the transfer itself.

Dillwyn v Llewelyn concerned title to land. It did not concern estoppel, nor does it stand for the proposition that promises which are relied upon are enforceable.

[40] See ch 4.
[41] *Guest v Guest* (26) [5].
[42] *Dillwyn v Llewelyn* (1862) 4 De GF & J 517, 45 ER 1285.

There was no promise of any future action. The father stated that the land was, without more, *now* the son's, something which had been accepted. Absent the formality requirement, there was a gift. *Dillwyn v Llewelyn* only applies to informal gifts of rights where the legal formalities for transfer have not been complied with. It does not stand for the proposition that promises which have been relied upon are enforceable. Indeed, from the majority's judgment in *Guest v Guest* it is unclear why proprietary estoppel should be confined to promises to convey title to land at all. Why not enforce all promises that have been relied upon?

The true source of proprietary estoppel as a cause of action in our modern law was not *Dillwyn v Llewelyn* but, as Lord Leggatt observed in *Guest v Guest*, *Crabb v Arun DC*. In that case, which, in result, is rightly decided, Scarman LJ spoke loosely of the court crafting a remedy in order to provide 'the minimum equity to do justice to the plaintiff',[43] something which has led to a mushrooming of litigation over the last fifty years.

Lord Mansfield's statement that 'the common law . . . works itself pure'[44] reflects a Whiggish view of history that we should unsentimentally reject. Mistakes can be introduced just as much as they can be eradicated. Eventually the decision of the majority in *Guest v Guest* will have to be revisited and Lord Leggatt's dissent re-evaluated, but judicial inertia means that this is unlikely to happen in my lifetime.

VI. Conclusion: 'Unjust Enrichment'

As Alexander Waghorn reminds us,[45] judges have authority to determine for us what the law is in our jurisdiction. Once they have spoken, that is the end of the matter. Yet they have no power to determine the meaning of concepts, or what justice requires, both of which are independent of the positive law in any particular time and place. Consequently, whether the reasons given by judges are good cannot be determined by the law itself. This means that the judicial rejection of the omnibus concept of 'unjust enrichment' as an organising idea, even by such great judges as Lord Diplock[46] and Scrutton LJ,[47] cannot have been determinative of this point, nor is its endorsement by other judges in the modern era.

One common tactic in attempting to dispense with the idea of 'unjust enrichment' has been to push the examples said to exemplify it into other, more familiar, areas of law.[48] Two approaches are common. First, attempts to explain

[43] *Crabb* (n 27) 198.
[44] William Murray (later Lord Mansfield), argument for the claimant in *Omychund v Barker* (1744) 1 Atk 21, 23.
[45] See ch 15.
[46] *Orakpo v Manson Investments Ltd* [1978] AC 95 (HL) 104.
[47] *Holt v Markham* [1923] 1 KB 504 (CA) 513.
[48] See, eg, Steve Hedley, *Restitution: Its Division and Ordering* (Sweet & Maxwell 2001) 224.

the claimant's right to restitution of the mistaken payment of money, or other transfer of 'property', as based upon a pre-existing property right of the claimant.[49] Secondly, seeing the right to restitution of work done at another's request in terms of an expanded law of contract.[50]

These attempts to make do with *fewer* reasons for restitution are exactly the wrong move. Restitution is in fact justified by a diverse variety of different reasons, which are neither reducible into other more familiar categories nor into one 'uber' category of 'unjust enrichment'.

The main problem with the first approach is that payments of money do not necessarily entail any transfer of property, or the loss and gain of a property right, however loosely defined, at all. The mistaken payment of money from my overdrawn bank account, with further drawings at the bank's discretion, to your overdrawn bank account is a common example.

The second approach, seeing claims such as *Deglman* as contractual, or to enforce the promise made, is also very problematic. The Statute of Frauds 1677 meant what it said, that 'noe action shall be brought' upon agreements within its scope unless they are proved in writing. As William Day's chapter explores,[51] in claims of this kind the existence and meaning of the condition under which the work the nephew did for his aunt is determined by the terms of the agreement with his aunt. This condition is not found in the mind of the claimant, nor that of the defendant, nor of both of them, but in their agreement as objectively made by them together. The claim was not, however, to enforce a promise made by the aunt. We return therefore to where we began. Although the claim was based upon the agreement between the parties, that does not entail that it was contractual because it was not to enforce any promise made. The case falls within the law of agreement, but not within its subset, the law of contract.

There are, of course, many claims for restitution that are independent of any extant agreement between the parties (for example, claims for restitution of payments made under an agreement avoided for duress). Trying to determine what the boundaries of 'unjust enrichment' are, when restitutionary obligations arise for a diverse number of reasons, with claims governed by quite different rules, with different subject matters, is like trying to classify mermaids and griffins. A task that is beyond me.

[49] Samuel Stoljar, *The Law of Quasi-Contract* (2nd edn, Law Book Co 1989) esp 5–10, 113, 250; Charlie Webb, *Reason and Restitution* (OUP 2016) 84.
[50] Stoljar (n 49) 187–90, 232–35. Compare Steve Hedley, *A Critical Introduction to Restitution* (Butterworths 2001) 30–54
[51] See ch 9.

Index

For the benefit of digital users, indexed terms that span two pages (e.g., 52–53) may, on occasion, appear on only one of those pages.